ALSO BY LAURENT DUBOIS

A Colony of Citizens

Avengers of the New World

Soccer Empire

Haiti

Haiti

The Aftershocks of History

Laurent Dubois

Metropolitan Books

Henry Holt and Company   New York

Metropolitan Books
Henry Holt and Company, LLC
Publishers since 1866
175 Fifth Avenue
New York, New York 10010
www.henryholt.com

Metropolitan Books® and ® are registered trademarks of
Henry Holt and Company, LLC.

Library of Congress Cataloging-in-Publication data
Dubois, Laurent, 1971–
  Haiti : the aftershocks of history / Laurent Dubois.—1st ed.
    p. cm.
  Includes bibliographical references and index.
  ISBN 978-0-8050-9335-3
1. Haiti—History.   I. Title.
  F1921.D83 2012
  972.94—dc23   2011020162

Henry Holt books are available for special promotions and
premiums. For details contact: Director, Special Markets.

First Edition 2012

Designed by Kelly S. Too

Printed in the United States of America
1   3   5   7   9   10   8   6   4   2

For Georges Anglade, whose writings
illuminated the past and present of Haiti,

and for all those who, like him,
died in the earthquake of January 12, 2010

CONTENTS

Haiti

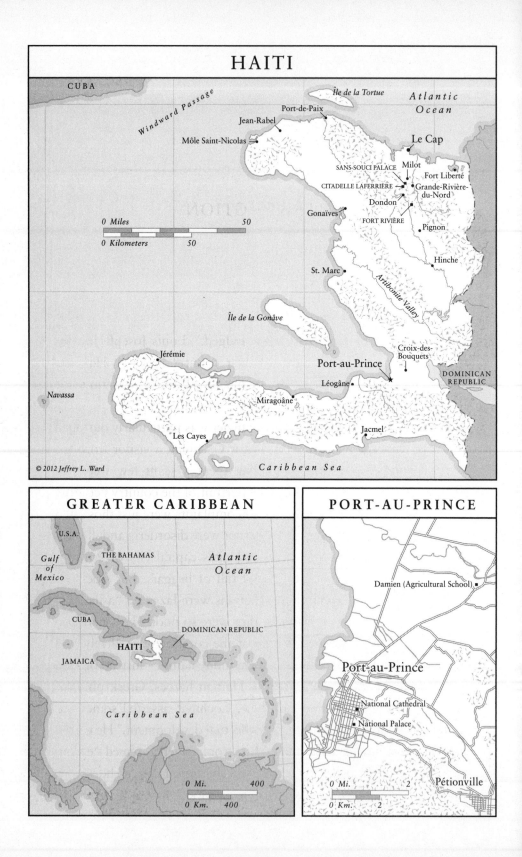

INTRODUCTION

"For eighty years Haiti has been judged," Louis-Joseph Janvier wrote in 1883. Since the birth of their country in 1804, Haitians had been incessantly "accused" by outsiders, and it was time for them to respond.[1]

A Haitian student living in Paris, Janvier was particularly outraged by a set of newspaper articles by Victor Cochinat, a visitor from the French colony of Martinique. Having spent a scant few weeks in Haiti, Cochinat had penned a cutting portrait of the country's culture, its people, and its politics. Some of his complaints were just those of a grouchy traveler: the porters in the harbor were disorderly and ill-clad, there was no set price for anything, Haiti's capital city of Port-au-Prince was dirty and unpleasant and full of beggars. But Cochinat quickly extrapolated much more. Haitians were lazy and "ashamed" of work, he wrote, which was why they were so poor. They spent too much money on rum. The children of the country were "lively and intelligent," but their parents gave them funny names—instead of Paul or Jacques, they chose the names of Haitian heroes, Greek philosophers, and French writers—and these, Cochinat asserted somewhat mysteriously, "interfere with their intellectual development." He teased that Haitians, having freed themselves from slavery, seemed "enamored" of the whip, using it against their children. Haiti, as he saw it, was a farce, a "phantasmagoria of civilization." It was a nation of

"admirals without boats, generals without soldiers," and schools without teachers: a hopeless and absurd place with no future. Its attempt
to look like a modern country was nothing more than a "joke."[2]

Seething, Janvier wrote a sardonic six-hundred-page history of
"Haiti and its visitors." Many of these visitors had, like Cochinat,
breezed through Haiti and then penned authoritative-sounding con-
demnations of the entire country. Janvier demanded at least a shred
of objectivity. Was Haiti the only country with beggars in the streets?
He'd noticed quite a few in Paris. Was it wrong for parents to name
their children after great figures, in the hopes that their children
would achieve great things? Janvier found himself having to remind
his readers that Haitians were real people, living in a real society.
They had their problems, to be sure, but they could not be reduced
to mere caricatures, presented with no sense of context or history.

Janvier himself knew Haiti's challenges intimately. When he was
born in 1855, Haiti was dominated by the unpopular emperor Soulouque, and of the five presidents who had ruled by the time he
wrote his book, four were violently overthrown, with the country
torn apart by civil wars. Janvier served his nation as a diplomat, a
judge, and a politician, trying to confront the forces—both external
and internal—that were holding the country back. He also became
one of Haiti's great intellectuals; his fourteen books included several
novels, a critique of European racism, and the classic study of Haiti's
constitutional history. His defenses of his beloved land were eloquent,
impassioned, erudite, and often funny.

But Janvier wasn't able to bring much change to Haiti; and he
didn't make much of a dent, either, in the overwhelmingly hostile
and distorted views held by most outsiders about the country. A few
years after Janvier died, yet another Haitian president was overthrown in a bloody coup. The country was then occupied by the
U.S. Marines, several of whom wrote popular accounts that portrayed Haiti as a dismal, backward place, full of lazy (if sometimes
charming) peasants in the thrall of Vodou. In the decades since then,
a succession of economic troubles and dictatorial regimes like that

of François "Papa Doc" Duvalier have reinforced the negative stereo-types. When Haiti appears at all in the media, it registers largely as a place of disaster, poverty, and suffering, populated by desperate people trying to escape.

On January 12, 2010, Haiti was struck by one of the deadliest earthquakes in modern history, which killed upwards of 230,000 people and left millions homeless. The country's National Palace, Port-au-Prince's historic cathedral, and the headquarters of the U.N. mission in the country were demolished. As troops and relief work-ers rushed to help, the familiar tropes emerged again. Nearly every mention of Haiti in the press reminded readers that it was "the poor-est nation in the Western Hemisphere," a moniker incessantly repeated like some dogged trademark. The coverage often made the country sound like some place entirely outside the West—a primitive and incomprehensible territory—rather than as a place whose history has been deeply intertwined with that of Europe and the United States for three centuries. And when people wanted to know how Haiti had come to be so poor, and why its government barely func-tioned, pundits offered a plethora of ill-informed speculation, like so many modern-day Cochinats. Many seemed all too ready to believe that the fault must lie with the Haitians themselves.

The day after the earthquake, televangelist Pat Robertson famously opined that Haitians were suffering because they had sold them-selves to the devil. A more polite version of the same argument came from *New York Times* columnist David Brooks, who accused Haiti of having "progress-resistant cultural influences," including "the influence of the voodoo religion." Why else would the country be so poor, so miserable, when its immediate neighbor the Dominican Republic—right there on the same island of Hispaniola—was a comparatively prosperous Caribbean tourist attraction? Many called openly for Haiti to be made a protectorate. Brooks advocated "intrusive paternalism" that would change the local culture by pro-moting "No Excuses countercultures." Against such claims, other voices responded by placing the blame for the situation entirely on

outside forces: foreign corporations, the U.S. and French governments, the International Monetary Fund. Nearly all of the coverage
portrayed Haitians themselves as either simple villains or simple
victims. More complex interpretations were few and far between.[3]

But the true causes of Haiti's poverty and instability are not mysterious, and they have nothing to do with any inherent shortcomings
on the part of the Haitians themselves. Rather, Haiti's present is the
product of its history: of the nation's founding by enslaved people
who overthrew their masters and freed themselves; of the hostility
that this revolution generated among the colonial powers surrounding the country; and of the intense struggle within Haiti itself to
define that freedom and realize its promise.

III

A little more than two hundred years ago, the place that we now
know as Haiti—then the French colony of Saint-Domingue—was
perhaps the most profitable bit of land in the world. It was full of
thriving sugar plantations, with slaves—who made up nine-tenths
of the colony's population—planting and cutting cane and operating the mills and boiling houses that produced the sugar crystals
coveted by European consumers. The plantation system was immensely
lucrative, creating enormous fortunes in France. It was also brutally
destructive. The plantations consumed the landscape: observers at the
time already noted that alarmingly large areas of the forests had been
chopped down for construction and for export of precious woods to
Europe. And they consumed the lives of the colony's slaves at a murderous rate. Over the course of the colony's history, as many as a
million slaves were brought from Africa to Saint-Domingue, but the
work was so harsh that even with a constant stream of imports, the
slave population constantly declined. Few children were born, and
those that were often died young. By the late 1700s, the colony had
about half a million slaves altogether. It was out of this brutal world
that Haiti was born.[4]

In August 1791, slaves on the sugar plantations in the north of the colony launched the largest slave revolt in history. They set the cane fields on fire, killed their masters, and smashed all the instruments used to process the sugarcane. They took over the northern plantations, gained new recruits, and built an army and a political movement. Within two years, they had secured freedom for all the slaves in the colony. In 1794, the French government—then in the hands of the radical Jacobins—recognized that freedom and extended it, abolishing slavery throughout the French empire.

Between 1794 and 1801, Saint-Domingue remained nominally a French colony, led by Toussaint Louverture—a former slave, now a French general. Louverture defended the territory from English invasion and sought to maintain the colony's plantation system, intent on proving to the world that it was possible to produce sugar and coffee without slavery. But when Napoleon Bonaparte sent troops to resurrect the order that had been destroyed by the 1791 uprising, the population, faced with the prospect of a return to slavery, rose up again. With Haiti's declaration of independence, the revolution was complete.

The aftershocks of that revolution reverberate throughout Haiti's history. The country emerged in a world still dominated by slavery, and the nations that surrounded it saw its existence as a serious threat. For decades France refused to recognize Haiti's independence, maintaining that it still had sovereignty over its onetime colony, and the governments of England and the United States followed France's lead. Haiti's political isolation and the constant threats directed at it weighed heavily on its early leaders, who keenly felt the burden of proving to the world that a black nation could succeed. To defend against possible attack, they poured money into building fortifications and maintaining a large army. Being Haiti, it turned out, was costly. What's more, this emphasis on military readiness meant that, from the start, civilian concerns were often subordinated to the army's needs.

The colony of Saint-Domingue had been built and populated

with just one goal: to produce crops for export. This old order inevitably haunted the newly independent Haiti. Like Louverture before them, the men who first ruled the fledgling country—among them several ex-slaves—saw the reconstruction of its plantations as the only viable economic course of action. What else was there to sell besides sugar and coffee, after all, in order to buy the goods and the guns they needed to survive? But the former slaves who made up the vast majority of the population had a very different plan. They were not going back to the plantation system. Instead, they took over the land they had once worked as slaves, creating small farms where they raised livestock and grew crops to feed themselves and sell in local markets. On these small farms, they did all the things that had been denied to them under slavery: they built families, practiced their religion, and worked for themselves.[5]

The deep division over what Haiti should be has shaped the entire political history of the country. Haiti's rural population effectively undid the plantation model. By combining subsistence agriculture with the production of some crops for export, they created a system that guaranteed them a better life, materially and socially, than that available to most other people of African descent in the Americas throughout the nineteenth and early twentieth centuries. But they did not succeed in establishing that system in the country as a whole. In the face of most Haitians' unwillingness to work the plantations, Haiti's ruling groups retreated but did not surrender. Ceding, to some extent, control of the land, they took charge of the ports and the export trade. And they took control of the state, heavily taxing the goods produced by the small-scale farmers and thereby reinforcing the economic divisions between the haves and the have-nots.[6]

In the past two centuries, this stalemate between the ruling class and the broader population has led to a devastating set of authoritarian political habits. Over time—often convinced that the masses were simply not ready to participate in political life—the Haitian governing elites crafted state institutions that excluded most Haitians from formal political involvement. Although reformers occasionally pushed for a more liberal democracy, the elites always closed ranks whenever the question of sharing political power with the rural population arose. A simple fact illustrates the depth of this political exclusion. The majority of Haitians speak Kreyòl, a language born of the encounter between French and various African languages in the eighteenth century. Until 1987, however, the only official language of the government was French, which only a small minority in the country could read or even understand. For almost all of Haiti's history, most of its population has literally been unable to read the laws under which they have been governed.[7]

Haiti is often described as a "failed state." In fact, though, Haiti's state has been quite successful at doing what it was set up to do: preserve power for a small group. The constitutional structures established in the nineteenth century made it very difficult to vote the country's leaders out of office, leaving insurrection as the only means of effecting political change. Haiti's twentieth-century laws have grown more liberal, but its government still changes hands primarily through extraconstitutional, and often violent, means. And despite a powerful wave of popular participation in the past decades, the country's political structures remain largely unaccountable and impermeable to the demands of the majority of Haitians.

III

Haiti's domestic divisions were not the only—or even the most significant—source of its problems. Over the course of the nineteenth century, foreign governments gained more and more control over the country's economy and politics. France did so in a particularly cynical and devastating way. When the French finally granted recognition to Haiti, more than two decades after its founding, they took a kind of revenge, insisting that the new nation pay an indemnity of 150 million francs (roughly $3 billion in today's currency) to compensate the slaveholders for their losses. To pay the indemnity, the

Haitian government took out loans from French banks, which added interest payments to the crushing debt load. Though the amount of the indemnity was later reduced to 60 million francs by France, the cycle of debt only worsened. By 1898, fully half of Haiti's government budget went to paying France and the French banks. By 1914, that proportion had climbed to 80 percent.[8]

As Janvier furiously put it, Haitians had been forced to pay for their land—"this little stretch of land of which we are the masters," which they were "jealously keeping" for their descendants—not once or twice but three times. They first paid for it through their ancestors, with "two centuries of tears and sweat." Then the Haitians paid for it during their revolution, through the "massive quantity of blood" spilled to win liberty and independence. And, after all that, they still had to pay for it in cash that passed from Haiti into France's treasury for generations.[9]

What might have been done with this money in Haiti itself? How much could have been created with it? We will never know. The indemnity was certainly not the only force sapping Haiti's finances. The government maintained a massive military, and corruption and mismanagement also took their toll. So did the country's civil wars, and the repeated demands from foreign merchants in Haiti—sometimes literally backed up by gunships—to be compensated for property lost during the fighting. But the indemnity represented a constant leak of funds out of the country for nearly a century. Ultimately, of course, the cost was borne by Haitian farmers, the descendants of the same slaves who had been "lost" by the French slaveholders.

The demands of the French were soon surpassed by the pressures of a new and powerful imperial force. Military officials of the United States considered Haiti strategically important, while American entrepreneurs were eager to build new plantations in Haiti as they had elsewhere in the region. In 1915, the marines landed in Haiti, ostensibly in order to reestablish political order after a bloody coup. They stayed for twenty years.

The U.S. occupation transformed Haiti in ways that are still playing out today. The United States, like other colonial powers, touted its building of schools and roads, and it is still recognized and appreciated for having brought significant medical assistance. But while the United States justified the occupation as a project to improve and democratize Haiti's political institutions, it ultimately exacerbated the rift within the society. As more and more U.S. agricultural companies entered Haiti, they deprived peasants of their land. The result was that, for the first time in its history, large numbers of Haitians left the country, looking for work in nearby Caribbean islands and beyond. Others moved to the capital of Port-au-Prince, which the United States had made into Haiti's center of trade at the expense of the regional ports. In the decades that followed, the capital's growth continued, uncontrolled and ultimately disastrous, while the countryside suffered increasing immiseration.[10]

The U.S. occupation also deepened Haiti's economic and political dependence on outside powers. During the second half of the twentieth century, the extent of foreign support has often been one of the most important factors determining the political destiny of Haitian rulers—frequently more important than popular support within the country. When the legitimacy of a political leader is established by outside forces rather than a nation's own population, of course, the results are rarely good for that population. François Duvalier and his son Jean-Claude, the Haitian dictators whose regimes were legendary for their brutality and terror, used U.S. support to stay in power for decades while driving hundreds of thousands of their countrymen into exile. Today, U.S. influence over Haiti is so well established as to seem almost unremarkable. After the 2010 earthquake, Haitians noted with little surprise that Bill Clinton, in his role as cochair of the international commission overseeing Haitian reconstruction, often seems to hold more power over the country than does Haiti's elected president.

All these factors have contributed to a powerful sense of political exhaustion surrounding Haiti's future. A succession of military regimes has left the country with almost no functioning social infrastructure.

Ever since popular president Jean-Bertrand Aristide was violently overthrown in 2004, Haiti has been policed largely by foreign troops under U.N. command. Haiti's proud independence has been eroded, too, by the thousands of foreign organizations that have flocked to the country over the years with projects for improvement and reform. For all their work, though, hunger, poverty, and disease still stalk much of the population. In the cities, the last decades have seen an increase in violent crime, including drug trafficking and kidnapping, while the situation in rural Haiti, where the majority of the population still lives, is increasingly desperate. The soil is severely depleted; generations of intensive agriculture and deforestation have taken their toll. As the population has grown and parcels of land have been divided into smaller and smaller bits, the social and agricultural strategies that worked well for Haitian peasants into the early decades of the twentieth century have become increasingly unsustainable. At the same time, the solutions prescribed by foreign powers and international organizations have largely turned out to be ineffective, or worse.

❙ ❙ ❙

"Ladies and gentlemen, come and see," beckons novelist Lyonel Trouillot in a searing account of life in contemporary Haiti. "This isn't a country here but an epic failure factory, an excuse for a place, a weed lot, an abyss for tightrope-walkers, blindman's bluff for the sightless saddled with delusions of grandeur . . . Proud mountains reduced to dust dumped in big helpings into the cruciform maws of sick children who crouch waiting in the hope of insane epiphanies, behaving badly and swamped besides, bogged down in their devil's quagmires." "Our history," he laments, "is a corset, a stifling cell, a great searing fire."[11]

That history, however, represents the only foundation upon which a different Haiti might be built. And it can—indeed must—serve as a source of inspiration, and even hope. Despite all its tragedy, Haiti's past shows the remarkable, steadfast, and ongoing struggle of a people to craft an alternative to the existence that others wanted to impose on them. Throughout Haiti's existence, reformers and rebels have attacked authoritarian leaders and exclusive institutions in the effort to bring something better into being. Even when these attempts have failed, they serve as touchstones, sources of inspiration for confronting Haiti's present crisis.

"Haiti disturbs," sociologist Jean Casimir likes to say. It disturbs, of course, because of its poverty and its suffering. But it also disturbs because, throughout its history, Haiti's people have repeatedly turned away from social and political institutions designed to achieve profits and economic growth, choosing to maintain their autonomy instead. The Haitian population has been told for two centuries, as it is told today, that it must change, adapt, modernize. No doubt some change is needed; but what has largely been offered to Haiti's population in the guise of foreign advice is simply a precarious place at the bottom of the global order.

Haitians have consistently refused such offers. In 1883, Janvier explained that he was more than happy for outsiders to come to Haiti to enrich themselves through commerce. "But please," he asked, "spare us your advice . . . We want to do things ourselves." Haitians might be "stubborn" and "proud" in their independence. But they had their reasons. No one else in the world had ever "paid as dearly for the right to say, while stomping their foot on the ground: 'This is mine, and I can do with it what I want!' "[12]

Faced with various envoys, missionaries, and experts from inside and outside the country, many Haitian communities have—often with impressive patience and a marked lack of hostility—steadfastly resisted all attempts to make them abandon their historic aspirations. A population born of slave revolution, they have insisted on holding on to a way of life predicated on refusing the return of the plantation system or anything that looks like it. They have paid more and more for that refusal as their situation has grown increasingly difficult. Nevertheless, under incredible duress, Haitians remain as determined as ever to make their world on their own terms, to use it to their own ends and not those of others.

The social cohesion that has resulted from this long historical process was made dramatically visible by the 2010 earthquake. Many outside observers expected that, given the massive difficulties and lack of security in Haiti even before the disaster, there would be a complete social breakdown—as there might well be in many places where the state has essentially evaporated. But as aid workers and journalists arrived in the country, they were surprised at the level of organization they encountered. Television anchors kept asking expectantly when the looting was going to begin, but reporters in Haiti instead described most communities as rapidly mobilizing to deliver mutual aid. In many disasters, of course, common citizens are the first responders to the crisis, and Haiti was no different: neighbors, family members, passersby dug people out of the rubble with hammers, rocks, or their bare hands. But even after the initial rescue work was done, when the solidarity of emergency response might have given way under the strain of dealing with the catastrophe, the people of Haiti largely continued to look after one another. In many areas Haitians got no assistance at all for many days, even weeks. It was not the government but the networks that crisscross the country—neighborhood organizations, religious groups, extended families—that tended the injured, set up camps, fed one another, sang and prayed and mourned together.

The fact that they had to do so much on their own is appalling. But that they did it also shows clearly that Haiti, despite its massive poverty and its almost total lack of a functioning government, is not a place of chaos. Life in Haiti is not organized by the state, or along the lines many people might expect or want it to be. But it does draw on a set of complex and resilient social institutions that have emerged from a historic commitment to self-sufficiency and self-reliance. And it is only through collaboration with those institutions that reconstruction can truly succeed.

The Haiti of today cannot be understood without knowledge of its complex and often tragic history. Against visions of Haiti that see it only as a place of disaster and failure, a country lacking democratic principles and civil society, the pages that follow also highlight Haiti's legacy of political struggle in the country, and Haitians' historic insistence on fashioning a way of life predicated on equality and autonomy. For it is now more vital than ever to remember that Haiti has had its triumphs, as distant as they often seem. Haiti's founding revolution—the only successful slave revolt in the history of the world—has continued to resonate in Haiti's society and culture for the past two centuries. The promise of that revolution, disparaged and undermined by the powerful both within and outside Haiti, has remained unfulfilled. But it has never disappeared.

INDEPENDENCE

"In the end," Jean-Jacques Dessalines announced on January 1, 1804, "we must live independent or die." Six weeks earlier, Dessalines, the revolutionaries' general-in-chief, had secured the decisive defeat of the French forces at the Battle of Vertières. Now, surrounded by the main commanders of his army, he called into existence a new nation: Haiti. On the same day, those commanders named him "Governor-General for Life" of the newborn country, making him its first head of state.[1]

Like the majority of the population he spoke to, Dessalines had once been a slave. The slogan "Liberty or Death," printed above the official independence decree, had a particularly potent meaning in Haiti. Defeat at the hands of the French would have meant literal death for the revolution's leaders, and a return to slavery for the rest. In victory, they guaranteed themselves the freedom to build new lives and a new society.

Haiti's independence had been won at a terrible cost. The new nation's ports and many of its plantations were in ashes. Combat, hunger, and disease had killed vast numbers of people—as many as 100,000 during 1802–03 alone. As Dessalines surveyed the new country, he saw a land haunted by the dead. "Men and women, girls and boys, let your gaze tend on all parts of this island: look there for your wives, your husbands, your brothers, your sisters . . . what have they become?" He also invoked the memory of those who had died as slaves on the plantations, their misery the wellspring of the colony's fabulous wealth. The French "barbarians," said Dessalines, had "bloodied our land for two centuries," and their influence would not be easy to throw off. "Le nom français lugubre encore nos contrées," Dessalines declared—"The French name still glooms our lands." The unconventional transformation of the adjective "lugubre"—"lugubrious"—into a verb captured just how deeply the history of French colonialism shadowed the newborn country. Against all this loss, the new country's leader offered an absolute commitment to a liberated future. "We have dared to be free," he proclaimed; "let us be thus by ourselves and for ourselves."[2]

The expulsion of the French seemed to hold out the promise of a completely new system for organizing the Haitian society. But as Dessalines quickly realized, the colonial order could not be exorcised by fiat or decree. The Haitian population and its leaders, after all, inherited a finely tuned plantation machine, a place whose entire mode of being was driven by the production of sugar and coffee for export. That was the initial condition from which the new country had to be built, and it proved inescapable. Colonial Saint-Domingue had been constructed around a hierarchical social order, an autocratic and militarized political system, and an export-oriented economy. From the moment of its founding to the present day, Haiti would find itself burdened by all three.

At the same time, however, the Haitian Revolution was an act of profound—and irreversible—transformation. Few other generations in history have achieved what the Haitian revolutionaries managed to do. If not for their victory, slavery would almost certainly have continued in the colony for at least several decades more, as it did in all the societies that surrounded them. By defeating the French forces, they created a space where former slaves could exercise cultural and social autonomy to a degree unknown anywhere else in the Americas. While Dessalines and other Haitian leaders eloquently articulated a passionate refusal of slavery, it was the people of Haiti who truly gave content to that refusal. Melding traditions and beliefs carried from Africa, the spirit of resistance born on the plantations of Saint-Domingue, and the confidence and knowledge gained from the triumph over the French, they created a new culture and way of life driven by an unceasing emphasis on independence and personal freedom.

Despite its drama and historic importance, many of the most important aspects of Haiti's revolution are startlingly difficult to document. We know much about its leaders, who left plentiful records of their actions and perspectives; we know far less about the experiences and the views of the masses of slaves who so dramatically changed the world in which they lived. Yet it was the culture of these masses, forged in bondage—the Kreyòl language, the Vodou religion, the focus on community, dignity, and self-sufficiency—that ultimately enabled them to destroy slavery and produce something new in its place.

III

Haiti has had many names. When the Atlantic currents brought Columbus to its shores on his first voyage, he baptized the island La Española, which in English became Hispaniola. The small outpost that Columbus set up on the northern coast of Hispaniola was the first European settlement in the Americas, though an ill-fated one: by the time he returned, all the settlers had been killed by indigenous inhabitants. The Spanish soon built a new settlement on the southeastern coast of the island, however, which they dubbed Santo Domingo, after the revered founder of the Dominican order. The town gave its name to the Spanish colony of Santo Domingo, which, centuries later, would become the Dominican Republic. French colonists, arriving on the western half of the island in the late seventeenth century, took the Spanish name and translated it, giving the title of Saint-Domingue to what would soon become their most precious American territory. Of course, long before the Europeans appeared, the indigenous inhabitants had their own names for the land. Among them, as early Spanish chroniclers noted, was Ayiti—"land of mountains." It was this name that the founders of Haiti reached back to in 1804, seeking to connect their struggle for freedom from slavery with the earlier battles of indigenous peoples against Spanish invaders.[3]

The island of Hispaniola was the starting point for European conquest of the Americas. By the middle of the sixteenth century, Hispaniola's indigenous population of perhaps 500,000 to 750,000 people was almost completely eliminated through war, forced labor, and disease. Santo Domingo became America's first colonial city, with a cathedral and university, and the Spanish imported African slaves to work on sugar plantations. As Spain conquered vast territories on the mainland of South America, however, Santo Domingo lost its importance, becoming mainly a stopover point for Spanish ships on their way to Europe. The ships' cargoes of silver drew English and French pirates to the region, and the Spanish government, unable to protect settlements on the western half of Hispaniola against pirate raids, removed them altogether. Soon French settlers from the famous pirate haven of Tortuga, just north of Hispaniola, moved in on the Spanish territory and began building plantations on the island's northwest coast. For a few decades they remained essentially illegal squatters, but in 1697 Spain officially ceded the territory to France.

By the late seventeenth century, the English and French empires in the Americas were increasingly fixated on growing one particular crop: sugar. The geographical fault lines that lie under Haiti and the rest of the Caribbean created a series of islands that turned out to be the perfect place for the cultivation of sugarcane. Haiti had the region's highest mountains, which sent water down to a series of large, flat plains. These abutted well-protected bays, ideal for anchoring ships. The island, furthermore, is situated right at the end of a highway crossing the Atlantic: a strong current flows from Europe directly toward it. Another set of currents lead from Africa straight to Haiti as well. The territory became one of the key points in the "triangle trade" that created the Atlantic economy of the eighteenth century: manufactured goods were brought from Europe to Africa, slaves from Africa to the Americas, and slave-produced crops from the Caribbean back to Europe.

French Saint-Domingue grew to become the most profitable colony in the world. By the late eighteenth century, it was the world's largest producer of sugar, exporting more of it than the colonies of Jamaica, Cuba, and Brazil combined. At the same time, Saint-Domingue also grew fully half of the world's coffee. It was a small territory, covering only about 10,600 square miles—about the size of Massachusetts. Yet it was more valuable to France than all the thirteen colonies of North America were to England.

An official estimate of the colony's population in 1789 reported that Saint-Domingue contained 55,000 free people and 450,000 slaves. But because slaves were taxed, they were also broadly undercounted; in all likelihood there were at least half a million of them. The slaves outnumbered the free population by ten to one in the colony overall, and by a much higher proportion on many of the plantations. In the parish of Acul, where the 1791 insurrection began, there were 3,500 slaves surrounding 130 free people.[4]

The free population was also deeply segmented and divided. It included fabulously wealthy white planters and powerful officials; poor white migrants managing slave gangs or working in the ports; and what were known as "free people of color," men and women of African descent who were not slaves and who indeed often owned slaves and plantations themselves.* According to official estimates,

---

* Historians often refer to the free people of color as "mulattoes," but that can be misleading, since not all were of mixed European and African ancestry. Skin color was certainly important: light-skinned men and women gained certain social privileges thanks to the fact that they were considered closer to being white. But there were also free people with no European ancestry, and some who were African-born but had managed to gain freedom and grow wealthy in Saint-Domingue. Officials at the time, and historians writing since, often use the term "free blacks" to describe the latter group, but here I will use the general term "free people of color" to designate all those people in the colony who were partly or wholly of African descent and were not slaves.

the colony's free population was divided more or less evenly between whites and people of color. Notably, the free men of color made up a large portion of the local police as well as of the colonial militia. The major task of that militia force, in Saint-Domingue, was not to defend the colony from external threats but to protect the territory from its potentially overwhelming enemy within: the slave majority.[5]

Although the colony produced some cotton, indigo, and a great deal of coffee, most of the slaves toiled on sugar plantations. Harvesting cane is backbreaking work, made risky by the razor-sharp spines of the tall stalks and the insects and snakes nested in the fields. Once cut, cane has to be processed quickly, so enslaved workers—usually women—worked day and night feeding the cane stalks into large stone mills, where it was all too easy for hands and arms to be pulled in and crushed. Other slaves supervised vats of boiling cane juice that produced the sugar crystals. A small number of slaves also worked as artisans, constructing barrels and buildings, or as domestics in the opulent plantation homes. A privileged few occupied positions as *commandeurs*, slave drivers transmitting instructions from masters and managers to field hands and making sure that these orders were followed. The drivers were viewed with both respect and fear—they were the ones who whipped any slaves who disobeyed—and were informal leaders within the plantation. It was a well-ordered system, a combination of "field and factory," in the terms of anthropologist Sidney Mintz, that brought together advanced technology and carefully designed labor management. But it also exhausted the soil through one cane harvest after another, and began a process of deforestation as swaths of trees were cut down to build plantation houses and the thriving port towns.[6]

Although masters controlled slaves in part through the promise of material rewards—extra food, better work, and sometimes even freedom—they depended most of all on terror. Slaves were branded with their masters' initials (often after having been already branded once by slave traders in Africa) and quickly learned that any resistance would be met with whipping or worse. Each plantation in

Saint-Domingue had a post ready for public punishments, which were carried out in front of the assembled workforce. Some contemporaries described brutally creative tortures devised by particularly sadistic masters, such as cutting off arms and legs, or burying slaves up to their necks and leaving them to be attacked by biting insects.

Slaves died in stunning numbers in the colony; each year, between 5 and 10 percent of the slave population succumbed to overwork and disease. Death outpaced births, and only a constant stream of imports sustained the laboring population. Some contemporaries were dismayed by the brutality and inefficiency of the system. They proposed reforms they hoped would increase the locally born slave population: a few weeks of rest from field labor for pregnant women, and rewards for those who had several children. But it was cheaper to let slaves die and buy more from Africa, so that is what the planters did.

Of the half-million slaves in Saint-Domingue on the eve of the 1791 revolt, about 330,000 had been born and raised in Africa. Most of them were quite recent arrivals; more than 40,000 had stepped off the slave ships just the previous year. Their African background—as well as their experience of the Middle Passage and plantation labor—shaped their politics, their practices, and their hopes for what life after slavery should be like. Though they were at the bottom of the social pyramid, they profoundly influenced the society's culture and therefore its future.[7]

The largest number of slaves in the colony came from the central African region broadly known as the Kongo. Captured by slave raiders or in battle, they were shipped to Africa's Atlantic coast and then loaded onto slave ships for the weeks-long voyage to Saint-Domingue. Arriving in Saint-Domingue, they found themselves in a cosmopolitan world, a mélange of different languages and cultures. None of them would likely have defined themselves as "Africans," but rather as members of particular groups or kingdoms: Kongo, Ibo, Fon, Poulards. And the newcomers were immediately mixed with enslaved people who were "creoles," born in the colony itself.

Creoles and African-born slaves had very different perspectives, to be sure, but at the same time they also shared a great deal. Most creole slaves, after all, had African parents, while the African arrivals necessarily became creolized, part of a New World culture in formation. "I'm a Creole-Kongo," a Vodou song declares.[8]

As they suffered together through the trauma of plantation life, Africans and creoles developed their own rituals of healing, mourning, and worship. Such ceremonies, along with dances and communal meals held on the margins of plantations, carved out a place where the enslaved could temporarily escape the order that saw them only as chattel property. The rituals combined religious practices from a wide variety of African traditions, including Christianity: the royalty of the Kongo had converted to Catholicism in the sixteenth century, and that religion was widely practiced in the region. Over time, the hybrid form of worship became known by the West African name of Vodou. It was an extremely open and fluid religion, welcoming new arrivals. Contemporary Vodou bears the traces of this openness: its pantheon includes many different *lwa*, or gods, who share certain rituals but also retain their distinctiveness. The different *nanchons*—nations—of *lwa* bear signs of their varied origins in different parts of Africa, and Vodou songs often emphasize the way in which many groups came together to create one common tradition of worship. One, called "Sou Lan Mè"—"On the Ocean"—uses the experience of the Middle Passage as a metaphor for the broader creation of a new life in Haiti. In the hold of the ship, on the turbulent waters of the Atlantic, it announces, "we all became one." Sung within Vodou ceremonies, the song is another reminder of the way in which the new culture was born out of a common experience of captivity, exile, and ultimately resistance.[9]

Saint-Domingue also gave birth to a new language: Kreyòl. What began as a rough-hewn form of communication for the linguistically diverse population of the colony—speakers of French, dialects such as Breton, and different African languages—became the native tongue of most children in the colony, slave and free alike, who developed and solidified the language. By the mid-eighteenth century, Kreyòl was spoken by almost everyone in Saint-Domingue, from wealthy masters to African-born slaves. It was the lingua franca of the plantations and the towns alike, and poetry, songs, and plays were written and performed in Kreyòl.[10]

Born in the harsh world of the plantations, these cultural achievements turned out to be potent political weapons. Masters and officials had always tried to contain the slave majority as much as possible. Colonial laws restricted the movement of slaves, mostly keeping them under constant surveillance on the plantation, and severely punishing any runaways, known as maroons. But slaves nonetheless found opportunities to circulate and thereby build connections with slaves from other plantations. The development of Kreyòl and Vodou facilitated such connections, creating communities of trust that stretched between different plantations and into the towns. These communities were what made it ultimately possible for the conspirators of 1791 to organize a coordinated assault on masters, sugar, and slavery.

The 1791 uprising also drew on a particularly useful skill that many of the recently arrived slaves had brought across the Atlantic. The slaves who arrived in Saint-Domingue from central Africa in the late eighteenth century came from a region torn apart by civil wars. Many were former soldiers, sold to European slavers after being captured in battle. They were well versed in the use of firearms and experienced in military tactics involving small, mobile, autonomous units. The governors and masters of Saint-Domingue had seen only living merchandise stepping off the African ships docked in their harbors, and they were confident that their methods for controlling these slaves would work as they always had in colonies throughout the Americas. What the masters didn't see was that the boats had brought literally thousands of soldiers to their shores. The new arrivals carried in their minds all the tactics and experience required to start—and win—a war. All they needed were weapons and an opportunity.[11]

| | |

In the middle of 1789, news of the French Revolution began arriving in Saint-Domingue from across the Atlantic. The upheaval in France sent shock waves throughout the world, but it created a particularly significant opening in Saint-Domingue. It weakened the French empire's central government and its system of colonial rule. At the same time, the revolution produced and sent into circulation a new, radical language of rights that could be put to use in contesting the existing social order. Among the first to take advantage of this new situation were Saint-Domingue's free people of color, who saw an opportunity to remedy their exclusion from the colony's political life. It was their initiative that launched what can be considered the first stage of the Haitian Revolution—though no one at the time would likely have predicted that these events would lead to the end of slavery, and eventually of the colony itself.

In the prospering territory of Saint-Domingue, many free people of color had become quite wealthy. White planters who fathered children with their slaves rarely acknowledged the mixed-race offspring officially, but it was relatively common practice to free them and give them land. By the time of the revolution, some families of color had been free for two or three generations. They bought their own plantations and slaves, and they became particularly involved in the colony's lesser crops: indigo, cotton, and especially coffee. The plains that were best for cultivating sugar were mostly controlled by French colonists, but even in the mid-eighteenth century there was still plenty of land to be had in the mountains of Saint-Domingue, and these plots were ideal for coffee growing. Some free people of color who got into the coffee boom early made fortunes as a result; others invested in waterfront property in Port-au-Prince and ended up perfectly positioned to become successful merchants in the port town. Since there were almost no schools in the colony, such families often sent their children to France, where they received elite educations.[12]

Of course, not all free people of color were wealthy; some of them led a very modest existence on the margins of free society. And not all were creoles: the group also included African-born men and women who had managed to gain their freedom. But rich or poor, light-skinned or not, all the free people of color were discriminated against by a set of laws which constantly reminded them that, simply because they were not white, they were a step below in the colonial hierarchy. They were prevented from practicing law and medicine, from holding local administrative positions, even from buying luxury clothes and furniture. Starting in 1784, an activist named Julien Raimond repeatedly petitioned the royal government to strike down these laws, but to no avail. After 1789, leading free people of color in the colony took advantage of the new political context to again demand equality with whites. They didn't attack the institution of slavery itself—after all, wealth in Saint-Domingue was rooted in slavery, and many of them were slaveholders themselves—but they insisted that there should no longer be racial distinctions between free people in the colonies.

Despite the French Revolution's egalitarian rhetoric, the Saint-Domingue planters and the French government refused to make any serious concessions to the free people of color. As a few lucid observers at the time realized, this was a major strategic mistake. When pamphlets and lobbying in Paris failed, free men of color took up arms in their cause. They had long made up the majority of the militia and police in the colony and thus had ready access to weapons. Their first uprising, led by a man named Vincent Ogé, was crushed, and in 1790 Ogé was captured and publicly broken on the wheel. After this defeat, some of Ogé's companions proposed increasing the size of their forces by arming their plantation slaves. As skirmishes erupted throughout the colony, free men of color began leading their slaves into battle. Whites responded in kind. Soon, slaves everywhere were being given weapons and asked to fight on one side or another of a steadily expanding conflict.

Suddenly, what had begun as an intense but contained struggle over social privileges among the free population of Saint-Domingue had expanded to involve the other nine-tenths of the population. The colony, where the slaves vastly outnumbered their owners, had long been a tinderbox, and the French Revolution had now tossed a match into it. Within a few months, the slaves would no longer be fighting on behalf of their masters, but for themselves.

At a religious ceremony held in August 1791, slave conspirators in the north of Haiti finalized their plans for insurrection. Among those who oversaw the ceremony was an enslaved man named Boukman, who emerged as the movement's main early leader. He and his network of conspirators organized the uprising brilliantly, and when a few days later the slaves rose up simultaneously on sugar plantations throughout the north, they took the colonial power structure by surprise. As the insurgents swept across the plain setting fire to cane fields, their terrorized masters fled to the port town of Le Cap. Boukman was killed in an engagement with French forces, but his fellow fighters pressed on, and one by one the world's most profitable plantations became military camps for a new army of insurgent slaves.

The insurrection's leaders knew that the odds were massively against them. Slave revolts had broken out constantly in plantation societies, but they had been essentially suicide missions. The rebels knew that slavery was everywhere: behind any one group of masters or troop of soldiers there was always another. If they were to succeed, they would need strong allies.

The Saint-Domingue insurgents found such allies in the colony's free people of color, many of whom decided that joining the slave revolt was their best chance for gaining equal rights from the French government. The alliance was a potent one, bringing together the military skills of enslaved Africans with those of colonial soldiers and police. At first, the rebelling slaves had mainly used the tools of their labor—machetes and cane knives—as weapons, though they also found some pistols and rifles on the plantations. Free people of color, however, brought rifles and even cannon into the insurgent camps.

Many of the revolutionaries were intent on vengeance, and one infamous leader named Jeannot ordered the whites whom he captured to be whipped and tortured. But other slaves understood that such actions were a political liability. They ordered Jeannot to stop and, when he didn't, executed him. In fact, many white prisoners found that, while they were certainly threatened by their captors, they were treated relatively well. Several were recruited as secretaries, writing letters for the insurgent leaders.

One of the most prominent advocates for humane treatment of whites was Toussaint Bréda, who, early in the conflict, had taken on a new and soon legendary last name: Louverture. Like many of those who became leaders in the revolution, he had known life in several different strata of the colonial society in Saint-Domingue. Born a slave, he had served as a coachman on a large sugar plantation in the north of the colony. He received some education from his godfather—a free man of color—and was given his freedom as a relatively young man. He did well for himself, managing a small plantation near Le Cap and briefly owning his own slave. At the beginning of the insurrection, he helped his white former masters to safety before joining the rebels, an act that earned him valuable trust among local planters and for which he was long lauded by his biographers. Louverture was a consummate tactician and a tireless negotiator, whose brilliant military and political strategies shaped the insurrection into a powerful, even unstoppable force. One of the most dramatic figures in the history of the modern world, he was at once frightening and fascinating to his contemporaries.[13]

Louverture astutely made use of the geopolitical conflicts of the moment. European empires shared a common commitment to slavery, but they also coveted one another's Caribbean territories and had fought unceasingly over them for centuries. When the slave uprising began in 1791, England and Spain both saw it as a marvelous opportunity to take over the coveted colony of Saint-Domingue. The Spanish, working from across the border in Santo Domingo, reached out to the slave insurgents, offering to give them weapons and commissions as Spanish officers if they would help secure the colony for Spain. Louverture took advantage of the proffered weaponry, which turned his army into a powerful military force. Later, when he no longer needed the Spanish, he unceremoniously turned on them and drove them from the colony.

The English unwittingly assisted the insurgents in their own way. In their bid for control of the colony they reached out to French planters, who by 1792 were increasingly suspicious of the French state—now in the hands of the radicals, some of them prominent abolitionists. Several of the planters made it clear that they would be willing to support England's ambitions for Saint-Domingue in order to preserve slavery in the colony. Dealing with France's enemy, however, created a significant new opening for the slave insurgents. The isolated French governors of the island, facing the possibility of mass treason among white planters, found they had no one to turn to for preventing the loss of the colony except the revolutionaries themselves.

In June 1793, two French Republican commissioners—Léger Félicité Sonthonax and Étienne Polverel—made a stunning decision. Reaching out to the armies of slave insurgents that surrounded Le Cap, the commissioners promised that if these rebels fought for the French Republic, they would be granted freedom and citizenship. The first to respond were a group of rebels led by an elderly Kongo-born man named Pierrot. He became an officer in the French army, his troops Republican soldiers. Other insurgents soon followed, shoring up the vulnerable position of the French commissioners. Understanding their power, the insurgents pressed for their families to be freed as well, and Sonthonax and Polverel agreed to do so, steadily expanding their offer. Still, many rebels, including Toussaint Louverture, remained aloof and kept fighting on the side of the Spanish and against the French. Under pressure from the insurgents and desperate to secure the loyalty of the population of Saint-Domingue, Sonthonax and Polverel took an even more radical step in August 1793: they abolished all slavery in the colony outright.[14]

A delegation of elected representatives from Saint-Domingue, including the African-born Jean-Baptiste Belley, traveled to Paris and presented the news to the National Convention. They argued forcefully that emancipation was both morally right and strategically vital. While white planters had happily consorted with England, France's enemy, the black former slaves in the colony had made themselves the Republic's most valuable and steadfast defenders in the Caribbean. The delegates were so persuasive that in February 1794, the Convention decreed slavery abolished not just in Saint-Domingue but throughout the former French empire. They extended the rights of French citizenship to "all men, of all colors," creating the legal foundations for the first multiracial democracy in the New World.

It was a remarkable victory for the revolutionaries of the Caribbean. By crafting an alliance with progressive forces in France, they had managed to convert to their cause the government of one of the most powerful empires on earth, whose fortunes had been built on the foundation of slavery. It was an action without precedent, and without preparation. No one in France, not even the more radical abolitionists, had envisioned that slavery would be abolished as suddenly as it was in Saint-Domingue. None had imagined that the former slaves would gain not just freedom but also the rights of citizenship. France's abolition of slavery did not grow out of French abolitionists' plans and deliberations; rather, it was the direct result of the 1791 slave uprising and the successful military campaign waged over the course of two years by an army of determined insurgents.

But the dramatic victory also created major problems. What would the economy of Saint-Domingue look like after slavery? How would the plantation system work? Broadly united in a common struggle for liberation, the coalition that won freedom in 1793 would find itself deeply divided over precisely what that freedom should mean.

III

How do you get from slavery to freedom? Throughout the nine-teenth century, the question haunted and challenged many political leaders. But it initially arose in all its complexity in Saint-Domingue, where it fell to Toussaint Louverture to manage the first large-scale emancipation process in the Americas. As soon as he heard that the National Convention had abolished slavery throughout the empire, Louverture rapidly rallied to the French side. Having established himself as the main leader of the insurrection, he now became a French general. Within a few years, he was named the governor general of the colony by the French government.

After their initial slavery-abolishing proclamations in 1793, Son-thonax and Polverel had hurriedly issued a series of decrees that sought to contain the economic and social impact of emancipation. According to these regulations, former slaves were obligated to remain on their plantations. No longer slaves but not fully free either, they were called "cultivators," and in return for their labor they received a quarter of what was produced on the plantation, to be divided among themselves. Rapidly put together in a moment of crisis, these regulations ended up having a remarkably long-term impact on the territory. They became the foundation not only for Louverture's administration, but also for many of the laws enacted by Haitian leaders after independence.

Both the French commissioners and Louverture might, of course, have chosen another solution: breaking up the plantations and giv-ing the land to the slaves. After all, as at least one commentator noted during the revolution, the slaves had worked for no pay for a long time. People who fled from France or its territories after 1791 were officially considered traitors by the French government, and the state took over their property. In Saint-Domingue, that meant that the military regime led by Toussaint Louverture was now in control of estates abandoned by the planters and could dispose of them as it saw fit.

Louverture never really considered breaking up the plantations, however. He saw the continuation of the plantation system as the only viable choice for his people. How else, after all, could the economy of an export-oriented colony function? During his time as leader of Saint-Domingue, Louverture steadfastly defended the plantation system, telling the ex-slaves that they had to prove to the world that it was possible to produce sugar and coffee without slavery. He argued fervently that in order to preserve their hard-won freedom, the ex-slaves of Saint-Domingue had to accept the restrictions that would keep plantations going.

In practice, this meant that Louverture offered up the sequestered land for rent. Those who leased the plantations paid the ex-slave cultivators a quarter of what was produced and gave another quarter to the state. The rest was theirs. It was a very lucrative proposition, and the people who were best placed to take advantage of this opportunity were members of Louverture's regime—especially the army's higher-ranking officers and generals. Their military power allowed them to dominate the state, and that in turn gave them access to valuable properties in the colony. This equation, established over the course of the revolution, would long haunt independent Haiti.[15]

For the plantation laborers, the process must have seemed particularly cynical. Louverture was the one who insisted on the maintenance of agricultural policies, set up by Sonthonax and Polverel, that forced ex-slaves to keep working as "cultivators"; and his generals doubled as agricultural administrators, using the armed forces to police the plantations and punish anyone who sought to run away from them. Saint-Domingue's social hierarchy was no longer based on race or on chattel bondage; like the overall population, the army was comprised mostly of ex-slaves, many of them African-born. But with the military hierarchy offering the only definitive escape from plantation toil, the path to power in the colony was still closed off to all but a small group of men.

Plantation laborers knew that their condition had changed for the better, but they also resented the many continuities between the old regime and the new. Some of them put up resistance reminiscent of what slaves had done before the revolution: running away to the mountains or the towns, or even turning to violent rebellion. (Louverture decisively crushed such revolts, including one led by his adopted nephew Moïse.) Others fought back in more subtle ways, taking advantage of provisions in Sonthonax and Polverel's 1793 decrees that set up democratic assemblies on the plantations. These assemblies, in which laborers could vote on details of their work routine, elect their own leaders, and discuss problems or complaints, were clearly cherished by the cultivators. The laborers quickly put the assemblies to good use in lively debates, making choices that often frustrated plantation managers and officials.

Women were especially active in these assemblies. Because they could not join the army, and because mothers with young children found it more difficult to simply run away from the plantation, in many areas women came to make up the bulk of the labor force. Accordingly, they had a particularly powerful interest in shaping the structure of labor on the plantations, and they frequently took the lead in the debates. They complained about the fact that while they did essentially the same work as men, they were paid less. And they pushed for the cultivators to spend less time working in the sugarcane fields and more time developing the small plots of land that they depended on to feed themselves and their families—plots whose history and significance stretched back to the days of slavery.[16]

In Saint-Domingue as in most other slave societies, masters trying to figure out how to feed a large slave population had settled upon a kind of compromise. Instead of purchasing expensive provisions, they allowed the slaves to farm scattered plots of land for themselves or else to work collectively on provision grounds for the whole plantation. The plots given over to the slaves were often difficult to cultivate: all the best land was kept for growing sugar, coffee, or cotton. Still, slaves took full advantage of the opportunity, developing productive gardens, planting fruit trees, and raising livestock in tiny spaces. What they didn't consume themselves they sold in local markets. (These markets also provided a place for slaves from different plantations to meet and talk, connect and conspire.) The garden plots were so productive, in fact, that by the late eighteenth century they produced most of the food eaten in the colony by slaves and masters alike. From a tiny, self-serving concession by the owners, the slaves had carved out a measure of autonomy. Over time they came to consider the plots of land essentially theirs.[17]

After the insurrection began on the northern plantations, masters and managers throughout the colony found that the increasingly hard-to-control slaves were turning away from field labor and toward expanding their individual plots or the collective provision grounds. Sugar and coffee were not particularly useful to them, the slaves made clear; potatoes, livestock, and fruit were. It was a quiet, nonviolent revolt, but no less emphatic for all that.

Under Louverture's regime, the little garden plots assumed even greater importance. Working on the same plantations for meager wages seemed a poor recompense for the costs of insurrection. Having survived the brutality of the slave system and then the violence of the revolution, the ex-slaves strongly believed that the land should be theirs; land ownership would give freedom its full and true meaning. Through their emphasis on self-sufficient agriculture, they built what Haitian sociologist Jean Casimir dubs a "counter-plantation" system, one based on a steadfast resistance to plantation labor in all its forms.[18]

Louverture never yielded to the counter-plantation resistance. Indeed, his use of force against unwilling plantation laborers led to persistent rumors that he was in league with the white planters and was planning to reestablish slavery. Thousands of planters had fled the island during the insurrection, heading to Jamaica and to U.S. cities such as Philadelphia, Charleston, and New York, but there were plenty who stayed in the colony, and Louverture developed an uneasy but stable compromise with them. They found that, while they had lost their direct ownership and immediate control of the laboring population, they could still survive, and in some cases even thrive, under Louverture's regime. Indeed, he did so well by the remaining planters that many of those who had fled in the midst of war between 1791 and 1793 soon returned, attracted by the relative stability and the prospect of regaining control of their plantations.* For a few years during the late 1790s, two groups of landowners—some of them former masters, others former slaves—broadly cooperated in running the colony.[20]

In 1801, a commission composed almost entirely of white planters wrote a constitution for the territory of Saint-Domingue that made Louverture governor-for-life of the colony and gave him broad political powers. At the same time, the constitution established even more draconian agricultural provisions, solidifying and expanding regulations that forced laborers to continue working on the plantations. It was, in effect, a charter for a new colonial order, one in which slavery and racial hierarchy were dismantled but plantation production—and even white ownership of many plantations—was preserved.[21]

In the short term, this regime was an economic success. Under Louverture, coffee production reached nearly the levels it had achieved before the insurrection of 1791, while sugar production—severely affected by the widespread destruction of sugar processing machinery during the uprising—was steadily increasing. In the long run, however, the Haitian population's hunger for land ownership and autonomy meant that the plantation system was doomed. Although the governments that came in the wake of Louverture

---

* The return of the masters to their former plantations resulted in some remarkable scenes. In the late 1790s, one French visitor who was seeking to reestablish control over a family-owned plantation found that although he was welcome to stay on the property that he considered his, the workers were no longer interested in serving him. When he asked for food, they told him that there were some potatoes ready to be harvested in the field: he could help himself. The visitor was shocked by the cheekiness of the response, though it was in many ways remarkably humane, even hospitable. The former slaves didn't take revenge or refuse his presence; they just made it clear that times had changed, that they were no longer bound to obey his commands, and that they were now all living on the land together as equals.[19]

would, like him, attempt to maintain and rebuild the plantation system—at times with tentative success—they could never truly reverse the process that began with the revolution of 1791 and the emancipation of the slaves two years later. The people of Saint-Domingue were determined to take control of their lives, and they would build their society around that resolve.

III

Although Saint-Domingue was still a French colony, Louverture often acted like the head of an independent state. Besides trading with the United States, for instance, he established a series of trade agreements with England—even though England and France were at war. And while Louverture always professed loyalty to France, he clearly didn't fully trust the country's commitment to emancipation. He made sure to keep his army well supplied with guns and ammunition, largely purchased from the United States, ready to work with France but also to fight it if necessary. He had reason to be concerned. Over the preceding years, many Frenchmen had attacked Louverture's regime, painting damning portraits of a "despotic" governor and plantations overrun by lazy and violent ex-slaves. As long as there was a strong parliamentary system in France, Louverture had eloquent defenders who managed to hold back such challenges. But he knew how rapidly the situation might change.[22]

In November 1799, Napoleon Bonaparte carried out a coup in France, naming himself first consul. With the help of his brother-in-law, Victor Emmanuel Leclerc, he eliminated the parliament, silenced public debate, and centralized power in his own hands. Napoleon's approach to colonial policy was shaped by a small group of advisers, several of whom were convinced that it was time for the experiment in emancipation to come to an end. Napoleon was particularly incensed by Louverture's 1801 constitution, which he considered an inexcusable attack on his authority. He also knew that the timing was right for a strike: the French had begun peace negotiations with the British, and Napoleon had received assurances that any ships he sent to Saint-Domingue could travel unmolested across the Atlantic. He decided to act.

In late 1801, Napoleon placed Leclerc in charge of a massive military expedition to Saint-Domingue. Publicly, he proclaimed his commitment to liberty in the colonies and announced that the troops had an innocuous mission: to help buttress the defenses of the territory and keep order there. But he gave his brother-in-law detailed secret instructions: Leclerc was to either co-opt or destroy the black generals and prepare the way for the reestablishment of the old colonial order. "Rid us of these gilded negroes," Napoleon pleaded, "and we will have nothing more to wish for."[23]

When Louverture saw Leclerc's armada hovering off the shores of Saint-Domingue, he decided to stage a tactical retreat. Realizing that he wouldn't be able to hold the port towns, he ordered his officers to burn them to the ground, leaving nothing behind for the French. One of Louverture's highest-ranking generals, Henry Christophe, who was in command of Cap Français when the French troops arrived, set his own mansion there alight before proceeding to the rest of the town. Dessalines, then the commander at Gonaïves, did the same. Christophe and Dessalines then led their troops into the mountains to begin the campaign of resistance against the French.[24]

Not everyone in the colony was united behind Louverture, however. Back in 1798, a rival general, André Rigaud, had refused to serve under Louverture's authority and had created his own autonomous regime in the south of Saint-Domingue. Louverture soon crushed the uprising, and Rigaud fled to France, along with two prominent officers who had supported him: Alexandre Pétion and Jean-Pierre Boyer. Now, Napoleon invited Pétion and Boyer to be part of the Leclerc expedition. He also sent along Louverture's two sons, who had been studying in France, with a personal letter from the emperor to their father. The presence of all these familiar figures from the colony in the French armada reassured many people in

Saint-Domingue that Leclerc had in fact come only to assist the colony's armed forces and help assure internal stability. So while Christophe and Dessalines followed Louverture's orders, some of his other top generals welcomed the French troops and gave their support to Leclerc.

Haiti's war of independence thus felt to its combatants more like a civil war, creating profound divisions within the population and pitting different parts of the Saint-Domingue military against one another. After all, for most of the previous decade, Louverture and his troops had all served under the French flag, fighting for the Republic. They had successfully defended the colony against Spanish incursions and a large-scale English invasion. Leclerc's forces fighting in Saint-Domingue in 1802 were bewildered to find, during one battle, that their opponents were singing French revolutionary songs. The two armies had the same anthems.

Even with only partial support from his army, Louverture held the French at bay, drawing Leclerc's troops into a series of exhausting engagements in the interior of the colony. He knew that if he could last long enough, the rainy season would bring yellow fever to the unacclimated French forces, weakening them enough that he might be able to triumph. But after a few months of fighting, Louverture realized he was in a precarious situation, his troops exhausted and stretched too thin to hold out. In April 1802, Henry Christophe surrendered to the French, and Louverture and Dessalines followed soon afterward. The three of them made a deal: if they could keep their rank and privilege as generals, they would help the French destroy the vestiges of resistance in the colony. Having distinguished themselves in battle against Leclerc, Dessalines and Christophe now used their considerable military talents fighting fiercely *for* the French.

Louverture was not with them. Suspecting that his submission was only a temporary ruse and that he was just waiting for an opportune moment to attack the French again, Leclerc reneged on the deal, arrested Louverture, and deported him to France. On leaving the island, Louverture famously declared: "In overthrowing me, you have cut down only the trunk of the tree of liberty of the blacks; it will grow back from the roots, because they are deep and numerous." Leclerc warned the French government, "You cannot hold Toussaint far enough from the ocean or put him in a prison that is too strong." They locked him in the Fort de Joux prison in the Jura mountains, where he grew ill in his cold cell and died in April 1803, months before Haiti's declaration of independence. Until his last days, he repeatedly wrote to Napoleon insisting on his loyalty and asking for a chance to defend himself against Leclerc's accusations. He got no response. When Louverture's jailers discovered his corpse, they found a piece of paper tucked into the bandanna wrapped around his head. On it Louverture complained one last time of being arbitrarily arrested and sent off "as naked as an earthworm," with no chance to respond to the charges against him: "Is it not to cut off someone's legs and order him to walk? Is it not to cut out his tongue and tell him to talk? Is it not to bury a man alive?"[25]

Napoleon and his advisers were convinced that once the leadership in Saint-Domingue was firmly under their control, the French could proceed comfortably to the reestablishment of slavery in the colony. They remained blind to a reality that a few observers outside of France saw quite clearly: the revolution in Saint-Domingue had transformed its entire population. Despite all the limits that Louverture had placed on liberty to keep the plantations going, the former slaves had begun to construct a new social order of their own, and many of them were ready to die rather than go back to slavery. So even after all the major leaders in the colony had gone over to the French side, the resistance didn't stop. Plantation laborers everywhere kept fighting Leclerc's forces, organizing themselves into small bands that took refuge in the mountains. They were relentless and resourceful. One group sent a riderless horse in front of the French line, enticing soldiers to come out and capture it, and then gunned them down. A group of women attacked the French troops while wearing mattresses to protect themselves from musket fire. As one early account of the war put it, "everywhere the land harbored enemies, in the woods, behind a rock; liberty gave birth to them."[26]

In August of 1802 the rainy season began, and, as Louverture had predicted, the French troops fell prey to yellow fever. As more and more of them died from combat and disease, Leclerc found his mission increasingly hampered by its own contradictions. With few French soldiers left at his disposal, the only way to fight the rebels in the mountains was to depend fully on the very same "gilded negroes" that Napoleon wanted to eliminate from the colony. And in order to maintain their loyalty, he had to keep convincing them—and the population at large—of France's good intentions. But the longer Leclerc stayed in Saint-Domingue, the more he found it impossible to hide what he had really been sent to do. Some of Leclerc's officers were openly contemptuous of blacks, and after Napoleon reopened the French slave trade, a few had started buying and selling slaves. In desperation, Leclerc even asked Napoleon to censor French newspapers: they had been publishing racist jokes, and infuriated residents of Saint-Domingue took this as further proof that France had turned against emancipation.[27]

Dessalines, Christophe, and other officers who had switched sides now faced a choice. The French were losing the war, and continuing to fight on their behalf might well be suicidal: if the rebels won, they were not going to be gentle with black officers in the uniforms of the French. In October 1802, Dessalines secretly met with Alexandre Pétion, who was guarding Le Cap for the French. Pétion and Dessalines had fought against each other a few years before, during Rigaud's rebellion, and they came from different sectors of Saint-Domingue's society: Dessalines a former plantation slave, Pétion a free man of color. The two of them agreed, however, to take their troops and join the rebels in the mountains. Christophe and his soldiers followed soon after. Dessalines sent a simple parting message to the French: they should "return to Europe."[28]

Facing increasingly steadfast and unified resistance, Leclerc recommended a "war of extermination" against the population of the colony. "Here is my opinion of this country," he wrote to Napoleon in October 1802 after the defection of Dessalines. "We must destroy all the blacks of the mountains—men and women—and spare only children under twelve years of age." He conceded that some of the blacks who lived in the plains of the colony, where its sugar plantations once thrived, might be salvageable. The French needed to kill only half of them.[29]

Leclerc died of yellow fever not long afterward, and as the French found their erstwhile comrades turning against them, they responded with growing paranoia. Fearing that the ever-decreasing number of black troops who remained loyal to France might join the insurrection, Leclerc's successor, General Donatien Rochambeau, began executing them, dumping them into the harbor with weights around their necks. He also gassed prisoners, locking them in the holds of ships and asphyxiating them with burning sulphur. But Rochambeau's tactics only succeeded in solidifying and unifying the opposition, sending black soldiers who might have remained with the French into the arms of the rebels.* The insurgents gained other converts as well: several units of Polish troops, who had been enlisted in the French army after the occupation of their own land, now defected to Dessalines, who welcomed them.

For a decade, France had been an ally and indeed guarantor of emancipation. Now it had become the enemy of an entire people. In May 1803, Dessalines gathered the rebel generals together at the Congress of Arcahaye, and they vowed to destroy the French pres-

---

* The French were not the only ones to execute their prisoners. Dessalines's forces responded to Rochambeau's atrocities by hanging their white captives on the hills outside Le Cap in view of the French troops. Marcus Rainsford, an Englishman who wrote about the conflict, included in his book two parallel engravings illustrating the cycle of violence. One shows a French soldier pushing a black prisoner into the water, with a French tricolor flag overhead; the other depicts the hanging of a white officer by black troops under a palm tree. The second engraving is regularly reproduced as a representation of the Haitian Revolution, but the first is usually left out. Outside the country, Haiti's independence is all too often remembered as a case of blacks indiscriminately killing whites. But in Haiti itself, Rochambeau's brutality has never been forgotten.[30]

ence on the island. To symbolize their oath, Dessalines created a new flag for his army. Taking the French tricolor, with its bars of red, white, and blue, he ripped the white out of the middle of it and tossed it away. The remaining red and blue bars were sewn together to make the new flag of the revolutionary movement, which would soon become the flag of independent Haiti. Over the next few months Dessalines managed to lead a diverse and fragmented army to victory, uniting the entire nation for a brief but crucial moment in the pursuit of one common goal.

▌▌▌

"Dessalines is leaving the North / Come see what he is bringing," a traditional Haitian song invites us. The song narrates the final triumph of Dessalines over the French. What is the secret to Dessalines's victory? A *ouanga nouveau*, the song tells us—a kind of "new magic." A *ouanga*, in Haitian Vodou, is an object that concentrates and transmits power, and it can take many forms. According to the song, Dessalines's magic took one form in particular: as he marched to defeat the French, his power came in the shape of muskets, bullets, and "cannons to chase away the whites."[31]

And chase them away he did. Dessalines's stunning victory in November 1803 effectively ended the French campaign in Saint-Domingue, enabling Haiti to declare its independence a few weeks later. Of the tens of thousands of French soldiers and sailors sent to the colony between 1801 and 1803, only a few thousand survived the conflict. Having set out to tame the insufficiently respectful colony, Napoleon wound up losing it altogether. Haitians understood how remarkable their victory was, and the first years of independence were filled with joyous, almost unbelieving celebrations. Officers and their wives, decked out in jewels and clothes of silk and Indian madras, went out to the countryside for barbecues set at long tables in alleys of mango trees. Young Haitians performed plays dramatizing the great moments in the war for independence. One of

Dessalines's officers always attended the shows in a large hat upon which was written, in red letters, "Haiti, the tomb of the French."[32]

Outside Haiti, however, Dessalines is usually remembered not for his heroics against the French but for his attacks on the white planters who chose to remain in the new country. His call for an end to French influence certainly had an ominous undercurrent; and while Dessalines declared "peace to our neighbors," seeking to reassure the empires with slave colonies in the Caribbean that he had no intention of spreading insurrection, he remained (like Louverture) deeply suspicious of the French. In February 1804 he accused the planters who had stayed in Haiti of conspiring against the new regime and working to facilitate a French return. He also produced a letter from 1802, signed by many of the planters still in the country, in which they declared their support for the brutal tactics of Rochambeau. In the course of the next few weeks, roving groups of soldiers and residents acting under orders from Dessalines carried out mass killings of most of the French whites who still lived in Haiti—perhaps as many as several thousand people. In a famous proclamation, he presented the killings as both an act of self-defense and a justified act of revenge for the crimes of the past. "Yes, we have paid back these true cannibals crime for crime, outrage for outrage," he announced. "I have saved my country. I have avenged America."[33]

These killings were not, as is often said, indiscriminate massacres of all the whites in Haiti. Indeed, white North American merchants traded in Haiti undisturbed during this period; one of them even hosted a large dinner party attended by Haitian officers while the massacres were under way. Dessalines also placed some French whites whom he considered to be allies of Haiti, as well as the Polish defectors from the French army, under his protection. They had, after all, embraced the cause of independence from France. Indeed, one Frenchman—nicknamed "the good white"—was among those who signed the Haitian declaration of independence.[34]

In newly independent Haiti, these protected whites became Haitian citizens, and several of them even ended up serving in high-ranking military positions under the new regime. Officially, they also stopped being white: in his 1805 constitution, Dessalines decreed that all Haitians would "henceforth only be known generically as blacks." In so doing, he made blackness not so much an issue of color as of allegiance to the project of freedom and independence. The same constitution, however, made it clear that while some approved whites could become part of Haitian society, new ones would face severe restrictions: "No white man, regardless of nationality, may set foot in this territory as a master or landowner, nor will he ever be able to acquire any property." In a country where most of the population had once been the literal property of whites, this stipulation—maintained almost without exception until the U.S. occupation of the country in the early twentieth century—was meant as a shield against the return of the past.[35]

In his proclamations—which were disseminated throughout the Americas and translated and published in many U.S. newspapers—Dessalines wrote eloquently of the determination of Haiti's people to create a radically new order. Haiti was going to be a beacon for the oppressed everywhere, he promised, carrying out vengeance for the brutalities of colonial rule and offering a social structure in which blacks were not only free but politically and economically empowered. The proclamations established the idea that Haiti offered a home for people of color throughout the Americas who longed for freedom and citizenship.[36]

While carrying on this remarkable international media campaign, Dessalines also made diplomatic overtures to the Americans and the British in nearby Jamaica. These were the nearest and most powerful merchant powers, and the obvious entities to approach as outlets for Haiti's agricultural products. He ran into some resistance: Britain and the United States were both committed slaveholding powers, and officials in both countries passed laws preventing Haitian merchants and sailors from visiting their shores. They feared what their slaves might learn from the Haitians and were intent on limiting the impact of what Haiti had achieved. At the same time, however, the United States and Britain were eager to profit from Caribbean commerce, and although Dessalines was unable to gain official recognition of Haitian independence from either country, he did develop trade relations with both. These were crucial for Dessalines's regime, since the goods he acquired included large quantities of weapons and ammunition.[37]

Aware of Haiti's vulnerability and marginal status, Dessalines was determined to provide Haiti with a powerful military infrastructure that could stand up to any new invasion. Empires in the Caribbean had traditionally focused primarily on repelling naval assault, but Dessalines knew that Haiti had no navy to speak of, and little hope of building one that could face the massive armadas of the European empires. Moreover, Haiti's military had its roots in slave insurrection and guerrilla warfare, and throughout the revolutionary wars, the insurgents had always drawn strength from their redoubts in the mountains. Even when they lost control of the towns and the plains, they were never wholly defeated in the heights, and they had beaten the French largely by successfully drawing their enemies into a series of devastating engagements in the interior. Dessalines had lived through—indeed, had led—many of these military successes. To defend Haiti, therefore, he created a string of fortifications on the mountaintops and in the interior of the country, expanding a few existing forts and building new ones. Some of these forts were placed to defend the country from incursions from Spanish Santo Domingo, then occupied by a French general with a few thousand soldiers who encouraged his troops to capture Haitians and sell them into slavery. But the forts were also meant to provide the Haitian army with a place to retreat to and withstand a siege by the French.[38]

While such military projects were driven by understandable fears, they did divert a huge portion of Haiti's already strained resources. The money, of course, could have done much good elsewhere: in the construction of schools, in the rebuilding of towns or agricultural infrastructure. The large-scale irrigation projects that had sustained Saint-Domingue's flourishing colonial economy lay in ruins after years of warfare, and hopes of reviving sugar production required mills and boiling houses. Instead, Haiti got a string of forts that, in the end, were never used against a foreign enemy at any time in the nineteenth century. (Much later, they did briefly serve as redoubts for insurgents fighting a different foe: the United States Marines.)

This early phase of defensive militarization also had political consequences, helping to solidify an order in which military leaders came to both embody and control the Haitian state. There was a long history to this political formation. War, after all, had brought freedom to the population in 1793, and had preserved that freedom when it was threatened in 1804. Toussaint Louverture had ruled the colony simultaneously as its top general and its political head, and Dessalines and the country's other founders had also served as army officers. Military leaders, they believed, were the only ones capable of guiding and protecting the fragile new nation.

Named Haiti's head of state by an assembly of generals, Dessalines organized his new government around military structures. He justified the concentration of power in his hands by presenting himself as a symbol and guarantor of the liberty of Haiti. Indeed, the country's independence declaration itself had been written as a message from Dessalines to his countrymen: "Remember that I sacrificed everything to rally to your defense," he commanded, "family, children, fortune, and now am rich only in your liberty." He emphasized that he had struck fear into the hearts of slave owners everywhere: "My name has become a horror to all those who want slavery. Despots and tyrants curse the day I was born." But in the same breath he also warned the people of Haiti that those who refused the laws "which the spirit guarding your fate dictates to me for your own good" would deserve, and receive, the treatment that was appropriate for an "ungrateful people." The first document of Haitian independence thus contained a kind of threat, an assertion that the leader (aided by higher powers) knew best what the people needed and that they must submit to the new order or suffer the consequences. In 1805, Dessalines, seeking to secure respect from European nations, crowned himself emperor of Haiti and issued an imperial constitution that concentrated all political power in his own hands. His state council was made up of army generals, and his decrees and legislation were written by a small group of secretaries who were likewise drawn from the military staff.[39]

In retrospect these developments might seem inevitable, the result of both institutional inertia and external pressures. But Haiti's early leaders could have chosen a different path, organizing a constitutional convention and an election rather than simply creating a state out of the military. It would certainly have been difficult—in part because, unlike the British colonies in North America, French Saint-Domingue possessed few institutions that could serve as foundations for a democratic order. The slaves, of course, had had no say in how the plantations were run, and even the tiny minority of free people had little input into the governance of the colony: almost all the power was concentrated in the hands of officials appointed by the king. Still, Dessalines and other postindependence leaders could have drawn inspiration from the Haitian Revolution, which had been a profoundly democratic social movement. Insurgent bands had met, debated, and organized, and starting in 1793 there were several elections that sent representatives to serve in the French parliament. Thanks to these and to the plantation assemblies that were so popular under Louverture, many ex-slaves thus already had at least some experience with democratic processes before Dessalines came to power.

One potential obstacle to democratic participation was the fact that only a small minority of Haitians could read and write, and most of them spoke only Kreyòl rather than French, the language of the government ever since the founding of Saint-Domingue. But Haiti wasn't the only place in which much of the population was illiterate in this period, and there were ways around the problem. Indeed, throughout the revolution, French administrators—starting with Sonthonax and Polverel—had issued proclamations in Kreyòl, which could be posted and read aloud by a literate individual to others. The leaders of independent Haiti could have opted for a similar strategy for mobilizing popular participation, but they chose not to do what even Napoleon had done for the population: translate official government announcements into the language of the governed. Perhaps they felt they didn't need to, confident that Haitians would trust them to defend their best interests. Perhaps they believed that the larger population was simply incapable of participating in an election, or that—given the massive problems faced by the new country—there was simply no time to set one up. Whatever their reasoning, the early years of independence represented a lost opportunity to channel the mass engagement of the revolution into a truly democratic order.

Widespread political participation, of course, would have opened the way for a profound challenge to the agricultural policies set up by Louverture and largely maintained by Dessalines. At the moment of independence, after all, most of the population was already clearly invested in the "counter-plantation" model, while Dessalines and other members of the elite were determined to keep the plantations alive. Like Louverture before him, Dessalines used the army to enforce his agricultural policies, preventing laborers from leaving the plantations. For most Haitians, his regime represented continuity with the oppressive labor practices of the past rather than a significant break with them.

Dessalines also followed Louverture's lead when it came to dealing with issues of land. Haiti was full of abandoned plantations; and while some Haitians who were related to departed French planters tried to use these family ties to assert ownership over the planters' old holdings, special commissions set up by Dessalines to examine the applications rejected most such claims. Instead, the commissions

placed the estates in the hands of the militarily controlled state, helping make it the country's largest landowner. Dessalines could thus
have carried out a distribution of land to the general population,
fulfilling the broad yearning for a full dismantling of the plantation
system. But although there are hints that near the end of his regime
he was considering some such experiment with land reform, during
his time in power he never embarked on that path. Like Louverture
before him, Dessalines seems to have been convinced that keeping
large properties intact was essential for maintaining the export-
oriented agricultural system—an ideology that put him on the same
side as the wealthy landowners, who also wanted to retain and expand
their sizable holdings. The debate, such as it was, revolved only around
the question of which group of elites would profit from Haiti's new
order—not what that order would look like.[40]

III

Today, Dessalines is widely and justifiably venerated for his role in
leading Haiti to independence. But the mythology surrounding him
tends to obscure the internal conflicts within the revolutionary
movement. The victory of 1804, after all, had been possible only
because some fighters—unlike Dessalines—had never joined the
French but had continued to resist even at the lowest point of the
conflict. Dessalines and his defenders argued that his time fighting
for the French was just a necessary ploy, providing him with the
opportunity to gather weapons and soldiers for the final push for
independence. Still, some of the insurgents—including Sans-Souci,
an African-born officer who had held much of the north in 1802
against French attacks led by Dessalines and Christophe—were not
sure why they should suddenly take orders from these fickle generals. Eventually, Christophe summoned Sans-Souci to a meeting, saying they needed to discuss the matter. It was an ambush: Sans-Souci
was killed, and his troops were brought under Christophe's command. Though in many ways Sans-Souci was one of the crucial

heroes of the Haitian Revolution, he remains largely forgotten to this day.[41]

In fact, the African-born majority of the new nation would largely find themselves marginalized. In his declaration of independence, Dessalines announced his determination to "forever ensure liberty's reign in the country of our birth." But most Haitians hearing him in 1804 were not born in Haiti; they had grown up in Africa and been brought to the colony as slaves. Perhaps Dessalines was speaking in symbolic terms, of Haiti as the country that gave birth to the Haitian people regardless of their individual origins. Still, whether deliberately exclusionary or merely careless, Dessalines's phrasing foreshadowed the second-class treatment that his regime and those that followed would often mete out to the African born majority.[42]

Dessalines had managed a political miracle by creating a broad coalition of insurgents and leading them to victory in 1804. But after independence, the sense of unity did not last: the tensions surrounding land ownership and the distribution of power were simply too strong. Caught between competing social forces, he was unable to count on support from either the Haitian oligarchy or the masses of laborers, and his regime rapidly unraveled. Even the soldiers in his army became increasingly disenchanted with his rule, depriving him of his most essential source of support.[43]

Dessalines faced particularly strong resistance in the south, where he had once led Louverture's troops against Rigaud. Touring the region in 1806, he was infuriated to find piles of dyewood being readied for shipment overseas: he had outlawed any export of wood because of worries about the consequences of widespread logging. Now he punished the merchants who were flouting the law, outraging them by burning the harvest they were preparing to sell. After a series of similar provocations, military leaders decided it was time to act. The imperial regime left little room for political opposition, but the people of Haiti were quite familiar with another mechanism for creating a change in government: armed revolt. Town by town, garrisons rose up against Dessalines, swearing to fight to the death against the emperor. Away from Port-au-Prince when he heard the news, Dessalines rushed back toward the capital, not realizing that many of his top generals had already turned against him. As he arrived at Pont-Rouge, north of the city, he was ambushed by a group of officers and unceremoniously gunned down. His reign as ruler of Haiti had lasted less than three years.[44]

Over the years, Dessalines's assassination at Pont-Rouge has become a legendary historical moment, a tragic testament to the way that Haiti's glorious independence so rapidly collapsed into violence. Dessalines was apparently ripped to pieces by an angry crowd after he was killed, and it fell to a woman named Défilée—who had been a camp follower in Dessalines's army units since the early days of the revolution—to make sure he got a proper burial. She is said to have gathered the pieces of his body in a bag and brought them to a cemetery, where he was buried in an unmarked grave. Early chroniclers of the event described Défilée as a madwoman, but over time she has come to seem like the only sane one in the midst of madness. In a 1967 play about the assassination, Haitian historian and playwright Hénock Trouillot has Défilée issue a powerful rebuke to those who assassinated Dessalines: "What the French could not accomplish, have they really done it, these monsters? . . . The father of our country? What will they say about us tomorrow?"[45]

In time, Dessalines's simple grave got a marker, and there are now many monuments and statues of him in Haiti, as well as streets and shops bearing his name. But perhaps the most vital and complex remembrance he receives takes place in Haitian Vodou, where Dessalines has gained the status of a *lwa*, or god, in the form of Ogou Dessalines, and where he is the subject of many songs that recount his deeds and channel his memory. Ogou is the god of war, and represents both sides of what soldiers have long meant in Haiti: forces of liberation, they can all too easily clash with the very people they are meant to defend.[46]

For Haiti's later leaders, Dessalines's short reign offered a cautionary tale: he had led the country to independence, but rapidly fell prey to social conflicts over what that independence should mean. After his death, it would be up to others to confront the challenge of turning the freedom that Haiti had gained into something meaningful, and sustainable, for its people.

2

THE CITADEL

"I am informed that you have mistreated your servants," King Henry Christophe of Haiti wrote to his nine-year-old son, Jacques-Victor-Henry, in 1813. "That is not commendable." Christophe knew what he was talking about: he had, after all, spent much of his life as a servant. Now, however, he was the ruler of an independent kingdom, reigning from a magnificent palace called Sans-Souci. His son was known as the "Prince Royal," and Christophe spared no expense in his education, putting him in the hands of the best tutors available. But he was disappointed with his son's writing skills—"I noted three erasures, and several other mistakes," he wrote disapprovingly in one letter—and concerned that the boy was not "docile" enough in following the commands of his teachers.[1]

Christophe felt the same way about his subjects. Like his son, they had been born as a free people in 1804. But the king believed that they needed to be educated, indeed transformed, before they could truly be independent. At stake was the future not just of Haiti, but of the entire black race. "Too long has the African race been unjustly calumniated," Christophe wrote in 1819 to the emperor Alexander of Russia. "Too long has it been represented as deprived of intellectual faculties, as scarcely susceptible of civilization or government by regular or established laws." By succeeding, Haiti could change that. Having freed themselves from bondage, Haitians could now disabuse the world of the "false assertions" that their masters—who "have had the impiety to degrade the finest work of the Creator, as if mankind had not one common origin"—had used to justify slavery throughout the centuries.[2]

Like other nations born of anticolonial revolutions, such as the United States in the late eighteenth century and the Latin American republics in the early nineteenth, Haiti struggled to gain allies and respect in a world still largely controlled by European empires. But Haiti also had an additional burden, one that Christophe clearly felt with particular force. No other country had faced such hostility, such resistance, even outright doubt about its very capacity to exist. The racist ideas that saturated the Western world at the time, coupled with the rage and fear that many slaveholders felt regarding black revolutionaries, raised the stakes immeasurably high for Haiti's early leaders. Many of those watching them were ready and eager to see Haiti fail.

Like Dessalines before him, Christophe poured money into national defense, most famously by constructing a massive fort—La Citadelle Laferrière—in the northern mountains. The fort had a practical purpose: if the French came back, the Haitian king and his army could retreat there and safely withstand a siege. To that end, the Citadel was packed with stores of ammunition and outfitted with a rainwater collection system. But the Citadel was also a symbol. Visible from miles away, it announced the Haitians' determination to stand firm against any possible return of the old order. Indeed, it was literally made partly out of brick and stone taken from broken-down former plantation houses.[3]

For Christophe's enemies at the time, and for many who have written about him since, the Citadel was a brutal folly, one that drove him to the ultimate irony: in order to assure freedom for Haitians, he turned them into slaves again. Visitors to the construction site described workers laboring in chains, carrying rocks up the hill under the watchful eyes of armed guards. Some contemporary chronicles state that thousands, even tens of thousands, of workers perished in the process. Christophe's defenders have sought to temper this image, claiming that the building of the Citadel was carried out as a massive public works project with rotating groups of laborers brought in from various plantations for short periods of work. Today, it seems nearly impossible to judge the truth of these competing accounts and reconstruct the precise experience of those who labored to build the Citadel. Over the last two hundred years, so many layers of history and myth have accumulated around the fort that its origins have become as inaccessible as Christophe had hoped the Citadel itself would be.[4]

Christophe was driven by a sense of urgency, as well as by a profound belief that it was vital to spread civilization within Haiti. In the ravaged postindependence landscape, he sought to build a resplendent new order, irrefutable proof of the justice of Haiti's cause. His country would be as economically successful and politically respected as the European states that controlled the seas and much of the world. At the top of Christophe's official newspaper, a quote from Voltaire summed up the regime's aspirations: "Each people has its turn to shine on the earth." Now it was Haiti's turn.[5]

| | |

The officers who assassinated Dessalines in early 1806 saw their act as a second liberation. "We have broken our chains!" they proclaimed, and they promised the people of Haiti that everything was about to get better. "Soldiers, you will be paid and clothed; cultivators, you will be protected; property owners, you will be able to keep hold of your property: a wise constitution will soon establish the rights and duties of all."[6]

The plot against Dessalines was led by Alexandre Pétion, the high-ranking army officer who had been exiled to France after supporting André Rigaud's rebellion against Louverture. He had then served as a valued commander in Leclerc's French forces before switching sides and joining the Haitian insurgents in the fight for independence.

During his long military career, Pétion had distinguished himself as a fearless soldier, and within Dessalines's military regime he became a powerful general. Dissatisfied with what he saw as Dessalines's tyrannical rule, however, Pétion started plotting an uprising against him as early as 1805, and by the spring of 1806 he had organized several officers into a conspiracy against the increasingly unpopular emperor. Before the ambush was carried out, Pétion also made sure to contact Christophe, whose actions against the French had secured him a permanent place in the pantheon of Haitian national heroes. Christophe wrote back that the conspirators could count on him not to interfere in the assassination.[7]

Behind the superficial rapport between Pétion and Christophe, however, was a prickly political question: Who would take the place of the fallen emperor? Pétion, the son of a white man and a free woman of color, had numerous supporters—especially in Haiti's western areas, around his native Port-au-Prince, as well as in the country's southern peninsula, where there was a significant population of landowning free people of color. He was also the one who had actually organized the overthrow of Dessalines. Christophe, however, commanded a loyal following in much of the nation's army, and he was the undisputed leader of Haiti's north—the country's largest and wealthiest region. After Dessalines was eliminated, Christophe seemed in many ways to be his most obvious successor.

For someone of such prominence, Christophe has a curiously clouded biography. Indeed, like Louverture, who during his life gave the impression that he had always been a slave and elided his experience on the other side of slavery, Christophe deliberately cultivated uncertainty about his early years. No one is quite sure where and when Christophe was born, or whether he was originally free or enslaved. Most historians, though, believe that he came to colonial Saint-Domingue as a cabin boy from the British island of Grenada and was set to work by a French planter who owned an inn in the northern city of Le Cap. Christophe eventually became the inn's maître d'—a position that, by bringing him into contact with many different sectors of the colony's elite, was in its way the ideal profession for the future leader of a fragmented land. After joining Louverture's forces during the slave insurrection, Christophe had risen rapidly through the ranks, overseeing both military and agricultural matters in his part of the country.[8]

The choice between Christophe and Pétion was not the only issue preoccupying the leaders of the revolt. They were also faced with a more fundamental question: What sort of political structure was best suited to Haiti's situation? In place of the unpopular emperor, they decided that the country should have a parliament and a president, and they sought to follow a more democratic process for establishing the new political order: residents of the various regions were invited to choose representatives who would then travel to Port-au-Prince and write a new constitution. We know little about the details of these discussions, and participation in the elections seems to have been limited to a small number of elites in the towns. Still, it was a significant step, for it laid the foundation for a constitutional regime rooted in some form of democratic politics.

The representatives who gathered to work on Haiti's new constitution were especially focused on deciding how strong the country's executive should be. There was broad consensus on the outlines of the new system: an elected senate would appoint a president and share power with him. But there were strong differences of opinion regarding the precise role that each body should take on. The two most powerful men in the country—Pétion and Christophe—did their best to influence this debate. Christophe understood that he was the strongest candidate to take over the executive branch, and wanted to make sure he would have ample power in that role. Pétion seemed ready to accept Christophe as the next president, but was intent on containing him by granting broad powers to the Senate. Pétion had the support of most of the representatives of the south and west of the country and managed to sideline Christophe's supporters from the north, and the new constitution fulfilled his wishes. The Senate was given control of the most crucial legislative issues: the budget, taxation, treaties, and declarations of war—in short, nearly everything having to do with the army and commerce. The executive branch was left with a largely symbolic role. Having set up the constitution in this way, the representatives then selected Christophe as the president.[9]

Christophe was not pleased. Before the constitution was even proclaimed, he marched his troops toward Port-au-Prince, which Pétion's supporters had established as the country's new capital. Pétion gathered his forces to respond. Three years into its independence, Haiti was now in a state of civil war. The armies of Christophe and Pétion battled one another throughout the country, but neither could vanquish the other. After much bloodshed, the conflict settled into a standoff, with each leader holding a part of the territory. Christophe established firm control of the northern areas around Le Cap as well as the central towns of Gonaïves and St. Marc and the rich Artibonite Valley. Pétion, meanwhile, ruled a somewhat less prosperous region that stretched westward from Port-au-Prince along Haiti's southern peninsula. More than a decade would pass after Dessalines's death before Haiti would be united again.[10]

III

On March 10, 1807, Pétion was ceremonially inaugurated as the president of the Republic of Haiti. His years as a soldier had left him with serious rheumatism, and he hobbled his way to the Senate podium on crutches. Still, once seated in the presidential chair, he delivered a spirited acceptance speech. Having been "entrusted with the happiness and destiny" of Haiti, Pétion declared, he was lucky to be able to depend on the "enlightenment," "wisdom," and "energy" of the Senate to help him rule. He proclaimed that his government would be run by and for the people: "May the weapons given to the people for them to defend their liberty be turned against my own breast if ever I conceive of the impious and audacious idea of attacking their rights." His regime would, he insisted, be different from that

of Dessalines—"a tyrant whose existence was an error of nature"—
and from that of Christophe, who because of his "wild ambition"
had plunged the country into civil war. To symbolize his commitment to an open and transparent democracy, Pétion opened up the
Senate to the public, inviting them to witness the senators' discussions.[11]

The political imagery of Pétion's government emphasized its links
to the revolutionary period in Haiti and France. The flag of the new
republic used the same design of a red and a blue stripe that Dessalines had adopted for the insurrection army, albeit with the stripes
placed horizontally rather than vertically. For the center of the flag,
Pétion designed a coat of arms featuring cannon and pikes surrounding a palm tree—a testament to liberation from enslavement that
recalled the "liberty trees" planted during the French and American
revolutions. (That coat of arms is still used on the Haitian flag today.)
The palm tree was surmounted by a Phrygian cap, the little floppy
red hat originally worn by slaves in ancient Rome that was used by
the sansculottes during the French Revolution to show their readiness
to upend the social order. The republican allusions of the regime even
extended to Pétion's luxurious private residence, a Renaissance villa
complete with a marble staircase and a large salon decorated with
Haitian-made paintings of classical generals such as Hannibal and
Julius Caesar.[12]

Below the coat of arms that Pétion designed for his republic's flag
was a motto testifying to his hope of avoiding the kinds of internal
conflicts that had led to Dessalines's downfall: "Unity is our strength."
It was an optimistic sentiment, for Pétion confronted the same tensions that had wrecked Dessalines's regime, most notably the issue of
agricultural policy. On taking power, Pétion did not immediately
institute any major changes: as in prior regimes, plantation laborers
were officially not allowed to leave the properties to which they were
"attached" as laborers, and could be imprisoned if found to be vagabonds. Over time, however, Pétion accepted the idea that people who
work for themselves have much greater incentive to work the land

productively than those who do not. Accordingly, in place of the traditional models of direct management of plantation labor, he encouraged landowners to set up a sort of sharecropping system known as *métayage*. In this arrangement, a landowner essentially handed over the cultivation of a property to those who worked on it, surrendering day to day control over their tasks. In return, the laborers gave the landowner half of what they produced each year. While this annual payment still represented a burden, of course, the new setup allowed the laborers to control the rhythms of their work and gave them the choice of what crops to grow from season to season.

Pétion also helped agricultural laborers by changing and simplifying the tax system. Instead of collecting a quarter of profits from each plantation, as had been done ever since emancipation in 1793, he instituted a "territorial tax" that was levied at the ports of export. Establishing a long-running tradition, the Republic of Haiti filled its state coffers largely thanks to the tax on coffee, which was a nearly ideal export crop: it could be produced relatively easily on both small and large plots of land, and there was significant demand for it on the world market. Combined with the *métayage* arrangement, the new tax system provided agricultural workers with larger profit margins than they had enjoyed before, garnering Pétion much support in the countryside.[13]

In addition, Pétion significantly expanded the ranks of the landowners in his territory—though this was based as much on necessity as on principle. Relatively early in his regime, having difficulty paying the troops he needed in the war against Christophe, Pétion pragmatically decided to offer land to his troops instead of money. The distribution process was not egalitarian: officers got more than rank-and-file soldiers, and the state retained some control over the properties. Seeking to stall the fragmentation of plantations into small plots, Pétion outlawed the sale of parcels smaller than about 30 acres, which effectively excluded many of the poorer members of society from purchasing plots of land. His policy thus tried to steer a middle course between keeping land exclusively in the hands of a small elite and allowing the masses to take it over outright. Nevertheless, under Pétion's rule, many former slaves in the republic were transformed into official property owners—sometimes gaining title to parts of the plantations where they had once been property themselves.[14]

Pétion's regime also famously provided assistance to the anticolonial rebels who, after Napoleon's 1808 toppling of the Spanish crown, began plotting revolutions throughout Latin America. Having established itself as the first independent nation in Latin America in 1804, Haiti offered both inspiration and practical support to these initiatives. In 1815, for example, Simón Bolívar came to Haiti after having failed in his first attempt to gain independence for New Granada. With Pétion's help, Bolívar mounted a second expedition the following year, and he repaid Haiti's support by making the abolition of slavery a part of his early program for independence. When that second attempt was also defeated by pro-Spanish forces, Bolívar traveled once more to what he called "the island of free men"—Haiti—to regroup. Although these early rebellions did not bear as much fruit as Pétion and others had hoped, their support for Bolívar and other Latin American revolutionaries remains a point of pride for Haitians, and one of the lasting legacies of Pétion's regime.[15]

Even as he was encouraging republican revolution in Latin America, though, Pétion crafted an increasingly autocratic regime in the Republic of Haiti itself. Soon after being appointed president in 1807, he persuaded the Senate to abdicate many of its powers, rendering moot the constitutional arrangement that had provoked war with Christophe in the first place. When some senators protested, Pétion's supporters pushed for placing the government entirely in presidential hands. By 1810, when Pétion was reelected, the Senate consisted of just five members, all of them firmly in his pocket.[16]

In 1816, the Republic of Haiti put into place a new constitution, with a system of legislative and executive power that in its broad

outlines remains recognizable in Haiti to this day. The new constitution created a bicameral legislature, with the Senate supplemented
by a Chamber of Deputies who could bring local concerns from the
communes (counties) throughout Haiti to the capital in Port-au-
Prince. The creation of the Chamber of Deputies was a significant
advance for democratic government: the deputies were elected by
universal male suffrage, with no restrictions on the right to vote
(though only property owners could serve as representatives). At the
same time, however, the new constitution set up a cozy and tightly
controlled relationship between the legislature and the executive
branch. The president was the only one who could propose a new
law, and the Senate was formed exclusively from candidates nominated by the president. In turn, the president was selected by the
Senate; once chosen, he was to occupy the position for life, and he
had the right to nominate his successor. Thus, although Pétion's
regime nominally established a democracy in Haiti, its broader and
lasting effect was the creation of a style of exclusivist, indeed oligar-
chical, rule constructed around extensive presidential power.[17]

III

Pétion's inclinations toward an autocratic regime were more than
matched by his counterpart in the north. For the first four years of
his rule, Christophe had been content to be president of the region,
aided by an appointed council of state. But he eventually decided
that in order to deal with his enemies inside Haiti and with the hostile world that surrounded the country, he needed the power and
respect granted to kings. Declaring himself king of the north of
Haiti, Christophe gave himself a series of titles, proclaiming himself "Destroyer of tyranny, Regenerator and benefactor of the Haitian nation, Creator of its moral, political and military institutions."
He boasted that he was the "first monarch crowned in the New
World," and the coronation ceremony at the resplendent palace of

Sans-Souci* was followed by eight days of dances and celebrations throughout the kingdom. Descriptions of the proceedings appeared in newspapers throughout Europe and the Americas.[19]

While Pétion's republic took its political imagery from the Haitian and French revolutions, Christophe's monarchy drew together a wide-ranging array of symbols from America, Africa, and Europe. Seeking to make a symbolic connection with the indigenous peoples who once inhabited Haiti, Christophe occasionally even claimed that one of his ancestors was a native Caribbean ruler. One of his favorite songs, performed often at court, was said to have been handed down from the indigenous Haitians, celebrating their fight against the Spanish colonizers and proclaiming they would "die rather than be enslaved." At the queen's suggestion, Christophe created a Society of Amazons, a corps of women who accompanied the queen and king on their processions. At the same time, he presented himself and his court as being linked to Africa, and his military police was known as the Royal Dahomets in reference to the great West African kingdom. An elite subgroup of about one hundred and fifty of them made up Christophe's personal guard, the nicely named "Royal Bonbons."[20]

The institutional heart of Christophe's regime, meanwhile, was the European-style hereditary landed aristocracy, complete with heraldic crests and mottoes, that he created to administer his kingdom. Each of these counts, dukes, and barons either commanded a sector of the government or was given control of a parish of the kingdom,

---

* There is an interesting debate about precisely why Christophe picked the name Sans-Souci for his palace. Many have assumed that it was a reference to the great palace of the same name in Potsdam, Germany. But Haitian anthropologist Michel-Rolph Trouillot argues that it may have been a different kind of homage: to his onetime enemy Sans-Souci, the Kongo-born officer he ambushed and killed in 1802. In naming his palace Sans-Souci, Christophe might have intended to bury the memory of his former enemy even deeper and make sure his time on the wrong side of the war would be silenced: now, the name itself would conjure up only an image of the king's grandeur, and not of his earlier treachery. Indeed, argues Trouillot, there is a chance that the palace was literally built on top of Sans-Souci's grave, or at least very close to it.[18]

charged with overseeing the plantations and assuring the discipline and productivity of the laborers. The king's nobles came from a highly diverse set of backgrounds, ranging from African-born survivors of the Middle Passage to light-skinned men who had been free during colonial times and achieved wealth and education in Saint-Domingue. Indeed, many of them had fought against one another during the conflicts of the Haitian Revolution before being united by Christophe as members of the kingdom's ruling class.[21]*

Alongside the notable military commanders, Christophe's aristocracy also included several remarkable Haitian writers, who produced an outpouring of texts that attacked European racism and articulated a vision of Haiti as a beacon of racial equality. Among them was Pompée-Valentin, the Baron de Vastey, who served as Christophe's lead secretary. Vastey wrote several works on Haitian history and eloquently exposed the "multitude of absurdities" he found in the work of French defenders of slavery. Their refusal to grant him his humanity, Vastey wrote, had almost driven him "to the point of throwing down my pen." "I am a man," he proclaimed; "I feel it in the whole of my being; I possess the faculties, mental and corporeal, which mark my affinity to a divine original"; and yet he had been required to "enter into a serious refutation" of those who refused to accept that he was "their fellow." Three of Vastey's books were quickly translated into English, and he is recognized today as one of Haiti's first great writers.[23]

Despite the individual accomplishments of Christophe's aristocrats, however, the idea of invented black royalty has struck many commentators over the years as inherently risible. As one scholar put it, there is "a degree of embarrassment at what are seen as the faintly ridiculous monarchic trappings of the régime; hurriedly thrown together, ersatz, gaudy imitation of European cultural models." To

---

* The European influence on Christophe's court extended to his patronage of the arts. He created an academy of painting and drawing at Sans-Souci and funded a theater in his capital whose repertoire included Voltaire's play *Zaïre*, the most popular French drama of the eighteenth century.[22]

some extent, this ridicule is the legacy of early historians from Pétion's Republic of Haiti. Engaging in a kind of historiographical battle that paralleled the country's civil war, they helped create a powerful image of Christophe as a megalomaniac ruling over an aberration: a black kingdom in the New World. To this day, the history of Christophe's regime always seems to be overtaken by the sense that his vision of a Haitian royal court was always implausible, always doomed, a kind of historical joke and interregnum.[24]

The durability of this view can be seen in one of the best-known accounts of Christophe's regime, Aimé Césaire's 1963 play *La tragédie du roi Christophe*. A poet, activist, and political leader from the French colony of Martinique, Césaire was fascinated by the history of Haiti and celebrated Louverture and the Haitian Revolution. When he turned to Christophe, however, Césaire presented him as a tragic figure and a bit of a buffoon and turned his court into a kind of farce. At a 1997 performance of Césaire's play in Paris, audiences roared with laughter when the characters of the "Duke of Marmelade" and the "Duke of Limonade" were introduced. Unaware that these are simply place names in Haiti—names given by French colonists—many viewers imagine them as the product of some kind of native ignorance and overactive imagination.[25]

However we may judge Christophe's regime from an aesthetic viewpoint, though, his wide-ranging and ambitious efforts aimed at creating a sustainable postemancipation state deserve more attention than historians have usually given them. Pétion, whose territory was less prosperous than Christophe's, could not maintain a particularly strong state apparatus; accordingly, he ceded some control over crop production to the agricultural laborers themselves, and he had little involvement with foreign affairs beyond his support for Bolívar and other revolutionaries in Haiti's vicinity. Christophe, on the other hand, actively sought to build up a strong state with a viable export economy, one that would have a major presence on the world stage. It was in support of this project that Christophe maintained—even expanded—the plantation system, keeping large plantations intact and making his handpicked group of elites into landed gentry who would keep a close eye on the agricultural work on their estates.

Christophe's aspirations for Haiti led not just to the construction of the Citadel and other buildings but also to major initiatives in legal reform and public education, as well as a strengthening of ties with British abolitionists. Only by establishing itself as a self-sustaining, economically thriving power, Christophe believed, could Haiti finally stop being subordinate to its former colonizers and be seen by other nations as an equal.[26]

III

In contrast to Pétion's relatively hands-off governing style, Christophe wanted to actively manage his subjects' lives. He produced an extensive corpus of laws known as the "Code Henry," which totaled nearly eight hundred pages and legislated seemingly all aspects of life in his kingdom. Some of its stipulations, for example, were aimed at environmental preservation and the establishment of food security. There were rather reasonable rules commanding property owners who wanted to set fire to their cane fields (as was commonly done at the end of harvest periods to clear the fields and enrich the soil) to first check with their neighbors, whose unharvested fields might burn as a result. There were also forward-thinking regulations meant to prevent deforestation: no one who rented a plantation, for instance, was allowed to cut down more than one-third of the trees on the property, and they were also told to avoid cutting down trees on the "summits of mountains." Property owners themselves were not subject to such restrictions, but they were ordered to plant large numbers of breadfruit, mango, and palm trees as well as to plant and maintain "precious" banana trees, all of which could provide abundant food over the long term.[27]

An even more important—and more sensitive—set of regulations dealt with the management of plantation workers. Like his predecessors, Christophe was faced with the problem of building an economy based on free labor in a land entirely constructed around slavery. In response, the Code Henry put particular emphasis on the need to balance the responsibilities of laborers with those of land-owners, laying out the "reciprocal obligations" of three groups: property owners, tenant farmers, and field workers. The property owners, among them Christophe's nobles, made up the smallest and most powerful group. Next down the ladder were the tenant farmers, known as *fermiers*; these were those who—through military service or other routes—had been able to gain access to rented land, which gave them a measure of independence. The field workers, or *agriculteurs*, on the other hand, were always "attached" to a particular plantation, where they were required to stay. Like laborers under Louverture, the *agriculteurs* were paid for their work with one-quarter of their plantation's yearly production, to be divided among them-selves.[28]

Unless they practiced some other profession, every *agriculteur* in Christophe's kindgom was ordered to work on a plantation. "The law punishes men who are lazy or vagabonds; all individuals must make themselves useful to society," Christophe decreed. Any agri-cultural worker who "left the plantation where they have chosen to live, in order to take refuge, without a valid reason, on another plantation, in the towns, cities, or in any other place where their residence is outlawed" would be considered a vagabond and pun-ished accordingly. Begging was "severely prohibited," and all "lazy people, beggars," and "women of bad character" would also be considered vagabonds. When caught, they were to be "sent back to their plantations"; if they were not already "attached" to a planta-tion, they would be placed on one by the authorities. What's more, the laborers were not allowed to leave the plantations during "work days" unless their manager requested for them a special permit from the local "lieutenant of the king." The Code Henry does suggest that *agriculteurs* had some choice in selecting which plantation they were "attached" to, though it provided no mechanism for them to later move from one to another. Having chosen a plantation, they were ordered to stay there, and in practice many probably toiled in the fields where they had once been enslaved.[29]

The Code Henry did not set out rules for the *agriculteurs* alone, however; it also carefully regulated the activities of property owners and tenant farmers. Plantation owners, for example, were required to provide health care for their workers, ordered to pay all expenses of doctors' visits and medicine. They were supposed to have not one but two hospitals on their property: the first a general care facility, the second—to be located some distance away from workers' houses— for those with contagious diseases. These were remarkably enlightened and progressive stipulations for the period, though it is difficult to know to what extent they were actually enforced. (The French Code Noir, which governed plantation life in colonial times, had similar provisions that commanded masters to provide health care and food to their slaves, but masters rarely did.) Still, even if the paternalistic and somewhat bucolic vision of plantation relations offered by the Code Henry did not quite match the reality of daily life as it was experienced by the *agriculteurs*, the detailed attempt to balance responsibilities of workers and landowners reflects Christophe's desire to maintain the plantation structure while providing the laborers with a certain level of protection and care.[30]

Indeed, some stipulations in Christophe's code show remarkable concern for the particular conditions of agricultural workers. "It is expressly outlawed," reads one article, "for property owners and tenant farmers of coffee plantations to have their products carried, either to the parish towns or to the ports, on the heads of the agricultural workers." The landowners and tenant farmers were ordered, instead, to provide the "animals necessary for the transport of the products of their plantations." This legislation might seem like intense micromanagement, but in all likelihood it represents the trace of some complaint by *agriculteurs* about the difficulty of carrying baskets of coffee to distant markets. Christophe's annual Festival of Agriculture, during which *agriculteurs* were invited to a celebration at Sans-Souci palace, might even have given the laborers a chance to speak to the king about plantation problems directly.[31]

The popular notion of the "tragedy" of Christophe—the vision of him as a cruel ruler who effectively reenslaved the population of Haiti—thus oversimplifies a much more complex reality. To be properly appreciated, the Code Henry needs to be read and understood in its broader historical context: that of nineteenth-century law in Europe and the Americas. This was a time when many countries, including Britain and France, also had tough stipulations against vagrancy and various laws giving employers significant control over their workers. For all their limitations, Christophe's regulations gave the *agriculteurs* some rights and methods of recourse: if landowners violated provisions of the Code, laborers could complain about their treatment to the royal authorities. Most strikingly, because Christophe's regime was not constructed around a racial hierarchy—people of African descent controlled and occupied essentially all levels of the system—escape from the plantation was a real possibility for a significant part of the population. Through service in the army or the administration, as well as through renting their own land, agricultural workers had steady access to mechanisms through which they could alter their situation.

For all these reasons, the Code Henry impressed, and indeed seduced, many contemporaries. The naturalist Sir Joseph Banks, a veteran of Captain Cook's first voyage to the Pacific and cofounder of the abolitionist African Institution, declared, "It is worthy to be written in gold; nothing I have ever seen which was written for the same purposes by white men is worthy to be compared to it." Many abolitionists hoped that Christophe's regime would serve to refute the racist theories of their opponents and prove that—despite the arguments of proslavery forces—emancipation did not necessarily mean the end of prosperity in the Caribbean. Christophe, in turn, actively reached out to international allies, hoping they would help him build a new world in Haiti.[32]

III

"Without a doubt," the prominent French priest and abolitionist the Abbé Grégoire wrote in 1815, "the most difficult problem to resolve would be how to appropriate all the advantages of European civilization, without including the vicious and hideous parts." Europe, he went on, had "done much for the spirit," but it had also "perverted reason" and "neglected . . . the education of the heart." Grégoire was writing about Africa, but he elegantly captured the dilemma facing the Haitian leadership: they looked to Europe for models of governance even as they ruled over a land that had experienced the worst of what the "perverted reason" of European empire had to offer.[33]

Many Haitians deeply admired Grégoire, who had been at the forefront of the battle for the rights of free people of color early in the revolution, and had given his strong support to Haitian independence. His 1808 work *De la littérature des nègres* presented an impassioned and richly documented defense of the capacities of blacks; Christophe ordered fifty copies of the book and published excerpts from it in his newspaper. Grégoire, however, was politically uncomfortable with Christophe's regime: he considered Christophe's elaborate ceremonies a waste of money, and he was appalled by Christophe's adoption of a monarchical system, arguing that a "nobility of paper" was just as absurd as the "nobility of skin color" that the white masters had enforced in Saint-Domingue. Even if the ex-slaves of the country didn't have much education, Grégoire insisted, that did not mean they lacked the capacity to elect their own leaders. Grégoire was happy to work with Pétion's republic, and he continued to be a steadfast supporter of "free Haiti" overall, but his antimonarchical views— shaped by the French Revolution—ultimately made it impossible for Christophe to rely on his support.[34]

No one else in France seemed particularly eager to help Christophe either. And Christophe, for his part, also had a deeply personal reason for wanting to avoid dealing with the French: he had lost a son to them. Late in 1801, Christophe had decided to follow the example of Toussaint Louverture—who had sent his two sons to France to be educated—and began making plans to send his first-born, Ferdinand, to school in Paris. After the Leclerc expedition arrived in early 1802 and Christophe burned Le Cap and started fighting against the French, of course, this no longer seemed like a good idea. But when he surrendered a few months later, Christophe went ahead with the project. The decision is puzzling, and Christophe was clearly uneasy about it. "If you had our skin," he confided in a white French general, "you would perhaps not share my confidence in sending my only son" to be "raised in France." But perhaps Christophe believed at the time that ultimately France would triumph in Saint-Domingue, and he and his son would then both be in a better position if Ferdinand had a Parisian education. It was a dangerous gamble, though, essentially making Ferdinand both student and hostage.[35]

For his first few months in Paris, Ferdinand was treated well. When news arrived that his father had once again turned against the French, however, he was transferred to a state orphanage and told he would learn to be a shoemaker. Ferdinand refused: he had come to Paris, he complained, "to get a fine education, not to be a cobbler." The teachers who had now become his jailers replied that he was nothing more than "a little brigand, the son of a bigger brigand who was massacring all the whites in Saint-Domingue." Ferdinand was beaten in the orphanage so badly that he eventually died from his injuries. His fate was covered up by the authorities, and Christophe never publicly mentioned Ferdinand again.[36]

It is not surprising, then, that instead of trying to repair his relations with Grégoire or perhaps connect with other potentially sympathetic Frenchmen, Christophe looked to France's great enemy, Britain. The king spoke English well; he liked the British, whom he saw as embodying the virtues of hard work and discipline, and he believed that his subjects liked them too. The ongoing war between Britain and France served Haiti particularly well since it kept their former colonizers largely tied up militarily, lessening the chance that they would try to reconquer their lost territory. Christophe (like Pétion in the south) cultivated the valuable trade with the nearby British colony of Jamaica, and ships shuttled back and forth constantly between the two islands.

But while the British government happily let their merchants trade with Haiti, they refused to recognize Haiti's independence, or even to dignify Haiti's representatives with the formalities extended to other diplomats. Like officials in the United States, British function-aries worked hard to prevent Haitians from actually spending any time in British territory. Britain had abolished the slave trade in 1807, but they maintained slavery itself in their colonies for three decades after Haitian Independence; and to deal on equal terms with Haiti, they assumed, would send a message to their own population that an antislavery revolt was acceptable.

Knowing that he couldn't depend on open support from the British government, Christophe instead sought to cultivate ties with British abolitionists, whom he admired for their successful cam-paign against the slave trade and their eloquent attacks on racism. He found particular allies in two of Britain's most prominent anti-slavery activists, William Wilberforce and Thomas Clarkson. Unlike Grégoire, Clarkson and Wilberforce were not uncomfortable with the idea of a monarchy, and they immediately responded to Chris-tophe's offer of friendship. They used their personal contacts and intimate knowledge of European politics to give Haiti's king advice on how to deal with Europe's political leaders. When Clarkson sug-gested to Christophe that he write to the emperor of Russia, for instance, Christophe hesitated: Could he really just write to the emperor without an introduction? But Clarkson took care of the necessary formalities and transmitted the letter, in which Chris-tophe called on Alexander to support Haitian independence and to oppose the slave trade. Clarkson later functioned as goodwill ambas-sador for Christophe in Europe, trying to get Haitian independence finally recognized. Of course, there was a limit to how much someone like Clarkson could do. As a writer who described himself as a "friend of Christophe" later noted, the king was perhaps liable to forget that the "philanthropists of Britain," like those elsewhere, didn't have access to "the treasury and the armed forces."[37]

Still, the abolitionists did assist Christophe as much as they could. One of their key initiatives involved helping Christophe to develop an extensive education infrastructure, which was admired by many contemporaries outside the country. Christophe's interest in education was of long standing: as far back as 1805, he had strongly criticized Dessalines for his neglect of teachers, angrily proclaiming that this lack of support for schools exposed Dessalines as "a barbarian with no idea of civilization, incapable of regenerating the nation . . . merely a brutal soldier, happy only when surrounded by bayonets." On taking power in 1807, Christophe declared that public education was—"after religion and liberty"—the most "precious" thing for any population, and that it would be "venerated" under his regime.[38]

It took most of a decade for Christophe to establish his education projects, and he was perhaps ultimately spurred on by a competitive urge: in 1816, Pétion recruited three teachers from France and created a prestigious secondary school, the Lycée de Port-au-Prince, which offered instruction in Latin, French, English, mathematics, navigation, history, music, and fencing. (Later renamed the Lycée Pétion, the school remains one of the elite institutions in Haiti, occupying, in the words of one historian, "the same place in the imagination of Haitians that Harvard does in that of Americans.") Not to be outdone, Christophe asked Clarkson and Wilberforce to send teachers to the Kingdom of Haiti, and he established an ambitious system of public education that stretched from primary schools to university-level classes. He created a special chamber to oversee the educational system, launched plans to create textbooks designed specifically for Haitian students, inaugurated schools for women, and installed teachers in all of his military's barracks, hoping in this way to educate his soldiers during their idle moments.[39]

The scope of Christophe's educational initiatives soon far out-stripped Pétion's efforts. Between 1816 and 1820, thirteen schools were functioning in the Kingdom of Haiti. It is estimated that as many as 72,000 students attended school at some point during Christophe's regime, which would have meant that nearly all the children in the kingdom received some public instruction. Chris-tophe believed that Haitians would be better off if they learned to speak English rather than French, and a significant amount of the instruction focused on teaching that language at the primary level. In higher education, meanwhile, one of Christophe's most lasting contributions was the creation of a chair of medicine in Le Cap, where a Scotsman named Duncan Stewart taught anatomy, disease treatment, and surgery. Stewart's school was so successful that it was one of the few institutions to survive Christophe's reign, for after his overthrow, the new president maintained Stewart in his post—though a "simulacrum" of an inauguration was held in order to make it seem that the new regime had actually created the post.[40]

I I I

Not all of the assistance from Christophe's British friends worked out quite so well. Hoping to increase the productivity of his king-dom's plantations—and thus gather more money for building his forts, palaces, and schools—Christophe reached out to his aboli-tionist allies for technical advice on agricultural matters. Wilber-force was enthusiastic about the notion, becoming the first of many outsiders over the decades to support the idea that foreign expertise could help Haiti's farmers and laborers become more efficient. He sent two plows to Haiti for demonstration purposes, along with two British plowmen to operate them. Clarkson was only a little more reticent, his main concern being that the transmission of technical knowledge might run up against linguistic difficulties. "I confess I cannot see how common ploughmen, who can only speak English, can instruct the Haytians, who can only speak French," he wrote.

What was needed, he went on, was "some middle man between the two, some very superior farmer, who should be able to speak French and English, and who should go about from farm to farm and explain to the Haytian farmer what the British ploughman wishes to communicate to him." The plowman could then teach the Haitians the "most judicious application of husbandry to the soil, and in various other departments connected with that science."[41]

We can imagine the slightly quizzical response of the residents in the north of Haiti as they encountered these foreign experts and their plows. As a contemporary account relates it, one of the plowmen had quite good luck: he was set up on a piece of land that been "prepared before his arrival," and with the assistance of the plow the plot was "cultivated with a great saving of manual labor, and produced a most abundant crop." The other Englishman, however, was placed further from Cap Haïtien, on a piece of land that needed to be cleared before it could be tilled. As a result, he needed "the assistance of a great number of laborers, in order to clear it of weeds, bushes, and cane roots before he could introduce his plough." He was, it seems, working on the ruins of an old sugarcane plantation, which was perhaps why the soil proved to be "less fertile" than the plot farmed by his countryman—the intensive cultivation of cane having tapped out the land—and the use of the plow "gained nothing in point of labour, and nothing in produce." Beset by difficulties and illness, tasked with carrying out an undertaking which was "likely to be the occasion of constant trouble and vexation," the second plowman often "lamented ever having quitted England." If he wondered what he was doing in Haiti, those who worked with him—heirs to a range of agricultural techniques that layered different crops on small plots, developed over generations to maximize productivity and minimize soil exhaustion—probably wondered the same thing.[42]

While these agricultural experiments were going on, Clarkson also liberally gave Christophe a great deal of advice—much of which sounds eerily familiar—about how to broadly reform Haiti's social organization. What Haiti really needed, he told Christophe, was a middle class. Where might they find one? In the United States, Clarkson suggested, among the "persons of colour" who were free and owned some property. The advantage to Haiti of such immigration, he explained, would be that such settlers would come with wealth, and could therefore provide that "connecting medium between the rich and the poor and which is the great cause of prosperity in Europe, but which cannot at present have been raised up in your Majesty's dominions." The movement in favor of the emigration of free African Americans out of the United States was gaining steam—Liberia would be created in 1822—and Clarkson put Christophe in contact with Prince Saunders, an African American from Massachusetts who came to Haiti to explore the possibility of bringing settlers there. Saunders was fascinated by Haiti's promise, and in 1818 he published in Boston a glowing description of Christophe's kingdom and a commentary on its laws.[43]

Clarkson admitted that some American emigrants might have some trouble adjusting to Haiti. For one thing, being "free men" in the United States, they were "accustomed to go where they pleased in search of their livelihood without any questions being asked them or without any hindrance by the Government. No passports are ever necessary there." That was not the case under Christophe's regime, which policed movement assiduously: plantation laborers were, after all, required to stay on their plantations and could not move freely about looking for work. Immigrants might also, Clarkson acknowledged, miss the "advantage" of "being tried by a jury of their own citizens" if they were accused of a crime. Of course, African Americans might gladly have accepted these trade-offs to live in a country that, for all its problems, was at least free from the constant threat and exercise of white supremacy.[44]

Christophe was enthusiastic about the plans for emigration from North America, and he committed to funding the journeys of immigrants, but his reign came to an end before he could see the project through. In general, his kingdom was noted for being largely hospitable to foreign traders, investors, and tourists; many British and

North American visitors came to his court and admired Sans-Souci
and the Citadel. One nation, however, was not impressed: France.
Indeed, the French government continued to insist that Christophe's
kingdom and Pétion's republic were not, in fact, independent countries at all.

I I I

More than a decade after the defeat of Leclerc's forces, many exiled
planters from Saint-Domingue still hoped to reverse what had happened and persistently lobbied for a new mission to reconquer the
former colony. A number of them held powerful positions in the
French government, and their pressure led France to officially
insist that it still had a claim over Haiti. Other European nations, in
turn, refused to extend recognition to Haiti until the former colonial
power did so. Indeed, when Britain and France were negotiating an
end to their conflict at the Congress of Vienna, the French signed an
additional secret agreement with Britain specifically regarding Haiti.
The British promised that they would not interfere if the French
attacked their former colony; in return, France formally accepted
Britain's right to trade with Haiti.[45]

It was an astounding gesture—what right, after all, did France
have to determine whether anyone traded with Haiti?—but it summed
up the prevailing attitude at the time. Haiti's declaration of independence was regarded by a surprising number of Frenchmen as just a
temporary setback. Some of the former planters laid out detailed
military plans for taking back the colony, arguing that the disaster of
the Leclerc expedition was a fluke, or else the result of mistakes that
could be avoided by the next commander. Others focused on asking
for increased financial restitution. The exiled planters had received
some state assistance since they had fled Saint-Domingue during the
revolution, but they wanted more. They demanded to be paid back
for all the property the revolution had taken from them, including

that most precious of property of all: the human beings, once enslaved, who had now become citizens of Haiti.

Some of the former colonists who aspired to return as masters were conservative royalists, committed not only to the old order of slavery but also to the structures of Old Regime France. For them, the Haitian Revolution was an example of the excesses of the French Revolution; Haiti, in their eyes, was the "last province of France still under the control of the Jacobins," and one that should fall to the counterrevolution like all the other parts of France. They added, furthermore, that all European empires had a clear interest in uniting to crush Haiti—"whose existence, let us be frank, is shameful for all colonial governments." "No one will accept, in the middle of the Caribbean, a foyer of revolt, a hideout for pirates and brigands, a school for revolution," one former planter declared. Another argued that the Haitian state was an illegal entity, since it had been founded by slaves and the law had always forbidden slaves to own any property. For those who believed, as these planters did, that "slavery is inherent to the black race," Haiti was an aberration, unnatural and untenable.[46]

Several writers unabashedly dreamed of genocide. An aristocrat who had served as an officer in Saint-Domingue during the revolution said that the only solution would be to take over Haiti and exterminate all males over six years old who lived there. A former colonist responded that this would not go far enough: it would also be necessary to kill all the women, since they could "whisper into the souls of their children the same spirit of revolt" that had animated the men. Haitians had to be completely erased from history in order to protect white supremacy and the colonial order. It was simply intolerable that "three hundred thousand Africans" had "stolen from thirty million Frenchmen the most beautiful and useful of their possessions."[47]

Other exiled planters, however, were a bit more strategic in their thinking. They granted that there was no going back to the old order. The revolution had forever destroyed the "kind of magic" that had "made it so that three or four whites could sleep in complete security, with their doors open, on a property on which there were four or five hundred blacks." All the Haitians now knew how easy it was to "ruin and slaughter" the whites, and they weren't going to forget it. There was, however, an example of possible compromise: the relative peace of Louverture's regime, when white planters had conceded political power to a black leader and consented to new labor structures while holding on to their property. When Napoleon attacked Louverture, some former colonists argued bitterly, he had destroyed a system that might ultimately have worked for the benefit of the planters and the French empire. (Napoleon himself had in fact concluded the same thing, admitting on his deathbed that targeting Louverture had been one of the great mistakes of his career.) Perhaps, some former planters imagined, a deal could be worked out with Haiti's new elites: the "mulatto" class of the island could serve in Louverture's place, as allies and intermediaries for rebuilding the plantation order. Together, the former planters and the "mulatto" elites could develop a new form of colonial rule in Haiti, possibly making it into a French protectorate.[48]

This notion got a more serious hearing in government circles than talk of military conquest. Most in the French military had little desire to go through a replay of the Leclerc expedition. They remembered all too well how Haiti had swallowed up tens of thousands of Napoleon's best troops. Clarkson, who visited France on Christophe's behalf, reported back that anyone in French government circles who proposed reconquering Saint-Domingue by force "would be considered to be mad." "Ridicule has generally accompanied the mention of any expedition to Hayti," Clarkson noted. Indeed, "as hopeless and disastrous as the Expedition of Leclerc" had become a byword in the military to describe something considered a particularly bad plan.[49]

French officials did believe, however, that the threat of force could be used as a bargaining tool to extract concessions from Haiti's leaders. In 1814, the French minister of the colonies, Pierre-Victor

Malouet—a onetime governor of the colony of Saint-Domingue—
sent envoys to Haiti to begin negotiations with Pétion and Christophe. The delegation began by proposing to Pétion that he place
Haiti back under the control of France. He categorically refused the
return of any form of French sovereignty, but he made his own counter-
offer to the French, one that would come to haunt Haiti for a long
time. What if the Haitian state paid an indemnity to France, Pétion
asked, which they could use to pay damages to former French planters? Having won its independence through revolt, Haiti could effectively now buy recognition of that independence once and for all.[50]

Perhaps, in making this proposal, Pétion was remembering how
slaves had sometimes bought liberty from their masters. It is also
possible that he genuinely had some sympathy for the plight of
planters who had lost property in Saint-Domingue: after all, though
he had participated in the final defeat of the French, Pétion had also
initially served as part of the Leclerc expedition. An indemnity was
an elegant way of solving the problem of political recognition: the
country would remain free and independent, but those who had
been victims of its revolution would receive some form of compensation. Once recognized, Haiti would have a much clearer political
and diplomatic status, as well as an easier time exporting its products. Pétion probably considered that, on balance, Haiti would benefit from the deal.

When Agostino Franco de Medina, another of the French envoys,
came to meet with Christophe, however, he got a rather different
response. Christophe had Medina arrested and searched, uncovering
a set of private instructions from Malouet. The king found these so
shocking, in both tone and content, that he ordered Medina executed. To justify the act, he published the papers that Medina had
carried—a move that effectively embarrassed not only the French
but also Pétion for having been willing to deal with them. As Medina's documents made clear, Malouet envisioned bringing not only
colonialism back to Haiti, but also slavery, or something close to it.[51]

In his instructions to Medina, Malouet never referred to Haiti, instead calling the territory Saint-Domingue and acting as if it were still part of the French kingdom. The French king, Malouet declared, was determined to make the "insurgents of Saint-Domingue" accept his sovereignty over their land. But while the king was ready to use force if necessary, he was also prepared to grant "concessions and advantages" to those who "promptly" offered him the "obeisance" he was owed. His envoys were told to seek out leaders who were "educated and enlightened," notably Pétion, and come to an agreement with them. Such leaders, Malouet predicted, would understand the fundamental truth: there would be no "tranquility and prosperity" in Haiti unless the "mass of blacks" were "returned to and maintained in the state of slavery, or at least a kind of submission similar to that which they were in before the troubles." The envoys were given some leeway in determining precisely how to assure this "submission" of the laboring population; but their goal, the instructions made clear, was to get as close to the "old colonial order of things" as possible.[52]

The documents which Christophe found on Medina blustered that the French king would never be cowed by the "exaggerated pretentions" of Haiti's leaders and would "make the full extent of his power felt if his favors are refused." Given that French armies had in fact been decisively defeated by Haitian troops, the tone was both bullying and a little deluded, which may be why Malouet labored to make the threat sound serious. There was "no doubt," he wrote, "that if the King of France wanted to send all his forces bearing down on a group of rebel subjects who make up barely one hundredth of the people of his kingdom, who have neither within them or among them the great military, moral, or material resources that Europe has, who will receive no support from outside," he could "reduce them, even if that means exterminating them." Haitians undoubtedly heard echoes here of the rhetoric of Leclerc and Rochambeau. Back in 1804, in justifying his killings of French planters, Dessalines had argued that the French would always consider themselves to be lords and masters of the country. Malouet's instructions confirmed such suspicions.[53]

Malouet's vision for the future of Haiti built on the idea—common in many accounts of the Haitian Revolution at the time—that if only the French government had made concessions to the free people of color when they demanded equal rights in the early 1790s, the colony would have been able to avoid, or at least contain, the insurrection of the slaves. Malouet wanted a replay, and this time France would get it right. Once they took back control of their former territory, the French government would offer a small number of leaders— including Pétion, whose skin color was almost white—"complete assimilation" with whites, along with honors and money. Somewhat darker skinned people would receive nearly the same political rights, just with "a few exceptions" that would place them a bit "below" the whites. And so on down the ladder: the darker the skin, the fewer the rights. The majority of the population—not only "the blacks who are working on plantations" but also "those who have escaped this condition"—would be "attached to the soil and returned to their former masters." And, just for good measure, the island was to be "purged" of all those rebellious blacks who were too dangerous to place on the plantations, for fear they would lead new insurrections. Finally, the new order would severely restrict the possibilities for emancipation, so as to avoid the creation of a new class of free people.[54]

Christophe had, in the previous years, created an entire state and aristocracy based on racial equality. Malouet, seeking to curry favor with Christophe's enemies to the south, proposed instead a reconstructed, even perfected, colonial order based on an intricate racial hierarchy. Christophe's arrest and execution of Medina exposed the plan, and the French king was forced to disavow Malouet's instructions, claiming that his minister had overstepped his bounds and that the documents didn't in fact express the vision of the French government. The first round of negotiations thus ended in a kind of victory for Haiti: from then on, the French no longer proposed any kind of return to the former colonial system. But they didn't give up trying to assert some form of control.

In 1816, the French sent new envoys to Haiti to reopen negotiations. The plan was to co-opt a portion of the Haitian leadership by offering them military positions and honors in the French army: the envoys arrived with twelve Crosses of the Legion of Honor and ten of the Order of Saint-Louis. In return for such titles, Haitian rulers were asked to place their country under the protection of France. Pétion, having been shamed by Christophe's actions the first time around, refused strongly, and publicly. In a printed proclamation "to the people and the army" of Haiti, he declared that there was no Haitian whose "soul is tepid enough" to accept anything but complete recognition of independence. Nature, he noted, had made Haitians "equal to other men," and if the French tried to take back the country, they would find only "ashes mingled with blood, iron, and an avenging climate." Christophe, for his part, refused even to receive this second set of envoys, so the negotiations once again went nowhere.[55]

Clarkson was disappointed that neither France nor England was acknowledging Haitian independence, and he eventually even suggested that Christophe should adopt Pétion's idea and pay an indemnity to France in return for recognition—though only if the amount were "reasonable and moderate" and could be paid "without any great sacrifice." Christophe found the idea of paying an indemnity to France unthinkable, but he did ask the English abolitionist to lobby the former colonial power on Haiti's behalf. Clarkson should begin, Christophe said, by trying to make the French government appreciate the history from Haiti's point of view. "The Haitian people, after shedding rivers of their finest blood, set themselves up sixteen years ago as a sovereign state, free and independent. Exercising its natural rights, the nation proclaimed its Independence before all men by its solemn Declaration of the 1st of January, 1804." The country based its claim to independence on the very "natural rights" which the French had enshrined in their own revolution. The old colonial order was "overthrown, destroyed from top to bottom"—it would not be resurrected. "A new and enlightened generation is replacing the former population; ideas, morals, customs, and even the habits of the people have undergone a total change . . . The last vestiges of that odious system have disappeared from the soil of Haiti." All that remained to complete this just and beneficial transformation was for France and other countries to formally acknowledge the irreversible facts.[56]

Through Clarkson, Christophe urged France to act with "justice and humanity" and to officially recognize what was clear to "every reasonable observer": the colonial power had made independence "inevitable" through its brutality, and now this independence could "in no possible way be destroyed." France's refusal to accept Haiti's autonomy had caused "astonishment, grief and regret." But the king of France could fix matters by offering immediate recognition. In return, Haiti would grant France trade privileges, giving it preferential access to markets and lower tariffs than other countries, though Christophe preemptively specified that he would not offer to France any kind of "exclusive right."[57]

As for the question of an indemnity, the document given to Clarkson burst with disbelief at the idea that France might ask Haiti to pay in return for political recognition. What, after all, were the colonists seeking to be reimbursed for? The most valuable aspect of their property had been their slaves: the people who were now free citizens of Haiti. "Is it possible that they wish to be recompensed for the loss of our persons? Is it conceivable that Haitians who have escaped torture and massacre at the hands of these men, Haitians who have conquered their own country by the force of their arms and at the cost of their blood, that these same free Haitians should now purchase their property and persons once again with money paid to their former oppressors?" As Christophe put it, "the ex-colonists are our natural and implacable enemies; they tortured us while it was in their power to do so, and they never cease to seek an opportunity to renew their torture." No true Haitian could consider paying an indemnity to them. "It is not possible; it is not for one moment to be considered. Free men could never accept such a condition without covering themselves with infamy!"[58]

It was a powerful statement, and a potent brief against the French approach to Haiti. But it was also, as Clarkson soon found out, impossible to deliver the message. As the abolitionist later explained to Christophe, he found himself caught up in a rather absurd dilemma. If he presented the French cabinet with Christophe's letter that named Clarkson as an official envoy for the Kingdom of Haiti, then, in the act of receiving the letter, the cabinet "would be acknowledging the Independence of Hayti at the very outset." The French government could not, it seems, even begin discussions about a treaty with "your Majesty as King of Hayti, because if the King of France were to allow your present title at [the] opening of the negotiation, he would be to all intents and purposes acknowledging your Independence." The envoys sent by France to Christophe and Pétion had skirted this issue by always using the name "Saint-Domingue," refusing to officially admit Haiti's existence in any of their documents. But now, negotiation seemed impossible, and Clarkson rapidly realized he was at a dead end.[59]

Frustrated, Clarkson wrote to Christophe that there seemed to be only two options. Christophe could acknowledge the French king as his "nominal sovereign" and secure "very favorable terms" for a trade treaty, or he could insist on an acknowledgment of independence—in which case, Clarkson noted prophetically, the French would "make you pay very dearly for it." It was, Clarkson suggested, perhaps better to wait. But Christophe was running out of time.[60]

███

In 1818, lightning struck the Citadel. The massive ammunition depot in the fort caught fire and exploded, destroying much of the building and killing many soldiers, along with Christophe's brother-in-law. It must have seemed a particularly potent omen. Christophe had poured his energy and that of his subjects into erecting the massive structure. But those who worked on it resented the cost and coercion involved, and many were clearly wondering what these projects were really worth. For a time, many of Christophe's subjects had found value in his regime: they were, we can imagine, impressed by and proud of his palaces, and reassured by the fortifications built to prevent the return of the French. But the kingdom stood on relatively weak political foundations. A number of Christophe's nobles had found their own ambitions frustrated, and were displeased by his tight control. Furthermore, the king's ambitious projects all depended on the willingness of his subjects to carry out plantation labor that supported the state. Nearly a decade into the experiment, many of the workers had grown tired of the inequalities and excesses of the system. In the end, it took only a stroke to bring it down.[61]

Attending mass in the town of Limonade in August 1820, Christophe suddenly fell ill. Though he was immediately attended by Dr. Stewart—the Scotsman who held the chair of medicine Christophe had set up in Le Cap—the stroke left him partly debilitated. Christophe's weakness emboldened members of his regime who were increasingly unhappy with his rule, and within a few months, several officers organized a conspiracy. Soldiers in Le Cap rallied in the streets, chanting: "Long live liberty! Long live independence! Down with the tyrant! Down with Christophe!" They quickly gained converts, and Christophe soon faced an insurrection among his troops. When he sent envoys to try to negotiate with the leaders of the rebellion, they responded that the people "had broken the chains of slavery" and "would no longer have a king." As more and more soldiers joined the revolt, even Christophe's bodyguards turned against him. Surrounded, Christophe shot himself in the heart. His wife and daughters carried his body up the long road to the Citadel and buried him in the center of the fort.[62]

The women in Christophe's immediate family were allowed to leave the country. They went to Britain, where they stayed with Clarkson for several months. "A more delightful family never entered a person's house," the abolitionist wrote. "Their dispositions are so amiable, their tempers under such complete subjugation, and their minds so enlightened, that it is a pleasure to live with such people." But Christophe's son Jacques-Victor-Henry was not so lucky: now sixteen, he was bayoneted to death by the rebels, along with the Baron de Vastey and several other members of the aristocracy of the kingdom of the north. Having lost his first son to the French, Christophe now lost another—the one he had named his heir—to his own subjects.[63]

Pétion had died two years before, in 1818, and had been succeeded by a longtime supporter, Jean-Pierre Boyer. After Christophe's death, Boyer's troops quickly took control of the north of Haiti, ending the schism in the country. The soldiers (together with some of Christophe's own former subjects) looted the Sans-Souci palace, though its walls and gardens would remain intact until 1842, when an earthquake brought down much of the building. The Citadel stands proudly to this day, watching over the plain. But what else was left behind by Christophe's regime? His efforts to impress outsiders with the grandeur of his regime bore some fruit, for he gained many admirers abroad. But the institutions he created—not only his royalty, but also his schools and universities—largely disappeared with him. Prince Saunders lamented in a letter to Thomas Clarkson that the schools and academies had been destroyed by the "unprincipled barbarians" who had overthrown Christophe. Wilberforce pleaded with Boyer to maintain the education system, but except for Dr. Stewart's medical school, the new ruler did not do so.[64]

Pétion's regime ultimately proved the more viable: the political order that he established laid the foundation for most of the Haitian governments that followed throughout the nineteenth century. But the differences between Pétion and Christophe are often misunderstood. Their conflict is frequently thought of as being rooted in skin color: the fact that Christophe was black and Pétion lighter-skinned makes it a little too easy to see the clash between them as a battle between "blacks" and "mulattoes," and because Boyer was also light-skinned, the Republic of Haiti is often considered to be the beginning of a long-standing political and cultural dominance on the part of a "mulatto elite" in Haitian life. But while Pétion's republic certainly channeled the aspirations of light-skinned elites, the political reality was significantly muddier than the oversimplified racial explanation would have it. Indeed, while they had different skin tones, Pétion and Christophe in fact shared quite similar roots. They both grew up in modest circumstances in midlevel urban professions. Despite his origins as a servant, and perhaps a slave, Christophe had long inhabited a world that was very different from that of most of the slaves toiling on sugar plantations. He had close ties with many free men of color, and quite a few of them became key members of his aristocracy. Overall, in giving privileged positions to free men of color—who were often literate and fluent in French, while the majority of the population spoke only Kreyòl and could not read or write—the regimes of Christophe and Pétion were more alike than different.[65]

The two regimes also resembled each other to a surprising extent when it came to their vision of the state itself. While Pétion ruled over a nominal republic that had the trappings of a democratic order and Christophe created a monarchy, both systems revolved around a famous general who anchored his power in a handpicked governing coalition. Both regimes were largely politically exclusive, creating and maintaining a relatively small group of leadership elites while doing little to provide for democratic participation by a larger segment of the population. Throughout their lives, both Pétion and Christophe remained convinced that it was the rulers who would civilize the population, not the other way around.[66]

The biggest difference between Pétion and Christophe—the one with the greatest impact on what was to follow—turned out to have much less to do with racial divisions or political structures than with their divergent attitudes toward government control of land. Because Christophe controlled a richer agricultural area and thus could afford a more powerful state apparatus, he was able to hold fast to the notion that Haiti needed large plantations in order to succeed, and he kept land ownership confined to his favored elites. He was, however, the last ruler in the country to successfully oversee a regime based on that colonial-era agricultural model. Pétion's poorer and less powerful state had led him to a more liberal system of land distribution, which essentially dismantled the plantation system in the south and west of the country; as one of his contemporaries put it, Pétion "republicanized the soil." His successors, in turn, quickly found that they had little choice but to continue those policies. The majority of Haitians were less concerned with how foreign governments saw their country than with defending their access to land: the only thing, they knew, that would provide them with real autonomy, dignity, and freedom. Two decades after independence, former slaves and their children—the first generation born in freedom—were steadily laying claim to their own territory within the nation. And they made clear that in their mind, there was no turning back.[67]

3

STALEMATE

A few years after the death of Henry Christophe, a journalist from the south of Haiti traveled north to explore what was left of the vanished kingdom. Hérard Dumesle was a longtime supporter of Alexandre Pétion; he was firmly convinced that Christophe had been a tyrant and the country was well rid of him. Nonetheless, Dumesle was curious to see the ruins of the monarch's regime. He was also interested in going to the place where the country had been born. It was in the north, after all, that the first slave uprising had begun in August 1791, there that freedom was won in 1793, there, too, that Dessalines had led his armies to final victory against the French. Dumesle sought out people who had witnessed these events and visited the key historical sites of the revolution, cultivating a kind of communion with the past. Upon returning home he wrote a narrative of his journey, one of the earliest accounts of Haiti's national history. He was trying to understand what had gone wrong in the decades since independence, and to find inspiration for a new social order that would fulfill the revolution's promise.[1]

Dumesle was born in 1784 to a free wealthy family of color in the town of Les Cayes, an important port in the south of the country. He was a voracious reader, and he spent part of the long carriage ride that took him up to the north of Haiti studying the writings of the eighteenth-century French naturalist the Comte de Buffon. It was, in a way, a curious choice for Dumesle, a man of mixed African and European descent: in his essay "Varieties of the Human Species," Buffon expressed concern about the impact of sexual relations between blacks and whites, and he wrote about racial mixing in the French colonies of the Caribbean with both fascination and disgust. Unlike some of his contemporaries, Buffon had concluded that all humans belong to a single race, but he also believed there was a hierarchy among the members of that race: light-skinned people were of superior intelligence to dark-skinned ones. His work therefore helped to justify legal restrictions placed on free people of color in the colonies, including members of Dumesle's own family. Dumesle, however, didn't seem to begrudge Buffon this aspect of his work. Instead, he found inspiration in the French thinker's descriptions of the constant changes and shifts in the natural world. Just as "flowers and fruits grow in a place once taken over by a pestilential swamp," Dumesle proclaimed, so, too, empires "succeed and replace one another"; and soon, he effused, Haiti would conquer its own space in the ocean of the world, even as other lands would find themselves flooded and destroyed. Already, Dumesle noted—sounding a lot like Christophe himself—the country presented a powerful refutation of the "ridiculous ideas" of racial difference. "Take a look at the tableau that Haiti offers to the universe, and dare deny our intelligence."[2]

While Dumesle was comfortable drawing on the thinking of the French Enlightenment, he also knew well the sufferings inflicted on his country by France's colonial regime. If he was a follower of Buffon, he was also an heir to the insurgents who had risen up against slavery. So he made a point of visiting what he believed to be the site of the secret ceremony that had launched the 1791 slave rebellion. Dumesle probably knew that a few Frenchmen had already written about this event—including Antoine Dalmas, a Saint-Domingue plantation surgeon who described how conspiring slaves had gathered "in the middle of an uncultivated woods" near one plantation and slaughtered a black pig "as a sacrifice to the all-powerful spirit of the black race." For Dalmas, the offering of the animal, "surrounded by objects they believe have magical power," was proof of the barbarism of the enslaved. "The greed with which they drank its blood, the importance they attached to owning some of its bristles, which they believed would make them invincible, reveal the characteristics of the Africans." Disparagingly, Dalmas had concluded that "it is natural that a caste this ignorant and stupid would begin the most horrible attacks with the superstitious rites of an absurd and bloodthirsty religion."[3]

Dumesle, in contrast, celebrated the conspirators and wrote admiringly about the grandeur of their ceremony. In Dumesle's telling, the slaves sacrificed not a pig but a bull, while calling on God and on the example of Spartacus to help them in their struggle for freedom. The moment was so moving for Dumesle that prose failed him, and he decided to write a poem about the event instead. In an unusual gesture for the time, he also included in the poem some text in Haitian Kreyòl: the words spoken by the man overseeing the sacrifice. Thanks to Dumesle's account, they have become some of the most famous words in Haitian history:

> *Bondié qui fait soleil, qui clairé nous en haut,*
> *Qui soulévé la mer, qui fait grondé l'orage,*
> *Bondié la, zot tandé? Caché dans youn nuage,*
> *Et la li gadé nous, li vouai tout ça blancs faits!*
> *Bondié blancs mandé crime, et part nous vlé bienfets*
> *mais dié là qui si bon, ordonnin nous vengeance;*
> *Li va conduit bras nous, la ba nous assistance,*
> *Jetté portrait dié blancs qui soif dlo dans gié nous,*
> *Couté la liberté li pale coeurs nous tous.*

> *This God who made the sun, who brings us light from above,*
> *Who raises the sea, and who makes the storm rumble,*
> *That God is there, do you understand? Hiding in a cloud,*
> *He watches us, he sees all that the whites do!*
> *The God of the whites pushes them to crime, but ours wants good deeds.*

That God who is so good orders us to vengeance.

He will direct our hands, give us help.

Throw away the image of the God of the whites who thirsts for our
     tears,

Listen to the liberty that speaks in all our hearts.[4]

Dumesle provided no name for the man who spoke the powerful words he printed, but subsequent historians have attributed the speech to Boukman, the most important early leader of the slave insurrection. Boukman left no written records, but he is now remembered for this rousing call to revolution, a sanctification of the uprising as holy duty, and revered as a kind of founding ancestor for Vodou itself.*

There is a certain irony in the fact that Boukman owes his legend to the writings of Hérard Dumesle, a man from a radically different background. A well-educated, light-skinned descendant of landowning free people of color, Dumesle was part of a group often depicted in harsh terms by those who write about Haitian history—a group long seen as a Francophile neocolonial oligarchy whose members used their privileged status as descendants of whites to establish themselves as independent Haiti's new elite. But while there is, no doubt, a certain truth to this portrait, the situation was always more complicated.

---

* Based on Dumesle's account, subsequent writers developed a fuller picture of what became known as the Bois Caïman ceremony, for the woods in which it was held, and recent historians have discovered a series of new archival sources that seem to confirm that a religious ceremony indeed took place in the week before the insurrection. Today, it is broadly considered Haiti's founding event: the moment when the seed of liberty was planted, leading first to the abolition of slavery and eventually to full independence from France. The Bois Caïman ceremony is also understood by many who practice Vodou as a generative moment for the religion as well.[5] However, in part because of this, it has also become the focus of evangelical groups in Haiti, many of whom consider the ceremony itself to have been the moment when a "pact with the devil" was made that has haunted the country ever since. The notion was made famous in the United States by Pat Robertson in the wake of the January 12, 2010, earthquake in Haiti, but he was simply repeating a view that is prevalent among many evangelicals, both missionaries working in Haiti and Haitians themselves. Indeed, several attempts have been made to exorcise the site where the ceremony is believed to have taken place, as well as to poison a tree—considered sacred by Vodou practitioners—located there.

Dumesle, like many other Haitian intellectuals before and since, real-ized that it was also, in a sense, Boukman who had created him. Though Dumesle celebrated the accomplishments of Alexandre Pétion and other light-skinned elites, he emphasized the uprising of the enslaved as the core of Haiti's historical experience. He understood that Haiti was at a historical crossroads after the fall of Chris-tophe, and that the various political aspirations that had divided the country in its first decades had to be reconciled somehow. Over the course of the next decades, Dumesle would come to believe that Haiti's institutions had failed to deliver on the democratic promises of its founding revolution, and that the only way forward involved overthrowing the country's established political order. The young political activists whom he inspired, many of them born after Haiti's independence, would be the first Haitian generation to battle their elders for control of the direction of the state—though far from the last.

I I I

From 1818 to 1843—a remarkable twenty-seven years—Haiti was governed by president Jean-Pierre Boyer. Indeed, for much of that time, Boyer ruled over not just Haiti, but the entire island of His-paniola. In November 1821, insurgents in Spanish Santo Domingo had risen up, seeking separation from Spain. They were inspired by the battles for independence in mainland Latin America and by the example of their island neighbor: some of them called the new nation "Spanish Haiti." As they fought against Spain, the insurgents lobbied Boyer for help. His response, driven in part by fear that an independent Santo Domingo might become a launching pad for new attempts by the French to reconquer Haiti, was to occupy the Spanish side of the island and proclaim it part of his dominion.[6]

The early years of Boyer's rule brought remarkable political sta-bility to Haiti, which drew a stream of migrants to the country. In an echo of Christophe's plans, the Haitian government subsidized the travel of six thousand African Americans in the mid-1820s. By some accounts, the total number of immigrants during this period was as high as thirteen thousand. Part of a broader, and highly controversial, movement among African Americans that saw emigration from the United States as the best hope for true freedom and equality, these settlers were given tracts of land in different parts of Haiti as well as in occupied Santo Domingo. Perhaps a third of the arrivals, disappointed by what they found, quickly returned home, but most of them seem to have stayed and became citizens. They found work as farmers and artisans, and soon blended into the general population.[7]

As these migrants would learn, however, Boyer's regime—while welcoming—also had a marked authoritarian side. Indeed, Boyer's very stable rule was predicated on tight control over political life in Haiti. The 1816 constitution under which he took power made him president for life and gave him wide-ranging powers. The legislative structure, originally developed by Pétion, was carefully designed to provide a little democracy but not too much. Haitians were given the opportunity to elect their representatives for the Chamber of Deputies, the lower house of the bicameral legislature; but the role of these representatives was severely limited. The Chamber of Deputies was subservient to the Senate, and the senators were chosen exclusively from candidates nominated directly by the president. The senators did have some power, and could contest the president's decisions; but since their appointment was dependent on presidential approval, the highest political reaches were inaccessible to those who were not part of the president's network. In a sense, while the setup superficially resembled those of the United States and other nineteenth-century democracies, it ultimately confirmed the military-style political structures established under the regimes of Dessalines, Christophe, and Pétion: nearly all the political power was concentrated in one man's hands, without any meaningful opportunity for democratic opposition or protest.[8]

The French abolitionist Victor Schoelcher, who visited Haiti during the later years of Boyer's regime, claimed that literally every decision, whether major or minor, seemed to be made directly by the president. Boyer, he wrote, was a "veritable dictator," more an "autocrat of all of Haiti's provinces" than a president. "He is infallible; he is the Republic, and even Louis XIV couldn't say with more exactitude: 'The state is me.'" Boyer was in charge of appointing people to every position: even professionals such as lawyers and notaries were considered to be "public servants" and therefore depended on his approval to practice. Schoelcher particularly lambasted Boyer for his cynicism as a ruler. The problem was not, he insisted, that Boyer was unable to do better, nor—as so many proslavery thinkers argued at the time—that Haiti's population simply didn't have the capacity for economic development and self government. Rather, Schoelcher wrote, the president and his supporters were clearly committed to "corrupting" Haiti's political order, and to keeping the population trapped in poverty and ignorance, because that was how they could most easily stay in power.[9]

Schoelcher pointed out that, in sharp contrast to Christophe, Boyer did almost nothing to encourage education in the country. His government funded only ten schools, each with about one hundred students and one teacher, for a population of at least 700,000. Boyer was, the abolitionist declared harshly, as little interested in providing education for his nation as the slave owners had been in educating their slaves. Indeed, his attitude went beyond simple indifference: when a landowner near Port-au-Prince had opened up a privately funded school for local students, he was pressured into closing it down. Boyer, it was said, had once declared that "to sow education is to sow revolution." Although the story is perhaps apocryphal, Schoelcher concluded that the president's policy was indeed quite calculated—and tragic. Having freed themselves from slavery, Schoelcher wrote, the "glorious" people of Haiti had given to their executive the task of bringing the country toward "civilization," but they had been "betrayed" by their leader. "The people did everything a people could do. Shame on those in power, not on the people." In

Schoelcher's view, asking a population deprived of schooling to make progress was like asking a man whose arms had been cut off to work in the fields.[10]

Education was not the only potential source of "revolution" that Boyer worried about. Like his predecessors, he exercised state control largely through the military, with local officers appointed as governors of rural districts; but living long enough in a particular region often led these officers to develop divided loyalties. After years or even decades of dispensing counsel and moderating disputes over land, water, and other resources, they frequently became more deeply attached to the areas they administered than to the central government in Port-au-Prince. When conflicts arose within the country, they often ended up representing the interests of their districts instead of following presidential commands. As Boyer and many leaders who followed him found out, in times of political crisis, the very generals who were the foundation of their power could easily become leaders of insurrections. Depending heavily on the military as a tool for governance was, it turned out, a double-edged sword.

What was true for officers held for their men as well. In principle, soldiers were under the strict control of the central government; in practice, however, starting with Pétion's regime, military service had become essentially a kind of militia service, which most men carried out while living and working at home. Soldiers were paid pitiable salaries, from which they were required to provide their own shoes, sabers, and epaulettes. They were not fed or housed by the state. Their duty was to show up for exercises once a week, on Sunday, while military bands played martial tunes—among them, decades after independence, the "Marseillaise," France's revolutionary anthem. The rest of the time the soldiers lived with their families and worked for themselves. Though they were sometimes mobilized for guard duty in the capital or for national wars, such as Boyer's invasion of Spanish Santo Domingo, the army was increasingly decentralized and thus no longer a fully reliable guarantor of presidential power.

Knowing the tenuousness of his hold on power, Boyer repressed all forms of political opposition. Hérard Dumesle was one of many who, in the 1820s and 1830s, would discover that there was a cost to speaking out against the president. Boyer was not the first Haitian ruler to crush dissent, but because his rule lasted so long, it had a profound impact on Haiti's political history, establishing an autocratic approach to the presidency as the country's norm. Anténor Firmin, a prominent Haitian intellectual of the late nineteenth century, would look back and see in Boyer the "true creator of the militaristic regime whose wounds, un-healable, still poison our national organism."[11]

The cost of the political structure established by Pétion and perfected by Boyer—the combination of nominally liberal institutions with thoroughly autocratic governance—was made startlingly clear in 1825, when Boyer finally gained Haiti's diplomatic recognition by France. Though the deal he made ended his country's political isolation, the president in fact offered Haiti a defeat disguised as a victory.

III

By the mid-1820s, the exiled planters of Saint-Domingue understood that France was never going to reconquer Haiti and they were never going to be able to go back. They did not, however, give up on demanding compensation for what they had lost. Since the French government had offered restitution to individuals who were forced into exile and dispossessed of their properties during the French Revolution, they argued, why shouldn't the former plantation owners of Saint-Domingue receive the same benefit?

In 1825, Charles X, the king of France, decided it was time to resolve the Haitian situation once and for all. He planned to follow essentially the same approach as that suggested by Pétion in 1814: Haiti would pay an indemnity to compensate the exiled planters, and in return France would recognize Haiti's independence. But exactly how to carry out this plan was not clear. After all, if France admitted that Haiti was an independent nation, then it would have no right to impose financial demands on it. On the other hand, if France was merely addressing a wayward colony—as the French government had maintained for the past twenty years—then they could not present to Haiti a treaty laying out the conditions of the agreement, since treaties could be negotiated only between independent states.

In the end, Charles X cut through this Gordian knot by issuing the demand for an indemnity as a royal ordinance: a diplomatic instrument which, in the words of one historian, was "as extraordinary in its form as in its content." Royal ordinances were traditionally used only to address internal matters within a kingdom, so the agreement—although it has often been described as a "treaty" between Haiti and France—really wasn't one. Rather, it was an order given by the French king to Boyer's government, which that government accepted. (The constitutionality of this arrangement was in fact challenged several times in both countries in subsequent decades, but to no avail.)[12]

The royal ordinance didn't use the term "Haiti," referring instead to "the French part of Saint-Domingue." This made some legalistic sense: while the state of Haiti under Boyer controlled the entire island, including Spanish Santo Domingo, France could not legally intervene in the status of the Spanish territory. But the terminology also reflected the sustained reluctance on the part of the French government to accept historical facts. More than two decades after the debacle of the Leclerc mission and Dessalines's declaration of independence, the French government still had difficulty uttering the name "Haiti."

In its content, Charles X's royal ordinance was deceptively simple. To address the "interests of French commerce," the "miseries of the former colonists of Saint-Domingue," and the "precarious state of the current inhabitants of the island," it laid out three articles. The first declared that the ports of the "French part of Saint-Domingue" would henceforth be "open to the commerce of all nations," with "equal and uniform" tariffs on trade—except that tariffs on French goods would be only half the standard rate. The second article declared that Haitians would deposit in the French treasury 150 million francs "to compensate the former colonists who request an indemnity," payable in five equal installments starting in December 1825. The amount was supposed to represent the value of the property held by French planters that was lost as a result of the Haitian Revolution, though the method of calculation was in fact rather vague. Finally, the third article offered something in return: "According to these conditions, we concede with this ordinance to the current inhabitants of the French part of the island of Saint-Domingue the full and complete independence of their government."[13]

Once the ordinance was written, Charles X sent Ange René Armand, the Baron de Mackau, to Haiti with orders to get Boyer's government to accept the conditions of the royal decree. According to Mackau's instructions (labeled "very secret"), the terms of the ordinance were "the only ones which his majesty deigns accept in granting independence to the government of Saint-Domingue." If the Haitian government balked at paying the 150-million-franc indemnity, Mackau was to reassure them that they could "easily take out a loan in France under acceptable conditions"; indeed, he was to "insist" that they not look anywhere else for such a loan. And if that offer still didn't persuade the Haitians to be "grateful" and sign the agreement, Mackau was to threaten them with the "interruption of all maritime commerce." A squadron of French warships would be waiting off the shores of Haiti, ready to carry out a blockade; and that blockade would end only "after the island has submitted itself, without any conditions, to the supremacy of France." In short, there was to be no compromise: either the Haitian government accepted the ordinance as written or it went to war with France.[14]

In command of the French warships that accompanied Mackau

was the Admiral Jurien de la Gravière. He was a striking choice: his personal history was a microcosm of all the reasons Haitians had to resist the French. Gravière had first visited Saint-Domingue in 1789 as a sailor on a slave-trading vessel arriving from Africa with a cargo of captives. Later, in 1803, he had captained a ship with a grisly mission: to fetch from Cuba 150 dogs specially trained to attack blacks, so that they could be used against insurgents in Saint-Domingue. Now, in 1825, he was in command of a naval squadron ready to sever the island nation from the outside world.[15]

On July 3, 1825, three French ships arrived off the coast of Haiti. Two of them anchored far enough away to be out of the range of the country's coastal batteries, while Mackau entered the harbor of Port-au-Prince on the third. He presented Charles X's ordinance to President Boyer, who set up a commission to examine it and respond to the French. The members of the commission, shocked by what they read, rejected the document immediately and categorically. As he had been ordered to do, Mackau responded that the French squadron was prepared to blockade the island. The Haitian commission replied pugnaciously that Mackau had better go move the ship he'd arrived in: the Haitian guns were ready.[16]

Before leaving, however, Mackau set up a personal meeting with Boyer in a last-ditch effort to salvage the negotiations. The Haitian president was much more conciliatory than his commission, though he complained that the indemnity was too large. Mackau reassured him: the amount could be renegotiated in the future, he promised, based on the friendly relationship between the two countries. And if Haiti couldn't pay immediately then French banks would be happy to offer a loan. After a brief conversation, Boyer decided to accept the deal. The essential point, he considered, was that after twenty years of political isolation and constant worry about another French invasion, his country finally had the opportunity for recognition and peace.[17]

Boyer never publicly shared the details of his negotiations with Mackau, or indeed even the terms of the deal he had made. The

Haitian Senate registered approval of the agreement after hearing it read publicly to them; then the document was locked away in a velvet case. When the French squadron—fourteen ships in all—sailed into the harbor of Port-au-Prince, Boyer did not mention that it had been poised to blockade the island, but simply announced that he had secured French recognition of Haitian independence. The French ships, he declared, had come "to salute this land of liberty" and in so doing had "consecrated the legitimacy of your emancipation." There were several days of festivities in Port-au-Prince, punctuated by toasts and songs celebrating the dawn of a new era of cooperation between the two countries. It was only several months later, when newspapers describing the agreement arrived from France, that Haitians found out that—without consulting the citizens of his country—Boyer had contracted a massive debt, one they would have to pay for generations.[18]

Many citizens were furious at Boyer for giving away Haiti's meager wealth to their former colonizer, and several officers even sought to organize an uprising to force the government to reverse Boyer's decision. There were other forms of scattered protest as well: in Port-au-Prince, a few angry residents harassed French citizens, while the following year a group of Haitians tried to prevent one of the first payments from being loaded onto a French ship. Over time, Boyer would come to realize that many considered what he had done a crime, one for which he could never be forgiven. But by then it was too late.[19]

To be fair, Boyer was confident that Haiti would be able to pay the indemnity. The country was agriculturally very productive, exporting coffee and dyewood along with other goods, and the government collected taxes from all the exports. He also hoped that French merchants, absent in the colony since 1804, would return after the agreement was signed, and commerce would boom. Boyer even imagined that with a little discipline and control the population could be made to go back to cultivating sugar, further boosting exports and filling state coffers. Those sugar dreams never came to pass, though, and while the opening up of trade did create some new opportunities for Haitians, the economic advantages did not counterbalance the cost of the indemnity.[20]

In November 1825, Boyer took out a huge loan from a French bank in order to pay the first installment of the indemnity. The terms of the loan were highly disadvantageous: the Haitian government was obligated to repay 30 million francs over 25 years at an annual interest rate of 6 percent, but the bank charged an additional 20 percent fee just to provide the money to Haiti, so in fact only 24 million francs went toward the indemnity. This arrangement helped create what Haitians came to refer to as the "double debt" of independence, with the original amount of the indemnity significantly increased over the long term by loan fees and interest. Though Boyer eventually brokered a deal that decreased the indemnity itself from 150 million to 60 million francs, the 1825 loan turned out to be only the first of many, and the repayments represented a constant drain on the Haitian treasury. With the indemnity, Haiti suddenly became a debtor nation, an unlucky pioneer of the woes of postcolonial economic dependence.[21]

From the French perspective, the deal between Boyer and Charles X marked the beginning of a bright new era for France in its former colony. The Haitian population "speak our language, and share our habits," one French writer enthused. He even asserted that the only memories Haitians had were French, since their links with Africa had been entirely "broken." Building on these connections, France would elevate Haiti by bringing its arts and sciences there, exchanging "all the treasures of the human spirit" for the "products of that fertile land." By recognizing Haitian independence, the writer exulted, France had gained for itself a much better form of control over the country than they could have achieved through war. In a way, he was right. The extent of French economic dominance in Haiti throughout the nineteenth century is starkly illustrated by the fact that when the National Bank of Haiti was founded in 1888, it was fully owned and controlled by a French bank.[22]

The indemnity was certainly not the only reason why the coffers of the Haitian state were empty throughout the nineteenth century. Money raised by taxing exports was wasted on a bloated army that served mainly to buttress the presidential regime; it was drained away by corruption and consumed by internal conflicts. Yet there is no doubt that the payment of the indemnity, and of interest on the loans that it required, profoundly sapped the public treasury. Year after year, Haiti's population watched as money that could have been used to build roads, ports, schools, and hospitals simply vanished. In 1838, according to Victor Schoelcher, about 30 percent of Haiti's total annual budget was spent servicing the national debt, and almost 50 percent went to the military. By contrast, less than one percent was spent on education. "Everything you need to know about Haiti's government is summarized in that," Schoelcher lamented.[23]

Would a different kind of leader have acted differently in the face of France's demands? Christophe, of course, had steadfastly refused to even hear of an indemnity. Pétion, who had originated the idea, ended up, under pressure, taking a similarly firm stance against the French. Boyer had much in common with his predecessor: like Pétion, he was born a free man of color in colonial Saint-Domingue, fought against Louverture and Dessalines as part of Rigaud's break-away government during the Haitian Revolution, was exiled to France, and came back to Haiti as a member of the Leclerc expedition. Like Pétion, he was a landowner himself, and on that basis perhaps sympathized with the plight of the white planters of Saint-Domingue who had lost their properties. Without the counterbalancing presence of someone like Christophe, Boyer in a way represented just what French officials and writers had for years hoped to find in Haiti: a pliant and cooperative elite, ready to work with France to create a new form of external control. Perhaps he had no real choice, facing the squadron of French ships and the threat of a blockade. Yet it is hard not to wonder whether it might have been better to fight than pay, especially in view of Haiti's previous military successes against France.

More generally, Boyer's choice shows how costly it was to the Haitian people to live in a political order organized around near-absolute presidential power and lacking in broader structures of accountability. If others had been present at the meeting between Boyer and Mackau, and if the Haitian head of state had felt that it was impossible for him to make such a consequential deal without any consultation, things might have turned out differently. Instead, he made the decision essentially by himself, confident that he knew what was best for the nation. Boyer could not accept, it seems, that all around him Haitians were busily creating a very different social order—a true alternative both to the slavery they had experienced and to the new forms of foreign dominance that their president was ready to allow.

|||

For decades—as Dessalines defended Haiti, as Christophe and Pétion fought each other, as Boyer consolidated power and negotiated with France—ordinary men and women had been building their own local communities. Drawing on traditions of farming that they had brought from Africa and developed in their plantation gardens, they took the plantations and created something new. Thanks to a remarkably strong and widely shared set of cultural forms—the Kreyòl language, the Vodou religion, and innovative ways of managing land ownership and extended families—they built a society able to resist all forms of subjection that recalled the days of slavery. More than the military leaders who claimed to represent the Haitian Revolution, these new settlers were the ones who truly pursued the core goals of that uprising.

By the 1820s, the establishment of the "counter-plantation" model was essentially unstoppable. Thanks to Pétion's distribution of land to his troops, some Haitians now had legal access to small farm plots; others simply squatted on privately-owned or state-owned land. Landowners soon found that they had little choice but to negotiate with rural residents. Many simply sold off their land piece by piece, while others became absentee landlords, living in towns and leasing small parcels of their land to farmers in exchange for half the crop produced. This *métayage* system, originally developed in Pétion's republic, quickly became an established method of agricultural production throughout the country.[24]

After Boyer agreed to the indemnity, he tried to reverse this process, considering it particularly urgent to rebuild the plantation system and increase tax revenues. In 1826 he inaugurated a new Code Rural meant to reestablish state control over agricultural production. The new legislation placed rural residents under a set of specific laws that gave landowners extensive powers over their laborers. Declaring, as earlier rulers had, that agriculture was the "principal source of prosperity for the state," Boyer decreed that any rural resident who was not employed by the government or working in another profession "must cultivate the land." He outlawed agricultural cooperatives, used by farmers to jointly buy needed supplies and agree on prices for their products, and forbade rural laborers to set up their own farm stands to sell what they produced. The code also limited the movement of rural residents, denying them the right to travel to towns or cities without authorization from a local official, and created a rural police to enforce these regulations. In addition, Boyer's new laws provided for so-called corvée labor, which allowed officials and the police to temporarily force rural residents to work on road repair projects without pay. One British visitor noted that corvée laborers were spared the whip by their overseers, but that the "bayonet or sabre is used in its stead (to prick them)."[25]

In effect, Boyer had created two classes of citizens in Haiti: urban residents, who were governed by the national laws, and rural dwellers, who were subject to a different, highly restrictive set of rules. And yet, while the Code Rural encouraged and enabled mistreatment and exploitation of rural residents by local officials and landowners, it was ultimately unenforceable. Over generations, Haitians had practiced and refined their resistance to various forms of coerced labor, and by Boyer's time many of them had gained an essential weapon in that battle: their own plots of land. Once they had a place to plant their own crops to feed themselves and their families, they could refuse or avoid forms of wage labor they considered too harsh or poorly paid. In response to Boyer's attempts to control and constrain them, rural residents perfected techniques of evading government officials, living as much as possible beyond the gaze of the state.[26]

The laborers' resistance made it impossible for Boyer to carry out his grand plans of reviving sugar production. As it turned out, he was not able to realize his goals even on his own two-thousand-acre plantation: after years of effort, only 2 percent of his land was successfully planted with cane. Meanwhile, Beaubrun Ardouin, one of Haiti's founding historians and a senator under Boyer's regime, found it similarly impossible to keep laborers on his coffee plantation. Those he tried to get to work for him had established "new properties for themselves and their families." On land that they owned or leased, rural residents could grow coffee for themselves just as easily, and make much more in the process. "Could I have stopped them?" Ardouin wondered. An English visitor to Ardouin's plantation noted that many laborers had essentially taken over the land that Ardouin considered to be his—going so far as to "appropriate to themselves almost the whole of the provisions which the land furnishes, sending on down a few of the rarer vegetables, beans, peas, and artichokes to their master." Throughout the country, landowners largely ceded control of cultivation to their tenant farmers. Increasingly, they had only very tenuous power over the land they held title to. Though the landowners could legally have tried using force against the laborers who resisted them, most of them realized that in practice, any deployment of police or soldiers

against the local population would result in at best only a temporary victory.[27]

Over time, many Haitian leaders—following the example of
Pétion—simply accepted the push for mass land ownership. In
1862, President Geffrard would sign a law allowing for the sale of
government-owned land in small parcels, and in 1883, President
Salomon, hoping to promote exports, carried out a policy of distributing small plots of land to anyone who committed to cultivating
coffee, cotton, tobacco, or indigo there. Over the course of the nineteenth century, then, the number of Haitians owning land—usually
no more than a few acres—increased dramatically. Although some
individuals and families certainly continued to hold on to large plantations, the overall level of distribution and fragmentation of land
ownership in Haiti was remarkable, surpassing that of any other
society in the Americas.[28]

The population did not just take control of the land. They also
developed a set of social and cultural practices intended to secure
this land ownership over time and to guarantee every rural resident
a measure of autonomy. The most visible and widely shared of these
practices, and one that has left a distinctive mark on the social geography of Haiti, was the system of the *lakou*. In its most basic sense,
a *lakou* (from the French *la cour*, or courtyard) refers to a group
of houses—sometimes including a dozen or more structures, and
usually owned by an extended family—gathered around a common yard. But the *lakou* also came to represent specific social con-
ventions meant to guarantee each person equal access to dignity
and individual freedom. The *lakou* system has had a profound
impact on life throughout Haiti, which has long been—and indeed
remains—a largely rural country. In the mid-twentieth century, 85
percent of the population still lived in rural areas, and while that
number has steadily declined in recent decades, to this day the
majority of the population resides outside the cities. What's more,
many of those who live in urban areas were born in the countryside,

and they have imported elements of the *lakou* setup to the cities as well.[29]

The *lakou* system developed largely in the absence of—indeed, in opposition to—the Haitian government. Unable to transform the national political system, rural residents found another solution: they created, as one scholar puts it, "an egalitarian system *without a state*." Profoundly innovative, this system was predicated on the "auto-regulation" of local communities. These communities took on many of the tasks of social organization that might otherwise have been supervised or legislated by the authorities, such as the regulation of inheritance, land ownership, and family relationships. In a sense, the *lakou* system was analogous to the Citadel built by Christophe—except that while his edifice was designed to withstand a siege from external attackers, the *lakou* enabled communities to repel a threat that came from within Haiti, from the state itself as it attempted to reconstruct the plantation order.[30]

The egalitarianism of the *lakou* system was rooted in the land ownership arrangements. Each individual or nuclear family owned their own land, through which they provided for basic necessities by growing food and raising livestock for their own consumption and for sale in local markets. They also grew export crops, such as coffee, in order to buy imported consumer goods such as clothes and tools. While the *lakou* involved some forms of communal assistance and exchange—relatives and neighbors might join together to help out with large harvests or the building of a house, for example—the system was generally constructed around close-knit family networks and emphasized self-reliance through working the soil. From the moment a child was born, it would literally become a property owner: the infant's umbilical cord was buried in the yard, and a fruit tree planted upon it. The fruit of that tree would then be used to buy clothes and other necessities for the child as it grew up, and the income thus generated could eventually provide the foundation for investment in livestock or even land. In principle, at least, the *lakou* thus divided power in a way that allowed rural residents to live and work as they wished, while preventing the consolidation of wealth, and therefore control, in the hands of any person within the community. In practice, of course, there were some disparities in wealth: certain peasants, for instance, were established on more productive plots or had better connections for selling their products, and were thus able to expand their holdings and consolidate their economic power. Even the wealthier rural residents, however, remained rooted in the codes of the communities where they lived.[31]

The antithesis of *lakou*-based autonomy was salaried work, which represented a surrender to the demands of another individual. Indeed, one scholar argues that whereas workers in many societies over the last two hundred years have accepted salaried work but sought to curb its excesses through government control or union organizing, the preferred strategy in Haiti has been to "refuse the entire system." The rural population, writes Haitian anthropologist Michel-Rolph Trouillot, was not willing to trade its liberty for money. "When it had to choose between a higher income and direct control of the labor process, it chose control."[32]

In order to preserve that control, the *lakou* system established its own set of customs to regulate land ownership and land transfers. The state had no part in these transactions, which were overseen entirely by community and family institutions. When several people in an extended family owned adjacent plots of land, for example, the formal title to the entire set of fields would usually be held by just one family member, who served as the interface between his *lakou* and the official world beyond. Meanwhile, the actual division of the land would be done within the family, leaving few if any written traces. As far as the *lakou* was concerned, the individual ownership was no less real for its lack of state recognition. When it came to their own fields, the family members could do whatever they wished, with just one signal exception: they could not sell the land to anyone outside the *lakou*.[33]

That, of course, might seem like a serious restriction. But most rural residents would not have wanted to sell their fields anyway, out of deep-rooted fear that the loss of one plot could open the door to the acquisition of larger pieces of property by outsiders who, by gaining control over land, would gain control over the community and its labor. Land transfers could take place within an extended family, of course, according to processes governed by consensus; but ceding land to an outsider was largely taboo. In essence, the limits on the sale of land were driven by the idea that it was always possible, if the community were not extremely careful, for the plantation to return. And indeed, over generations, these cultural restrictions on selling land have effectively protected Haiti's rural communities from encroachment by outside interests, whether from within the country or from abroad.[34]

Like any social system, the *lakou* had to keep the peace among its members. That was often a serious challenge, for in a situation of relative poverty and intense individualism, conflicts over property could easily turn violent. As a result, in many communities great care was given to the placement of boundaries—often "living fences" made out of cactus, for instance—to prevent livestock from causing damage to neighboring yards. The means of access to and from properties also required careful discussion, with many communities settling on a network of small paths with few large common roads: the roads might have been useful in some ways, but they would have taken land away from planting and opened up a danger of access from the outside. The location of spots for defecation, too, was a contentious question, regulated by a set of customs whose transgression could be a serious issue. Thus, while the rural residents preserved a sense of individual autonomy, they did so in a world governed by codes and coordinated by *lakou* leaders, usually the family patriarchs. Everyone was subject to a kind of reciprocal control from family and neighbors that maintained the delicate balance required for an egalitarian existence.[35]

Highly charged issues were softened by intensive habits of hospitality, with food shared either through communal dining or through the custom of sending part of whatever one family cooked to their neighbors in the *lakou*. Religious life, too, served to hold this world together. Each *lakou* included a set of family tombs, allowing residents of the countryside to do something that had been difficult if not impossible under slavery itself: to keep and maintain a cemetery, paying respects to the dead and through them honoring more distant ancestors in Africa. Such service to ancestors is an important part of Vodou practice, in which departed family members are seen as being connected to the broader pantheon of *lwa* (gods). The presence of the tombs served as a constant reminder of the origins of the family and the *lakou*, thereby emphasizing each family member's responsibility to maintain the community and the land that it was built upon. Naturally, some found this world constraining, even claustrophobic, and fled their communities—often going to the cities in search of education and new opportunities. Still, until the twentieth century, the Haitian countryside seems largely to have sustained and satisfied the population that lived there.[36]

Of course, though they were focused on individual autonomy, the *lakou* were never isolated from one another, or from the broader economic system of Haiti. Rather, they were the building blocks of a complex agricultural system tied together by a network of thriving and bustling markets. The Haitian geographer and novelist Georges Anglade, who mapped this network of markets in a 1982 atlas, described them as not just places for commercial exchange but a "fundamental aspect of rural life." Each market sustained the region around it, providing a site for the exchange of news as well as for the organization of social events, political action, and secret societies that governed life in much of the countryside. The markets helped "an infinite number of small intermediaries" to "share the crumbs" of rural production: "merchants, resellers, brokers, porters, artisans who all work to get a few cents." The work of buying and selling in the market was "scattered," Anglade writes, precisely in order to "provide resources to the greatest number of people, notably peasants without land," who hired themselves out to work for other peasants in their gardens. Outsiders often saw (and still see)

Haitian markets as chaotic and incomprehensible, but their form in fact reflects their evolution over time to serve specific purposes, channeling commerce in particular ways for the communal good. Since the markets were one of the main places where rural residents encountered government officials, their fragmentation had another benefit as well, making it all the more difficult for the state to track, control, and tax the trading that went on there. In this way, the markets also allowed the rural population to resist those who sought to control them from outside.[37]

The form of agricultural and social organization developed in the Haitian countryside in the nineteenth century was highly productive, even if it didn't supply Boyer with the tax revenues he had been counting on. While the *lakou* system never generated the massive profits that planters and French merchants had gained from the slave economy, it provided the former slavers and their descendants with a relatively comfortable and sustainable life. Indeed, Haiti at this time was a magnet for immigrants. In addition to African Americans drawn by Boyer's travel subsidy, men and women from Germany, Corsica, Syria, and other countries came to Haiti in significant numbers during the second half of the nineteenth century. Migrants also arrived from other parts of the Caribbean. Hundreds came from Guadeloupe and Martinique after slavery was abolished there in 1848—considering that, even though they were now legally free, they would find a truer independence in Haiti. Thanks to a broadly shared Kreyòl language, they were able to integrate themselves into the society relatively quickly, joining in the creation of Haiti's remarkable culture.[38]

I I I

"The first step one takes into Haiti is a little frightening, especially for an abolitionist," the French antislavery activist Victor Schoelcher wrote in his account of the journey he took to Haiti in 1841. "I desired, I feared, I hoped." He had read ardently about Haiti's struggle for freedom, and he admired Toussaint Louverture and other heroes of the fight for emancipation. He wanted contemporary Haiti to provide further proof to the world that slavery was unnecessary and that the Caribbean could thrive without it. But he worried that he would find instead that the proslavery voices were right, and that he would encounter only "disorder and barbarism" in the former colony.[39]

As it turned out, Schoelcher had kind things to say about many of the Haitians who welcomed him during his travels. Ultimately, however, he found himself disappointed. He was shocked by the scrappy look and habits of Haitian soldiers, and claimed that the material conditions of free Haitians were little better than those of the slaves in other parts of the Caribbean. Schoelcher tried to take the sting out of his remarks by arguing that the situation was a result of bad leadership—Boyer's unwillingness to fund education, for example—rather than of any inherent incapacity on the part of the Haitian people. But in a curious way, his descriptions of Haiti at times dovetailed with those peddled by the proslavery advocates of the day, who gleefully circulated images of Haitian peasants descending into a mire of laziness and poverty when deprived of the benefits of white tutelage and mastery.

Schoelcher wrote that areas that had once been covered with thriving sugar plantations had become sites of "misery and sterility," with residents growing nothing more than food for themselves and a bit of cane to make alcohol. The *lakou*—scattered houses connected by narrow paths—looked to him like slave huts. He lamented that the women went around bare-breasted and the children naked, that whole families were sleeping together in one room and surviving on meager rations of bananas. Schoelcher was upset to find that Haitians had not developed the desire for consumption that "gives birth to industry and forces us to work" while also "refining" a people's sensibilities. Theirs was a "negative happiness," he wrote: "they live from day to day and, thanks to their liberty, they are happy and content despite their poverty." Desiring little beyond one's basic needs might be a fine "natural philosophy," he claimed, but it precluded mental progress.[40]

Haitian peasants, Schoelcher concluded, were ultimately being condemned to an "animalistic" existence. What was worse, by allowing this to happen, the country's leaders were doing harm not only to themselves but to the entire abolitionist cause. "The crime of Haitian barbarism is not only mortal for your Republic," he expostulated, "but can be called a universal crime." By giving comfort to all those who defended slavery, it helped to keep millions of men and women in chains. "Have you not thought about what you are doing? Have you not considered the responsibility that weighs on you? Are you not afraid that one day the voices of four million of your brothers will be raised against you in the universe's tribunal, accusing you of having slowed down their emancipation?" From the trees of liberty planted throughout Haiti, Schoelcher wrote, had come nothing but "bitter and disappointing fruit."[41]

It was a strange accusation: certainly the responsibility for holding millions of people in bondage lay with slave owners and their governments, not Haitian farmers. And it shows how even a leading abolitionist like Schoelcher could remain essentially blind to the antislavery revolution that was still under way in Haiti. The rural culture he condemned was driven by a historically constituted set of aspirations and a determined search for autonomy. To him, however, it looked like a retreat into primitivism, a criminal step backwards. Such charges against the country's rural population were in fact startlingly common during that time. Propagated by defenders of slavery and abolitionists alike, portrayals of Haiti's rural culture as atavistic, isolationist, and unsustainable took root in the nineteenth century, and they have never gone away. As Louis-Joseph Janvier noted furiously in 1882: "There are tons of idiots who have never used their ten fingers for anything, and who wander around constantly repeating, inanely: 'Haitians are very lazy.'" Such views were common among foreigners, and they have been shared by

many elites in Haiti as well. In 1842, an article in the *Patriote* newspaper declared that "polygamy and laziness" were the "two major
vices that afflict our population." Since the early nineteenth century,
Haiti's peasants have repeatedly been accused of refusing progress
and rejecting the benefits of consumption, depicted by their own
rulers as subjects in desperate need of reform who were holding the
country back.[42]

I I I

If they were so vilified, of course, it was partly because they had been
so successful. Through their social and cultural institutions, the rural
population of Haiti managed to steadfastly refuse plantation labor
and construct something else in its place. The ruling class—largely
composed of men who had already owned significant amounts of
land in 1804, either because they had been among the wealthier free
people of color in Saint-Domingue or because their military rank had
enabled them to acquire land during the revolution—found itself stymied when it tried to reproduce the colonial economy. Within a few
decades of Haiti's independence, many of its leaders had realized that
they couldn't rebuild the plantations or stop the country's majority
from pushing for land and autonomy. What they could do, however,
was channel and contain that push, surround and stifle it. Unable to
control the bodies or the work of the rural residents, Haitian elites
instead focused on controlling the nation's points of access to external markets: the port towns.

As Michel-Rolph Trouillot put it, nineteenth-century Haiti
became "a republic for the merchants." By funding its activities
almost entirely through the taxation of exports and imports, the
government "persistently siphoned off the meager resources of the
peasantry, so that this peasantry came to finance the state while having no control over it." This arrangement created an enduring tension within Haitian society. The elites were able to retain their

positions of wealth and power, but only by abandoning the drive for equality and liberty that had inspired Haiti's revolution in the first place. The rural inhabitants, meanwhile, carved out their own way of life in the countryside, but came to regard the state as a largely predatory force, at its best when it was absent altogether. With neither side able to prevail and gain control of the entire country, the situation settled down into a grinding stalemate.[43]

The government's emphasis on the taxation of foreign trade had evolved gradually in the first decades of Haiti's independence. During the Haitian Revolution, the state had taxed agricultural production in a simple way: a quarter of what was grown on each plantation was literally handed over, in kind, to local authorities, who then sold it themselves on behalf of the state. Since plantation labor and production were closely controlled, and many estates were run by military officers, this form of taxation was a fairly efficient and reliable means of collecting revenue. (Christophe used a similar system of taxes to support his plantation-based regime.) Such an approach, however, was much less well suited to the increasingly dispersed and scattered agricultural production of the early nineteenth century. Accordingly, when he became president in 1807, Pétion focused on levying duties on imports and exports, and by the time of Boyer's regime, the Haitian government had come to depend exclusively on this form of taxation to raise money for the state. The import-export duties were collected not in the fragmented countryside but in the well-controlled port towns, where the coffee produced in the interior was sold to foreign merchants and exchanged for goods arriving from overseas. Indirectly, of course, the costs were still borne by the rural farmers, who received less for their export crops and paid more for the imported goods that they bought.[44]

After sugar, coffee had been the second most important crop in colonial Saint-Domingue, and it became the key export for independent Haiti. Despite forceful attempts by Louverture, Christophe, and Boyer, large-scale sugar production never returned to the country. (A few scattered sugarcane fields always remained here and there, but they were mostly used for the production of rum.) Coffee, however, was a very different kind of crop: its cultivation and harvesting was less brutal, its processing less complicated. Rural Haitians after independence found coffee ideal because its production could be carried out on a small scale and sustained with little outlay of money. In parts of the country where old coffee plantations sat empty, rural residents could simply harvest beans from coffee trees that were growing wild. Coffee was also a useful crop because there was significant demand for it on the global market, and the Haitian product was of high quality. Indeed, it was the equivalent of today's coveted shade-grown organic crops, with the label "St. Marc Coffee" considered a benchmark for quality throughout the world in the nineteenth century.[45]

However, on the long journey of prime Haitian coffee from bean to cup, Haitians were generally able to take part in—and profit from—only the earliest stages of the process. There was good money to be made in the coffee business, and it drew foreign merchants to Haiti in large numbers. (Germans were especially well represented among these merchant ranks.) Because they offered essential access to transatlantic trade networks, the foreign merchants soon gained substantial control over Haiti's export trade, becoming a powerful presence in Haitian society. Their interest in the country was entirely pecuniary: as Michel-Rolph Trouillot bluntly puts it, the merchants were essentially "uninterested in the fate of the nation." Nonetheless, Haitian leaders—even as they publicly presented themselves as proud defenders of Haiti's national sovereignty—increasingly allowed the foreign merchants to monopolize the country's international commerce, on the theory that economic gains made through this alliance would be worth the price. Over the course of the nineteenth century, the power of foreign merchants in Haiti continued to increase, and they proved a constant source of economic pressure and political instability.[46]

Meanwhile, the state became completely dependent on the taxation of exports for its own survival. "The peasant's coffee was for the government," quips one historian, "what the sheep's wool is for the shepherd." In 1810, 73 percent of government revenues had come from intake at customs houses; in 1842 that percentage was up to 92, and by 1881, duties on exports and imports comprised over 98 percent of state income. The indirect taxation was much less visible than direct levies, but it was also the opposite of a progressive taxation system, since it placed the heaviest burden on the country's poor majority: the rural farmers, for whom export crops were—at least potentially—the most profitable product of their land. "The state was spending," writes Michel-Rolph Trouillot, "but it was the peasant who was footing the bill."[47]

There was, of course, nothing unique to Haiti about merchants pursuing profits and the government imposing taxes on trade. What made the situation unusual was the fact that customs duties became nearly the only source of wealth in the society. After the breakup of the plantations, Haitians aspiring to riches and elite status no longer had the option of large-scale land ownership, and the dominance of foreign merchants made it difficult for Haitians to prosper in the import-export trades. That left control of the state as one of the few obvious sources of potential affluence and social advancement. The great number of aspirants to state power, in turn, made those who did have control of the state particularly concerned with holding on to their positions—which meant spending large amounts of money on the military and constantly compromising with the demands of foreign merchants and governments.[48]

Was this what Louverture, Dessalines, and Boukman had had in mind as they fought to establish a new order? Many under Boyer's regime felt as if the promise of liberty and dignity that had inspired the nation's founding had turned into a strange, nightmarish farce. Their country, so hard won, was being handed over to outsiders all too eager to take control, or milked by elites who had little concern for the general welfare. They watched with alarm, fearing that the very generation that had secured Haiti's independence was now allowing it to slip away.

III

By the 1830s, young activists in Haiti's various port towns as well as in Port-au-Prince were increasingly bold in their challenges to Boyer's rule. Opposition newspapers multiplied, attacking the government's authoritarianism and demanding greater rights. Such attacks took courage. The activists knew that just a few years after Boyer became president, he had been harshly criticized by a writer named Félix Darfour, who accused Boyer of having "sold the country to the whites" through the indemnity agreement. Darfour wrote to the Chamber of Deputies, laying out a series of grievances and complaining of the exclusion of darker-skinned Haitians from political power. In response, Boyer arrested Darfour and had him tried in a military court, even though Darfour had never been a soldier. Convicted of sedition, he was sentenced to death and executed.[49]

A decade after Darfour's death, however, the opposition press was flourishing, part of an increasingly vibrant public sphere in the country. Everyone, it seemed, had a plan for reforming Haiti. One writer lobbied for the abolition of Catholicism in favor of Protestantism and the abolition of French in favor of English. The Chamber of Deputies, meanwhile, was increasingly populated with critics of Boyer. Though it had little power to institute real reform, the Chamber often became a forum for passionate speeches against the president.[50]

Among the most vocal members of the opposition was Hérard Dumesle. In 1832, a few years after publishing the account of his journey to the north of Haiti, he was elected deputy for Les Cayes and led the call for a profound reform of Haitian society, ranging from modernization of commerce to greater investment in public education. Boyer would have none of it and expelled Dumesle from political office. Dumesle continued to speak out, however. Within a few years, he was reelected, and was named president of the Chamber by the rest of the deputies. Victor Schoelcher, who was in Haiti at the time, characterized the choice as a "declaration of war" against Boyer. The president quickly cracked down, expelling Dumesle from the Chamber again, outlawing public meetings, and arresting opposition figures. When a local teacher and some of his students collected money to present Dumesle with a medal acknowledging his political service, the teacher was fired.[51]

Under the 1816 constitution, all Haitian men over the age of twenty-one could participate in the local elections that chose parliamentary representatives. In 1841, however, Boyer raised the voting age to twenty-five, hoping to stall the electoral progress of the reformers. The political conflict was very much a generational one: although Dumesle was already in his sixties, many of his comrades and supporters were significantly younger. The older politicians in power were mostly veterans of the war of independence, and they depicted the reformers as young idealists who didn't truly understand the threats Haiti faced. The reformers, meanwhile, saw those in power as a sclerotic group who used old glories to justify their stranglehold on the government even as they sold out the country—a corrupt, authoritarian regime unconcerned with Haiti's national interests. Many young Haitians were thoroughly demoralized. "It seems as if there is no future," Schoelcher noted on his visit, "there is no tomorrow."[52]

Though they came mainly from Haiti's elite professional classes, the young reformers sought to create an alliance with the rural farmers who made up the majority of the population. At a time when some political leaders argued that Haiti should revoke the constitutional ban on ownership of property by foreign whites in order to attract international investment, the reformers fervently defended the prohibition. Foreign merchants and property owners, they argued, represented a threat to Haiti's small farmers. An 1841 editorial proclaimed that giving foreigners access to land would be "fatal to our political existence": outsiders would create large properties by absorbing smaller ones, which would mean returning to a kind of colonial rule. "They will be the masters and we the workers—they the exploiters and we the exploited." Inspired by the ideas of

Charles Fourier, Henri de Saint-Simon, and other French radicals of the time, the young reformers imagined an alternative to the hierarchical labor relations of Boyer's Code Rural: small farmers would form associations and cooperatives, gathering around "a central common" with buildings and factories that could be used collectively. What they were imagining was a kind of large *lakou*, albeit one that brought together not just an extended family but a broad community of laborers committed to growing crops for export in an egalitarian arrangement.[53]

One young opposition member, the twenty-four-year-old James Blackhurst, tried to put these ideas into practice. Schoelcher, who visited Blackhurst's experimental sugar plantation, noted that unlike other landowners in the area, Blackhurst was easily able to find laborers to work in the cane. The difference was that Blackhurst treated his workers well and lived "fraternally" among them, his dwelling as simple as the rest. "You are in the house of a peasant, sir," he announced to his visitor. Blackhurst also ran his farm as a cooperative and didn't keep too much of the profit for himself. What's more, Schoelcher effused, the young reformer knew that "a society, like a field, gets overgrown with weeds when you don't tend to it," and he was planning on setting up a school at his farm. In the meantime, he periodically gathered all the "most intelligent" laborers and delivered lectures to them on various topics, sometimes inviting guests to give talks as well. Schoelcher saw hope for Haiti in Blackhurst and believed that his cooperative agricultural model might make it possible for the country to start exporting sugar to European markets once again.[54]

Blackhurst's experimental farm, just a few miles from the capital, openly flouted Boyer's Code Rural, and was typical of increasingly bold actions on the part of the reformers. By the early 1840s, Boyer was facing challenges from all sides. In Santo Domingo, a rebellion against Haitian rule was gaining more and more popular support. At the same time, the Haitian government was struggling to deal with a mounting financial crisis. Then, in May 1842, a massive earthquake struck the northern part of the country, killing perhaps half the residents of Le Cap and demolishing the Sans-Souci palace. (Christophe's massive Citadel was mostly undamaged.) The tremors were also felt in Port-au-Prince, and the dislocation and suffering caused by the disaster increased the sense of crisis in the country. In the face of these calamities, the government seemed "without will and without means," and its inaction was strongly criticized by the opposition.[55]

In the election of 1842, the reformers won a majority in the Chamber of Deputies. Boyer's response was unsubtle: he placed troops in front of the parliament with orders to admit no one but his supporters. Led by Hérard Dumesle, the excluded parliamentarians created the Society for the Rights of Man and the Citizen and organized a series of dinners and meetings. The gatherings at Dumesle's home, outside the southern town of Les Cayes, culminated in a proclamation that attacked Boyer's regime as well as the 1816 constitution upon which it was based. The "vicious" constitutions, the manifesto declaimed, had made it too easy for leaders to forget the fundamental truth: that the people were the real sovereigns of the nation. The document crystallized sentiments that were shared widely throughout Haiti's towns and villages. As desire grew throughout the country for a more liberal political order, activists converged on Les Cayes to plan a revolution.[56]

In January 1843, the Les Cayes insurgents, led by Dumesle and his cousin Rivière Hérard, announced that the fortieth year of Haitian independence would be the "first year of the Regeneration." Taking up arms, they marched on the nearby town of Jérémie, which harbored a garrison of government troops, but the town's population welcomed them warmly and the army regiments joined the uprising instead of fighting it. When Boyer sent reinforcements from Port-au-Prince to crush the revolt, those troops did the same thing. A British officer reported that when one group of soldiers was ordered to attack the rebels, they "refused to fire upon their countrymen and, when repeatedly urged to advance by their Commandant, they went over in a body, and recommended to the General if he valued his life to make the best of his way back to Head Quarters." The rebellion, in fact, was strikingly peaceful, consisting largely of speeches and mass protests in the streets rather than armed conflict. "This extraordinary mode of revolutionizing a Country," the British officer wrote, "with scarcely any of the attendant scenes of Bloodshed, rapine and violence (so common in such cases in European Civilized Countries)," presented "a case almost unparalleled in History." Urban women played a major role in the revolution, speaking out in favor of the uprising and taking part in military operations. During one of the rare pitched battles, a group of women dragged two cannon from a fort outside of Léogâne and set them up to fire on Boyer's advancing troops, killing thirty soldiers. Later, Boyer himself was surrounded by a "disturbance of women, who followed him and cursed him, abusing him in the most scathing manner." Within two months, Boyer abdicated, going into exile in Jamaica. His palace in Port-au-Prince was invaded and looted, with furniture smashed and portraits of the departed president destroyed. Hérard Dumesle led a triumphant march into Port-au-Prince, greeted with "delirious enthusiasm" by the population.[57]

It was a remarkable democratic explosion, the greatest the country had seen since the days of the Haitian Revolution. "Democracy," one contemporary observer wrote, "flowed full to the brim. And what democracy!" While the movement did not actually include all segments of Haitian society—the main actors were residents of cities and towns, and the leaders were largely professionals—it nevertheless represented a significant break with Boyer's enclosed and authoritarian system of power. After two decades under his leadership, urban Haitians enthusiastically and fervently debated alternative forms of government, from "American federalism" to the more centralized model of postrevolutionary France. Many wanted to organize town meetings that would choose representatives and produce legislation. One newspaper effused that such meetings would become "the great occupation of the national elite, the rendezvous of the enlightened, the intelligent and the capable," creating an "immense" good in the society. The U.S. consul in Les Cayes, who watched the movement develop, reported back approvingly, noting his belief that the reforms would ultimately benefit American commerce and U.S. relations with Haiti in general.[58]

The leaders of the movement that overthrew Boyer chose Rivière Hérard as the provisional president and put him in charge of creating a new constitution. Elected representatives from throughout the country gathered in Port-au-Prince and formed a constitutional convention. The debates were attended by large and boisterous crowds, largely drawn from Port-au-Prince's professional classes and from students of the city's elite schools, who alternately booed and applauded orators as they took the stand. One of the fiercest discussions, as before, concerned the provision prohibiting whites from owning property in Haiti. The Chamber of Deputies at the time included a number of representatives from the Spanish half of the island; several of them considered themselves white and asked that the stipulation be removed from the constitution. Other representatives, however, rushed to defend the provision. One deputy who regretted the "isolation from the great human confraternity" caused by the exclusion of whites nevertheless defended the law, arguing it was less a manifestation of prejudice than an expression of fears that Haitian independence might be compromised. In the end, the provision was maintained.[59]

"Mr. President, we bring you the little monster," announced the representative who handed the final draft of the 1843 constitution to Rivière Hérard for ratification. It was substantially more liberal than those that had preceded it, and included a constitutional guarantee of the right to political assembly and the right to a trial by jury in criminal cases. There were also changes to the electoral process: senators would no longer be selected from nominees put forth by the president, but chosen by direct elections. Likewise, the president was no longer to be appointed by the Senate. Instead, as in the United States, the population would vote for electors, who were then charged with choosing the new head of state.

Along with these improvements, however, the new constitution also added suffrage restrictions that had not explicitly existed before. The voting age was rolled back to twenty-one, but now voting would be open only to certain classes of men: those who owned property, those who were renting land under a contract of at least nine years in duration, or those who could prove that they practiced a "profession" or were employed in some kind of "industry." Those last categories sounded quite broad, but it was not obvious how they would be interpreted. What is more, it was not clear that many rural residents— particularly those who rented plots of land for the short term, worked as informal day laborers, or practiced the system of *métayage* would retain the right to political participation.[60]

Such concerns were largely overlooked by the urban residents and professionals who were the driving force behind the 1843 uprising. They saw the new constitution as a crucial move forward, one that would guarantee greater political liberty. But the reform movement soon met with resistance from a key group: the military. Even before the constitutional debates were completed, military leaders made it clear that they would have no scruples about opposing the new regime. They did so in part because they resented the way that revolutionaries had taken over positions in the army. The opposition movement, after all, had finally triumphed thanks to the military's support; yet instead of expressing gratitude, the uprising's leaders—as one historian laments—had "thrown themselves frenetically on the epaulettes," naming themselves officers and generals as they rallied their supporters. And once in power, the reformers insisted on retaining the military ranks they had taken on during the revolt. They understood that political power in Haiti was always intimately tied to military power, and they were well aware that every president before Hérard had been a veteran of the war of independence. The established army officers, many of whom had joined the revolt once it was under way, were of course not particularly pleased by the spectacle of young lawyers and journalists taking up positions of command within the Haitian army. One of them complained about the pretensions of these "newcomers who have never warmed themselves around the fire of a bivouac."[61]

In February 1844, there was a new outburst of violence in the long-standing struggle for independence in Spanish Santo Domingo. Rivière Hérard departed with troops to try to repress the revolt, without success: the independence of the Dominican Republic was declared in May 1844. Back in Port-au-Prince, Hérard Dumesle headed the government in his cousin's absence, but he found critics of the new regime—both military leaders and reformers who felt that the new constitution had not gone far enough—mounting strong attacks against him in the Chamber of Deputies. Long the victim of authoritarian tactics during his years in the opposition, he nevertheless now used the same tactics himself, and dispersed the assembly.[62]

The reform movement that ultimately overthrew Boyer was driven by hopes that the spread of popular democracy would bring an end to the militarized, authoritarian style of politics that had dominated Haiti since its independence. But in the end, faced with internal dissent and resistance from the established military leaders, the reformers also fell into the trap of equating military might with political authority. Seeking to preserve their power and institute their new constitution, the leaders of the opposition soon found themselves stuck in the very political model they had hoped to abolish. Both Hérard Dumesle and Rivière Hérard quickly chose to dispense with their commitment to open debate and parliamentary procedure in favor of heavy-handed tactics of rule. They justified this strategic choice by arguing that it was the only way to confront deep-rooted resistance to change, particularly within the military. But they would soon also demonstrate the limits of their own commitment to change, as the 1843 revolution faced its most serious challenge: the political mobilization of small farmers in the countryside who, disappointed with the limits of the reforms, saw an opportunity to push for an even more profound transformation of the Haitian order. As historian Leslie Manigat puts it, Dumesle and his fellow activists had believed that once they passed their constitution, the revolution would be over. In fact, it was just beginning.[63]

III

"The bandit Acaau came barefoot," dressed like a peasant, "in a species of canvas packing-sheet and wearing a little straw hat." Behind him came the Army of the Sufferers, demanding a change in their condition. They wanted "respect for the Constitution, Rights, Equality, Liberty." But more than that, they wanted access to more land in order to secure a better existence as farmers. The "bandit," Louis Jean-Jacques Acaau, saw his mission as divinely ordained: speaking to a crowd convened by the sound of a conch in one public square, he "publicly vowed not to change his clothing until the orders of 'divine Providence' were executed." And what had providence ordered? "The poor people" were "first to chase out the mulattoes, second to divide up the mulatto properties." At this point, several eyes in the crowd turned and picked out light-skinned peasants who were standing and listening eagerly to Acaau. However, he proclaimed, pointing to them: "Oh—those are blacks!" A man named Joseph, a worker at a nearby rum distillery, stepped out of the crowd and concurred: "Nègue riche qui connaît li et écri, cila mulâte; mulâte pauve qui pas connaît li ni écri, cila nègue"—"The rich black who can read and write is a mulatto; the poor mulatto who can't read or write is black." From then on Joseph became one of the standard-bearers of the movement. Respected for his knowledge of both Vodou and Catholic prayer, he led Acaau's troops on their campaign with a candle in hand.[64]

So Maxime Reybaud, former French consul in Haiti, described the movement that erupted in 1844 and briefly threatened to upend the social order in Haiti. Reybaud's accounts, written under the pen name Gustave d'Alaux for the popular French magazine *Revue des Deux Mondes*, are deeply racist. Yet it is from this text that the often-cited Kreyòl proverb about the tight links between color and class—spoken by a Vodou-practicing rural insurgent, no less—comes to us. Just as Dumesle ended up channeling the words of the departed Boukman, so a supercilious Frenchman gave us the gift of Acaau's words. If they have remained so famous, however, it is because they point directly to the complexity and dynamism of politics, class, and color in Haiti. As Joseph and Acaau insisted, the real problem wasn't really the color of one's skin: it was whether you had access to the wealth and education you needed in order to be truly free.

Acaau's army, which mobilized thousands of supporters, was dubbed the Piquets after the pickets they carried into battle as rudimentary weapons. As one Methodist missionary in the country wrote, these were "sticks of different sorts of wood; they sharpened the edge, and applied poisonous gum to it, so that any wound which might not be dangerous, would through poison become so. The sticks were from 8 to 10 feet long." The Piquets were successful fighters, defeating government troops in several engagements and taking over a large swath of the south of Haiti. The political goals of their movement are difficult to document with precision, since they are known to us almost exclusively through the fragmented observations of largely hostile observers such as Reybaud. "Up to now," Louis-Joseph Janvier noted in his introduction to an 1884 book called *Le vieux piquet*, "those who have written the history of the *piquets* were their enemies or their assassins." Nevertheless, we can glimpse from these writings the broad political agenda that shook Haiti for several months in 1844.[65]

Acaau's movement took root in the south, a region with a long history of rural resistance. It was in the southern mountains, for instance, that the former maroon Goman had created a separate republic in 1807, holding out against Pétion's regime until 1819. Farmers in the south had, of course, followed political events during the final years of the Boyer regime, concerned about what the new order would mean for them. The majority of the peasants spoke only Kreyòl, while the debates and legislation of the 1843 revolution were in French. That fact itself was a source of political exclusion. But rural residents tried to overcome that barrier by gathering in public places and having someone who could read French explain the articles to them in Kreyòl. The lack of direct access to political documents meant that rumors played a powerful role in spreading news and inciting action. The uncertainty about precisely who would have the right to vote, for instance, led many to worry that they would be excluded from the political process. Many peasants also believed—wrongly—that the new constitution included provisions for the dispossession of small-scale landowners and the reconstruction of large properties. There were even whispers that legislation requiring the municipal government to register all newborns and conduct censuses had a sinister goal: the return of slavery. Such rumors tapped into profound fears of a return of plantation agriculture, and with it the destruction of the way of life that the peasants had painstakingly constructed. More broadly, many rural residents seemed to fear—rightly, as it turned out—that for all its sound and fury, the revolution of 1843 would end up merely replacing one authoritarian regime with another.[66]

Maxime Reybaud had a simple name for what the Piquets represented: "black communism." Just as the European communists demanded "reduced work and increase of salaries," he opined, so the peasants of Haiti were demanding "reduction of the price of foreign merchandise and augmentation of the value of their crops." Many owned small plots of land, but they wanted access to larger properties in order to have a more secure existence. And they wanted to be able to profit more fully from their labor instead of seeing their meager earnings disappear into the state treasury and the pockets of foreign merchants. In fact, however, the Piquets' agenda covered more than just the economic concerns that Reybaud described. Acaau also demanded that the state provide access to national education, and he tried to bring a truly participatory and democratic form of politics to Haiti. The leaders of the 1843 revolution had come from Haiti's urban, educated classes, and when they threw themselves into insurrection, they had dressed as military officers—like the members of the government they were opposing. Acaau, in contrast, tapped into a very different kind of political symbolism. He brought together crowds of farmers, few of whom had participated directly in the early uprising, speaking to them in Kreyòl and drawing on the symbols of Vodou and popular Catholicism. Though he was wealthier than many of his rural followers and could have afforded different clothes, he made a point of dressing in the traditional garments of the peasantry, "to show in actions the kind of equality and participation they were speaking about in words."[67]

The Piquet uprising began soon after Rivière Hérard's constitution was promulgated in late December 1843, and Acaau's followers marched along almost exactly the same route—from the southern province toward Port-au-Prince—as the forces who had overthrown Boyer a few months earlier. The new revolt starkly exposed the limits of Dumesle's earlier revolution; and for all their earlier idealism, Dumesle and Rivière were not willing to negotiate with Acaau's movement or address its demands. They responded instead with guns, sending troops to repel the Piquets.[68]

The Piquet uprising made it clear that in Haiti a little bit of revolution could be a very dangerous thing for the elite. Emboldened by the moderate reforms that Dumesle and his fellow activists carried out, Acaau pushed for a truly democratic order, one that would give real political power to the entire Haitian population. But such democracy would necessarily mean not just political change but a wholesale social transformation: if all the rural residents—the clear majority of the Haitian people—actually gained access to the presidency and the parliament, they would be able to use state institutions to demand more land and more control over the economy in general. And that would inevitably threaten, and probably destroy, the arrangement that the country's elite had crafted in the decades since independence, the "stalemate" that kept them in power and the peasants at bay.

The threat was a serious one, and many in the political class feared that Rivière Hérard and Hérard Dumesle were not up to the task of containing it. Soon, the ranks of the elites opposing the two leaders included not just military officers and members of Boyer's bureaucracy but also Dumesle's former supporters, professionals who had served in the Chamber of Deputies or participated in the opposition press but now were worried about dangerous social upheaval. They found a solution they believed would placate the rebels: replacing President Hérard with a man named Philippe Guerrier. An elderly veteran of the wars of independence, Guerrier had been a high-ranking member of Christophe's regime, where he was dubbed the Duc de l'Avancé. Famed for his military prowess, he sported a crest decorated with a porcupine and the motto "He who rubs against me will get pricked." By 1844, though, Guerrier no longer posed any political threat. His candidacy was the first case of what would come to be known as the "*politique de doublure*," whereby light-skinned elites choose a black president whom they think they can easily manipulate. Guerrier's selection was meant to mollify the mass of the population without surrendering political control. And, in a way, it worked. Guerrier offered Acaau a high-ranking government position as general and commander of the region of Les Cayes—which he accepted. Other leaders from the Piquet movement were also brought into the fold.[69]

Having reestablished control over the state and much of the countryside, the governing elite set to work creating yet another constitution, one that would prevent future threats to order by rescinding the more radical innovations of the 1843 document. The constitution of 1846 gave power largely back to the executive while diminishing the rights of the population. Political assemblies, for instance, were allowed only as long as their goals were not "contrary to public order." Voting rights remained essentially the same, but the creation of a number of intermediary electoral institutions—as well as restrictions on who could serve as an elector or a representative—introduced new obstacles to popular control over the government. Most significantly, the Senate returned to being a body selected from the president's nominees rather than chosen through direct elections, with the president in turn appointed directly by the Senate—and named for life. Furthermore, the president was once again given the power to dissolve the parliament under certain conditions. The closed circuit of the Senate and the president left little room for democratic change or reform. The only way for an outsider to take power—one that would be used again and again over the course of the nineteenth century—was to raise an army and march on the capital.[70]

This reversal created an atmosphere of defeat among reformers, putting an end to democratic aspirations even among some of the most fervent political activists. They found themselves disappointed by the behavior of their own leaders, who seemed all too ready to take on the habits of those they had opposed. And they were alarmed at the breadth and intensity of the political movement that emerged in the countryside, which seemed to threaten the foundations of the economic order that sustained urban life in Haiti. A generation of intellectuals ultimately reacted to the events of 1843 and 1844 by concluding that the Haitian population simply wasn't ready for democracy. The prominent light-skinned intellectual Romuald Lepelletier de Saint-Rémy declared emphatically that the "black race" had to return to the "second rank" in the country, leaving power to the educated, light-skinned elites. Honoré Féry, a major participant in the 1843 revolution, confessed in 1855 that the older generation had been right to warn the young agitators that they could not apply "what was happening elsewhere" to the "backward" people of Haiti. The politician and historian Thomas Madiou similarly wrote in 1878 that it had been a mistake to imagine that ideals of democracy could be applied to the "semi-barbaric population" of

Haiti. It was impossible, he said, to imagine a people of such "profound ignorance," barely capable of practicing agriculture effectively, "choosing its President, its Senators, its Deputies, its judges."[71]

Hérard Dumesle and Acaau were both part of a new generation of political activists who found themselves disappointed with the political regimes of postindependence Haiti. As a young man traveling in the north of the country, Dumesle had channeled the spirit of Boukman, and as an opposition politician he attacked Boyer's authoritarian regime and stood up for free speech and greater democracy. Once in power, however, Dumesle quickly adopted the style of the very regime he had opposed, and he soon followed Boyer into exile in Jamaica. Acaau, meanwhile, represented the promise of an even greater change, giving voice to the huge segment of the Haitian population that lived on the margins of the nation's political institutions. Ultimately, though, Haiti's elites did not yield to the demands of the Piquets, which threatened to upend the country's social order. Over the following decades, political movements in different regions of Haiti would often mobilize peasant groups with promises of land reform, but once in power they delivered little. The stalemate in Haitian society only solidified, with the state remaining largely unaccountable to its citizens. After Guerrier, the government passed through the hands of a rolling series of elites who, despite different regional and social origins, largely resembled one another. As the Haitian secretary of the interior and agriculture noted in an official report soon after the Piquet uprising, the rural population of the country had become a "distinct class," separated from the urban dwellers by an "almost unbridgeable demarcation."[72]

Acaau, for his part, was never completely co-opted by Guerrier's government. He tried using his position there to continue the push for broader democracy in Haiti, and in 1846, after those efforts came to naught, he organized another uprising in the south. This second attempted rebellion also ended in failure, and Acaau committed suicide in despair shortly thereafter. His ghost, though, would long haunt Haitian politics. Shortly after his death, Céligny Ardouin, a leading political figure who had helped engineer the presidency of Guerrier, wrote that it was vital to "avoid the appearance of a new Acaau." A modern historian of French-Haitian relations likewise concludes his work by warning that both foreign and Haitian leaders need to "watch out," for "a new Acaau can always appear." The specter of Acaau serves as a constant reminder that one day a truly democratic movement—one that channels the political aspirations of the entire Haitian population—might appear again, and this time succeed.[73]

4

THE SACRIFICE

In December 1859, an elaborate official funeral was held in the cathedral of Port-au-Prince. The Haitian president, Fabre Geffrard, oversaw the proceedings, while the head Catholic priest of Port-au-Prince officiated a high mass. In the nave of the church was the coffin, draped in black, lit up by candles, and decorated with an inscription naming the deceased as a "martyr for the cause of the blacks." After a rousing eulogy, it was carried to a cross at the edge of town by a large procession that brought together many of the town's most prominent citizens. But the coffin was never placed in the ground, for it was empty.[1]

The ceremony was held to honor the abolitionist John Brown, who had been executed days earlier in Charles Town, Virginia. Brown had never visited Haiti, but the country's history had long visited him. He knew the tale of its antislavery revolution by heart and enjoyed recounting it to other abolitionists. According to an English journalist, it was the example of the 1791 uprising that convinced Brown that with the proper trigger, slaves "would immediately rise all over the Southern States." Brown probably sought to imitate his Haitian forebears' tactics, too, when he chose the valley town of Harpers Ferry, for he knew that Haitian rebels had won by attacking towns and then retreating into inaccessible mountains to regroup.

And as he awaited execution after his plan failed, Brown took solace in reading a biography of Toussaint Louverture.[2]

After his father's hanging, Brown's son wrote that Louverture's spirit was speaking to the slaves of the United States. They could hear it, if they listened, "among the pines of the Carolinas in the Dismal Swamp and upon the mountain-tops, proclaiming that the despots of America shall yet know the strength of the toiler's arm, and that he who would be free must himself strike the first blow." A Haitian newspaper similarly addressed itself to the slaves of the United States: "Liberty is immortal. Brown and his companions have sown this Slave-land with their glorious blood, and doubt not that therefrom avengers will arise."[3]

It was fitting that Brown's largest funeral service was held in Haiti, where the president effectively welcomed him posthumously as an honorary Haitian. Perhaps Geffrard also suspected that his country might soon have another reason to be grateful to Brown. For decades, even as American merchants flowed in and out of Haiti, the Haitian governments had consistently been spurned—or simply ignored—when they requested political recognition from the United States. Haitian leaders had seen this rejection as both a chafing insult and a barrier to their country's full accession to the rights and privileges of an independent nation. But there was no changing the situation—until, that is, the United States descended into civil war. That created an opportunity, and an opening, for the half-century of American refusal to be overturned at last.

In 1859 there were signs as well that Haiti might soon find a more favorable reception from the only other major power that was still refusing to deal with the island nation: the Vatican. Haitian elites were convinced—and insisted to their country's skeptical population—that recognition from the Vatican and the United States would prove to everyone that Haiti truly belonged on the global stage. Few of them foresaw the dangers that broader engagement with the world might bring—the insecurity that could result as foreign visitors and governments increasingly criticized the country and intervened in its affairs with ever greater forcefulness. The denial of sovereignty, it turned out, could take many forms.

▮ ▮ ▮

Haiti and the United States grew up together. The North American colonies, especially New England, depended on and profited from extensive trade with the French colony of Saint-Domingue. John Adams commented in 1783 that the Caribbean was an essential part of the "natural system" of North American commerce: "We are necessary for them, and they necessary for us." Trade between Saint-Domingue and North America was officially restricted—the French and British empires discouraged trading with competitors and sometime enemies—but that didn't stop people on either side. Like many other colonies in the Caribbean, Saint-Domingue, with its many small ports and sheltered bays, was in any case basically impossible to police. North American merchants brought lumber and food, especially meat and flour, which were vital in sustaining a colony that was already suffering from deforestation and focused obsessively on the production of sugar and coffee for export rather than food crops for local consumption. And they took home sugar, cotton, and large quantities of molasses, which was transformed into rum in New England.[4]

The Haitian Revolution didn't halt the trading, and even created new opportunities for commerce. The United States was where Toussaint Louverture bought most of his guns and ammunition, which eventually enabled his army to defeat Leclerc. While many in the United States, especially slave owners like Thomas Jefferson, were horrified by the events in Haiti, others were happy to make a profit there. Not even the mass killings of French planters ordered by Dessalines in 1804 dissuaded North American merchants from trading with the newly independent nation; indeed, some seem to have sold him weapons. Dessalines himself apparently exclaimed at one point that only someone who "does not know the whites" might think that the massacres would unfavorably affect trade relations with outsiders. "Hang a white man below one of the pans on the scales of the customs house, and put a sack of coffee in the other pan; the other whites will buy the coffee without paying attention to the body of their fellow white."[5]

In the first year after Haiti's declaration of independence, no fewer than forty ships sailed between Haiti and the United States. When several merchants held a large banquet in 1805 on board a ship in the New York harbor to celebrate a successful trading voyage to Haiti, the guest list included prominent judges, officials, and two generals. The assembled luminaries first drank to the "Commerce of the United States . . . May its sails be unfurl'd in every sea and as free as the winds which fill them." For their next toast, they emptied their glasses to "the Government of Hayti; founded on the only legitimate basis of authority . . . the people's choice! May it be as durable as its principles are pure."[6]

Although French envoys, smarting from the loss of Saint-Domingue, pressured the U.S. government in 1806 into prohibiting trade with Haiti, the law was repealed in less than three years, and the embargo was never taken very seriously by merchants. By the 1820s, Haiti's exports to the United States were worth more than two million dollars per year (the equivalent of more than $30 million today), and Haiti was providing one-third of all the coffee consumed in the United States. Haiti brought in a steady stream of imports as well, making it among the top ten U.S. trading partners, just behind Germany and ahead of Brazil. Because Haiti was the only independent country in the Caribbean, with the rest of the region under the control of European empires that restricted trade, it was the one place U.S. merchants could trade freely, and they took full advantage of the opportunity.[7]

While the United States was happy to make profits from Haiti, however, the American government consistently refused to recognize it as a political entity. In 1822, Boyer wrote to President Monroe requesting political recognition for Haiti. He reminded him that

Haiti had been independent for almost two decades and was in constant communication with the United States. Boyer also invoked the countries' common history: "The Haitian people do not think that the American people, who in another epoch found themselves in the same situation and felt the same need, can refuse them the justice that is due them." Monroe, though, saw things differently. The letter, along with a later appeal brought by one of Boyer's allies in the United States, was stamped "Not to be answered." Instead, the American government settled on a policy that was, to put it gently, two-faced, leaving Haiti in a curious diplomatic limbo. As the U.S. secretary of the treasury put it, Haiti was considered to be "neither independent nor part of the mother country." This created some absurd difficulties, similar to the issues that had confronted French envoys trying to arrange meetings with Pétion and Christophe. When, in early 1824, U.S. senators requested that a commercial agent be sent to Haiti carrying a letter of introduction to President Boyer, John Quincy Adams—then serving as secretary of state—explained that there were "difficulties" involved in such an arrangement. A letter addressed to Boyer, the presidential cabinet determined, would be "a mode of recognizing the free government of colored people in Hayti," and it was not "advisable either to recognize them for the present or at any time in that manner."[8]

The reasons for such refusal were articulated clearly in a magazine article published in 1823. The article admitted that Haiti had a stable government, and indeed could be considered more liberal as a society than many nations in Europe. The problem was that its leaders were black, and the history of how they had come to power offered a potentially inflammatory example. Just a year earlier, the U.S. South had been shaken by the discovery of a conspiracy organized by a slave named Denmark Vesey, who was said to have been inspired by the Haitian Revolution. "The time has not yet come for a surrender of our feelings about color," the article proclaimed, "nor is it fitting at any time, that the public safety should be endangered."[9]

The refusal to recognize Haiti stood out especially in the context of the wave of revolutions that swept through Latin America during the 1820s, when several countries won their independence. In 1825, in response to this changing geopolitical landscape, President James Monroe famously laid out what came to be known as the Monroe Doctrine, casting the United States as a defender of these newly established republics. While Monroe promised that his government would not interfere in "existing colonies or dependencies" of European powers in the Americas, he also promised to oppose any European invasions in nations "who have declared their independence and maintained it, and whose independence we have, on great, consideration and on just principles acknowledged." Such invasions, Monroe warned, would be considered "the manifestation of an unfriendly disposition toward the United States." Haiti, however, was carefully excluded from the principles set out in the Monroe Doctrine. President Monroe, who had refused Boyer's request for recognition, made clear that the policy of noninterference applied only to independent nations the United States had already acknowledged as independent. Haiti did not qualify.[10]

The policy infuriated Haitians, of course. An 1824 editorial in Haiti's main newspaper lamented that once upon a time, the United States had led the way—it was the nation "from whose example we have learned to conquer our rights." Now, however, the United States had decided to "tread under foot those principles, which they have made to ring through the world." "They who act thus," the writer warned, "do not prove that they have made a good use of their long civilization."[11]

When France finally recognized Haiti in 1825, other European powers, including Prussia and Holland, followed its lead and sent consular agents to the country. It was yet another opportunity for the United States to change course. If Haiti's defeated colonial masters accept the existence of the country, why not the United States? In 1826, the U.S. Congress debated whether Haiti should be included in the Congress of Panama, which was to bring together a series of newly independent Latin American republics. The answer was, once again, a resounding no.

Unsurprisingly, Southern representatives were particularly steadfast in their opposition to recognizing Haiti. A representative from Louisiana evoked the terrifying plight of Southern planters trapped between the "black population" of Mexico on one side and Cuba and Haiti on the other. But some northerners were just as virulent. One representative from Massachusetts, Edward Everett—later U.S. secretary of state—declared dramatically, "I would cede the whole continent to anyone who would take it—to England, to France, to Spain: I would see it sunk to the bottom of the Ocean, before I would see any part of this fair America converted into a continental Hayti, by that awful process of bloodshed and desolation by which alone such a catastrophe could be brought on." Even American independence, Everett suggested, was less important than preserving whites from black rule. Several politicians argued that any connection with Haiti might actually ignite revolt in the United States. "The peace of eleven States in this Union," a Missouri senator declared, "will not permit black consuls and Ambassadors to establish themselves in our cities, and to parade through the country, and give their fellow blacks in the United States, proof in hand of the honors which await them, for a successful revolt on their part." "Our policy with regard to Hayti, is plain," Senator Robert Hayne of South Carolina declared. "We can never acknowledge her independence." As one historian wryly notes, rarely have political leaders "pleaded with so much eloquence for the maintenance of such base principles."[12]

There were, of course, some who challenged these dire visions of Haiti's influence. Indeed, in 1838 and 1839, when a "gag rule" prevented abolitionists from addressing Congress on the question of slavery, they turned to Haiti as a proxy cause, presenting more than two hundred petitions demanding that the United States recognize the Caribbean nation. For critics of slavery, the achievements of the Haitian Revolution represented a powerful refutation of dominant racist theories about the incapacities of blacks for leadership and self-governance. If Haiti could abolish slavery, might not the rest of the world follow its example, and justice finally prevail? For several prominent writers from the early 1800s onwards, Louverture's struggle and martyrdom represented a universal striving for freedom.[13]

Support for the recognition of Haiti also came from many of the U.S. merchants and naval officers who actually had firsthand experience of the country. One officer, who spent three months there in the early 1830s, wrote admiringly of President Boyer. He also described how the officers had "no hesitation in dancing and flirting with the St. Domingo ladies, although some of them were as black as the ace of spades," and mentioned his discovery that the "young women, in grace and lady-like manners, compared most favorably with young women in the best society." He found the supposed contradiction fascinating, describing one young woman "who was as black as a negress could be, but had the most exquisite figure, small black hands and feet, and beautiful teeth. She had been educated at a convent in Paris, was a very accomplished musician and dancer. Notwithstanding her ebony color, all of us vied with each other in securing her hand for the waltz or the quadrille." All in all, the officer concluded, they had a wonderful time in Haiti, despite the fact that they were "among niggers."[14]

III

By the mid-nineteenth century, the only major power other than the United States that still did not recognize Haiti was the Vatican. Starting with Toussaint Louverture, Haiti's leaders had generally practiced Catholicism and had urged their country's citizens to do the same. But most of the few Catholic priests present in Haiti during the revolution had left the country after its declaration of independence—one of them sneaked out of Port-au-Prince disguised as a sailor—and for the next few decades there was no established Catholic church in the country. Following France's lead, the Vatican refused to recognize Haiti's independence during the first decades of the nineteenth century, so the country remained outside the official system of Catholic bishoprics, parishes, and religious brotherhoods. Starting in the 1820s, the Vatican did begin to negotiate with Haitian leaders about once again sending priests to the country. But the negotiations foundered repeatedly because Haitian governments wanted a level of control over the activities of Catholic priests in the country that the Vatican was not willing to grant.[15]

The lack of formal Vatican approval did not stop the Haitian population from practicing Catholicism, so Haiti still needed priests, whether Rome wanted to send them or not. And there were always a few who were ready to answer the call. Considered renegades by the papacy, they were a small, remarkably international group. Some came from Latin America, others from Corsica and France; the head priest of Port-au-Prince, who would officiate at John Brown's ceremonial funeral, hailed from Senegal. Their motives for coming to Haiti were as varied as their origins. Some French priests traveling to the country were inspired by the legendary French abolitionist the Abbé Grégoire, who had corresponded with Toussaint Louverture during the 1790s about setting up a Haitian church and had publicly supported the country's independence. Others, having been defrocked or run into conflicts with their superiors, found Haiti a welcome refuge.[16]

The Catholic Church derided the "renegade" priests as debauched opportunists who got rich selling sacraments to gullible Haitians, and the French abolitionist Victor Schoelcher—shocked during his 1841 visit to find many of them living openly with women—wrote that it was "impossible to imagine anything more perverse than the Haitian clergy." But Haitian communities clearly appreciated their services, and despite their unofficial status, the priests in Haiti oversaw active and well-attended churches. In 1842, when Bishop Joseph Rosati of St. Louis, Missouri, traveled to Port-au-Prince, he was "extremely pleased" by what he found. "The Church is spacious, very decent, the grand altar is of marble, the sacred vestments & vessels are rich and clean," he reported; it was "quite full of people" for two masses on Sunday as well as on feast days. Rosati noted that the service was performed "with as much decency & solemnity as in the Cathedrals of Europe" by a parish priest, two assistants, and a dozen choirboys "dressed in surplices and red cassocks" along with a "number of other singers." They walked into church led by a Swiss guard in full uniform and carrying a halberd. To top it all off, Rosati effused, "the Gregorian chant is well performed, the singers knowing very well the *note*." Indeed, one could be forgiven for wondering whether Haitian Catholics needed papal approval at all.[17]

Haitian president Boyer, however, considered the lack of official recognition by the papacy to be an insult and a barrier to the country's full acceptance by the international community. He also believed that the Catholic Church would be a valuable ally in his project to improve the Haitian population. He and the Vatican tried hard to come to an agreement that would balance the demands of both parties: the papacy sent five missions to Haiti between 1821 and 1842, and the bishop of Charleston, South Carolina, spent a full five years in Haiti. But just when the deal was almost ready, Boyer was overthrown in the revolution of 1843. Almost two decades would pass before the Vatican would hold talks with Haiti again.[18]

III

As Haiti struggled to gain recognition and respect from major foreign powers in the mid-nineteenth century, its difficulties were increased by the sharply negative opinions that most outsiders held regarding Faustin Soulouque, who ruled the country from 1847 to 1859—holding power longer than any nineteenth-century Haitian head of state other than Boyer. At a time when the country's leaders were often criticized by foreign observers, Soulouque was particularly vilified, dismissed as a buffoon and made the target of scathing parody. The verdict from most modern scholars has also been harsh; one recent study of Haiti summed up Soulouque's reign as "twelve years of tyranny" and "the greatest disaster the country experienced in the nineteenth century." Against such judgments, however, a few historians have offered a different reading, portraying Soulouque—in the words of one recent defender—as "a man of high intelligence, a realist, a pragmatist, and a superb if ruthless politician and diplomat."[19]

Soulouque's regime is especially remarkable because it was produced entirely by accident, the result of a seemingly clever maneuver by Haiti's political elites that turned out to be a severe miscalculation. In their plan, Soulouque was never supposed to be anything more than a puppet. The elderly veteran Philippe Guerrier, who had been installed as president in 1844 in part to placate Acaau's supporters, died after only eleven months in office, and two successors to Guerrier also held the presidency for less than a year apiece. In February 1847, the Haitian senators thus found themselves searching once more for a presidential replacement while facing ongoing peasant uprisings in the south of the country. Hoping to apply once more the *politique de doublure* that had worked with Guerrier, they turned to Soulouque, whom they saw as both a useful symbol and an easy-to-manipulate figurehead. The head of the presidential guard in Port-au-Prince, Soulouque was a sixty-year-old military officer nearing the end of a long career. He was also a black ex-slave, in contrast to most of the members of the Senate, who were light-skinned and often the descendants of free people of color. According to a possibly apocryphal story, Soulouque was so surprised when told of his new position that at first he took the whole thing for a practical joke. But it was Soulouque who ultimately played the real joke on those who had chosen him.[20]

Once in power, Soulouque proved both ambitious and politically savvy. He rapidly got rid of the senators who had elevated him to the presidency, and a few months later ordered the killings of a group of prominent men—part of the traditional political elite—whom he suspected of conspiring against him. He then set about creating a new governing class, replacing the landowners and professionals who had traditionally dominated politics with supporters drawn from the middle ranks of the military. After crowning himself emperor of Haiti in August 1849, Soulouque followed Christophe's model and institutionalized this new elite as a hereditary aristocracy. The times, of course, were now different, and Soulouque's court, even more than Christophe's, was derided by many Europeans as an absurdity. But, as under Christophe's reign, the nobility was essentially Soulouque's way of constructing a governing coalition, binding together military officers and intellectuals, blacks and mulattoes, in support of his rule.[21]

Soulouque's regime became a famous subject of satire in France, partly because making fun of the Haitian emperor was a way for the French to make fun of their own ruler, Louis Napoleon. Napoleon was no particular friend of Haiti, which he once called a "land of barbarians." But after he crowned himself Napoleon III in 1851, putting an end to three years of democratic renewal, his furious critics accused him of imitating the Haitian leader. Karl Marx, in his legendary account of Napoleon's rise to power, lampooned the court of Napoleon III as "a noisy, disreputable, rapacious bohème" that had the "same grotesque dignity as the high dignitaries of Soulouque." The comparison deeply bothered the French ruler. When satirists in Paris described the creation of Versailles as *soulouquerie*, turning the Haitian emperor's fabled excesses into a derogatory tag, Napoleon issued an edict specifically prohibiting the use of that word.[22]

But if Soulouque was usually dismissed by external critics as stupid and inept, it was also in part precisely because he proved rather stubborn in the face of outside pressures, granting few concessions to foreign governments. He was particularly wary of the United States, being deeply concerned about the growing American power in the region. Part of the problem was that during the 1840s and 1850s—especially during the "forty-niner" California gold rush—Central America became one of the major routes for North American travelers going from the East Coast to the West. Instead of crossing the North American continent, it was often easier and less expensive for travelers to get to California by heading south, traveling by boat through the Caribbean, overland across the Panama isthmus to the Pacific, and by boat again to their destination. Only in the 1860s would the construction of transcontinental railways largely put an end to this travel pattern, and by then the U.S. commercial and political involvement in the Caribbean and Central America was firmly established.[23]

Soulouque was also aware that some Southern planters had an ambitious plan for the Caribbean: they dreamed of taking over Cuba and making it into another slaveholding state of the United States. In addition, a few looked to the Dominican Republic as a place for American companies to set up plantations for growing sugar and fruit. Indeed, the entire region was seen by many, according to one historian, as "an undeveloped paradise—a veritable Garden of Eden—anxiously awaiting the enterprise and appreciation that only Americans could bestow." Annexationists saw the population of the Caribbean as being in desperate need of help and discipline from the north. "With swelling hearts and suppressed impatience they await our coming, and with joyous shouts of 'Welcome! Welcome!' will they receive us," one journalist wrote about the Cubans. Another proclaimed that in the Caribbean and other regions to the south, "decaying nations and races invite our coming."[24]

Though annexationists mostly focused on Cuba, which had a thriving plantation system, Soulouque's regime in Haiti was singled out by some as a particularly backward place that called out for external control. Several U.S. citizens had claims against Haiti dating back to the period of Christophe—the king, they said, had defrauded them of money—and in 1850, the United States sent three warships to Port-au-Prince in their support. It was a surprising gesture, for the cost of the expedition almost certainly outstripped the amount of money at stake. But sending warships became an increasingly common maneuver for both the United States and European nations, a way for their governments to make it clear that they were ready to use force against Haiti when they deemed it necessary to protect their citizens and their substantial business interests in the country.[25]

Soulouque's government declared it knew nothing about the Christophe matter, and negotiations over the payment of the claims dragged on for years. While the claims were relatively small, the fact that they were not paid promptly incited a set of violent and racist denunciations of Haiti—and particularly of Soulouque—in the American press. "Several outrages on the persons and property of American citizens have been committed by the authorities of the so-called nigger Billy Bowlegs, Faustin Emperor the First, for which redress should be demanded," fulminated the *New York Herald* in April 1850. If the Haitians didn't respond, the article went on, then "the big black nigger, the Emperor himself" and his "equally black constables or officers, should be severely punished." Clearly, the *Herald* writer concluded, the "nigger population of Haiti" had "very hostile feelings towards the United States" and should be "licked into good behavior." The metaphors were as brutal as they were clear: Haiti was a slave, the United States the master. Another newspaper piece, published the next day, went a step further, arguing that if Haitians continued to be recalcitrant, then all of them should literally be reenslaved. There were, this article declared, ten thousand men who would "volunteer to colonize St. Domingo the instant the administration gives a hint that it is desirable." They were ready, on a moment's notice, to "abolish the negro butchery business": "St. Domingo will be a State in a year, if our cabinet will but authorize white volunteers to make slaves of every negro they can catch when they reach Hayti."[26]

Such talk, of course, was bound to set an ex-slave like Soulouque on edge. In 1855, partly because of his fears that the United States might gain control over the Dominican Republic and attack Haiti from there, he decided to invade the eastern half of Hispaniola. It was not a new idea: Dessalines had also tried to occupy Haiti's eastern neighbor, and Boyer had succeeded in placing the entire island under his government for more than two decades. The 1855 invasion, however, was poorly planned and poorly led. Within a few weeks, the Haitian troops were routed and in retreat.*[27]

Soulouque's power within Haiti, built in large part on his control over the army, was dealt a severe blow by the failed Dominican campaign. As a result, he found himself without much popular support a few years later when the United States decided to take over a small piece of Haitian territory: Navassa, a tiny island lying between Jamaica and the Haitian mainland. About eight square miles in size, uninhabited, and pockmarked with caves and rocky outcroppings, Navassa was a particularly inviting place for seabirds, and over centuries the island had become a massive repository of bird excrement mixed with bird corpses. At the time, U.S. farmers concerned about the decreasing yields of their land had begun turning to the use of fertilizers, and bird excrement—guano—was one of the best and most prized of these. It was sold by various countries, notably Peru, but U.S. businessmen were eager to get their hands on a cheaper source of the material.[28]

In 1856, the U.S. Congress passed the "Guano Islands" act, which authorized the government to take possession of islands that could supply the valuable product. (In time, the United States would claim seventy such islands.) The act also stipulated that U.S. citizens could take over guano-rich islands only if no other country either occupied or claimed them, which seemed to render Navassa beyond its reach: while no Haitians had ever settled on Navassa, it had always been considered part of the Haitian territory, and indeed was explicitly mentioned as such in several of the country's constitutions. Haiti

---

* Soulouque's attack on the Dominican Republic had ironic consequences: justified by him as a way of preventing foreign control on the island, it ultimately had the opposite effect. Some of those who resisted the Haitian invasion began lobbying for a return to Spanish colonial status, and in March 1861 the president of the Dominican Republic officially restored the country to Spain. Having become independent from Spain when it was taken over by Haiti in 1822, then independent from Haiti in 1844, the Dominican Republic was now once again in the hands of a European power.

based its claim on long precedent: the island's history as part of Saint-Domingue went back to the fifteenth century. Nevertheless, in 1857 a U.S. ship captain landed at Navassa, and on the basis of the "Guano Act" claimed it as territory of the United States.[29]

Soulouque protested that any exploitation of the guano on the island had to be carried out under a license from his government, and at first the American settlers accepted the conditions, allowing the Haitian flag to be raised on the island. Soon, however, the United States sent navy forces to Navassa, and an admiral sailed a warship into the harbor of Port-au-Prince to intimidate the Haitians into backing down. The show of strength succeeded. Within a few years the United States had built a small colony on Navassa, using African American and Haitian laborers to collect guano and ship it north. Despite complaints by Haitian diplomats, who documented their country's claim to the island and pointed out that its acquisition contravened the terms of the "Guano Act," the U.S. government refused to cede possession.[30]

Conditions on Navassa were harsh, and in 1889, workers revolted and killed five people. Lawyers defending the workers argued that U.S. courts couldn't condemn them because the incident had not taken place on American soil. The case went all the way to the Supreme Court, which eventually ruled that U.S. law did cover Navassa. A few decades later, in 1916, the U.S. government officially annexed the island as a territory, which it remains to this day—a little-known outpost in the Caribbean that now attracts only birds and ornithologists. For Haiti, its loss represented both a lost opportunity for the country to develop a new and profitable export and a threatening demonstration of ever-expanding U.S. control of the region.[31]

III

Even as the United States began to shadow Haiti in the late 1850s, however, the country's insurgent history took a kind of revenge on its northern neighbor. As tensions between the northern and southern states intensified, the example of Haiti's revolution proved to be a constant presence, exacerbating the conflict that ultimately led to civil war. The orator Wendell Phillips, for example, drew huge crowds to speeches he gave celebrating Toussaint Louverture. Many orators and writers had compared Louverture to Washington and Napoleon over the previous decades, but Phillips went further, arguing that Louverture was actually a greater figure than either of these. "I would call him Napoleon, but Napoleon made his way to empire over broken oaths and a sea of blood," he declared. "I would call him Washington, but the great general had slaves." If such high praise seemed surprising, Phillips told the crowd, it was only because "you read history not with your eyes, but with your prejudices." In fifty years, he assured them, when the muse of history wrote the list of the greatest men of all time, she would dip "her pen in the sunlight" and "write in clear blue, above them all, the name of the soldier, the statesman, the martyr TOUSSAINT LOUVERTURE."[32]

Antiabolitionist forces, meanwhile, saw Haiti as the embodiment of an existential threat. One response to Wendell Phillips, for instance, complained that he "blasphemes the name of Washington" by placing "above him on the roll of fame, a midnight assassin and robber, a carrier of the brand into peaceful homes at night, a butcherer of babes and violator of women." For such critics, the Haitian Revolution was circumscribed by the obsessively repeated phrase "the horrors of Santo Domingo," meant to immediately trigger visions of black insurgents killing babies and raping white women over the bodies of their dead husbands. A popular history book described the Haitian Revolution as a time when "virgins were immolated on the altar; weeping infants hurled into fires." In the aftermath of John Brown's raid on Harpers Ferry, a college professor explained that if the South didn't secede from the Union, they would be "St. Domingois'd."[33]

Drawing on narratives of the Haitian Revolution that claimed the slave uprising had been incited by French radicals, Southern secessionists drew an analogy to their own situation. Southern planters were like the whites of Saint-Domingue, they argued, surrounded by slaves who were docile under normal circumstances but could turn to violent revolt when prodded into action by outside agitators. The lesson of the Haitian Revolution was therefore clear: if they wanted to survive, U.S. slave owners had to escape from Northern abolitionists before these meddlers managed to start a slave revolution in the South.[34]

The Southern secessionists, though, also seem to have curiously under-studied the event they so often referred to. Keen to evoke the way in which outside agitators had supposedly stirred up the slave revolt in Saint-Domingue, they forgot what happened next: by reaching out to the English in an attempt to preserve their slave-holding privilege, French planters had turned themselves into traitors against their own country. Meanwhile, the slave insurgents, by standing with the French Republic, came to take on the role of saviors and patriots. Some parts of that history repeated themselves during the Civil War, as Southern slaveholders chose secession and African American leaders and soldiers effectively used military service in defense of the Union as a platform from which to attack slavery and demand full citizenship in the United States.

More immediately, the secession of the southern states also finally opened the way for U.S. recognition of Haiti. In December 1861, President Lincoln declared that he saw no "good reason" why the United States should "persevere longer in withholding our recognition of the independence and sovereignty" of its Caribbean neighbor. While some in Congress still opposed recognition—arguing, for instance, that Washington society was not yet ready to receive a black minister representing Haiti and allow him to sit in the Senate gallery as a diplomat—Lincoln had a powerful ally in Massachusetts senator Charles Sumner, an impassioned abolitionist and clever politician. Sumner judiciously argued the case for recognition by highlighting its strategic usefulness, insisting that the United States needed to "provide a check to distant schemes of ambition" of European empires seeking to expand their control in the Caribbean. He pointed to a series of alarming developments in the region, particularly the return of the Dominican Republic to Spanish rule in March 1861—a clear violation of the Monroe Doctrine. The American government, facing a more serious problem at home in 1861, was in no position to take action against Spain. But, Sumner argued, by recognizing Haiti, the United States could counterbalance the influence of the European empire on the island.[35]

Trade considerations also entered into the discussion. In a letter that was read in Congress as part of the debate over recognition, a U.S. commercial agent in Haiti complained that the refusal of diplomatic relations was "altogether disastrous of our commerce, & almost destroys the political influence of our government & its commercial agents." A "prompt & cordial recognition of Haytian nationality," he claimed, would "diffuse among those whole people a satisfaction which can hardly be understood in America." By making the gesture of recognition, "followed up on our part by even only the ordinary civilities of official intercourse," the United States would be able to "hold this island in the hollow of our hand." There was, the agent insisted, "no nation whose friendship, good opinion & protection the Haytian people so strongly desire & seek as those of the United States."[36]

After some deliberation, both the Senate and House passed the measure. On June 5, 1862—nearly six decades after Haitian independence, and almost four decades after France had officially recognized the independence of its former colony—the United States at last officially accepted the nation's existence. In early 1863, the first Haitian diplomat arrived in Washington, though the legation soon moved to New York, to the appropriately named Liberty Street. The U.S. government, meanwhile, gained much in return, for Haiti allowed Union warships to use its ports, which became important bases in the battle against the Confederacy. A U.S. coaling station was set up in Le Cap, and U.S. sailors and officers frequented the town and dined with local officials. One of them even found time for a bit of tourism, making the trip up to Christophe's Citadel.[37]

I I I

By the time of U.S. recognition, Haiti was no longer ruled by Emperor Soulouque and his court. Fabre Geffrard, one of Soulouque's generals, had overthrown him in 1859 and reestablished Haiti as a republic. Geffrard reversed many of the policies of the previous regime, decreasing the size of the army, which had expanded under Soulouque, and returning power to the traditional elite of the country, the wealthier and often light-skinned landowners and professionals. Like Boyer in the 1820s, Geffrard also enthusiastically worked to bring African Americans to Haiti, advancing them money to cover travel costs and offering them credit to buy land. An organization called the Haitian Bureau, funded by Geffrard's government with $20,000 (the equivalent of about $500,000 today), set up offices in several U.S. cities, including New York and New Orleans, and brought more than two thousand American emigrants to the country in the early 1860s.[38]

A key figure in the Haitian Bureau was Joseph Theodore Holly, a deacon in the Episcopal Church who had spent most of a decade ardently promoting Haiti as a homeland for African Americans. It was a place, he argued, where they could truly be at ease under a black government instead of perpetually on the run from the threats of slavery and white supremacy. Haiti was "the first nationality established by our race," Holly proclaimed, and "every colored man should feel bound to sustain the national existence of Hayti." In his speeches and writings, Holly celebrated the achievements of the Haitian Revolution. Joined by several collaborators, including John Brown's son, he traveled around New England recruiting settlers to join him in moving to Haiti. They would embark on what he called a new

"Mayflower expedition" gathering "sable pioneers in the cause of civil and religious liberty." He was choosy about who could go, seeking "unobtrusive, industrious, peaceable, intelligent, moral, progressive and useful citizens." (They must, he specified, "not be like the Irish.") In May 1861, Holly and a hundred of his followers sailed from New Haven, seen off by a large crowd. Though the journey was not without its difficulties, on their arrival in Port-au-Prince, several of the pilgrims were elated. "As I walked the streets of the capital I felt as no colored man in the United States can feel," one wrote, enjoying the sight of politicians, judges, and generals who all shared his color. "I am a *man* in Hayti where I feel as I never felt before, entirely free," another reported.[39]

Geffrard offered the newcomers a home on an estate he owned near Port-au-Prince, but the conditions were difficult. Many of the settlers died from disease, including Holly's mother, his wife, and two of his young children. Still, Holly remained loyal to Haiti, as did many of those who had traveled with him. He soon married again, taking as his wife another member of the settler community, and he ended up raising ten children who became Haitian citizens. Several of them trained as doctors and engineers in the United States and other countries before coming back to work as professionals in Holly's adopted homeland.[40]

Holly devoted himself in particular to work as a missionary for the Episcopal Church, convinced that Haiti offered a "splendid opportunity" for conversion. Although he received much less help from Episcopal churches in the U.S. organization than he had hoped or expected, his efforts eventually led to the creation of a permanent Episcopal presence on the island. In 1874 he was named the first Episcopal bishop in Haiti, establishing the Orthodox Apostolic Church—the country's first national church, and also the first church founded under Anglican auspices outside English-speaking countries. Invited to England in 1878, he became the first black man to preach at Westminster Abbey. Although his church started out relatively small, with only two thousand members by the time of Holly's death in 1911, it has remained a central institution in the country, and today boasts ninety thousand members.[41]

Holly was not the only one seeking souls in nineteenth-century Haiti: his coming coincided with the arrival of a stream of Catholic priests from France. Geffrard, who like many other members of the elite sent his children to be educated in Catholic schools in France, had made it a priority to bring the Catholic Church back to Haiti, and after taking power he dispatched two envoys to Rome. In 1860, just as Haiti was on the verge of winning recognition from the United States, a concordat largely based on the model proposed by Boyer in 1842 was finally signed between Haiti and the papacy. More than half a century after its declaration of independence, Haiti was at last formally recognized by the Catholic Church.[42]

A new era of Catholic activism now began. Despite Haiti's long history as a country of practicing Catholics, the priests who arrived after 1860 saw themselves as missionaries. Unlike their predecessors, who tended to concentrate in the larger towns, they fanned out to the many parts of the country that had no churches. A priest working in the isolated village of Jean-Rabel reported in 1871 that the church there was little more than a "hangar," and he began taking up a collection from the local community to build a new one. He ended up with a group of Catholic volunteers, who first gathered stones from the ruins of an old government building, then tramped to a nearby plantation and brought back stones from the owner's collapsed house. With the new church built, the priest of Jean-Rabel organized a nighttime procession for the feast day of Saint Joseph, with a statue of the Virgin Mary carried through the streets. The priest effused that the event was as beautiful as any he had seen in France, and he noted that it convinced several young people to become regular churchgoers. Still, the process of implantation was a slow one, and not every place was as devoted to church building as the village of Jean-Rabel. In 1886 the church at Furcy, a community of thriving small farms in the high mountains above Port-au-Prince, was a wooden shack with a small bell mounted beside it.[43]

The new generation of priests considered it one of their major missions to moralize Haitians. A report from 1861 complained that not only young children but even those as old as ten or twelve walked around naked in the streets of the towns, while adults "dare announce their lack of modesty by bathing in a state of complete nudity" in public places, even along the stream that crossed the Champ de Mars in the center of Port-au-Prince. An even more serious problem, in their eyes, was the near-total absence of marriage in the society, or at least of marriage as Catholic priests understood it. A priest in Jacmel reported in 1868 that of the nearly twelve hundred children he had baptized, only nineteen were born of parents who had been married in the church, and priests elsewhere found a similar situation. In fact, though, most of these children were born of unions that had been formalized by the community, frequently through a practice known as *plaçage*. A man wishing to live with a woman wrote a letter to her and her parents requesting permission to establish a permanent union. If they accepted, a ceremony took place at the woman's house. *Plaçage* allowed a man to form multiple unions in parallel, but it also required from him fidelity to his wife or wives. And, within the broader institution of the *lakou* system, it was understood that each wife and her children were to have access to their own plot of land. Most priests, however, saw these practices as backward and barbaric, marks of vice. As one despairingly wrote in 1867, in the area of Môle Saint-Nicolas all he could see was "bigamy, trigamy, all the way to septigamy." The situation was partly understandable, the priests concluded, since it was the result of the absence of the Catholic church for several generations, but that only made their task—what one priest called the "rehabilitation of Christian marriage"—all the more central. In the end, the church managed to effect only a partial change in social practices, with *plaçage* continuing as a common mechanism for forming unions in Haiti to the present day.[44]

Another major mission of the Catholic priesthood in Haiti involved helping Geffrard to expand access to education, especially in rural areas. Geffrard's education minister wrote that the Catholic Church could be a valuable ally in pursuing the work of "civilizing" Haiti, and the Catholic bishops were made part of the government commissions overseeing national education. By 1885 there were nine new schools staffed by Catholic priests and funded by the Haitian state, which provided the buildings, paid the teachers' salaries, and offered scholarships to the students. More were opened in the following years.[45]

One of the most important of these schools, the Petit Séminaire Collège Saint-Martial, was originally set up as a seminary but soon became a college providing secondary education for several hundred pupils. The school had a swimming pool, a natural history collection, and a magnificent library boasting books from as far back as the sixteenth century. In 1873, its students became famous and beloved in Port-au-Prince when some of them, led by a German-born priest, formed the city's first fire company. A couple of years later the company obtained a steam pump, which allowed them to rush to the scene of a fire and send a strong stream of water into the flames. "Progress is penetrating into us through every pore," wrote a journalist who witnessed the students using the pump to put out a fire, applauded by a cheering crowd. "The hammer of civilization is destroying, stone by stone, the Great Wall of China that was built around our island."[46]

III

Haiti's growing recognition by and engagement with the outside world carried a significant cost, however. As the nineteenth century went on, Haiti's leaders became increasingly concerned with the views that European countries and the United States had of their nation. Some decided that it was crucial to embark on a kind of internal civilizing mission, purifying the country of the "primitive" influences that they, like many outsiders, saw as an obstacle to Haiti's progress. President Geffrard, for instance, decided early in his administration to strike at what he and other political elites considered a scourge: the Vodou religion. Foreign observers criticizing Soulouque's reign had taken particular glee in portraying the emperor as a man in the thrall of Vodou and cannibalism, and Geffrard was determined to change the international image of the country. "Let us rush to eliminate the last vestiges of barbarism and slavery—superstition and the shameful practices surrounding it—from our land," he commanded in 1863.[47]

Geffrard didn't need to invent new laws to attack Vodou: many of its practices had been criminalized for decades. President Boyer's 1835 penal code declared that "all makers of *ouangas*, *caprelatas*, *vaudoux*, *donpèdre*, *macandals* and other spells will be punished by one to six months of imprisonment" along with a fine, and they could incur more serious punishment if the other "crimes or offenses" were committed in "preparing or carrying out their evil spells." In addition, the law prohibited "all dances and other practices that are of a nature to maintain the spirit of fetishism and superstition in populations." Boyer's code also criminalized the use of substances that "without causing death, produce a lethargic effect"—a stipulation clearly aimed at zombification, a set of practices that would long fascinate and frighten observers in Haiti and beyond.*[48]

Before Geffrard's time, such anti-Vodou laws had rarely been enforced. Many of the country's military officers and elites practiced the religion and had little appetite for carrying out repression against it. The arrival of Catholic priests, however, gave Geffrard a new kind of police force to help him confront these religious practices. Quite a few of these priests, unsurprisingly, had decided even before they left

---

* It is difficult to know whether the use of such poisons had been directly observed, or whether Boyer's lawmakers were themselves reacting to one of the many rumors about Vodou that circulated in nineteenth-century Haitian society. Whether zombification was real or not, its incorporation into the legal code of Haiti served—in the nineteenth and twentieth centuries—to confirm to outside observers that the country was apparently full of dangerous, even murderous, religious practices.

for Haiti that Vodou was a problem for the country's population, locking them in the "rudest of pagan superstitions." Such prejudices did not go away when they landed. One priest writing from Haiti in 1861 decried what he called the "diabolical meetings" of the religion, claiming that Vodou worshippers splattered religious objects with human blood. Another, describing Vodou as a "hellish invention," lamented that the "drums and dance" were a serious obstacle to the conversion of the "ignorant masses." Priests looking for converts in Haiti were also appalled to find that most of those who practiced Vodou considered themselves faithful Catholics—indeed, Vodou ceremonies usually began with Catholic prayers. Such cross-pollination, of course, only added to the priests' anxiety.[49]

Haitian communities had their own internal conflicts about the proper uses of spiritual power. Local secret societies, which efficiently shielded themselves from outside observers and occasionally even cultivated rumors of ritual murder as a way to keep prying eyes out, caused particular concern. And practitioners of Vodou sometimes accused each other of witchcraft, condemning those who called on the spirits for the purpose of harming others or for personal gain.[50]

In 1864, eight Vodou practitioners in the town of Bizoton, outside Port-au-Prince, were accused by townspeople of having killed and eaten a young girl named Claircine. Their trial became a sensation, covered in detail in the Haitian press, and the government invited members of the foreign diplomatic community to attend the proceedings. Among those who accepted the invitation was the British consul general, Spenser St. John, who would later include a detailed account of the trial in his book *Hayti; or, The Black Republic*. St. John noted that the accused had all been beaten in order to force confessions. One of them, a woman named Roséide Sumera, had made as much clear during the trial: when the prosecutor declared that she had confessed to the crime, she acknowledged that she had done so, but added that he should "remember how cruelly I was beaten before I said a word." These interrogation methods apparently did not bother St. John. The prisoners were convinced that they would be protected by "the Vaudoux," he wrote, and "it required the frequent application of the club to drive this belief out of their heads."[51]

The prosecutor's evidence centered on the remains of a girl, including a skull, which he claimed had been recovered near the scene of the crime and which were displayed during the trial. Of course, there are other possible explanations for the appearance of human remains than murder and cannibalism. They may, for instance, have been in the process of being prepared for funerary ritual, or perhaps for use in religious ceremonies, which sometimes make use of bones and skulls gathered from cemeteries. But combined with the extracted confessions and with statements from witnesses—in particular, one young child who claimed to have seen the killing and cooking of the victim— the evidence had the desired effect. After a two-day trial, the eight men and women, several of them elderly, were sentenced to death and killed by a firing squad. The government made the execution a major public event, scheduling it on a market day to assure the largest possible audience. The prosecutor, though, was only partially satisfied, having confided in St. John during the trial that "if full justice were done, there would be fifty on those benches instead of eight."[52]

The trial was in many ways directed at outsiders, an announcement that Haiti was ready to rid itself of what the editor of Haiti's government newspaper called its "interior savages." By targeting and criminalizing a subset of rural Haitians, Geffrard sought to brand Vodou as inessential, something that could easily be purged from the nation. In doing so, he hoped to free Haiti as a whole from being associated with these practices. The accused at the Bizoton trial seemed to understand that, in a sense, they were the ones being sacrificed to placate powerful external forces. "Why should I be put to death for observing our ancient customs?" one elderly woman on trial demanded.[53]

Geffrard's attempt to reassure foreign observers largely backfired, however. Instead of proving to outsiders that Haiti was free from "superstition," the Bizoton prosecutions were repeatedly cited as evidence that the country in fact harbored practitioners of ritual cannibalism. In his book, Spenser St. John was clearly eager to paint Haiti as a land of barbarism and savagery: he included a chapter titled "Vaudoux-Worship and Cannibalism" and then, just for good measure, followed it with another specifically titled "Cannibalism." (He did allow that there was a split in Vodou between those who only sacrificed animals and others, a minority, who practiced human sacrifice.) Though he hadn't personally witnessed the kinds of ceremonies he accused Haitians of practicing, St. John had clearly been welcomed into several Vodou temples, which didn't seem particularly menacing: he described one as a "spacious" place "papered with engravings from the *Illustrated London News*" and "pictures of the Virgin Mary and various saints." Still, despite the relative openness of various Haitian hosts, he seemed quite certain that at its heart, Vodou was somehow deeply sinister.[54]

Without any firsthand experience of rituals to draw on, the best St. John could do was to rehash a detailed description of a ceremony provided by Moreau de Saint-Méry in 1796 and insist that religious practices had remained essentially unchanged since then. He also located two supposed eyewitness accounts of child sacrifice—one by a French priest, another by a U.S. visitor who claimed to have been initiated into the secrets of Vodou by Dominican friends. Both writers described sneaking into ceremonies disguised in blackface, and both said that they saw a child being sacrificed and tried, unsuccessfully, to stop the proceedings.[55]

Such accounts were titillating, but a little too easy to dismiss as embellishments or full-out invention. In the trial at Bizoton, however, St. John felt he had found undeniable proof that cannibalism was rampant in the country. Though he complimented Geffrard on his efforts, St. John declared that the trial had done little to stop the practice of human sacrifice. "People are killed and their flesh sold at the market; children are stolen to furnish the repasts of cannibals;

bodies are dug from their graves to serve as food, and the Vaudoux reign triumphant," he announced. No important holiday passed, he claimed, without child sacrifice. These dramatic claims helped to make St. John's book into a bestseller, and his success attracted numerous imitators. In 1891, one writer admitted that he had never actually seen a Vodou ceremony, but he nevertheless described the religion's rituals in vivid detail—complete with Vodou practitioners "throwing themselves on the victims, tearing them apart with their teeth and avidly sucking the blood that boils from their veins." Each day, he wrote, forty Haitians were eaten, and almost every citizen in the country had tasted human flesh. Such writings multiplied throughout the late nineteenth and early twentieth centuries, shaping the way that Haiti was perceived throughout Europe and the United States.[56]

As they watched increasing numbers of outsiders arrive in their country, meanwhile, some rural Haitians similarly saw *them* as carriers of an old but vividly remembered barbarism. Wandering near the ruins of the Sans-Souci palace in the 1870s, for example, the U.S. traveler Samuel Hazard found that many Haitians harbored hostility toward his countrymen. "Why do you dislike the Americans so much?" he asked. The invariable answer was that "the Americans wanted to come and take their lands and make them slaves." Hazard did his best to be reassuring: the Haitians, he said, had nothing to fear from the United States, which had freed its slaves and was generously educating them. Of course, his Haitian interlocutors might have felt some reasonable suspicion at the lateness of the American conversion to the cause of emancipation, which they themselves had fought for three-quarters of a century before. But more importantly, Hazard's literal interpretation of the threat of a return to slavery also missed the point. In Haiti, the colonial past served as a metaphor, a specter of forced labor and external control. Taken in this way, the Haitians' perspective on U.S. intentions was in fact quite clear-eyed. The long-desired recognition of Haiti by the United States opened the way for more and more

American involvement in Haiti and its political life. During the coming decades, U.S. corporations and banks would gain an increasing foothold in Haiti, and in their wake would come U.S. marines. In the end, the fear of the return of a certain kind of slavery turned out to be perfectly justified.[57]

5

LOOKING NORTH

"Will Haiti work?" an anxious Anténor Firmin wondered in 1905. One of Haiti's most celebrated intellectuals and statesmen, Firmin had spent his life grappling with three demons: European racism, U.S. expansionism, and Haitian authoritarianism. Now, living in political exile at the twilight of his career, he wrote a book comparing Haiti's history to that of the United States and evaluating the possible benefits and threats to Haiti from its northern neighbor. The United States was now the most powerful political force in the region, Firmin advised his countrymen, and Haiti had to find a way to deal with it.[1]

Firmin did not think that Haiti should give itself over completely to U.S. influence. He brushed off, for instance, the notion that Haitians should abandon French and turn to English as the main language of their country—an idea first proposed by Christophe in the 1810s and echoed by some Haitian intellectuals in the late nineteenth century. At the same time, however, Firmin distanced himself from those who considered the United States a profound danger to Haitian sovereignty. Instead of "getting caught up in an irrational suspicion," he wrote, Haitians should instead "study the question with history books in their hands." Among foreign powers, he argued, the United States was the one that had shown itself "most respectful of their rights as an independent people." Firmin was well aware that the United States had been the last power to officially recognize Haiti's independence, but during the decades of his active political life he had seen more British and German gunships than American ones brazenly intervene in Haitian affairs. More importantly, Firmin had an idealistic conviction that the United States would always remain true to its founding principles and therefore respect the independence of other countries. In any case, he added as if to reassure himself, the United States didn't need Haiti. Of all the great "occidental powers," they had the lowest population density—fewer than twenty-five people per square mile—and therefore the least need for colonies.[2]

The key for Haiti, Firmin wrote, was to figure out how to thrive under the "colossal shadow" cast by the United States—how to "grow, develop, without ever letting itself be absorbed." In this task, he thought, Haiti could count on help from the Americans themselves. It was in the United States' best interest to make sure that Haiti "strengthened and civilized itself," so that European powers would no longer "molest" the country. In the long run, the United States might even become Haiti's savior, providing what the country needed to become "an active and laborious civilization." The Americans "have capital of all kinds," Firmin noted: "money, machines, experience of hard work, and the moral energy necessary to confront difficult circumstances." They could "offer us that helping hand we have been looking for throughout the past century."[3]

Firmin also thought that the United States could serve as an institutional example. The alternation of parties in power, he wrote, guaranteed political stability. He effused that of all the countries in the world, the U.S. social and political system combined liberty and equality in the most successful fashion. American citizens, he argued, put the national good over individual ambitions. Firmin even downplayed the continuing racial discrimination in the United States. He celebrated Lincoln, and while he admitted that African Americans had yet to secure full rights, he predicted confidently that the problem would be fully resolved within a century. Going further, he asserted that the United States could actually provide a model of racial egalitarianism for Haiti, which suffered from its own conflicts between mulattoes and blacks.[4]

For all its optimism, though, Firmin's analysis also carried a note of caution. With such a dominant neighbor, Haitians urgently had to solve their own problems; otherwise they would be inviting disaster, opening the way for the violation and destruction of their precious sovereignty. The power of the United States, its "almost undisputed preponderance" in the hemisphere, was inescapable, he wrote, and Haiti needed to act accordingly. "Instead of putting ourselves in the position of trying to block an impetuous and irresistible torrent," Haiti had to allow itself to be "productively watered" by the flood of U.S. power. Otherwise, Firmin warned, "we'll be carried away trying to block it, in a gesture as reckless as it is hopeless."[5]

III

Growing up in Le Cap in the 1860s, Firmin got an early education in the vagaries and violence of Haitian politics. He was nine years old when Soulouque was overthrown by Geffrard, and within a few years insurgents had in turn risen up against the new president. Among them was a prominent officer named Sylvain Salnave, who set up his headquarters in Le Cap. Fighting to remain in power, Geffrard secured military support from the British, and in 1865, British warships bombarded Le Cap on two occasions, targeting its public buildings and reducing its forts to rubble.[6]

Salnave, for his part, sought assistance from the United States, hoping that U.S. warships would help him blockade Port-au-Prince. "Since we are an American nation like the United States," his officers wrote in an appeal for aid, "we wish to unite ourselves in a close bond of political and commercial friendship with your government." With U.S. military assistance, Salnave explained, he could overthrow Geffrard. Then, once he won, he would be in a position to offer the United States special military and commercial privileges.

Most significantly, Salnave was prepared to provide access to a spectacular naval station in Haiti: the port of Môle Saint-Nicolas.[7]

The Môle sits astride a beautiful and protected bay on Haiti's northwestern tip, directly across from Guantánamo Bay in Cuba. Dubbed the "Gibraltar of the West Indies," it was described by a British officer in the late eighteenth century as the best harbor he had ever seen—perhaps the best "in the world," and one that could shelter any European navy. Salnave knew that the United States, which had made frequent use of a coaling station set up at Le Cap during the Civil War, needed such ports. But he overestimated the American government's interest at the time. His offer was rejected. "We have no purposes or designs of acquisition or aggrandizement within the territory of Hayti," wrote the U.S. secretary of state.[8]

Even without U.S. aid, Salnave garnered enough support within Haiti to establish himself as president in 1867. But his rule was short-lived. In 1869, his opponents invaded Port-au-Prince and attacked the National Palace. Salnave had turned it into an armory, packing it with guns and ammunition, and when the shelling started, the palace exploded. It was a fitting symbol for Haiti's political situation, as competing groups appeared ready to sacrifice nearly everything for control of the state, even the state itself.[9]

The second half of the nineteenth century was a time of seemingly constant civil war in Haiti. Between 1843 and 1889, there were twelve presidents and nearly as many constitutions: eight in all, along with several constitutional amendments. Almost always, the changes in government came as the result of a military campaign in which the president was ousted by a rebel at the head of a regional army. The new constitutions, as historian Claude Moïse points out, were never the "result of a national consensus," or even of "agreement among the ruling classes." Instead, they were largely tools used to maintain control of the state and to divide up the spoils that came with it. The discussions surrounding each new constitution focused primarily on just one question: how much power the president would have within the system.[10]

And yet Haiti enjoyed an oddly stable form of instability. While control of the national government in Port-au-Prince constantly shifted as the result of civil war, the local political structures in most of Haiti's regions remained largely unchanged. The military commanders of each district ran the local governments and managed much of the administration of people's daily lives—policing communities, overseeing taxation, and distributing government resources. Though there were certainly other influential groups, especially in the towns—merchants, journalists, professionals—local power remained in the hands of military leaders. And although the district commanders were sometimes replaced when a new government came to power in Port-au-Prince, many stayed in their positions for years, even decades, providing a certain continuity despite the frequent changes in leadership on the national level.

In a district outside Croix-des-Bouquets, for instance, an officer named Caliska Calice held sway for nearly four decades. A French merchant who visited him around 1904 wrote that Calice had used his influence to "assure calm" in his district on behalf of the many national governments that had succeeded each other over the decades. He had a comfortable life: he greeted his visitor wearing a pink bathrobe decorated with red flowers and showed him around his property, which included a large garden producing corn, manioc, and potatoes, surrounded by large and productive palm trees. There were several buildings organized around a courtyard, where Calice acted as a judge for local conflicts, hosted dances and cockfights, and dispensed medical and psychiatric help to those who needed it.[11]

The Haitian army, thus, was used not so much to defend the country as to run it. Military service remained the primary route to social advancement, especially because officers got not only a salary but also often local power and access to land. Over time, the army became both bloated and top-heavy. Each new president brought to power by insurrection incorporated a new group of officers into his regime, and they often stayed on even after their benefactors were overthrown. "The only thing left to do," one president quipped, was to "issue a decree making everyone a general." In 1867 there were about 20,000 soldiers in Haiti (in a population of 700,000 or so), and of these, a startling 13,500 were officers.[12]

The military was far from unified or centrally controlled. The civil wars often pitted army divisions from different regions against the president in Port-au-Prince. Though the insurgencies frequently involved a patchwork of groups, they generally coalesced either in the north of the country or in the southern peninsula—regions that operated with considerable economic autonomy. Indeed, nineteenth-century Haiti can best be described as a confederation of eleven largely independent regions, each with its own port town, merchant elites, landowners, and market system. The regions specialized in the production of different crops, with the north focused largely on coffee and dyewood exports, for instance, while some plains in the south concentrated on growing cane for the production of rum and for local sugar consumption. Port-au-Prince was one of the larger ports, of course, and as the center of the government it occupied a unique role in this broader matrix. But it was not the dominant economic and political center that it would become in the twentieth century. Le Cap essentially functioned as an alternative capital, with a thriving economic life. Many residents in the north resented the central government in Port-au-Prince, as did their counterparts in the south, nursing grievances that could easily fuel uprisings against the state.[13]

Direct popular participation in Haiti's political institutions, meanwhile, remained quite limited. Theoretically, nineteenth-century constitutions granted the right to vote to most Haitian men over the age of twenty-one. But for reasons that remain unclear, theory and practice diverged substantially, and even in urban areas, very few people voted. In Port-au-Prince in 1870, only nine hundred men were registered to vote. By 1888 the situation had improved somewhat, but nevertheless, of fifty thousand residents of Port-au-Prince, only four thousand were registered, and no more than eight hundred actually voted. In smaller towns and in the countryside, voting was even rarer, and elections were often manipulated by local officers. The majority of Haitians were thus almost totally excluded from the political process.[14]

Insurrection, on the other hand, was open to all. Regional leaders who wanted to overthrow the central regime gathered followers from among the general population, taking advantage of the fact that Haitians on the whole were well armed and many had experience in military conflicts. Most of these leaders presented themselves as populists, making vague promises about a more equitable distribution of land and money. But while each new regime created some turnover within the ruling class, little changed in the broader structures of power. Most of the political promises made by insurrectionary leaders were never fulfilled, setting the stage for a continuing cycle of uprisings.[15]

The constant threat of insurrection in turn shaped government action. Once they gained power, even leaders who saw themselves as liberal reformers and decried the repressive nature of the previous government quickly became convinced that they could survive only by eliminating their enemies. They responded harshly to all forms of opposition, even those channeled through parliamentary means, seeing disagreement as a threat to national governance rather than a constitutive part of it. With a new uprising threatening Port-au-Prince every few years, political leaders could nearly always claim that the security of the government was in danger and on that basis justify almost anything. Indeed, Haitian president Lysius Salomon, who ruled from 1879 to 1888, admitted with striking candor: "I like coups d'état. You can't govern without them." The trick to ruling, he went on, was to "take as much advantage as possible" of a crisis—whatever its provenance—in order to justify a stranglehold on executive power. In 1908, one Haitian observer wrote that governments resided in the National Palace as if they were "camped in enemy country," always ready to carry out "extreme measures" against their own citizens like an occupying army.[16]

But in fact no president had a monopoly on violence within the heavily armed and regionalized society of nineteenth-century Haiti. If a ruler angered residents of a particular region, he might quickly find himself facing a dangerous uprising. The result was a balance in which regional armies served as a counterweight to the ambitions of central power, thus providing a mechanism to contain Haiti's rulers. Heads of state who committed crimes of corruption or violence were never tried in the court of law, but they could be held to account, as one nineteenth-century observer put it, through the "summary judgment of revolution." Given that the state was still primarily focused on extracting wealth from the countryside, the power of the quasiautonomous regions served as a significant and necessary means of protection for rural Haitians.[17]

The frequency of insurrection did not mean that Haiti was constantly in the midst of widespread war. Campaigns were often relatively short, and many who fought in them quickly returned to their normal lives. In comparison with the major nineteenth-century wars in the United States and Europe, casualties seem to have been low. And while the conflicts usually culminated in attacks on the capital, they were scattered across different parts of the country, and some regions were spared altogether. Many Haitians were only peripherally involved in the political battles, and their lives were largely shaped instead by the social institutions in their rural communities. Indeed, the instability of the central government was probably perceived by many as an advantage. If the state offered little, it also lacked the power to take too much away.[18]

Most rural residents focused the majority of their energy on cultivating their plots of land, which often continued to provide them with a comfortable existence. In 1948, a seventy-year-old man in the Marbial Valley in southern Haiti recalled his life as a child in the late nineteenth century. When spring came, he remembered, "it was a pleasure for the eyes to contemplate our gardens. The beans were ripening, corn was spiking up, the branches sunk under the weight of the calabashes." Alongside his father's house was a large plantation of coffee trees, whose harvests would enable the family to buy what they couldn't grow for themselves. His father was so comfortable that he did something that would later be unthinkable: he cut down a grove of profitable coffee trees, his son recalled with some wonder, just "to build his house!"[19]

I I I

The thriving rural regions also brought prosperity to the port towns of Haiti, which benefited from the flow of peasants' exports. The wealth of the port towns in turn continued to draw speculators and merchants from outside the country, who were happy to keep trading with Haiti regardless of who presided over Port-au-Prince. But the civil wars that racked the country during the second half of the nineteenth century did make it vulnerable to foreign intervention in new ways. Now, when violent outbursts caused property damage, foreign citizens frequently demanded compensation for their losses from the Haitian government itself. The fact that the destruction had taken place at the hands of one or another pretender to power, they argued, made the state responsible. These citizens had the support of their own governments, who repeatedly threatened to use force in the pursuit of individual claims.

Private citizens abroad frequently call on their governments for help, of course, but the actions in Haiti were by all accounts extreme, amounting to brazen international extortion. Foreign governments and merchants consistently armed and sometimes openly supported various combatants in civil wars—as the British did with Geffrard in the 1860s—only to complain later that they had lost property during the conflicts. Having encouraged crises in the country, they then demanded that the Haitian state pay for what had happened to their citizens as a result. It was what one scholar has dubbed "a veritable expatriate industry of damage claims."[20]

In 1872, for instance, Germany sent two warships into the harbor of Port-au-Prince, demanding that Haiti pay some outstanding claims from German citizens. When the Haitian president refused, the Germans captured two Haitian warships in the harbor. After that, arrangements were quickly made to pay the German claims, and the two captured ships were released. Such capitulation only embold-ened German merchants in their later dealings with the Haitian government. In 1885, one Haitian quipped that "Haiti is in the pro-cess of becoming a colony of Hamburg." But the Germans were not the only ones who used this approach. In 1886, the British pursued a similar course when one of their citizens was arrested in Haiti, sending a warship into Port-au-Prince and successfully pressuring the Haitian government to release the man. French citizens also made claims against Haiti; these totaled more than a million francs, and the French government likewise threatened to send gunships if the sums were not paid. "We are dupes of their politics," one Haitian writer lamented regarding the foreign powers, "victims of their intrigues, slaves of their capital."[21]

The 1805 Haitian constitution had made it illegal for foreigners to buy property in Haiti or for whites to become Haitian citizens. These provisions were maintained in subsequent constitutions, but foreign merchants found a way around the problem by marrying into Haitian families. Their Haitian wives could purchase and hold property in the country; at the same time, since the men remained foreign citizens, they could still demand indemnities from the Hai-tian government with the support of their home governments. By the 1870s, this merchant strategy had become so common that Hai-tian governments decided to enact additional restrictions surround-ing Haitian citizenship. They took particular aim at Haitian women who married foreign men, eventually decreeing that if a Haitian woman married a foreigner she would lose her Haitian citizenship and would have to sell any property she owned within three months. Such nationality codes were shaped by deep-seated fears that foreign merchants might gain access to too much political and economic power in the country—yet another threat to the always-besieged Hai-tian sense of sovereignty.[22]

The nationality laws, however, ultimately did little to prevent outsiders from gaining influence in Haiti, for the state itself was increasingly beholden on a massive scale to foreign banks. In 1874 and 1875 the Haitian government took out huge new loans from banks in France. The 1874 loan was meant primarily to cover the costs of paying the 1825 French indemnity, but it was extremely costly, with high commissions, so the next year the government decided to take out a second, much larger loan, in part in order to cover the expenses of the first. Within a few years, government debt skyrocketed from 16 million to 44 million francs.[23]

Despite such massive expenditures, the Haitian government spent relatively little during these years on infrastructure development within the country. Instead, the whole process of foreign loans became a kind of racket as more and more bankers and merchants rushed to offer high-interest loans to Haiti, often promising significant kickbacks to the government officials who signed them. In addition to large loans like that of 1875, the Haitian government soon took out many short-term loans to cover its immediate costs, and in the following decades, government debt—long a major drain on the state treasury—began to spiral out of control. Through the 1890s, about 25 percent of Haiti's state budget went to paying off debts (and roughly 30 percent to support the military). By 1898, fully 50 percent of the state budget was consumed by loan repayments, and by the 1913–14 budget year, that amount had climbed to over 67 percent.[24]

These loans also had another long-term consequence. The increasing stake that French bankers had in Haiti led them in 1880 to create the Banque Nationale d'Haïti, which effectively took over the treasury of Haiti itself. The BNH, which was owned by the Société Général de Crédit Industriel et Commercial, printed Haitian money, charging the government a commission for doing so, and served as the depository for all Haitian tax revenues. Moreover, since there were no other banks in Haiti until the early twentieth century, the BNH had a monopoly on commercial banking activities in the country—the only official source for loans to private individuals or small businesses. The possibility of such business lending, of course, could well have contributed to improvements in the commercial and agricultural life in Haiti. But the BNH wasn't really a national bank: it was a French bank, whose accountability was to its French shareholders and not the Haitian people. This meant that the Haitian government, unlike the governments of most other nations, did not have the ability to set fiscal policy or embark on economic initiatives through the country's bank. The only benefits the BNH really provided for Haiti ultimately accrued to a very small segment of the population with government connections. The state, always a fruitful prize, became an ever greater one.[25]

The symbolism of German warships capturing Haitian ships in the Port-au-Prince harbor, or a new batch of Haitian currency arriving from the Direction de la Monnaie in Paris, was unmistakable. The country's hold over its economic destiny seemed increasingly tenuous. And as the twentieth century approached, German merchants and French bankers were joined by the latest foreign power on the scene, one that would ultimately have an even greater impact on Haiti: the United States.

III

It was the steamship that made Haiti into a place of vital interest to the U.S. government. In the mid-nineteenth century, the adoption of steam power brought both new advantages and new complications for the navies of the great empires. Traditional sailing used a resource that, if fickle, was also free and often in endless supply: the wind. Steamships were better in many ways: they went faster, were bigger, and depended less on the vagaries of currents and breezes. But they needed to burn coal to make the steam that drove them, and thus they needed depots where they could stop to get that coal. For Britain, France, and Spain, the problem was not a serious one: they had colonies across the globe, and they built depots there for their

steamships. If the United States wanted to compete with these countries, it needed to set up coaling stations, too, notably in the Caribbean. However, only a few locations there were not under the firm
control of one of the other major empires. Because they were independent, the Dominican Republic and neighboring Haiti ironically
became the most likely candidates for U.S. takeover.[26]

Thanks to such considerations, the 1870s saw the return of the
dreams of Caribbean annexation that had been popular in the American South before the Civil War. These aspirations, however, now
came from very different quarters, with President Ulysses S. Grant as
their most powerful new proponent. To build support for the idea,
Grant enlisted the assistance of the famed abolitionist Frederick
Douglass, who enthusiastically embraced the proposal. This was a
change of heart for him: before the Civil War, Douglass had been a
vocal opponent of Caribbean annexation, which he saw as leading
only to "more slavery, more ignorance and more barbarism." After
the war, though, Douglass saw annexation as a way of spreading the
progressive values of U.S. society. At the time, he had reason to be
optimistic, for it seemed possible that the federal government was
going to truly guarantee the social and political rights of African
Americans. And while Douglass was well aware of the broader forces
driving U.S. designs—"Almost every great maritime nation," he
noted, "has some footing and foothold in the Caribbean sea but our
own"—he also saw U.S. expansion as a way of bringing prosperity
to the region. "It may, indeed, be important to know what Santo
Domingo can do for us," Douglass declared in 1871, "but it is vastly
more important to know what we can do for Santo Domingo." It was
a statement, as the historian Millery Polyné points out, whose form
and meaning anticipated American president John F. Kennedy's inaugural address of ninety years later, envisioning the United States as a
force for progress and democracy in the hemisphere.[27]

As Haitians watched warily, the attention of the United States
focused first on the Dominican Republic, which was undergoing its
own series of political upheavals. In 1861, Spain had retaken its

former colony at the invitation of Pedro Santana, the Dominican president at the time. Their control proved short-lived, though: in 1865 the Dominican Republic threw off the Spanish mantle for the second time. But Dominican independence seemed to be a tenuous affair. In 1869, the new president of the Dominican Republic, Buenaventura Báez, signed a deal with an American envoy allowing the United States to annex the country if the United States took over the responsibility for $1.5 million in debt (roughly equivalent to $24 million today) that it owed to various creditors. In a way, the proposal, which enraged many Dominicans, was the reverse of the arrangement that Boyer had made with Haiti's French indemnity: Báez was willing to sacrifice political independence for relief from economic dependence.[28]

The annexation deal depended on ratification by the U.S. Congress, where it quickly ran into significant opposition. Senator Charles Sumner, who had been instrumental in helping Haiti win U.S. recognition, argued that the proposal was a violation of international law. Sumner was also convinced, as he wrote to a friend, that annexation would "menace Hayti," and he was determined to prevent that from happening. The Haitian minister of foreign relations, Stephen Preston, agreed with Sumner about the danger of a U.S. presence on the island. He kept in close touch with the American senator, and hired journalists in the United States to mount a press campaign against Dominican annexation.[29]

Báez and his supporters tried to woo the United States in part by emphasizing the contrast between their country and Haiti. They presented the Dominican Republic as a nation populated mainly by whites and, recalling the many cases of Haitian occupation, warned that they could easily be overrun by a black government. Báez accused his opponents of being in league with the Haitians and of intending to create in a situation in which "the African race shall dominate this island." But this attempt to appeal to American prejudices failed. Indeed, when the U.S. Congress voted against the annexation scheme, one newspaper reported that they had done so mainly out of racism, concluding that "we have negroes enough at home without annexing an island full of them."[30]

Grant did not give up easily on his vision for the Caribbean, and two years later he sent a "fact-finding" mission to the Dominican Republic. Among its members was Frederick Douglass, who, on his return to the United States, went on a speaking tour promoting Dominican annexation. But despite support from Douglass and others, Grant was ultimately unable to overcome the mix of congressional opposition and general indifference to his plans. He later lamented that the United States had lost a great opportunity to solve several problems at once. If they had annexed the Dominican Republic, Grant explained, it could have become a "new home for the blacks, who were and I hear still are oppressed in the South." As Southerners watched hundreds of thousands of their laborers leave for the Caribbean, Grant imagined, they would have been forced to understand "the crime of Ku-Kluxism, because they would see how necessary the black is to their own prosperity." The United States, meanwhile, would have saved itself the trouble of importing tropical products. "We should have grown our own coffee and sugar, our own hardwoods and spices . . . We should have made of St. Domingo a new Texas or a New California." And along the way, Grant added, "we should have had Hayti"—suggesting that once a part of Hispaniola became U.S. territory, the rest of the island would inevitably have come under U.S. control as well.[31]

Haitians and Dominicans who opposed annexation knew that it had been a close call. When President Báez was overthrown in April 1874, the new Dominican government immediately began negotiations with Haiti for a treaty that was signed in September of that year. The core of the agreement between the countries was a promise by both nations to "maintain with all their strength and with all their power the integrity of their respective territories." Neither country was to "cede, compromise nor alienate in favor of any foreign Power

either the whole or any part of the territories or of the adjacent islands
dependent on them." Finally, they pledged "not to solicit or consent
to any foreign annexation or domination."[32]

The treaty brought to an end the long-standing tradition in Haitian politics of periodically invading the eastern side of the island.
Haitian leaders had repeatedly sought to forestall any foreign control
on Hispaniola, which they considered a threat to their sovereignty,
by simply taking over their neighbor. Now, the two countries assumed
joint responsibility for keeping their shared island under the control
of its inhabitants. In its way, the 1874 agreement was a version of
the Monroe Doctrine, which had insisted that European powers
should not meddle in the affairs of independent nations in the Western Hemisphere. The Haitians and Dominicans made a similar point
with their treaty—but they targeted the doctrine of nonintervention
at the United States, which they deemed to be the most dangerous
foreign power of all.[33]

I I I

Given the international tensions caused by U.S. expansionism, it is
perhaps not surprising that many Haitians at the time had a negative view of their northern neighbor and lamented the rising power
of the United States. "You are good at making machines," one Haitian writer complained after spending a long train ride in Europe
sitting next to a painfully talkative American, "but have a hard time
coming up with ideas." Many Haitian leaders described the United
States as a hopelessly materialistic, uncouth, even backward country, not to mention a deeply racist one. In 1873 the prominent politician and intellectual Demesvar Delorme urged his compatriots to
turn their backs on the United States and focus instead on Haiti's
long-standing connections to France.[34]

A few prominent Haitians—including Anténor Firmin—did try
to speak up for the United States, arguing that it would be a much
more useful partner for economic development than France had

ever been. (Firmin, after a stint as a schoolteacher, had become a well-known lawyer in Le Cap; though of humble origins, he was now a member of the town's elite, married to the daughter of the deceased former president Salnave.) In Firmin's view, the country had much to gain from establishing U.S. connections. He probably agreed with the Haitian politician who declared that a "marriage of love" with France was an impossible dream, and that Haitians ultimately had no choice but to join in "a marriage of convenience" with the United States.[35]

Firmin and Delorme would clash again in the late 1870s, when they found themselves on opposite sides of a political debate that divided Haiti's intellectual class throughout the final decades of the nineteenth century. Firmin became a key figure in the powerful Liberal Party, whose slogan was "Government by the Most Competent" and whose political philosophy was undisguisedly antipopulist. Many of its members argued that only Haiti's elites had the education and capacity necessary to confront the country's challenges and that Haiti was simply not ready for popular democracy: "The supremacy of numbers assures the supremacy of ignorance." Delorme, meanwhile, became a major presence in the competing National Party, which responded to the Liberal Party's claims with its own slogan: "The Greatest Good to the Greatest Number."[36]

Both parties openly framed their arguments in terms of skin color. The Liberals made no secret of the fact that the elites whom they put forward as Haiti's best hope were mostly light-skinned. The Nationals, on the other hand, believed that Haiti's problems were mostly caused by mulatto politicians and by the weakness of black leaders who had allowed mulattoes to manipulate and use them. Louis-Joseph Janvier, one of the great theorists of the National Party, made a point of praising Christophe and other black rulers throughout Haiti's history.

The analogies to early Haitian history ran deeper than Janvier would probably have been willing to admit, however. Just as Christophe and Pétion had presided over nominally different styles of government—a kingdom in the north, a republic in the south—yet ruled in similarly autocratic ways, so, too, the National and Liberal parties ended up much alike despite their differing self-presentations. Both were interested in small-scale democratic reforms and in increasing intellectuals' involvement in government; neither envisioned a real expansion of political participation to include the masses of rural Haitians. When the National Party came to power, they did help bring more blacks into the political class. But, their slogan notwithstanding, they didn't address the fundamental divide between that elite and the rest of the population—the deeper structures of power and exclusion in the society—which remained largely unaltered.[37]

What's more, the divisions by skin color were also never as absolute as the two parties would have it. After all, Christophe, the black leader lauded by the Nationals, had carefully assembled an aristocracy for his court that included many notable light-skinned men. Meanwhile, Firmin, that staunch proponent of the Liberal elites, was himself black, as were a few other prominent members of the Liberal Party. In the late 1870s, when Firmin ran for local office in Le Cap, the National Party opposition attacked him by declaring that he was "as light-skinned as a white man"—but that was a calculated lie.[38]

Firmin lost the election in Le Cap, and a few years later he decided to move to Paris. There he found himself among other expatriates from the Caribbean and Latin America. The Puerto Rican nationalist Ramón Emeterio Betances organized a salon in the city at which various thinkers from throughout the region gathered, talked, and plotted. Firmin was also invited to join the Anthropological Society of Paris, of which Louis-Joseph Janvier was already a member. Though they had some welcoming allies, Janvier and Firmin found themselves largely in hostile territory. At the time, the ideas of the Comte de Gobineau, who had penned his famous *Essay on the Inequality of the Human Races* in the 1850s, dominated European thought on the question of the origins of the human species and the reasons for differences in color and culture. As they took their seats at the Anthropological Society, the two Haitians thus joined an organization where most members strongly believed that black people were inherently and irredeemably inferior. It was, as Firmin wrote, a rather strange situation. Although he initially kept quiet, not wanting to stir up trouble and be perceived as an "intruder," the experience left him in a fury. Soon he found a way to channel the experience into something productive: he published *The Equality of the Human Races*, an impassioned refutation of Gobineau and the dominant racial theories of the day.[39]

Firmin's book skewered the European intellectuals, famous and obscure, who had lined up behind spurious theories of racial difference. In one short chapter, called "Prejudices and Vanities," Firmin simply listed racist comments by "men who are generally considered authoritative voices in science and philosophy," from Immanuel Kant to Ernest Renan. Clearly, he wrote, the notion of the inequality of the human races was "deeply rooted in the minds of the most enlightened men of Europe"—so deeply that "they seem incapable of ever discarding it." Yet none of these intellectual luminaries had ever offered solid support for that idea: they believed in the inferiority of blacks, Firmin argued, not because that belief was reasonable or logical, but because the history of slavery and colonialism had produced, shaped, and ultimately naturalized that prejudice.[40]

It was high time to change the situation. There was, Firmin insisted, only one human race. If anthropology were to be a true positivist science, it needed to escape from the thrall of untenable racist theories based on scattered anecdotal evidence and devote itself to its real calling: the study of human societies, in all their complexity, through careful scientific method. Firmin's book took its readers on a journey from Egypt to India to Africa, showing the flimsiness of the support for the principle of racial inequality. And he argued that Haiti, in particular, provided a clear refutation of all the assertions of racist science: a nation of blacks had produced brilliant poets, statesmen, and intellectuals.

In a playful response to the "scientific" idea that whites were inherently more beautiful, Firmin even included in his book a list of some particularly good-looking Haitian men. He recalled seeing, among the aides-de-camp of a Haitian general, "a young Black man so mesmerizingly handsome that one could not take one's eyes off his face." He also described another "handsome specimen of the Black race," the director of the customs office at Le Cap: "I still remember how visiting foreigners who came through the town's port often neglected the business at hand to gaze admiringly at this man whose handsome features were enhanced by his black skin." The "physical beauty" of such men, Firmin suggested, gave "the lie to the fanciful descriptions of ethnographers." Though his tone was lighthearted, Firmin was making a serious point. For each supposed "scientific observation" deployed to justify racist theories, he could provide an opposite example. Of course, his observations were based on his personal experience as a Haitian; but those of the supposed scientists on the other side were just as personal, the product of their own European background, and not in any way universal.[41]

Firmin's work was largely ignored by European anthropology, which continued for decades to focus on racial differences and hierarchy. It would take another generation before a new set of thinkers, led by Franz Boas in the United States, began to dismantle the racist "science" that Firmin had lambasted. And it took much longer yet for Firmin to begin to assume his rightful place in the history of anthropological thought; the first English translation of his work was not produced until 2002. In Haiti, however, Firmin's powerful attack on European racism gained him many admirers and established him as one of the country's most revered intellectuals.[42]

III

Firmin returned to Haiti in 1888 and found the country in the midst of yet another civil war, one not unlike the conflict which he had experienced during his teenage years in Le Cap. A coalition of regional armies had overthrown the president and put a general from the west of the country, François Denys Légitime, into power. But an officer from Le Cap, Florville Hyppolite, had immediately launched an insurrection against Légitime. Hyppolite's movement was nourished by longstanding grievances among residents of the north, who had complained for decades about the fact that the central government collected enormous revenues from the agriculturally productive region and provided almost nothing in return. (As one rebel group had put it in the 1870s, a few "plumed generals" in Port-au-Prince were "fattening themselves on the sweat of the North.") Hyppolite pledged that he would allow the region to control its own finances, enabling it to escape such exploitation.[43]

Firmin decided to support the uprising, and Hyppolite, impressed by his intellectual and political credentials, named him the movement's minister of exterior relations. Firmin's primary mission was to get U.S. backing for the insurrection. Like Salnave several decades earlier, Hyppolite hoped that if he promised trade concessions to the United States and discussed the possibility of allowing them to have access to a naval base in Haiti, he could gain valuable military assistance against his opponent. He understood the political reality of late-nineteenth-century Haiti: any struggle for power within the country now depended upon support from outside.[44]

For the most part, the U.S. government found the ongoing civil wars in Haiti perplexing and concerning. "The situation is becoming intolerable," wrote one exasperated State Department official in 1888. "Hayti is a public nuisance at our doors." But in 1889, James Blaine, appointed as secretary of state by the newly elected President Benjamin Harrison, saw an opportunity in the conflicts within Haiti. Blaine was a major proponent of a diplomatic approach known as Pan-Americanism, which sought to create networks of cooperation and trade between nations of the Western Hemisphere. In the opening speech of the International American Conference that he organized in Washington in October 1889, Blaine declared that "friendship and not force, the spirit of just law and not the violence of the mob should be the recognized rule of administration between American nations and in American nations." Increased trade and better communication, he proclaimed, would enable each nation to "acquire the highest possible advantage from the enlightened and enlarged intercourse of all." Blaine's Pan-Americanism was also driven by less lofty motives: he was especially concerned that the huge profits to be made by trading with Latin America were making their way "to England, France, Germany and other countries" instead of to the United States.[45]

Blaine proceeded carefully in developing his policy toward Haiti. He first contacted Stephen Preston, Haiti's minister to Washington, who was representing President Légitime. Withholding official recognition from Légitime's government, Blaine confronted Preston with a series of demands. He wanted Haiti to grant the United States a naval station in Haiti and to agree to be represented in European countries by the U.S. envoys to those countries. Preston—surprised particularly by the second demand, which he considered an infringement on Haiti's sovereignty—rejected both proposals.[46]

Having gained little from Légitime, Blaine turned his attentions to Hyppolite's insurgent movement. Firmin had already succeeded in getting Hyppolite a steady supply of high-end weapons—one shipment, for example, included seventeen Gatling guns—from an American merchant named William P. Clyde, who owned a fleet of steamships called the West India Line. Now, the U.S. government provided Firmin with arms shipments as well as naval support, giving Hyppolite's insurgency the edge it needed to triumph. In October 1899, he took over Haiti's presidency, and he brought Firmin to Port-au-Prince with him.[47]

The U.S. press had a high opinion of Firmin, complimenting him by describing him as the "Haitian Blaine." Hyppolite's opponents, however, were quick to attack the new regime by criticizing its cozy relationship with the United States. A group calling itself the League for the Maintenance of National Independence denounced Hyppolite as a tool of foreign interests, claiming that he had made a secret deal to cede the port of Môle Saint-Nicolas to the Americans. Firmin and Hyppolite both denied the allegation, but William Clyde claimed that one of their agents had indeed offered the United States access to a port in return for American support during the insurrection. While the truth about the matter is difficult to determine, it was all too easy for people to believe that such a deal had been made, given how openly Hyppolite had cultivated and depended on U.S. support in his struggle for the presidency.[48]

It was also abundantly clear to Haitians that Blaine and the U.S. government were in fact avidly eyeing Môle Saint-Nicolas, unlike their predecessors who had rebuffed Salnave in the 1860s. In his inaugural address, U.S. president Harrison had made a point of mentioning that "the necessities of our navy require convenient coaling stations and dock and harbor privileges." The navy ordered one of its admirals, Bancroft Gherardi, to gather a "full and detailed description of all coaling stations in the West Indies," and the Môle was high on the list of sought-after spots. When Harrison had to choose a new minister to Haiti, he therefore carefully looked for someone who might be able to successfully negotiate a delicate deal with the Black Republic. The man he settled on was Frederick Douglass.[49]

It was an inspired choice. Stephen Preston rejoiced when he heard the news, calling it a "miracle" and effusing that, at least for the moment, the danger "of attempts to annex a part of our territory" had passed. Blaine, meanwhile, wrote to Douglass that his appointment to Haiti was a potent symbol of the American desire to secure "the peace, welfare, and prosperity of that warring and dissatisfied people." Back in 1861, Douglass had written proudly of Haiti as "a refutation of the slanders and disparagements of our race," but his plans to visit the country had been interrupted by the U.S. Civil War. Nearly thirty years later, he would finally be able to spend time in the land he admired.[50]

Douglass's appointment, however, came in a very different context from either the 1860s or the early 1870s, when he had optimistically labored on behalf of annexation of the Dominican Republic. By the late 1880s, many of the gains of Reconstruction had been reversed, and Douglass was much more subdued about the extent to which the United States could serve as a progressive and democratic force. Within a few years, a Supreme Court case involving Homer Plessy—a Louisiana man descended from migrants who had come from Saint-Domingue to New Orleans in the early nineteenth century—would signal the federal government's official acceptance of racial segregation. As he arrived in Haiti, Douglass thus found himself in a curious and uncomfortable position, distrusting to a large extent the true intentions of the country that he served.[51]

III

As he settled into the presidency, Hyppolite began what had become a nearly unavoidable ritual for new national leaders in Haiti: rewriting the constitution. For decades, constitutions had come and gone in Haiti with remarkable rapidity. A nineteenth-century proverb put it succinctly: "Constitusyon sé papié, bayonet sé fer"—"Constitutions are made of paper, bayonets of iron." Rebel leaders usually won the presidency by making sweeping promises to their supporters in rural areas: if they won, they claimed, they would expand political rights, carry out land reform, decentralize public institutions. Once they attained power, producing a new constitution was the best way to show that they were serious about reform. But often the constitutional changes were mostly cosmetic, or else designed to make it easier for the new president to hold on to the position he had just won. None of the constitutional revisions really fulfilled perennial popular demands: increased political access for the masses and limitations on presidential power. The 1889 constitution produced by Hyppolite was, in a sense, no different: though it clarified some key issues, in many ways it maintained the structure of earlier documents. The main difference was that, as things turned out, it would remain in force for nearly thirty years.[52]

Firmin was an active participant in the writing of the new constitution, and he was proud that he did achieve one major change: the
elimination of a long-standing article that made it impossible for
whites to become Haitian citizens. In 1804, Dessalines had allowed a
certain number of whites who had supported independence to become
Haitian citizens, but the 1816 constitution made it clear that other
whites would not be eligible for naturalization. From then on, Haitian constitutions had consistently declared in one form or another
that all "Africans and Indians" could become Haitian citizens, but
"no white" could do so. But Firmin, among others, believed that it no
longer made sense to maintain a racial barrier around Haitian citizenship, and the 1889 constitution declared: "Any foreigner can become
a Haitian citizen by following the regulations established by the law."
It was a significant shift, but also only a partial one. Hyppolite's constitution still maintained the long-standing exclusion of whites from
land ownership, and it made clear that this applied even to those
whites who had been naturalized as Haitian citizens.[53]

During the constitutional debates Firmin also pushed for provisions that would contain executive power, but he had only partial
success. In the end, the president ultimately retained the right to
nominate senators as well as to veto legislation. Firmin did manage
to remove an article allowing the president to dissolve the parliament at will, a significant victory. And the constitution introduced a
significant innovation by answering the demands for decentraliza-
tion that had been a central part of the insurrection. State finances
were now decentralized, with regional taxes going into regional coffers. The change was aimed in part at decreasing corruption in the
government, something Firmin would pursue directly over the following years, earning himself many enemies in the process.[54]

Having promulgated the new constitution, Hyppolite and Firmin
quickly turned to the pressing question of how to deal with the
United States. When the Haitian president first met with the newly
arrived Frederick Douglass, the American diplomat made a pitch for
happy globalization. "The growing commercial intercommunication

of various nationalities, so important to the dissemination of knowledge, to the enlargement of human sympathies and to the extinction of hurtful prejudices," he effused, was not a "menace to the autonomy of nations." Hyppolite, a little skeptically, agreed that there was nothing wrong with international exchange, but he added that "each nation has the right to be proud of its autonomy."[55]

Sympathetic and knowledgeable about Haitian history, Douglass was well aware that Haitians had good reason to be sensitive about the threat of external forces. He warned Secretary of State Blaine that it did not help the American cause when a U.S. Navy ship arrived to inspect the harbor of Môle Saint-Nicolas without permission from the Haitian government. It was too easy for opponents of the new regime in Haiti to seize on such actions as proof that the government was ready to "sell the country to the Americans." In fact, the U.S. Navy regarded the Môle as very nearly theirs already; a report by Admiral Gherardi had concluded that if they approached the Haitians with the right mixture of firmness and strategy, the port could be acquired with little difficulty.[56]

Douglass left Haiti for much of 1890, returning at the end of the year with official instructions to begin negotiations for the Môle. On New Year's Day 1891, he called on Firmin. It was a remarkable meeting of minds: the two men, though of different generations, were major intellectual figures who had worked throughout their lives to defeat racism. There was no time for learned discussion, however. Firmin focused on expressing his worries about the intentions of the United States; Douglass, in return, tried to reassure his Haitian colleague that while his government was indeed interested in acquiring a coaling station, they would do so only through "proper means" that were "consistent with the peace and welfare of Haiti."[57]

Such reassurances probably pleased Firmin, but back in the United States, Douglass was getting a reputation for being a bit too sensitive to the Haitian perspective. One of his strongest critics was U.S. entrepreneur William Clyde, the owner of the West India Line. In 1889, having helped Hyppolite get into power with arms sales, he negotiated a contract with the Haitian president that would give his company a monopoly concession to run steamships between the United States and seven Haitian ports. Clyde also offered Hyppolite the right to transform these steamships into warships if needed, as well as to use them to carry troops, weapons, and ammunition within Haiti itself. In return, the Haitian government was to subsidize the steamship operations, paying Clyde $480,000 over the course of five years (the equivalent of $11.3 million in today's currency). According to Clyde, Firmin originally signed the deal but then temporized, deciding not to submit it for final approval to the Haitian legislature. Firmin clearly realized that, given the ongoing criticism of Hyppolite's close relationship with the United States, the opposition would seize on news of this contract to attack him. A frustrated Clyde asked Douglass to pressure the Haitian government to finalize the deal. When it became clear that this wasn't going to happen, Clyde insisted that the Haitians should pay him for the "time and money" he had expended trying to set up his concession in their country. Douglass, with a dose of incisive humor, responded disbelievingly to Clyde: "Then, sir, as they will not allow you to put a hot poker down their backs, you mean to make them pay you for heating it!" Clyde was not amused. "In his eyes," Douglass wrote, "I was more a Haïtien than an American."[58]

In March 1891, an article in the *New York Herald* attacked Douglass for, among other things, being black. If it was to gain the respect of Haitians, the article argued, the United States needed a white diplomatic representative, "for the people [in Haiti] look upon a colored man as one of themselves, whereas they unwittingly recognize the superiority of the white race, although they will never admit it." They needed, the author suggested, a strong white hand to guide them: "To let Haiti alone is to allow her to follow her own path back to barbarism." Douglass responded that Haitians would see right through a white diplomat who tried to "play the hypocrite and pretend to love negroes in Haïti when he is known to hate negroes in the United States." Furthermore, he insisted, strong-arm tactics were not necessary. "The American people are too great to be small," Douglass wrote hopefully, and it was their duty to treat Haiti with respect and justice. If, instead, the United States planned on preying on Haiti's weaknesses and fears, on acquiring concessions through the "dread of our power," then Douglass admitted he was not the right person to represent the United States. "I am charged with sympathy for Haiti," Douglass declared. "I am not ashamed of that charge."[59]

The attacks against Douglass worked. Though Secretary of State Blaine realized that he couldn't get rid of Douglass entirely without inciting an outcry in both Haiti and the United States, he also concluded that he couldn't trust him to get the Môle. So Blaine sent Admiral Gherardi to Haiti, where he essentially took over the negotiations with the Haitian government that should have been under Douglass's control. Looking back bitterly on the negotiations later on, Douglass wrote that the overweening attitude of Gherardi had the opposite of the intended effect, undermining his government's chances of getting what they wanted. In his first meeting with Firmin and President Hyppolite, Gherardi aggressively claimed that a promise had already been made to lease the Môle to the United States years before by an agent of Hyppolite who had traveled to the U.S. during the insurrection. When Firmin disagreed, the admiral responded with a set of veiled threats, declaring ominously that if his request were refused, the United States would have to force Haiti into assuming its "moral obligation." He also told Firmin that "it was the destiny of the Môle to belong to the United States." Douglass, meanwhile, attempted to be more conciliatory, as well as more vague, arguing that the concession would be "consistent with the autonomy of Haïti" and a "source of strength rather than weakness." He proposed that providing the United States with a coaling station would help Haiti to end its national isolation and "touch the world at all points that make for civilization and commerce."[60]

In many ways, Firmin likely agreed with Douglass; his later writings about Haiti's relationship to the United States present similar arguments about the need for open trade. He also understood that given the strategic importance of the Môle in the Caribbean, both the United States and European powers would continue to covet the site. Firmin saw that the United States was clearly the rising power in the region and probably saw the Môle negotiations as a remarkable opportunity. If a deal went through, Haiti could gain income from leasing the port to the Americans, and could also press them for better trade policies and other concessions. In its relations with foreign powers, Haiti had few bargaining chips, but the port was one of them.

The problem was that, given popular fears about the implications of U.S. control—rooted both in long-standing worries about a loss of autonomy and in knowledge of the racism of their neighbor to the north—it was extremely difficult for the Hyppolite regime to negotiate without opening itself up to the dangerous charge of selling out the population to foreign interests. Firmin knew Haitian politics, and the particular situation that his government was in, well enough to realize that it would be extremely difficult to accept the U.S. request. Indeed, Firmin told Gherardi and Douglass as much in their first discussion. He admitted that "if someone must have" the Môle, it should be the United States, but he explained that such a concession would be the end of Hyppolite's government. So he stalled for time, asking for further documentation from the U.S. officials.[61]

In April 1891, an increasingly impatient Gherardi, along with Douglass, went to see Firmin and press him on the Môle issue. This time, they had backup, of a sort: the U.S. Navy sent four warships into the harbor of Port-au-Prince, adding to the three American warships already anchored there. The population of the town was, of course, alarmed by the display of force, and Firmin, under pressure, promised a final response on the request. But to the surprise of the U.S. envoys, it was a polite but firm no.[62]

Firmin agreed that, in principle, the cession of Môle Saint-Nicolas could have been arranged to the benefit of both countries.

The problem, however, was in the details. In addition to asking for a long-term lease of the Môle, the United States had insisted that Haiti must also promise not to rent any part of its territory to any other government, nor grant any "special privilege or usage rights" to another foreign power. This was more than an articulation of the Monroe Doctrine—it sought to set up a privileged deal in which territorial control would be given to the United States and no one else. For Firmin, it was too much. To accept such a condition, he wrote, would constitute an "outrage against the national sovereignty of Haiti and a flagrant violation of Article 1 of our Constitution for, in renouncing our right to dispose of our territory, we will have tacitly accepted its alienation."[63]

The other problem, Firmin explained, was that the United States was being a bully. The fact that they had sent warships to Port-au-Prince—a clear attempt to threaten Haiti—made it impossible for Haiti's government to accept the U.S. request, for if they did so, the Haitians would "seem to cede to foreign pressure and therefore, *ipso facto*, to compromise our existence as an independent people." This was especially true, Firmin added, because U.S. newspapers had been spreading "lies" and declaring that an agreement to grant Môle Saint-Nicolas to the United States as a naval station had already been made. Firmin wrapped up his refusal by insisting that it was not an act of "ill will" on Haiti's part and that his country remained committed to maintaining its relations with "the most glorious and the most generous Republic of the New World and perhaps of the modern World."[64]

Firmin was clearly proud of his message to the United States: he reprinted it in his 1905 book as a reminder of what he had accomplished. And he was celebrated in Haiti for having stood up to its overbearing neighbor the United States. "Firmin's pen," notes one historian, "managed to displace the seven beautiful, brand-new warships, planted in the harbor of Port-au-Prince during the negotiations." The action gave him enormous political legitimacy—he became "a hero, a legend," even "a messiah" in the eyes of many

Haitians, who had watched the U.S. warships nervously for days. When the last of the warships left, there was a "great sigh of relief" in the town, and Firmin emerged bearing the mantle of a new national hero.[65]

In fact, though, Firmin's success was owed largely to his contact with an astute observer of U.S. policy in Washington itself. The Haitian minister to the United States, Hannibal Price—the son of an Englishman and a Haitian woman—was a skilled politician who had cultivated many connections in the capital. He reported that U.S. public opinion would not support aggression against Haiti, and that the Republican Party would likely lose seats in the next election, leaving Harrison and Blaine in a weak position to press the matter. Price concluded that the show of force the U.S. Navy had staged in Port-au-Prince was, in fact, just theater. When Firmin wrote his response to Douglass and Gherardi, he had in hand a telegram from Price that read simply: "The fleet for the purpose of intimidating. Do not yield. Nothing will happen."[66]

III

Firmin was not alone in trying to figure out how to deal with, and contain, the United States. Throughout the Caribbean, particularly in Puerto Rico and Cuba, insurgents and intellectuals were wondering about the same thing. In 1893, Firmin met with the legendary Cuban leader José Martí in Le Cap. The two discussed the struggle for Cuban independence and shared ideas about uniting independent nations in the region into a Caribbean Confederation that could more easily resist incursions from outside. Firmin also traveled widely during the 1890s, posted by the Haitian government as a diplomat in France, England, and Cuba. He was in Paris in 1898 when the United States occupied Cuba and Puerto Rico. Though many nationalists in those countries, struggling for independence from Spain, at first welcomed U.S. support, they were soon dismayed to find that the occupying power had more than simple assistance in mind, and intended to exert control over the political process. Firmin recalled later how Ramón Betances, who had for years fought for Puerto Rican independence, was devastated when he realized that his island had merely traded one empire for another, going from a Spanish colony to an American one. He grew ill and died, with Firmin among those at his bedside. His memory probably haunted Firmin when, years later, he reflected on the dangers that U.S. hegemony might pose to Haiti.[67]

Though he was often abroad, Firmin kept in close contact with his home country and was invested with the hopes of young thinkers and activists in Haiti. For decades, all of Haiti's presidents had been officers or generals, usually with their own loyal armies who could be mobilized to fight for them when necessary. Firmin, by contrast, was not a military man—his greatest victory on Haiti's behalf had been won with his pen, not with guns—and he was admired for his intellectual challenges to European racism. Over the course of the 1890s, he garnered an increasingly vocal following: students, youthful militants, and educated members of the middle class came to constitute what was known as Firminisme, a movement pushing for liberal reform, progress, and democratization.[68]

In March 1896, Hyppolite—setting out to confront an insurrection in the south of the country—fell from his horse, was struck by a heart attack, and died. Briefly, Firmin became part of the government of his successor, Tiresius Antoine Sam. He resigned from Sam's staff in 1897, however, apparently because he despaired of being able to root out the corruption that tied government officials to the merchant houses. In addition, the Haitian government seemed increasingly unable to assert its authority when dealing with foreign powers. In 1897, for instance, a German merchant named Emil Lüders was sentenced to a one-year prison term in Haiti after he fought with police who had come to arrest one of his employees. The German kaiser personally intervened in the case, making a series of dramatic demands against the Haitian state. He wanted Haiti not only to release the prisoner but also to remove the judges who had sentenced him, fire the police who arrested him, and pay an indemnity of $5,000 (more than $125,000 in today's currency) for each day Lüders spent in jail. Haitian President Sam quickly set Lüders free and appealed to U.S. diplomats to help mediate with the Germans regarding their other demands. The United States wasn't much help, however, and the Germans soon sent two cruisers into the harbor of Port-au-Prince with a simple message: Sam must pay an indemnity of $20,000 or they would bombard the town. Seeing no alternative, Sam acquiesced. The U.S. minister to Haiti, William F. Powell, was disgusted by the affair and by the fact that the United States had not defended Haiti. "This is the first time in my life I have ever had cause to be ashamed of being American," he wrote. It was, effectively, an international holdup carried out by Germany against Haiti, but no one outside the country publicly complained.[69]

Sam's acquiescence, which contrasted sharply with Firmin's resolute stand against U.S. expansionism, seriously undermined his legitimacy in Haiti. Under pressure, he agreed to step down in May 1902, creating an opening for the activists who wanted to see a change in Haiti's political structure. Like earlier constitutions, the 1889 constitution stipulated that the elected National Assembly would name the president—a process many saw as a recipe for cronyism and corruption. An uprising in Port-au-Prince calling for direct presidential election led the National Assembly to disperse, and the country burst into political activity, with commissions gathering in the major towns to select organizers for nationwide balloting. It was an echo of 1843, when a new generation had thrown themselves into politics hoping to reform a broken system. Decades earlier, Firmin had belonged to the elitist Liberal Party; but after a few decades of public life, he had come to support a broad expansion of political rights, seeing it as a necessary foundation for reform. On his arrival in Port-au-Prince a few weeks after the end of Sam's term, he was greeted by several thousand supporters shouting "Long live Firmin!" He was, in fact, probably in a position where he could have easily gathered an army to establish himself as the new president. Some suggested he should, and some later regretted that he hadn't. But he was committed to gaining power without the use of force.[70]

Delegates from throughout the country converged on Port-au-Prince to decide how, exactly, the presidential election should be held. The debates were quite intense, and, it seems, haunted: at one point, a framed photograph of the departed President Sam suddenly detached itself from the wall and fell on the head of one of the delegates, Michel Oreste—who would himself serve a brief and ill-fated few months as president a decade later. The delegates settled on an American-style system in which voters throughout the country would select electors who pledged to vote for a certain candidate. All the citizens of Haiti who fulfilled the requirements set out in the constitution—who owned or rented land, practiced a profession, or could prove some kind of employment—were invited to sign up for the elections. Large numbers of people rushed to do so: some twelve thousand soon registered in Port-au-Prince alone. Firmin rapidly emerged as a favorite candidate, especially among young reformers. They even created an impromptu armed guard for him: each night, one of them later recalled, up to fifty "young enthusiasts" of Firmin camped out in the house where he was staying, ready to defend him if necessary. They were enthralled with the "magnetism" of their leader. In Le Cap, one young supporter went so far as to marry Firmin, in a sense: he changed his last name from Paret to Paret-Firmin.[71]

There were still some notable barriers to political participation, both legal (even the relatively broad suffrage rules excluded some men and all women) and cultural (the Kreyòl-speaking rural population remained on the margins of the political process). Nevertheless, the political mobilization inspired by Firmin represented a significant expansion of democratic participation. Firmin found broad support both in his native Le Cap and in towns throughout the country. Lawyers and teachers were firmly behind him; so was an association of artisans—masons, boat builders, tailors, shoemakers—calling itself the Société des Coeurs Unis. The voter registration offices were flooded with partisans of Firmin eager to take part in the election. It was clear that he had a significant lead over the other candidates.[72]

The problem for Firmin, however, was that the military structures in the country remained a major part of the political landscape. The officers who served as local governors still had tremendous influence in their districts, and they were concerned that Firmin's anticorruption initiatives and other political reforms might upend their stable role as power holders. As the campaign progressed, an elderly general named Nord Alexis began to mobilize the military to oppose Firmin. Alexis had been a fixture of political and military life in the north for decades: in 1867, he had led an insurrection against Salnave, and a seventeen-year-old Firmin had been among the armed citizens who repelled one of his attacks on Le Cap. Now the two men came into conflict again.[73]

Alexis mobilized his followers by declaring that Firmin was an elitist intellectual who would hand Haiti over to the whites. Firmin's supporters, meanwhile, accused Alexis of trafficking in registration cards and finding other ways to manipulate the election—a weighty charge, since the military commanders in Haitian towns were in charge of overseeing the election process there. These suspicions appear to have been well-founded. In June 1902, for example, Alexis sent a letter to one of the commanders in the north of Haiti. Enclosed in the letter, Alexis wrote, were "the names of some citizens that I have chosen to be elected as deputies" in the commander's area, and he hoped the commander would "do everything you can to have them elected." A generous reading of the message might see it as simply an endorsement of certain candidates. It's pretty clear, however, that Alexis was actually telling the military commander to make sure that these delegates ended up being chosen, legally or not.[74]

As the election approached, the political tensions boiled over into violence. In Le Cap, soldiers attacked a group of people waiting to register to vote in a neighborhood whose population largely supported Firmin. One man was killed and three seriously injured, while the town police stood by and did nothing. Then, on June 28, the day of the election itself, soldiers supporting Alexis came out in force, occupying the streets in Le Cap and frightening the population away from polling stations. Firmin's partisans decided to respond in kind, arming themselves and attacking the soldiers. Soon, in Le Cap and other parts of the country, a new civil war was under way.[75]

Firmin, who had always been committed to using only democratic and constitutional means, now found himself in a role he had always sought to avoid: that of a general. And in a military conflict, Alexis had the upper hand. Firmin was soon forced to flee Le Cap, and his house was looted. Jewels and furniture were taken, the building stripped down to its doorknobs and tiles, and the thing that Firmin probably treasured the most—his library—was ripped apart and scattered.[76]

Despite Alexis's efforts, Firmin actually won the majority of the votes in many places, and he garnered a significant majority in the electoral assembly. But once the fighting began, the vote counts no longer mattered. Haiti's next president would be chosen in the same way that the country's leaders had so often been determined: on the battlefields. As Alexis gathered his troops in Le Cap and other ports, Firmin blockaded those towns thanks to his control of an impressive warship named the *Crête-à-Pierrot*, after the fort where Dessalines had famously resisted a siege by the French in 1802. The ship was commanded by Hammerton Killick, one of Firmin's loyal supporters. In early September 1902, however, after the *Crête-à-Pierrot* stopped a German ship carrying a large shipment of weapons and ammunition to Le Cap, Alexis called on the German government to help him seize what he called a "pirate ship." A German warship pursued the *Crête-à-Pierrot*, and Killick, realizing his ship couldn't escape, ordered his sailors to evacuate and then blew it up—along with himself—to prevent the vessel from being captured by the enemy. The act was heroic, but it also largely ended Firmin's campaign. Alexis assumed the presidency in December, and Firmin ended up in exile in St. Thomas, without his books and with many regrets.[77]

The democratic political movement that Firmin and others had sought to build in Haiti was defeated, the new politics overtaken, once again, by the old. In 1908, after a few years in St. Thomas—and after the publication of his book praising the United States as a model and potential ally for Haiti—Firmin sought support from the United States for another attempt at wresting Haiti's presidency from Alexis. His requests were rebuffed. In fact, the ship carrying the weapons that Firmin's partisans were planning to use was intercepted by the United States, and in the end the new pro-Firmin movement was crushed before it got off the ground. Firmin spent the rest of his days in exile and died in St. Thomas in 1911.[78]

III

Throughout his life, Firmin had attacked European prejudice and defended his country's sovereignty from U.S. bullying. He had also thrown himself into several attempts to transform the political system in Haiti. But like an earlier generation of reformers, he was compelled to turn to military force, unable to circumvent the deeply rooted political practices of the country. Instead of bringing about a new political configuration, his efforts became just another piece of the ever-worsening crisis of the Haitian state.

Firmin knew that if Haiti could not end the cycle of political violence, the cost could be quite high. In 1904, the U.S. president had issued what became known as the Roosevelt Corollary to the long-standing Monroe Doctrine. While reiterating that the United States would not accept European intervention in the Americas, Theodore Roosevelt added that the United States itself might sometimes need to intervene if a country was incapable of guaranteeing its own political stability and was therefore vulnerable to foreign occupation. It was an interesting and cynical twist: the danger of foreign occupation might require foreign occupation. What it meant, worried Firmin, was that if Haiti were to fall prey to a "demeaning and incurable inner sickness" that made it weak and unstable, then "Uncle Sam would reach out his long arms, to prevent us from choosing the hands of another." A French journalist, Firmin noted, had recently forecast that Haiti would be annexed by the United States. "It is ineluctable and certain," the journalist had intoned, "that a few hundred thousand half-barbarian individuals, living in a land that could feed several million, have no right to resist its development by people more civilized than they are." The situation was summed up more ruefully in 1907 by a young Haitian intellectual named Dantès Bellegarde, who quipped—repeating a famous phrase attributed to Mexican president Porfirio Díaz about his own country—that "God is too far, and the United States is too close."[79]

Firmin tried to take solace in the idea that any effort to take over Haiti would inevitably fail. "There is no doubt that Haiti is ready to fight, to the last breath of the last citizen, to conserve its independence," he wrote. The history of the Haitian Revolution was "still there, still very fresh in our memories, nobly inspiring" and even "seductive," calling out to Haitians to relive it if necessary. Firmin imagined a doctor examining a Haitian confronted with a threat to national independence: he would hear, in his heart, a "fire that suddenly alights to either save everything or destroy everything." In the face of a common threat from outside, Firmin predicted, all the divisions and individual "egoism" in Haitian society would disappear: "We will resist still, the elderly showing the young how beautiful it is to bury oneself in the ruins of the nation rather than to survive its ruin." Haitians did not have to succumb to "unenlightened and sickly suspicion" about the designs of foreigners, but rather could feel confident that in the face of any threat, they would always find salvation in their capacity for "heroic fury."[80]

In his last days, however, Firmin sounded less certain. All he knew for sure was that, in one way or another, Haiti's unstable situation would not last. "After my death," he wrote with a mix of foreboding and hope, "one of two things will happen: either Haiti will fall under foreign control, or it will resolutely adopt the principles in the name of which I have always struggled . . . No people can live indefinitely under tyranny, injustice, ignorance, and misery."[81]

6

OCCUPATION

In December 1914, the USS *Machias* dropped anchor in the harbor of Port-au-Prince and a detachment of U.S. marines disembarked. They proceeded to carry out what can only be described as an international armed robbery. Entering the Banque Nationale d'Haïti, they removed from the vaults $500,000 worth of gold belonging to the Haitian government—the equivalent of $11 million today. Then, in broad daylight, they took the gold back to the harbor, loaded it onto their gunboat, and shipped it to New York. Louis Borno, the Haitian minister of foreign relations, denounced the seizure as a "criminal act," but no one—neither bank employees, state officials, nor Haitian soldiers and policemen—dared step in to stop it.[1]

The official justification for the raid was that the seized gold might be required to cover Haiti's debts to U.S. bankers. The Haitian government indeed owed large sums of money to banks in many countries, including the United States. In 1883 Haiti had at last paid off the "double debt" contracted with France in 1825— both the indemnity levied in return for recognition and all the loans it took out in order to cover that indemnity—but it had taken out many other loans in the intervening years. The Haitian government, however, had been assiduous in making all its debt payments as required. In fact, they were so committed to paying off their loans that they found themselves with little money to do anything else: by the 1914–15 budget year, a staggering 80 percent of all the money coming in through customs and taxes was being immediately spent on debt service. Given the situation, Haiti had little choice but to keep taking out yet more loans just to keep functioning. As this cycle continued, it was increasingly easy for foreign bankers to claim that there was a danger they would eventually not be repaid. That was the ultimate message of the *Machias* incident: the Haitian government, the United States had concluded, could no longer be trusted with its own money.[2]

The raid was the culmination of a process that, over the previous years, had placed Americans firmly in charge of Haiti's national bank. In 1909, at the urging of the State Department, two U.S. banks had purchased a majority stake in the institution from the French, and they soon established complete control over its operations. Roger Farnham, the vice president of the National City Bank in New York, took on the additional title of vice president for the Banque Nationale, and the French tricolor that had flown in front of the bank since its founding was soon replaced with the Stars and Stripes. In a way, the marines who landed in December 1914 simply carried out a transfer between the two institutions that Farnham managed.[3]

The shift in power came as the United States increasingly established itself as Haiti's main trading partner. In 1870, 46 percent of Haiti's imports came from France, and just under 40 percent from the United States. By 1905, however, France accounted for only about 10 percent and the United States for 71 percent of all the country's imports. As a French diplomat noted, many Haitians were alarmed by the change, seeing the Americans not just as foreign whites but as "those whites who had the most outrageous scorn for black people." These opponents of U.S. power urged the country to forge trade alliances instead with smaller European nations. ("What Haitians find seductive about Belgium," a Haitian official explained to a French minister in 1910, "is that they don't have an armed navy.") But most Haitians understood what Anténor Firmin had argued in his writings: the ultimate question was not whether Americans would dominate trade in the region—that, after a time, became a certainty—but how deeply the United States would come to control Haiti itself.[4]

The United States, for its part, was eager to solidify its grip on the Caribbean nation. Indeed, with Farnham in control, the Banque Nationale was at the center of a rather cynical plan: to bring on a financial emergency so that the United States would be called on to resolve it. A few months before the USS *Machias* carried out its raid, the U.S. ambassador in Haiti told the State Department that the Banque Nationale was considering ending all advances of funds to the Haitian government. When "confronted by such a crisis," he explained, Haiti would have no recourse but to "ask for the assistance of the United States in adjusting its financial tangle and American supervision of the customs houses would result." The United States had already taken over direct supervision of customs collection in the Dominican Republic, and on several occasions over the course of 1914 it proposed a similar arrangement to the Haitians. Under such an agreement, the entire financial system of Haiti would be directly in the hands of the United States, which would collect the government's receipts, pay off its debts, and oversee the entire budget.[5]

Haitian leaders, unsurprisingly, were not eager to sign off on such a blatant surrender of sovereignty. But they knew that thanks to its control of the bank, the United States was in a strong position to pressure the Haitian government to do its will. Solon Menos, the Haitian ambassador in Washington, D.C., warned his friend Louis Borno in early 1915 that "through a system of progressive strangulation" the United States aimed to force Haiti's government to "reach out for the chains." Any misstep, Menos wrote, would be used as a pretext by the United States to intervene. American troops had already taken the government's reserves from the Banque Nationale; it wouldn't take much for another detachment of marines to assume control of the customs houses.[6]

A few weeks later, Menos again wrote to Borno from Washington. He was alarmed by a small but telling detail about his interactions with the State Department: the U.S. officials were getting increasingly jovial and jokey with him. They mentioned the political violence in the country with what Menos felt was a certain undisguised glee. Secretary of State William Jennings Bryan informed him one day that rebels had taken the town of St. Marc and suggested once again that it was time for Haiti to accept the need for U.S. control. Menos understood what was happening, but he saw no way out. Neither did Borno. Indeed, like all of Haiti's political class, Borno would soon find himself part of a nation under occupation, its government taking orders from the United States Marines.[7]

III

The U.S. tradesmen who did business in Haiti throughout the nineteenth century were never as connected with Haitian communities as the merchants from Germany and other European countries, who often married into Haitian families to circumvent constitutional limitations on foreign ownership of property. But during the early years of the twentieth century, several U.S. companies did manage to make inroads into Haiti by gaining government contracts for agricultural and infrastructure projects. American corporations participated in the expansion of the wharf in Port-au-Prince and helped to establish the country's first electric company. Most important, they became involved with Haiti's nascent railroads.

In 1905, Haitian businessmen had created the Compagnie Nationale des Chemins de Fer d'Haïti—the National Railroad Company— with the goal of building a railway between Port-au-Prince and Le Cap. They hoped that the railroad line would integrate the agricultural regions of the country's north, northwest, and west, particularly the Artibonite Valley. The project ran out of money, however, and in 1910 a U.S. investor named James P. MacDonald acquired the company. Desperate to get the railroad constructed with foreign capital, the Haitian government granted him a series of major concessions. For fifty years, MacDonald was to have exclusive control of a twelve-mile-wide swath of land on either side of the railway line, where he proposed to create banana plantations. He also secured a monopoly on all future banana exports from the country. From the perspective of the Haitian government, the deal seemed like a remarkable opportunity to develop a new export, allowing Haiti to take advantage of the boom in banana consumption that was under way in North America.[8]

For the rural residents who lived in the region, however, the plan represented something very different: a profound threat to their carefully sustained and cherished autonomy. Generations of families and individuals had built their lives on the land granted to Mac-Donald, growing high-quality coffee, cultivating livestock, and harvesting acajou and other woods for export. Now, the same rich soil that made agriculture so productive in the area attracted the attention of foreign investors. MacDonald's project aimed to replace the local way of life with a new version of an old but still vividly remembered system: monoculture plantation production for export. There would be bananas rather than sugar, and wage workers instead of slaves, but the overall effect remained the same: if the plan succeeded, many Haitians would be transformed from independent farmers into field laborers toiling for a foreign master.[9]

The dispossession process began in earnest in 1911. Many peasants in the valley could not show legal title to the land on which they lived and were easily expelled. But even those who had titles were often dispossessed by the authorities who supported MacDonald's project. People were ejected from their homes without compensation, and their houses were razed or burned. Land prices in the region spiraled upward, so buying new land was nearly impossible for those who had lost theirs. Soon, desperate farmers began fighting back. With cries of "Down with MacDonald!" and "Down with the railroad!" they attacked the buildings of the U.S. company, destroying sawmills and lumberyards, smashing tools, and trying to intimidate Haitian workers into abandoning the construction sites.[10]

Popular anger created both a challenge and an opportunity for regional leaders. The situation could easily have led to intraregional conflicts between those deprived of land and those who still had it. Instead, however, local elites were largely able to channel the anger of the dispossessed into uprisings against the central authorities in Port-au-Prince. Military and political leaders in the north of the country declared that the poverty in the region was the result of its oppression by those in charge of the Haitian state, who were bowing too easily to U.S. influence. Gathering armies of followers anxious about losing land to outsiders, officers with presidential ambitions promised that once in power they would stop the dispossessions. Fueled by the peasants' fury and fears, the insurrections sweeping across Haiti grew in frequency and intensity. Rural armies became a constant presence in the countryside, foraging for food and looting properties. In some areas, rival bands burned houses in towns that had supported their enemies. As the unrest spread, the farmers in the afflicted regions paid the steepest price: many lost homes and crops to passing armies, women became victims of rape by marauding soldiers, and men were strong-armed into fighting and never returned.[11]

In Port-au-Prince, meanwhile, presidents followed each other in rapid succession. Some met with a violent end: Cincinnatus Leconte, who took over the presidency at the head of an insurrection in 1911, was sleeping in the National Palace less than a year later when a mysterious explosion ripped through the building, killing him and many of his followers. Other presidents, dogged by insurrections, resigned or fled into exile. Over the course of four years, from 1911 through early 1915, the Haitian presidency passed through the hands of seven different men, and the internal struggles left the government in shambles. Watching the disintegration of the Haitian state from Washington, President Wilson wrote to his secretary of state in April 1915 that "the time to act is now."[12]

The president of Haiti at the time of Wilson's message was Vilbrun Guillaume Sam, a son of the earlier president Tiresius Antoine Sam (whose abdication in 1902 had set the stage for the clash between Firmin and Nord Alexis). Like other Haitian leaders during this turbulent period, Vilbrun Sam found himself in a nearly impossible situation. With the Banque Nationale under American control and refusing to fund the government, the Haitian state was bankrupt. The pressure to make a deal with the United States was therefore constantly mounting. But there was also loud and passionate resistance to accommodating the United States in any form—a sentiment that was shared by many members of the Haitian parliament and the larger urban elite as well as by the rebel armies in the countryside.

Among the leaders of this anti-U.S. movement was Rosalvo Bobo, who had served in the cabinet of Vilbrun Sam's predecessor. Bobo was widely traveled and well educated, having studied in London and Paris and earned degrees in both medicine and law. He agreed that U.S. investment in Haiti was a necessary basis for economic advancement, but he vehemently opposed any surrender of control by his government to a foreign power. By July 1915, with strong support in the countryside and the capital, Bobo was on the verge of taking control of Port-au-Prince and overthrowing President Sam. Facing imminent defeat, Sam's military commander tried to cow the opposition with a gruesome act: he executed 167 political prisoners. Many of the victims were members of prominent Haitian families, and the city of Port-au-Prince erupted. Fearing for his life, Sam tried to take refuge in the French legation, but a crowd dragged him into the street and tore him to pieces.[13]

These bloody events provided the perfect pretext for a long-meditated U.S. intervention in the country. As Haitian historian Roger Gaillard puts it, the United States simply took preexisting plans for occupation out of a file drawer and, "having adjusted them to the circumstances, put them into application." Vivid depictions of Sam's death cemented the idea that Haiti was in desperate need of foreign control. Lost from the story, of course, was the way in which the pressures placed on Haiti by American banks and investors had pushed the country toward chaos in the first place. As

Gaillard notes, the United States had for several years helped to "ripen" political conflict in Haiti "according to its taste and its project." All that was left in 1915 was to pick the fruit.[14]

On the morning of July 28, 1915, the USS *Washington* steamed into the harbor of Port-au-Prince. Many Haitians recognized the ship, which had been extensively described by the local press, and they were well acquainted with its specifications—its tonnage, its 20 cannon, its complement of nearly 900 men. Some had seen the ship lurking in the harbor on previous occasions. This time, however, it had come to stay.[15]

▮▮▮

The U.S. occupation of Haiti was part of a broader sweep of American intervention in the Caribbean. In 1898 the United States had occupied Cuba and Puerto Rico, and soon thereafter it took over the construction of the Panama Canal, which was completed in 1914. These developments made the long-coveted Haitian port of Môle Saint-Nicolas even more important strategically for the U.S. Navy, which drew up a thorough plan for seizing it in case of a "military emergency." At the same time, with the outbreak of World War I, U.S. strategists became particularly concerned about the presence of Germans in the region. They knew that Haiti's powerful and well-established community of German merchants had occasionally bankrolled revolts in the country and had repeatedly called on their home government to back up their claims with gunboats. U.S. officials feared that it would not be too difficult for Germany to take another step and annex part of Haiti for use as a military base. Such concerns about German influence in the Caribbean helped justify U.S. involvement in Haiti and the Dominican Republic, as well as the U.S. purchase of the Danish West Indies in 1916.[16]

Fears of German expansion in the region turned out to be exaggerated: the German government does not seem to have had any plan to use its merchants to take control in Haiti. But in a time of looming war, such worries provided political ammunition for people who had a different reason to push for U.S. intervention in Haiti: businessmen interested in constructing plantations there. They found a receptive audience in the State Department, which had no in-house expertise in Haitian affairs and therefore turned to bankers and corporate leaders with experience in the country. In 1912, for instance, Secretary of State William Jennings Bryan summoned John H. Allen, then president of the Banque Nationale, to explain Haiti to him—though he doesn't seem to have learned very much. "Think of it!" Bryan exclaimed after the meeting. "Niggers speaking French!"[17]

One of those tapped for advice by the State Department was the railroad magnate James MacDonald, who told them that what Haiti really needed was employment. This, he argued, was something that could be provided only by outside investors constructing agricultural plantations in the country. Representatives from the United Fruit Company, a powerful player in Caribbean and Central American affairs, offered a similar perspective, informing the State Department that only an occupation by the United States could end the political conflict in Haiti and thereby open the way for business. To become a valuable economic satellite, like Cuba, Haiti was said to require massive corporate investment; such investment required political stability; and stability, U.S. officials concluded, could come only through a military occupation.[18]

One of the most persuasive and forceful advocates for intervention was Roger Farnham, the vice president of the National City Bank in New York and the Banque Nationale d'Haïti. As of 1913, Farnham also assumed the presidency of the National Railroad Company, which took over MacDonald's earlier railroad projects. As Farnham saw it, Haiti's problem was that an uncaring elite were oppressing and ignoring a poor population, which desperately needed U.S. assistance. He explained to Secretary of State Bryan that the political system in Haiti "constitutes a certain form of slavery for the masses, and no helping hand has been stretched out to the common people in an effort to improve their condition." In March 1915, Farnham warned that unless the U.S. government did something to tamp down the chaos in Haiti, American companies would no longer do business there. He urged Bryan to take control of Haiti's customs houses as a way of establishing a climate of financial stability conducive to economic development. Bryan was convinced, and helped convince President Wilson, who in any case had already decided that "the United States cannot consent to stand by and permit revolutionary conditions constantly to exist" in the Caribbean nation. Wilson did have a few misgivings after the fact: shortly after dispatching the marines to Haiti, he expressed concerns that the United States did not have "the legal authority to do what we apparently ought to do." But, he concluded, in the end there was "nothing for it but to take the bull by the horns and restore order."[19]

The strategic and economic arguments for the intervention were accompanied by a constant drumbeat of claims that Haitians were incapable of self-governance and needed to be saved from their own barbarism. The historian Hans Schmidt sums up the attitude: "The United States, as the self-appointed trustee of civilization in the Caribbean, was obligated to maintain minimal standards of decency and morality." For Haitians, of course, such claims rang rather false. As the Haitian intellectual Dantès Bellegarde would pointedly note in 1929, during the years of the occupation, lynching was commonplace throughout the American South. The butchery of World War I, meanwhile, represented a mass display of savagery that made the civil wars of Haiti look comparatively mild. And as a U.S. congressman later observed, the United States was also hardly a model when it came to political violence: like Haiti, it had seen three presidents assassinated since 1862, not to mention having had its own cataclysmic civil war.[20]

In 1915, though, U.S. critics of intervention were an isolated minority. Indeed, many in Washington were barely aware that it was happening: Wilson had ordered the marines to Haiti without consulting Congress. It would take several years before opposition to the occupation gathered steam in the United States. In the mean-time, U.S. plans went ahead with a clarity of purpose rooted in rac-ist certainty. As Secretary of State Robert Lansing, who replaced Bryan in 1915, explained in a letter: "The experience of Liberia and Haiti show [sic] that the African race are devoid of any capacity for political organization and lack genius for government. Unquestion-ably there is in them an inherent tendency to revert to savagery and to cast aside the shackles of civilization which are irksome to their physical nature."[21]

In July 1915, after the violent death of President Sam finally gave the U.S. government the pretext it had been waiting for, Lansing would effectively become the next ruler of Haiti. It was under his watchful eye that, as an article in *Time* magazine strikingly put it, the marines came ashore from their armored cruiser and "began forcibly soothing everybody."[22]

I I I

"It hurt. It stunk." So Private Faustin Wirkus, who later wrote a pop-ular account of his time in Haiti, described his first moments in the country. "We were not welcome. We could feel it as distinctly as we could smell the rot along the gutters." The Haitians lining the streets watched the marines with impassive expressions, taking stock of the new arrivals. "There was not a smile in sight. The opaque eyes in the black faces were not friendly. They seemed as indifferent as the lenses of cameras."[23]

The first marines to step off the USS *Washington*—330 of them—disembarked at Bizoton, to the south of Port-au-Prince, with orders to enter the capital and secure the port and commercial district. The marines were unsure what awaited them, but they were lucky: nei-ther the Haitian army nor the general population tried to fight back as they took control of the city. A man who saw the *Washington* arrive off the coast later recounted to the historian Roger Gaillard how he had watched boats carry the Americans ashore, "rifles in hand." "Everyone fled," he recalled. "Me too. You just had to see them, with their weapons, their swaggering and ostentatiously menacing attitude, to immediately understand both that they had come to hurt our country and that resistance was impossible." The next morning the man returned to the harbor, where he saw more troops disembarking. "I understood then that a new phase of our history was beginning. I could have nothing to do with these people." He fled to the woods, one among many who decided that if they couldn't fight they could at least disappear, becoming a new kind of maroons.[24]

As the marines filtered from Bizoton to central Port-au-Prince, gunshots echoed throughout the city. But they weren't directed at the intruders: gunfire was the traditional way of celebrating the arrival of a new president. Residents of the capital who were unaware of the U.S. invasion under way assumed that with the death of Vilbrun Sam, the popular Rosalvo Bobo would soon arrive and take over the National Palace. Two marines did die that night, one of them the nephew of the prominent labor leader Samuel Gompers, president of the American Federation of Labor; according to their captain, they were victims of "fanatics" who had fired on them from behind bushes and trees as they approached. In fact, though, as Haitian witnesses reported and the U.S. military later confirmed, the two marines were victims of friendly fire. Other U.S. troops, nervous in the dark, unfamiliar with the surroundings, had shot them by mistake. As for the Haitian army, there was one soldier, a young man named Joseph Pierre, who refused to either retreat or surrender when confronted by the marines. He was gunned down at his post, becoming a legendary martyr: the only one to stand up against the United States that night.[25]

In the next weeks, more U.S. troops arrived from the mainland and from the nearby base at Guantánamo Bay in Cuba. By late August, when a 300-strong artillery unit disembarked, there were two thousand American soldiers in the country. Having taken control of Port-au-Prince and Le Cap, they proceeded to occupy the other port towns. In each one, they seized the customs houses and began to disarm and disband the Haitian army units. Haitians had no way to get clear information about the precise intentions of the U.S. government, but it was clear that the marines were embarking on something much more extensive than just a simple operation to reestablish order and to protect U.S. interests after the unrest surrounding President Sam.[26]

Among those who watched the influx of marines were two young boys, part of the generation who would grow up under U.S. occupation. The poet Carl Brouard, who was thirteen at the time, later recalled how "melancholy widened our eyes" as he and his friends saw their country occupied. And the politician Roger Dorsinville, looking back on the arrival of the marines many decades later, remembered similar emotions. "I understood the newness of their presence by the stupefaction on the faces and the silence suddenly all around me," he wrote. Dorsinville watched the adults he knew sink into "stupor" and then "resignation." "The white soldiers had come to defile our independence: where were the ancestors? Finally the ancestors were no more."[27]

While much of the population watched and waited, unsure what was happening, Haiti's political leaders began trying to figure out a way to negotiate with the Americans. The historian Roger Gaillard summarizes their cautiously hopeful perspective: "'It's only a punitive expedition,' they thought. 'All in all, we probably deserved it. Now we just need to tread softly, demonstrate goodwill, promise not to do it again, and these gentlemen will leave.'"[28]

But who, precisely, was in charge of Haiti? Rosalvo Bobo, who commanded large armies throughout the country, was Sam's obvious successor, and a committee of prominent Haitians in Port-au-Prince was already preparing to name him the next president. But on August 6, Admiral William Caperton, the commander of the American forces in Haiti, had summoned Bobo to a meeting aboard a U.S. ship in the harbor of Port-au-Prince. The admiral's chief of staff, well aware that Bobo had opposed U.S. control over Haiti during the previous years, had informed him that Bobo was an "idealist and a dreamer" and "utterly unsuited to be Haiti's president." Caperton commanded Bobo to give up any intention of taking power by force and to disband his troops. If Bobo did so, Caperton said, the United States would allow him to become a candidate for president in a new election.[29]

Bobo agreed to the conditions, assuming that given his widespread popular support, he would not have trouble winning an election. Caperton, however, had other plans; he had already begun looking for an alternative candidate who would be more tractable in office. His first contact was J. N. Léger, a prominent political leader who had previously served as minister to the United States. But Léger refused to become a mere figurehead. "I am for Haiti, not for the United States," he declared. "Haiti's president will have to accept directions and orders from the United States and I propose to keep myself in a position where I will be able to defend Haiti's interests." Undeterred, Caperton approached another Haitian politician, Philippe Sudre Dartiguenave, who proved to be more pliable. As Caperton reported to Josephus Daniels, the secretary of the navy— who, along with Lansing, was overseeing Haitian policy—Dartiguenave understood that his country must accept all the conditions set by the United States, and he was willing to use his influence to make sure that others agreed.[30]

Having secured his candidate, Caperton went to work pressuring the National Assembly delegates to select Dartiguenave rather than Bobo. As an enticement, he declared that the U.S. military would stand behind those congressmen who worked with them, capturing and executing any rebels who attacked them. In a special session, the senators and deputies elected Dartiguenave with a large majority. His appointment was celebrated symbolically in August by a call-and-response cannonade between a U.S. gunship and a Haitian coastal battery. Many among the elite in fact welcomed the prospect of a bright new beginning after decades of turmoil, seeing the occupation as an opportunity to end Haiti's perpetual civil wars and pursue economic development. In mid-September, marine officers and Haitian political leaders came together for a cordial lunch at a prestigious club, the Cercle Bellevue.[31]

With Dartiguenave in power, the U.S. government rapidly proceeded to the next order of business: drafting a convention between the United States and Haiti that would establish an official basis for the marine presence in the country. The document they came up with had many familiar elements: the United States was to take control of Haitian customs houses and the state treasury, and the Haitian government was to promise not to cede or rent any portion of its territory to another foreign power. But the new proposal also included some additional stipulations. The marines were to create a new military structure that would replace the existing Haitian army. And the convention specified that appointments and nominations for all major Haitian state offices would be subject to approval by the president of the United States.[32]

Admiral Caperton wanted the convention to be signed as a treaty between two sovereign countries, legitimized by the approval of Haiti's president and both houses of the Haitian Congress. He knew that most Haitian politicians were already on the side of the Americans. Their opponents—though they included such prominent figures as Pauléus Sannon, the minister of foreign relations, who insisted that the proposal imposed too many conditions on Haiti—were a relatively small and isolated group. And as the negotiations began, Caperton sought to reassure any doubters. In an interview with a Haitian journalist on September 2, Caperton explained that the U.S. occupation was taking control of the customs houses only so that they could carry out their benevolent mission to "reestablish order, peace, and security for all in the country," and to provide employment to those who were "suffering." He wanted everyone to know that the United States had "the best of intentions for the good of Haiti" and had no plans to involve themselves in its long-term financial affairs. As soon as the "irregularities" that had been practiced under the previous regime were eliminated, Caperton declared, the Haitian government would once again have control of its treasury.[33]

The day after this interview, however, Haitians found posters on the walls of Port-au-Prince with a different kind of message from Caperton. The government of Haiti, the admiral announced, was facing "conditions it is incapable of controlling." Therefore, in order to "preserve fundamental human rights," Caperton was declaring martial law in Port-au-Prince and all the other areas currently under the control of the marines. The police of Port-au-Prince were placed under the direct supervision of a U.S. officer. The local commanders of the U.S. Marines would be dictating regulations as needed to assure order in the territory.[34]

As part of the new martial law regime, Caperton moved to muzzle the opposition press. On September 4, Haitian journalists and newspaper editors were summoned by a marine captain to a press conference. There they were told that "the situation of the press, under martial law, is exactly the same as in the United States," which meant that "there will be no attacks on freedom of the press." Nevertheless, the captain went on, the publication of "false or incendiary propaganda" attacking either the government of the United States or the government of Haiti was outlawed. The publication of "false, indecent or obscene" articles was also banned, as were "signed or unsigned" letters to the editor that might undermine public order. Anyone deemed guilty of violating these rules would be brought in front of a military tribunal and could face imprisonment. As Haitian journalists would soon find out, the U.S. officers were ready to enforce the new regime. Just a few weeks after the conference, the marines ordered a newspaper called *Haïti Intégrale* to be shut down and all its published copies to be impounded. When the editors refused, they were arrested, along with the newspaper's printer, by a detachment of marines, and were only able to avoid jail time by paying a fine to the Americans.[35]

Ernest Chauvet, editor in chief of the prominent newspaper *Le Nouvelliste*, was so taken aback by the actions of the marines that he traveled to Washington, hoping to speak to President Wilson directly. Chauvet had previously lived in the United States and was, as he wrote to Wilson, an "admirer" of the Americans. He had long worked to forge closer economic ties between the two countries, convinced that U.S. companies could help Haiti develop. "Above all," he explained to Wilson, "I was persuaded of the desire of the American people (and especially of its government) to act with fair play towards those with whom it has relationships." Because of this, Chauvet was convinced that the United States was making a terrible mistake in its approach to the occupation. If the United States had come, as it declared, to help "suffering humanity" in Haiti, then it had to "respect to the end" the desires of the people they wished to assist. Chauvet pleaded with Wilson not to impose the convention through force, warning that otherwise the occupation would end in bloodshed.[36]

As Chauvet waited in a hotel in Washington, however, he received no response. No one was listening. Even African American leaders denied his logic. Booker T. Washington, for example, published an article in which he celebrated the occupation of Haiti as the only way to civilize the blacks of that country. Likewise, W.E.B. Du Bois, whom Chauvet met in New York, told him that African Americans could do nothing for the Haitians, and that the current situation was beneficial for Haiti. Du Bois's only intervention was a letter to Wilson urging him to send black soldiers and officers to Haiti rather than white ones, in order not to irritate the population. As the Haitian ambassador in Washington wrote to a friend back home, there was little hope of changing U.S. policy. Nobody was going to take up the "disinterested defense of a weak people." As things stood, the ambassador concluded, "we must look only to ourselves to save the situation, and can count on no one else to break the spell."[37]

In Haiti, Pauléus Sannon, having similarly given up hope of reasoning with the United States, resigned from his position as the minister of foreign affairs. The proposed convention, he wrote, attacked the "national dignity" of his country, deeply undermining its sovereignty "to the profit of the United States." Even without the benefit of the convention, Sannon noted, the United States had already declared martial law. What would the Americans do once their power over Haiti was "consecrated" and they were free to invoke all the "exorbitant privileges" specified in the document? He could not in good conscience remain part of a government that had so easily surrendered its sovereignty to a foreign power.[38]

Sannon was replaced by Louis Borno, who had been the minister of foreign affairs during the *Machias* incident. A colleague later described Borno as someone who "sincerely believed that an American apprenticeship was necessary for our political and administrative education." The choice facing his country, as Borno saw it, was either to "disappear permanently into abjection, famine, and blood, or redeem itself with the help of the United States." He entered eagerly into the negotiations, and on September 16, after a few minor revisions, he signed the convention on behalf of President Dartiguenave. The agreement still had to be ratified by the Chamber of Deputies and the Senate, however, and Dartiguenave and the U.S. authorities put heavy pressure on the deputies to sign. They used a simple and effective technique: since the United States now controlled the treasury, they stopped paying the officials, making it clear that the money would start flowing again once the convention was signed. In early October, the Chamber of Deputies duly ratified the document, with only a small minority voting against. One despairing member, resigning in protest after the vote, described the convention as "moral slavery" and lambasted those around him who had just "re-forged" the chains that the Haitians had broken a century before.[39]

The Haitian Senate proved the toughest for Dartiguenave to convince. As the debate dragged on, everything seemed suspended in Port-au-Prince: in the words of one Haitian journalist, if you didn't want to deal with something, you just had to say that you would take care of it after the convention was signed. Then, after more than a month of discussion, the Senate committee examining the convention issued a report stating that the treaty was unconstitutional and could not be ratified. As the committee saw it, the proposed convention violated the constitution's first article, which proclaimed Haiti to be "one and indivisible, absolutely free, sovereign and independent." "There are sacred limits that the Haitian people cannot exceed," the report declared.[40]

Still, the bulk of Haiti's cultural and political elite disagreed with the senatorial committee. The popular singer August de Pradines, known as Candio, wrote a song ridiculing those politicians who "preferred the Cacos to the convention." The term "Caco"—which seems to have originally been derived from a small, fierce species of bird known in Kreyòl as the Taco—was used to describe the rural rebels who had carried out revolts during the previous years, and Candio's implication was clear. If the United States had occupied the country, it was only because Haitians had spent so much time fighting among themselves. Now there was nothing to do but to sign the convention, which would bring relief to an exhausted country. "The people will finally be able to breathe a little," Candio announced. "They are crushed. They are hungry." He spoke for many who believed that the politicians should have done something to save Haiti before the Americans came; now there was no point in complaining. "What?" one lawyer demanded in a newspaper editorial. "You are facing a military regime, the territory is occupied, and you have the naiveté to talk about sovereignty and the constitution?"[41]

On November 11, just a few days after its committee's report, the Senate voted to ratify the convention by a vote of 26 to 10. President Dartiguenave hailed the accord as "the most important event in our national history" and the "consecration of a new era." It would be, he proclaimed, the "foundation of national independence." Dessalines, presumably, turned over in his grave.[42]

The convention formally declared the Haitian government incapable of addressing its financial and military challenges and gave the United States sweeping power over the country's institutions. It created two innocuously named but tremendously powerful positions, receiver general and financial counselor, which would officially be filled by the Haitian president but with all the candidates nominated by the American president. The agreement also created a new military and police force, the Gendarmerie, to be run by U.S. officers appointed in the same way.

At the heart of the convention was a blinding paradox. The treaty presented the United States as the defender of Haiti's sovereignty, yet at the same moment that this sovereignty was confirmed it was almost entirely eviscerated. The convention prohibited the Haitian government from signing a treaty with any foreign power that would diminish the country's independence. But the document in which these words were included had itself reduced that independence to virtually nothing.[43]

III

As the central government in Port-au-Prince lurched toward an agreement with the Americans, the regional officers and soldiers of the Haitian army observed the proceedings with wariness and dismay. The country's culture, after all, had long emphasized the danger that whites might one day come back and try to gain control. Now the army watched in disbelief as their government allowed precisely that to happen. Faced with acquiescence on the part of the politicians, and exhausted from several years of intense internal conflict, most soldiers grudgingly accepted that they had little choice but to subordinate themselves to the arriving marines. For many, however, it was a devastating experience. One officer in Dondon later recalled that, when he told his troops that they would soon have U.S. marines as their officers, his men cried "tears of powerlessness." A corporal threw down his gun, proclaiming that he would rather die than be commanded by foreign whites.[44]

A few Haitian officers did try to take a more active stand against the United States. One of them was Charlemagne Péralte, the ranking commander in the town of Léogâne, an important hub south of Port-au-Prince. In mid-August, when a marine officer came to announce that the town was to be occupied, Péralte refused to hand it over without an official order from the Haitian president. Though a detachment of marines had already arrived by train from Port-au-Prince, Péralte told them to stay in the train station and had his soldiers surround the station so they wouldn't leave. Even with a U.S. warship hovering off the nearby coast, Péralte insisted that he was still in command and kept the Haitian flag flying over Léogâne headquarters.[45]

Péralte's refusal to hand over the town to the marines was courageous but mostly symbolic. President Dartiguenave soon fired him and replaced him with a more tractable officer, and Péralte packed up his belongings and went home. But he continued to wear his Haitian army uniform and, according to one account, ordered his soldiers to bury their guns before the U.S. marines could confiscate them. "You all accept working with the Americans," he chided his fellow soldiers. "I never will." As one of his friends later recalled, Péralte announced before he left: "I will not stay under the domination of the whites. You'll hear news of me."[46]

In mid-September 1915, another Haitian officer, Benoît Rameau, tried to drive the marines out of the town of Gonaïves. Rameau, once a domestic servant, had risen through the ranks of the army thanks to his support of regional insurrections in the previous decades, and he saw the arriving forces as a threat to his own position and his town. When the marines first arrived, Rameau wrote to the U.S. consul in Port-au-Prince explaining that he had no wish to fight the American troops but could not accept their control over his town. "For almost 112 years, we have been a free and independent people. Our sweat and our courage gave us our independence. In that time, we have never been governed by a head of state chosen by a foreign power." Receiving no response to his letter, Rameau decided to communicate instead by force of arms. He sent out a proclamation calling on all Haitians to join together and resist the intruders who had come "to re-establish slavery."[47]

A detachment of marines attacked Rameau's followers, and the disparity in weaponry between the two groups became strikingly clear. Over the next few weeks, Rameau's troops were repeatedly routed, and he was eventually captured and imprisoned. But this defeat did not end the fighting. Indeed, as the U.S. occupation became more firmly entrenched, the tradition of the Cacos—rebels in the countryside rising up against the central government in Port-au-Prince—became adapted, quite smoothly, into guerrilla resistance against the American forces. Near the town of Grande-Rivière-du-Nord, for example, the officer Josaphat Jean-Joseph set up a camp in the mountains and called on local soldiers to join him in repelling the invaders. They must remember Dessalines, Jean-Joseph wrote, "who, in giving us our country, had not given us the right to give it to the whites."[48]

Such opposition from the Cacos did not come as a complete surprise to the marines being shipped out to Haitian towns: they had been warned that Haitians might be "inclined to resist" U.S. attempts to restore order in the country. Aside from that warning, though, the preparation given to the American troops was remarkably limited. Before his departure, Private Faustin Wirkus learned only that there was "something going on in Haiti . . . which required the 'Marines to land, and take the situation in hand.'" The marines had a lot of questions, "but none of us could seem to get any idea as to where this Haiti place was . . . Somebody said Haiti was a land of black people—'just like Africa.'" The commanding officers, for their part, had rushed to libraries to find about the Black Republic, where they probably encountered the popular writings of racist observers such as Spenser St. John. One marine recalled that the officers taught them that Haitians were "devotees of Voodooism and past masters in the art of poisoning their enemies." Private Wirkus eventually learned from his superiors that a Haitian president had been overthrown and killed by a mob; he was also informed that President Sam had been a "brute throwback to his jungle ancestry."[49]

All of the marines were white, and they brought to the "land of black people" their own experiences and expectations from the racially segregated United States. Some historians have argued that there was a specific and purposeful policy of dispatching to Haiti marines from the American South, with the assumption that they would be particularly effective at controlling a black population. While there is no proof of such a policy, many of the marines were indeed southerners. One of the highest-ranking commanders in the early part of the occupation, for example, was Colonel Littleton W. T. Waller, who had led a bloody campaign in the Philippines in 1901. Waller was a Virginian, the descendant of a prominent family of slave owners; in fact, some of his ancestors had been killed in an 1831 rebellion led by Nat Turner, who was partly inspired by the example of the Haitian Revolution. Waller saw a continuity between what was needed to maintain order—that is, white supremacy—in the United States and in Haiti. "I know the nigger and how to handle him," he wrote. He reacted in disbelief at one point to the idea that the U.S. marines in Haiti might serve under the command of the country's president: "Did you ever hear of anything so fantastic in your life?" He was also wary about the notion of developing a Haitian gendarmerie, remarking that "you can never trust a nigger with a gun."[50]

Meanwhile, as Faustin Wirkus fired at Cacos who had taken refuge at the base of a cliff, he thought back to an amusement park game he'd played as a child, called "hit the nigger and get a cigar." He also recalled the orders he had received from his superiors: "Any Negro or any dark person out of doors after nine o'clock, whose behavior makes him seem like a sympathizer with the Caco rebels, is to be shot on sight by the patrol, if he does not surrender." But how, precisely, were those who were to be "shot on sight" to surrender? And what did it mean to "seem like" a Caco sympathizer? Years later, an odd pair of photographs published in a book by a writer sympathetic to the occupation suggested that for many U.S. observers, rural farmers were indistinguishable from Cacos. The photo on the left showed a bearded elderly man in ragged clothes and a hat. The caption read simply "A Peasant." On the right was the same man, now with a bag and a raised machete. The caption read "A Caco."[51]

As marines faced continued resistance from bands under the leadership of men like Josaphat Jean-Joseph, they enacted harsh reprisals. Entering the village of Bertol, for example, marine officer Chandler Campbell found the residents waving white flags from their houses. He questioned the local women about Caco activity, and he told them that "if in the future a single shot is fired" by rebels in the area, the marines would "return and burn all their houses and completely destroy their crops." This was not an idle threat. As his troops moved on to another town in early November 1915, Campbell recorded in his journal that his unit had gone "eastward burning all shacks in that direction." The next day's entry is "burned all shacks along route," and a week later "burned many shacks." What Campbell described as "shacks" were peasant homes, many occupied for generations. Sometimes the reprisals went further, targeting not only houses but entire villages. Catholic priests in the village of Dupity later recalled how, after a few shots were fired at marines from the heights near the town, they set fire to the whole area. "The chapel went up like the rest. Everything fell prey to the flames: chapel, presbytery, vestments, organ."[52]

In some towns, the marines were welcomed. The Cacos fighting against them, after all, were often the same bands who had been active in a given region over the previous years, attacking local farms, robbing women on the way to town, and looting shops for supplies. Many Haitians were tired of war. One merchant wrote in strong support of the U.S. troops, declaring that it was necessary for them to attack the Cacos and "massacre them to the last." When marines arrived in the town of Pignon, an officer recorded, they were greeted as "liberators" and told by local leaders that they were "freeing the Haitians from slavery." The words may have been heartfelt, or simply strategic: in the new order, the marines controlled the salaries of local employees, so the officer in charge of any particular town became "the paymaster for the loyal Haitians." And some U.S. commanders did make an effort to win over hearts and minds in rural Haiti by explaining what they saw as their mission. At Fort Liberté, for instance, marine officer Adolph Miller "sent for natives & held audience." Miller told them about the "American Idea in Haiti," which included using revenues from the customs houses to "employ several thousand natives to clean and pave the streets, put in sewers, a water supply system," and even an "electric light plant." "We will pay the natives daily so that they can accumulate a little money and get the wrinkles out of their belleys [sic]," he promised. In addition, Miller said, the marines would also provide villagers with protection, for they would "not stand for the [Haitian] Generals confiscating their farms, stealing their cattle," and "enforcing them into the army." Once the Haitians saw that the United States offered jobs, infrastructure, and security, he predicted, "they will be for us."[53]

But despite such reassurances, resistance to the occupation was widespread enough in the north of the country that the marines were forced to mount a coordinated campaign there against the rebels. The task was given to an experienced officer named Smedley Darlington Butler. A Quaker from Philadelphia who apparently saw no contradiction between his faith and a military career, Butler had previously fought in several campaigns, including the occupation of the Philippines and the repression of the Boxer Rebellion in China. Like many other officers, he carried strong racist attitudes to Haiti. He understood the Cacos to be "bad niggers, as we would call them at home," and described their leaders as "shaved apes, absolutely no intelligence whatsoever, just plain low nigger." He spoke of his Haitian domestic servant, Antoine, as an "ape man" and a "faithful slave." But he found the country exhilarating: "Oh the wildness of it all, the half-clothed, vicious natives, the wonderful scenery and fine clean air, there is no country like it that I have ever seen." And he had faith in the righteousness of his mission. "We were all embued [sic] with the fact that we were trustees of a huge estate that belonged to minors," Butler later said, "that the Haitians were our wards and that we were endeavoring to make for them a rich and productive property, to be turned over to them at such a time as our government saw fit." Still, he saw those Haitians who resisted the occupation less as children than as animals, and felt that he knew better than his higher-ups what was necessary to win against the Cacos. He derided the high-ranking U.S. military men, products of "a million dollar war college," who were "endeavoring to defeat an ignorant, treacherous crowd of niggers by 'constructive' warfare"—that is, through a combination of combat and negotiation with the enemy. Butler, by contrast, was an adherent of the "old-fashioned school" of war, which "believes the way to end a row with a savage monkey is to first go into the region or territory occupied by that monkey and find out how savage he is. If the monkey attacks you, return the compliment but only to a degree necessary to impress him with the danger he runs by repeating his attacks."[54]

The Cacos who confronted Butler's forces sought to draw on Haitian military traditions that stretched back to the slave insurrection of 1791. Like Haiti's original rebels, they avoided open and direct engagements with the superior firepower of their opponents, opting instead for guerrilla warfare. "The technique of the Cacos," one of them later recalled, was "to never stay more than twenty minutes on the battlefield once the outcome had been decided." They attacked suddenly, by surprise, then rapidly retreated into the hills to prepare for another engagement. Even their most successful raids usually involved occupying towns only long enough to seize guns from the local garrisons and take money and food to support themselves. Such guerrilla techniques had worked to startling effect in the eighteenth century, and the Cacos drew inspiration from the memory of those victories. In 1915, however, the dynamics were quite different. The marines had arrived as a modern army with the newest rifles and machine guns, while the outnumbered Cacos were primarily operating with the relatively antiquated weaponry of Haiti's regional conflicts: pikes, machetes, and a few old rifles. (These limited weapons partly explain why Haiti's constant civil wars seem to have produced far fewer casualties than the U.S. Civil War or European conflicts of the period.) Indeed, the last Haitian leaders to put substantial money into the defense infrastructure of the country were Dessalines and Christophe. And it was to their crumbling, century-old forts that the Cacos fled as they found themselves increasingly surrounded by the marines.[55]

In early November 1915, a few hundred Cacos under the command of Josaphat Jean-Joseph took refuge in Fort Rivière, not far from Christophe's Citadel. The rebels realized they were probably making a last stand, and they sent their families—who traditionally traveled with them—back home before preparing for a siege. But under the command of Butler, marines crawled through a small tunnel that led into the center of the fort, taking the Cacos by surprise. Other marines scaled the walls surrounding the fort and began firing from above with machine guns. Soon it was all over. In the wake of the battle, the marines burned sixty houses in the area surrounding the fort and then dynamited the structure. The corpses of the Cacos were still inside, so the ruins became a tomb, long seen by local inhabitants as a sacred and haunted place.[56]

The attack on Fort Rivière was widely celebrated in the U.S. press, especially because the victory was gained without a single marine casualty, and Butler and another officer received the Congressional Medal of Honor. In a 1917 visit to Haiti, Franklin Delano Roosevelt, then assistant secretary of the navy, accompanied Butler on a tour of the site. In the wake of the Cacos' defeat, Roosevelt was optimistic about the possibility of U.S. investment in Haiti. On the way to the fort, the group stopped at the ruins of Sans-Souci palace, which Roosevelt imagined could be an attractive place for American tourists to visit before they headed up to Fort Rivière to enjoy the "cool nights" there. At the fort itself, Butler narrated the battle for Roosevelt and declared that he and his troops had killed at least two hundred Cacos. He later included a swashbuckling and self-congratulatory account of the campaign in his memoir, which was published in 1933. In the book, Butler claimed that among the dead Cacos was the leader Josaphat Jean-Joseph, whom he described derisively as decked out in looted jewelry, including a gold watch chain.[57]

Haitian accounts of the event tell a different story. They describe fifty Cacos killed during the fighting, with perhaps the same number escaping and disappearing into the nearby hills. Indeed, while the battle at Fort Rivière represented a decisive victory for the marines, convincing the remaining Cacos to disband, few of them disarmed. As one man later recalled, the Cacos who had escaped from Fort Rivière went home, greased up their guns, wrapped them in palm leaves, and hid them in their attics, keeping the weapons ready for another day. And Jean-Joseph had not been killed. He escaped the fort and went to the Dominican Republic for a time, then returned to Haiti when he heard that U.S. troops had arrested his wife and his mother. Imprisoned for seven years, Jean-Joseph was released in 1922. In 1934, the year after the publication of Butler's memoir describing his gold-bedecked corpse, Jean-Joseph was living in Le Cap and working as a mason.[58]

III

Back in Washington, reading reports of the Haitian campaign, Secretary of the Navy Josephus Daniels was both pleased and a little alarmed. "Department appreciates excellent work done and gallantry displayed," he telegraphed to Admiral Caperton. But "in view of the heavy losses to Haitians in recent engagements," Daniels asked that the "offensive be suspended in order to prevent further loss of life." The war, he realized, could easily come to look like a massacre. Caperton replied reassuringly that most Haitians supported the marines and that the fighting had been "purely of defensive character," aimed at the "suppression of revolutionary activity against present Government and military intimidation of people, and for protection of life and property of innocent farmers and tradesmen, who form by far [the] majority population in these districts." The Cacos, he added, were "bandits pure and simple, owing no allegiance to the Government or any political faction, but organized under petty chiefs for sole purpose of stirring up strife against [the] Government and robbing, pillaging, and murdering innocent people." Caperton argued that the marines were not so much at war as simply protecting the Haitian population from bandits. Eventually, the U.S. Marines even issued an official order regarding terminology, instructing soldiers to stop using the term "Cacos" and to replace it with "Bandits" in all official correspondence. They were also to try to get the Haitians to follow suit, apparently: the order explained how the word "bandits" should be pronounced in French and in Kreyòl.[59]

The fact that the Caco resistance had often been led by officers from the Haitian army reinforced the determination of occupation authorities to disband that army and replace it with a different kind of order-keeping organization, a centralized one overseen by marine officers. In early 1916, they announced that all Haitian military officers would be removed from their positions. The new Gendarmerie, as provided for by the U.S.-Haiti convention, would have Haitian soldiers but American commanders. Smedley Darlington Butler, fresh from his successful campaign against the Cacos, was placed in charge of training the new units, and he eagerly took on the task of civilizing those he called "my little chocolate soldiers." "I am beginning to like the little fellows," he wrote as he worked with the new recruits. He styled himself a defender of the mass of rural Haitians, whom he described as the repressed, shoeless class, "the most kindly, generous, hospitable, pleasure-loving people" he had ever met. They were only dangerous, Butler said, when the elites, the one percent of the population who wore shoes, stirred them up with "liquor and voodoo stuff." Then they were "capable of the most horrid atrocities: they are cannibals." Still, Butler was convinced that his work would help create "a real and happy nation out of this blood crazed Garden of Eden."[60]

The Gendarmerie largely proved to be an effective tool in the war against the Cacos, and it also became the main institution for policing throughout the country. Butler recruited junior officers for the Gendarmerie from among career marines, inviting them to remain in Haiti as long as they wished, which allowed some to develop close ties to the Haitian soldiers they worked with. A young marine named Lewis Puller later recalled being particularly impressed by the drilling of the gendarmes, which he said made the cadets at Virginia Military Institute look "like amateurs," and by the commanding demeanor of their Haitian sergeant major. He found the gendarmes to be committed and dependable allies in the campaigns they participated in.[61]

An attempt to construct a viable coast guard for Haiti, however, met with a set of failures that read like a parable of early-twentieth-century Haitian history. One boat, *La République*, went up in flames in 1917 after a fire was accidentally started by a U.S. sailor; the next year, a ship called *Le Progrès* foundered on a reef. The ship *L'Indépendance* exploded in the harbor at Guantánamo Bay in 1922. The only vessel to survive the experiment, the ship *Haïti*, did so because it was sold in 1920.[62]

With the Haitian army officers who had served as regional governors removed from their posts, the U.S. marines essentially became colonial administrators. Each town and rural district was now overseen by a marine officer leading units of Haitian gendarmes, and these officers took over most of the tasks that had once been in the hands of the Haitian commanders, from tax collection to public works projects and judicial affairs. These marines exercised near-absolute power, but they did so with almost no knowledge or understanding of local conditions. Few spoke either of the languages of Haiti. When the U.S. Senate conducted an inquiry into the occupation in 1922, the chairman of the inquiry confided to the secretary of state that he was "amazed" to find that "not a single officer" in either the Navy or the Marine Corps in Haiti "spoke French with perfect accent and fluency." In time, some officers and soldiers did learn

Kreyòl, with a few becoming quite proficient in the language. But misunderstandings between marine officers and the populations under their control represented a continuing source of tension.[63]

Like colonial administrators elsewhere, marine officers depended heavily on the collaboration of Haitians in local communities. In addition to the Haitian soldiers whom they trained and deployed to battle Cacos, the marines also cultivated a network of spies. Paid in cash based on what they reported, these informants worked independently, finding out where Caco groups were camped and then leading marines to them, or infiltrating the ranks of the rebels as double agents. More broadly, the marines sought to make spies out of all the Haitians: they commanded that anyone who saw Cacos passing their farms or villages had to go immediately to the nearest Gendarmerie post and report what they had seen. Anyone who didn't do so would be suspected of sympathy with the rebels: their houses, and in some cases an entire village, could be burned as punishment. In time, the marines began issuing certificates of good conduct to locals who proved helpful, providing them with documents that they could show to occupation forces when they were stopped. But such enticements were counterbalanced by a harsh judicial system in which residents could be arrested for many crimes. The marines began strictly enforcing regulations against the practice of Vodou, for instance, jailing many *oungans* and *manbos* (priests and priestesses) during the occupation simply for conducting religious rituals. The punishment for cursing the U.S. occupiers, meanwhile, was nine months in prison.[64]

In larger towns the marines operated under the scrutiny of local town councils and judges, who sometimes complained to the authorities in Port-au-Prince about abuses, though rarely to much effect. In more isolated rural districts, however, marine officers had broad leeway in how they governed, and indeed acted with broad impunity. Faustin Wirkus, perhaps inspired by a reading of Joseph Conrad's *Heart of Darkness*, described three Americans in one outpost who looked "unlike any marines, officers or men, I had ever seen . . . Their eyes were sunken in their heads. They had bedraggled, untrimmed whiskers; their uniforms hung about them, slack and creaseless." One of them, Wirkus wrote, had developed a particular hobby: on a pole in front of the garrison, he stacked the "native hats" of all the local rebels he had killed. Some marine officers broke down completely: one in Les Cayes, for instance, was relieved of duty after randomly killing a local resident; he later committed suicide by jumping out a porthole of the ship taking him home. In fact, as the military itself later admitted, officers frequently abused their power, executing captured rebels or prisoners without trial and in some cases killing residents of the towns they commanded for refusing to provide information about the Cacos, or for no clear reason at all.[65]

Women were particularly vulnerable to abuse by the marines who controlled their communities. A Methodist Episcopal pastor working in Haiti who reported on the occupation for the Chicago *Defender* accused the marines of widespread rape, including the rape of young girls. He had also observed, he wrote, marines pressuring the Haitian gendarmes under their command "to procure native women for the use of the whites as concubines." Haitian women were said to be universally immoral and promiscuous; after just a day in the country, one soldier had confidently asserted that "all native women are of easy virtue and all its accompanying vices." Such attitudes helped justify and normalize coercive sexual relationships. Looking back on the occupation, one marine later wrote that "rape, I believe, implies a lack of consent. I never heard of a case where consent was lacking in Haiti's black belt." When it came to longer-term relationships with Haitian women, marines sometimes talked about such liaisons as being strategically useful—a mechanism for learning about the local culture—and occasionally referred to sexual partners as the "sleeping dictionary."[66]

The historian Roger Gaillard, who gathered oral testimony from many Haitians about the occupation, heard from a number of residents in Haiti's central plateau about one particularly sadistic local commander, Dorcas Lee William, whom they referred to by the

Kreyòl name Ouiliyanm. One story described how Ouiliyanm had humiliated the family of a local Haitian general by riding his horse into their house, having it shit on the floor, and then ordering the general's daughter to clean it up in front of him. A man remembered how Ouiliyanm used to walk into the local market and stare at people; if he determined they "looked Caco"—"based on clues only he knew"—he would beat them up. Two market woman died from the beatings they received from him. Another resident recalled how his sister-in-law had died at Ouiliyanm's hands. The marine commander had encountered her on a path outside the town and demanded that she tell him where the Cacos were hiding. When she replied that she didn't know, he shot her on the spot.[67]

Gaillard also heard about how Ouiliyanm once hung two brothers he suspected of being Cacos from a tree and lit a large fire under them, killing one and leaving the other burned all over his body. And in yet another incident, Ouiliyanm reportedly carried an elderly notary from the town to his police station in front of several witnesses, beat him nearly unconscious, then buried him alive in the courtyard. These stories were gathered by Gaillard in the early 1980s, and they might have been refracted through the more recent forms of terror that Haitians had experienced under the Duvalier dictatorship. Indeed, they were so dramatic that Gaillard himself wondered if they were all true. But he was deeply impressed by the way that, more than six decades later, Ouiliyamn's "terrifying shadow" still haunted the towns where he had ruled.[68]

When such abuses came to light, some high-ranking marines blamed them on Haitians and their culture. Questioned by the U.S. Senate about executions carried out under his command, for instance, Lieutenant Colonel Alexander S. Williams cited Haitian history to provide a justification. "For the unauthorized killing of prisoners," he declared, "there is an uninterrupted series of precedents running back to that established by the Cacique Coanabo in 1492." Coanabo was a chieftain ruling in the area where Columbus arrived that year, and he seems to have killed the Spaniards whom

Columbus had left behind to create a small settlement on the island. Similarly, Williams argued that Haitian soldiers recruited into the Gendarmerie brought callous brutality with them. "Our greatest problem in the organization of the Gendarmerie was the gendarme," Williams explained. The recruits were "utterly indifferent to the value of human life," he said; they were "prone to make the most of police authority, and very liable to exceed it." In fact, Williams told the Senate, it was the United States that had worked to civilize the gendarmes, to limit the brutality of the Haitians by punishing those who overstepped their bounds.[69]

Several years later, U.S. Marine Brigadier General Ivan W. Miller also claimed that any violence during the occupation had been made necessary by the culture of Haiti. "You have to remember that what we consider brutality among people in the United States is different from what they considered brutality," Miller explained. "Those people, particularly at the time there, their idea of brutality was entirely different from ours. They had no conception of kindness or helping people." John Russell, the high commissioner of the U.S. occupation for most of its duration, concurred, writing in 1929 that the "Haitian mentality only recognizes force, and appeal to reason and logic is unthinkable." Such arguments were apparently persuasive: even when military reports and a Senate inquiry turned up evidence of a wide range of abuses by marines, the perpetrators were almost never punished.[70]

These convenient justifications for the violence that U.S. soldiers perpetrated on Haitians ignored the ways in which structural changes brought about by the occupation facilitated the abuse. The Haitian army officers who had commanded Haiti's towns and rural districts throughout the nineteenth century had exercised tremendous power and could easily have acted as local despots; but the dispersed nature of the Haitian state had forced them to cultivate support among local populations. The lack of a powerful central government, and the frequency of insurrection, had provided villagers with opportunities to get rid of commanders who overstepped their bounds. That changed dramatically during the occupation, for the new Gendarmerie units had the firm support of the entire U.S. military command. The marine officers who commanded the gendarmes reported directly to their superiors in Port-au-Prince, and the local populations largely lost the mechanisms through which they had held the military leaders accountable. The change was a key part of a larger transformation in twentieth-century Haiti: what had been a highly regionalized economic and political order became firmly, and effectively, centralized. The authority of governors and merchants who had depended on the economies of local ports faded, superseded by the power that emanated from Port-au-Prince. The capital, whose influence had previously been counterbalanced by that of other towns and regions, increasingly became the exclusive center of economic and political activity, and in time a magnet for migrants from throughout the country.[71]

The Gendarmerie established by the marines was one of the few institutions created during occupation that actually outlasted it. Renamed the Garde d'Haïti in 1928, it became a powerful political force, the basis for a centralized military that would continue to shape Haitian life long after the Americans departed. But at its root, the Gendarmerie was an army created with one overarching goal: to crush internal resistance to the U.S. occupation. "It received its baptism of fire in combat against its countrymen," writes the Haitian scholar Michel-Rolph Trouillot; and the Gendarmerie, like the new Haitian army that emerged from it after the occupation, "indeed never fought anyone *but* Haitians."[72]

III

The first major task carried out by the Gendarmerie confirmed what many Haitians had long asserted: if white outsiders got control of the country, they would turn the people back into slaves. Within a year of the arrival of the marines, Haitian men found themselves taken from their homes, sometimes tied together in coffles, and put to forced labor.

It was all quite logical to the occupation authorities. Haiti needed new roads: it had become clear over the course of 1915 that one of the main problems in fighting Cacos was the difficulty of accessing the rugged terrain in which they operated. Better roads would allow the marines to move troops more quickly to combat zones. Such roads, of course, could also help improve the circulation of goods within the country, helping Haitian farmers to transport agricultural products to market and encouraging outside investment. But where to get the labor for this massive task? Haitian law provided an answer: the corvée. Article 54 of the 1864 Code Rural, which remained in effect in Haiti, allowed the government to conscript men as laborers on public works projects. These laws had not been enforced since Boyer's time, but they were still on the books.

In August 1916, invoking the corvée regulations, U.S. marines began using rural residents as road-building crews. On paper, the corvée was presented as a relatively humane institution. The men were to be paid, fed, and only made to work in the vicinity of their homes. Many in the U.S. administration considered it an effective and appropriate way of supplying labor needs for the development of infrastructure in the country. When Roosevelt traveled to the north of Haiti in early 1917, he encountered a group of corvée laborers who appeared quite happy to see the American visitors. Indeed, the hundred or so "natives" even presented a short performance, singing and dancing in honor of the august guests from the United States. Of course, the vision of the corvée as a harmless and even salutary arrangement was partly due to the Americans' assumptions about the place of blacks in their own society. On his trip to Haiti, Roosevelt was accompanied by John A. McIlhenny, a friend from New Orleans. At one luncheon that the Americans attended with President Dartiguenave and members of his cabinet, McIlhenny found himself unable to eat, staring intently at the Haitian

minister of agriculture seated across from him. "I couldn't help saying to myself that that man would have brought $1,500 at auc-
tion in New Orleans in 1860 for stud purposes," McIlhenny later
admitted.[73]

Among the marines who oversaw the system, a few did have misgivings. Colonel Waller, the Virginian who openly expressed racist
views about Haitians, said that he personally disliked the use of corvée labor. As he testified at the U.S. Senate a few years later, it did
not seem to be "the proper way or the economical way of getting
the work done," and it also struck him as "rather un-American." But
the orders were coming from above, so Waller followed them and
"made no effort to have it stopped." When Haitian officials tried to
resist the corvée, meanwhile, they had little success. In 1917, a Haitian town council objected to the use of local residents, but the
marines arrested the mayor and forced him, under armed guard, to
round up the workers. After being released, the mayor traveled to
Port-au-Prince to complain about the actions of the marines, but
to no avail.[74]

The corvée as it was actually practiced involved tremendous
abuse, which echoed the historical horrors of colonial slavery.
Dantès Bellegarde, who served as minister of agriculture in 1918
and energetically denounced the corvée, declared that it reminded
him of the "terrible epoch of the colony" of Saint-Domingue. Laborers who tried to escape from what Bellegarde called "concentration
camps" were frequently shot. Questioned about such shootings by
the U.S. Senate in 1921, an officer admitted that they did occur,
though he declared that the total number of laborers who died this
way was only "a hundred or less." A Baptist missionary who had
witnessed the corvée testified that he saw numerous bodies around
the construction sites of laborers he believed had been executed by
gendarmes. He estimated that more Haitians had "met their deaths
through the corvée thus illegally practiced" than "were killed in open
conflict with the Cacos."[75]

The "recruitment" of laborers was deeply traumatic for local residents. Sometimes it was done through brute force: a Haitian man testified in the Senate that one day in 1917 a "white man" and several others had come to his house to claim his son for the corvée. They struck the boy on the head and, as he was bleeding, dragged him away. The man never saw his son again. At other times, marines delegated the task of gathering laborers to the Haitian gendarmes, though this hardly improved the procedure. As one Haitian recalled, the U.S. soldiers would simply order, "bring me men," and "had no interest in how the orders were carried out." A victim of the corvée system described how the gendarmes came to his house early one morning and told him that he was under arrest. He was taken out to the road, where a group of other men were already tied up together, and added to the convoy. He was never told why he was arrested, because there was no reason, except that men were needed to build the roads. The Baptist missionary who testified in the Senate in 1921 declared that had seen many Haitians, including preachers and parishioners from his church, "roped tightly and cruelly together, and driven like slaves."[76]

Many men fled into the woods to avoid capture, making it increasingly difficult for the gendarmes to find laborers. One Haitian man, a local administrator at the time of the occupation, later recalled how a group of gendarmes took advantage of a wake to collect workers. Hearing the sound of singing, they stormed in, finding a group of men and women dressing a body for burial. They held their guns on the assembled party, tied up the men—including the carpenters who were building the coffin—and carried them away. The women, left behind, buried the corpse directly in the dirt.[77]

Though most corvée laborers worked building roads, they were also put to other tasks. One man recounted watching a marine overseeing the work of prisoners who were picking up dung in the streets of Hinche, an inland town along the border with the Dominican Republic. "It was his manner that struck me," the man recalled.

Riding a mule, the marine poked the prisoners with a stick, and prodded his mule to walk so close to them that its hooves tore their skin as they worked. The men cried out, cowed by the threats of the marine, while the townspeople had little choice but to look on, "terrified." Other marine officers were noted for their own forms of sadistic treatment. One of Roger Gaillard's interviewees claimed that he had watched an officer delivering the meager salaries of the workers through a form of highly choreographed torture. The officer lined up the laborers, placed their money on the ground a few steps in front of them, and stood there with a large attack dog. As the workers stepped forward to get their money, he let the dog lunge forward to growl and bite at them. Gaillard also heard accounts of recalcitrant workers being punished with a treatment that came to be known as the *baton-lamnò*, the baton of death. A marine would take the hat off a worker, throw it on the ground, and order him to pick it up. As the man did so, the marine would strike him forcefully on the back of the neck.[78]

In Hinche, the local commander targeted a particular neighborhood on the outskirts of town that he believed harbored "bandits" from the surrounding countryside. He put the neighborhood's residents to work constructing a new garrison for the Gendarmerie. They were neither paid nor fed. "Were those men prisoners?" a U.S. senator later asked a marine involved in overseeing the construction in Hinche. "They were not prisoners, but they were kept in a compound there," he responded. "Were they detained in the compound against their will?" the senator asked again. The marine's reply was equivocal. "They had no other place to sleep, probably . . . They were detained in the town. They were not allowed to leave the town."[79]

From the Haitian perspective, the situation was much less ambiguous. When Gaillard asked one man why he used the term "slavery" to describe the corvée, he answered succinctly: "One: the work isn't paid. Two: you worked with your back in the sun, wearing nothing but pants. Three: they only sent you home when you were sick.

Four: You didn't eat enough, just corn and beans. Five: You slept in a prison or at the construction site. Six: When you tried to run away, they killed you. Isn't that slavery?"[80]

Some Haitians decided that if the corvée was a new form of slavery, it deserved the same response given by their ancestors: revolt. The marines, who had turned to the corvée partly because they'd hoped that new roads would solidify their military control over Haiti, eventually found that they had in fact incited a new round of war through their use of the practice. In October 1917, a group of armed men stormed into Hinche, planning to attack the commanding U.S. officer in the town and free the prisoners held there. They were soon beaten back by the marines and gendarmes, but the local commander suspected that they had not acted on their own. He ordered the arrest of several prominent men in the town he thought were behind the attack, including members of the family of Charlemagne Péralte—the Haitian officer who had refused to let American troops into Léogâne. Péralte's home was burned and his brother's residence pillaged by gendarmes, with the furniture, art, silver, and porcelain carried off to furnish the houses of the marines. The looting was seared into the memory of Péralte's niece, who six decades later could still recite the precise inventory of what was taken, including her mother's jewelry and a treasured phonograph. Péralte and his brother, meanwhile, were sent to Le Cap, where they were convicted of having supported the attack on Hinche and condemned to forced labor. Charlemagne Péralte, former commanding officer in the Haitian army, began spending his days in a prisoner's uniform, sweeping the streets of Le Cap.[81]

III

"Haiti is a beautiful country," U.S. Admiral Caperton told a Haitian journalist in February 1916. "She can be proud of her ancestors who destroyed slavery and conquered a glorious independence." Caperton effused that there were many Haitians whom he was "happy and proud to count as friends." "The peasant class is docile, amiable and naturally happy," he went on. All that was needed for the country to flourish was for Haitians to create a "good government" for themselves. Once that was done, Caperton imagined, there would be "many more beautiful fields of sugarcane, vast plantations growing coffee, cotton, and fruit, and everywhere a happy, satisfied population." With "peace and order" spreading throughout Haiti, the government could "build schools everywhere in the magnificent land, so that all Haitians can elevate themselves mentally." This would lead to a flourishing of culture, an era of "great engineers, poets, artists." In the end, "everyone will be able to exercise their talents; everyone will be proud of being Haitian, and will thank God."[82]

But while the U.S. occupation authorities proclaimed that their only goal was "good government" for Haiti, they also wanted to make sure that the Haitian government was compatible with American economic interests and friendly to foreign investment. The 1916 convention, by giving the United States control over customs revenues and the state budget and establishing the Gendarmerie as a new police force, had already gone partway to fulfilling that desire. But Haiti's constitution still contained a provision that U.S. politicians, bankers, and corporate leaders saw as a barrier to their plans: the ban on foreign ownership of property. Erasing this ban would be no simple matter. Back in 1867, a Haitian writer had called it the "Holy Grail" of the country's liberty, and the provision was still tremendously popular half a century later.[83]

The U.S. authorities, and President Dartiguenave, were astute enough to realize they would face serious opposition if they tried to simply amend the constitution to allow foreign property ownership—especially in the Senate, which had been so reluctant to ratify the 1915 convention. So Dartiguenave tried to outmaneuver the opposition by dissolving the Senate and creating an assembly from the more tractable Chamber of Deputies. When senators protested the move, continuing to hold meetings (which were broken up by U.S.

troops), the president took a gamble, calling for elections in January 1917. Dartiguenave hoped to secure a more supportive set of deputies, but the move backfired. A group of charismatic leaders who opposed the occupation swept the first round of balloting, winning a majority in the Chamber of Deputies and putting themselves on track to gain a majority in the Senate as well.[84]

The opposition to Dartiguenave became even more intense after he made a controversial deal with U.S. authorities. The 1916 convention had given total control of Haiti's financial affairs to the U.S. for a period of ten years. But now the U.S. government told Dartiguenave that this time frame was too short. American bankers were willing to give Haiti a loan of $30 million (the equivalent of roughly $500 million today), but they needed reassurance that the money would be paid back responsibly. In order to provide that guarantee, the U.S. needed to extend its financial control for another decade, through 1934. Sténio Vincent, Haiti's interior minister, vociferously resisted the proposal, but Dartiguenave signed the agreement. In disgust, Vincent resigned from the government, joined the opposition, and campaigned successfully for a seat in the Senate. Suddenly, Dartiguenave found himself in a precarious position: the election had given him a Senate and a Chamber of Deputies firmly in the hands of antioccupation activists, among them a defector from his own cabinet.[85]

The activists were confident that they were now in a position to protect the constitutional ban on foreign land ownership, which they saw as an essential element of Haitian sovereignty. They underestimated the determination of the U.S. authorities, however. After the elections, as discussions about a new constitution began, the Americans informed Dartiguenave that if the Haitian parliament did not agree to remove the ban on foreign land ownership, he was to dissolve the legislature. If he refused, he would also be replaced, and a direct military government—similar to that which had been put in place in the Dominican Republic—would be installed in Haiti. Aware of the threat, the deputies worked furiously to wrap up a new constitution, with the ban preserved, and vote it into effect. But not quickly enough: the U.S. authorities in Haiti were determined to prevent the constitution under consideration from being enacted. Selected for the task, Smedley Darlington Butler marched troops into the legislature and, at gunpoint, ordered the deputies to disperse. He also seized all the papers of the constitutional commission in order to leave behind no trace of their work. Dartiguenave justified the action by declaring that the deputies had refused to "offer foreign capital the guarantees it deserves," and therefore had "stood in the way of the realization of the work of regeneration being carried out in concert by the two governments" of the United States and Haiti. Butler himself, though, later looked back on what he had done in Haiti (and elsewhere) with a more jaundiced eye. He described himself as having been little more than a "racketeer, a gangster for capitalism," a "high-class muscle man for big business," who had "made Haiti and Cuba a decent place for the National City Bank boys to collect revenues in."[86]

Deprived of its parliament, Haiti now found itself without any obvious path forward for putting a new constitution into place. The United States proposed an innovative solution, one for which there was no existing provision in Haitian law: in consultation with Washington, occupation authorities would draft a new document and then submit it directly for the approval of the population through a national referendum. Dartiguenave celebrated the idea, arguing that the foreign ownership ban did nothing for small farmers but only benefited large Haitian landowners who enjoyed a monopoly in some parts of the country. A referendum, he said, would finally sideline the politicians who "talked about sovereignty" merely as a way of "enriching themselves from the sweat of the workers." Now, the populace would have a chance to speak directly. "The sovereign power is you, the people. You are the nation," Dartiguenave declared. A State Department memo later made clear that from Washington's perspective, the advantage of the plebiscite was that it would skirt opposition from elected representatives while providing a pretense of democracy. "The people casting ballots would be 97% illiterate, ignorant of what they were voting for," the memo explained, and could certainly be pressured into casting their ballots as desired.[87]

Indeed, the United States took no chances with the election. Vocal opponents of the new constitution were arrested before the vote. Throughout the country, the referendum took place under the watchful eyes of U.S. marines backed up by Haitian gendarmes. As voters lined up at polls on June 12, 1918, they were offered a white ballot that signified a "yes" vote in favor of the new constitution, which they then dropped into the ballot box. Those who wanted to vote "no" had to request a different ballot. The result? 98,294 "yes" votes to 769 votes against. The proceedings were clearly a sham, involving no more than 5 percent of the population, but even those who tried to abstain faced reprisals: six leading professors at a medical school were fired when they refused to participate in the voting.[88]

The new constitution enacted by this process was largely a copy of the previous ones, but it made the key change to the ownership regulations. "Foreign residents" as well as "foreign companies" now had full rights to the ownership of property in Haiti. It had taken a military occupation, a dissolution of parliament, and a manipulated referendum, but American corporations had finally secured the clause they desired. Over the coming years, they would use it to transform Haiti's economic landscape.[89]

The 1918 constitution also included sections that sought to pre-emptively protect the occupation regime from accusations that the United States seemed to know would be coming. The document provided for the automatic "ratification of all the acts of the U.S. government during its military occupation of Haiti." It also declared that all Haitians who served under the authority of the occupation were exempt from any future legal action, civil or criminal. And while the new constitution nominally maintained the bicameral legislature, it also allowed the Haitian president or the U.S. government to defer legislative elections at will. Indeed, for the next twelve years the occupation authorities would refuse to hold any elections to replace the dissolved legislature. As a result, President Dartiguenave and his successor served with essentially no limits on their power except those imposed by the United States itself. In effect, the occupation propelled Haiti's political system backward by a century, returning the Haitian government to the days of 1806, when there had been no parliament at all.[90]

I I I

On September 3, 1918, Charlemagne Péralte escaped from forced labor in Le Cap. He had at least one accomplice: his Haitian prison guard fled the city with him. Péralte made his way back to his home town of Hinche, traveling—according to one account—disguised as a woman on a Vodou pilgrimage, singing religious songs and telling anyone who asked that he was going up into the hills to carry out a *ranvwaye nanm*, or "sending the spirit," a ritual for a recently departed family member. Setting up camp outside Hinche, he began to make contacts with friends and family, to gather guns, and to collect bullets and powder, which he stored in calabashes. Ever since the defeat of the Cacos at Fort Rivière in 1915, military resistance to the occupation had been sporadic and poorly organized. Péralte now set about creating a new movement, an insurrection aimed at ending the occupation's abuses once and for all by pushing the United States out of Haiti altogether.[91]

The first order of business was to seek out recruits. One man later recalled how Péralte came to visit his father, explaining that he was going to "fight a war against the Americans" and looking approvingly over the weapons the man had hidden in the house, including a Remington rifle and a .48 caliber pistol. Another Haitian remembered that his father, Dolciné Pierre, once hosted the rebel and two companions on his farm. The group sat together for a long time, and Pierre joyfully shook hands with them when they left. He then explained to his family that "a serious civil war was about to begin, a revolutionary war." Pierre, who had maintained his position as the local chief of the rural district where he lived, had told Péralte that he couldn't join the rebels himself. But he promised to help them get food and other supplies.[92]

Not everyone was ready to support Péralte. The man with the Remington and the .48 pistol, for instance, took his family away from the area rather than get involved in the war. And a trusted friend of Péralte, the godfather to one of his sons, met with him one day—the two talked at length under an avocado tree in a cane field—and then warned the local marine commander of Péralte's presence. (The officer didn't seem particularly concerned, replying: "Let him come, and he'll see who he has to deal with!") But there was one group that was particularly ripe for recruitment: the corvée laborers. In an isolated area near the village of Pignon, Péralte presented himself to a large group of workers building a road; he called on them to join him in revolt, and three hundred men followed him into the hills. Later, he located a house where corvée laborers were locked up at night by the marines and broke open the doors. "I'm fighting for liberty," he announced, inviting those who wished to "fight and die with me."[93]

By the fifteenth of October, Péralte was ready for his first attack, storming the town of Hinche with about a hundred soldiers. But the engagement ended poorly for Péralte's forces, who lost as many as thirty-five dead without inflicting much damage on the marines. And it came at a steep personal cost for Péralte himself: three of his brothers were in prison in Hinche, and in the days after the attack, all three were killed by their guards, who claimed they had been trying to escape. But none of that deterred him from his path. Péralte's October raid marked the beginning of a new Caco war, one that would soon outstrip the previous conflict in both the size of the revolt and the brutality used to suppress it.[94]

The fact that this new uprising began in a town in the northern part of Haiti was not mere happenstance. Colonel Clark H. Wells, the marine commander in charge of the region, was a particularly ruthless officer, whose methods for controlling the local population alarmed even his superiors. By the time that Péralte started gathering supporters for his uprising, for instance, the occupation authorities—responding to the urging of Haitian politicians and some marines—had already declared an end to the practice of the corvée. But it was only a limited abolition: corvée workers could still be used if there was a "real urgency" or a lack of funds for a given project. Taking advantage of the loophole, Wells continued to promote the use of forced labor in many areas under his command.[95]

Several months after the corvée officially ended, Albertus Catlin, who took over as high commissioner of the U.S. occupation in December 1918, encountered a large group of laborers outside the northern town of Maïssade. When he asked all those who were there involuntarily to cross to one side of the road, only three men stayed put. Major Richard Hooker, who was dispatched by Catlin on an investigative tour of the region, found similar cases. Outside Hinche he saw a group of 150 peasant laborers who were being paid only a tiny wage and carefully guarded, in what Hooker dubbed a "camouflage corvée." In Maïssade, meanwhile, he discovered that the local magistrate, in collaboration with the marine commanders, was using the corvée system to put fifty forcibly conscripted men to work on his own property.[96]

Hooker also found that other abuses abounded. He had to intervene in Hinche to stop a marine from hitting a market woman who had supposedly overcharged him for tobacco. In the town's prison, he saw three gendarmes beating a prisoner. And when he talked to Wells, the colonel told him quite unself-consciously that under his command "bandits" were simply "bumped off," with no trial or report of their execution. Hooker was so surprised that at first he thought the officer was joking, but Wells was completely in earnest.[97]

The execution of captured Cacos without a trial was in fact the standard practice in the area. "The orders down there were: the prisons are filled; we don't want any more prisoners," recalled Lewis Puller, the same young marine who had been so impressed with the drilling of the Haitian gendarmes. After a year in Haiti, Puller admitted in a letter to a friend that the tactics they were using could easily be seen as criminal. "You may rest assured that I was relieved when I found out that I had been ordered to Port-au-Prince to be decorated for killing Cacos," he wrote, "and not to be court-martialed for the same." Though he derided the occasional "misguided fool" in the United States who might "set up a howl over a few black bandits being knocked off," Puller also urged his friend to stay put at home. "You don't want to come down here . . . It's a dog's life." The NAACP magazine the *Crisis* published a terrifying photograph of one such summary execution. In it, a captured Caco, his hands severed, is about to be shot by a U.S. marine holding a pistol to his head. On the ground nearby is a previous victim.[98]

As they had in 1915, marines sometimes burned entire villages they considered friendly to the Cacos. A Catholic priest from the town of Thomazeau testified in the Senate that after a group of retreating Cacos stopped in his town, a Gendarmerie unit decided to punish the local population. They looted the houses, took the residents' horses, then burned down several hundred homes, along with the chapel that stood among them. For the next months, the homeless townspeople camped in the nearby woods, ready to flee at the first sight of the gendarmes. When the U.S. officer who commanded the detachment returned to the area two weeks later, the priest confronted him. The marine insisted that the town had given shelter to Cacos, though he admitted that he should have interrogated the inhabitants before burning their houses. He apologized only for having destroyed the chapel, saying he hadn't realized that the modest structure was a house of worship.[99]

A few observers in Haiti at the time also wrote descriptions of the occupation's abuses. In March 1919, the French vice-consul in Haiti produced a hair-raising summary of recent reports of violence. A marine officer in St. Marc had beaten a seventy-five-year-old woman, a relative of the former town mayor, unconscious in the street and then had his dog attack her. The same officer had imprisoned a local official and tortured him by burning much of his body with a hot iron, seeking a confession about a theft, and had executed four teenagers for minor thefts they had committed. Another officer had gunned down a woman because she refused to give him information about the location of Cacos. In the prison at Le Cap, 10 percent of the prisoners, on average, were dying. "With such approaches to 'civilization,'" the vice-consul wrote, "it is not surprising that the people are exasperated and the peasants would rather die fighting than submit to the caprices of such individuals." With a measure of hope, the vice-consul concluded by saying that the cabinet in Washington must not be aware of the situation, otherwise they would surely be acting to correct it.[100]

The Haitian government publicly denied the importance of the new Caco uprising, attributing it to the ambition of a few embittered leaders who hadn't understood that the "time of revolutions is over" and to "ignorant peasants" who followed such leaders into battle. But some politicians realized that the situation was veering out of control. Louis Borno, the minister of foreign relations, suggested in a letter to a Catholic bishop that what was needed was a "general amnesty" for the Cacos, most of whom had been "propelled into revolt by the abuses caused by the occupation." It was a generous thought, but also perhaps a naïve one, for Péralte's movement—unlike the earlier Caco resistance—was not only protesting the terms of U.S. rule and the overbearing behavior of the marines. Rather, its clear political and military goal was to rid Haiti of the occupation entirely. "The worst of it," wrote Charles Moravia, Haiti's ambassador in Washington, to Secretary of State Robert Lansing, "is that as it develops this movement of brigands is acquiring the character of a struggle for liberty."[101]

Moravia, who at the beginning of the occupation had celebrated the United States as "the enemy of Sovereign Despotism," laid out a devastating summary of the occupation's problems: the imposition of martial law, the privileging of U.S. officials over qualified Haitians in bureaucratic appointments, the daily brutality suffered by rural populations at the hands of gendarmes. Many in Haiti, he insisted, wished to collaborate with the U.S. forces in order to bring peace and progress to the country. But that desire didn't compensate for the "deprivation of certain liberties guaranteed by the constitution" and the "bad treatment to which they are constantly exposed." Like the French vice-consul, Moravia retained confidence in the best intentions of the United States, which he described as the "honored champion of Civilization, defender of the rights of Humanity." He was confident that, having established the fundamental right to the "pursuit of happiness" in its constitution, the United States was bound to help others exercise that same right. But to do that in Haiti, Moravia wrote, they would need to gain an understanding of the "true needs of the people, its mentality," and find ways to pursue improvement without "unnecessary violence."[102]

Moravia's examination highlighted the increasingly difficult situation faced by the Haitian leaders. In many cases, they had welcomed the U.S. occupation, seeing it as a necessary step to resolving the country's profound problems. But they now found themselves unable to defend their population from the brutality of the U.S. regime. The Caco rebels had stepped into the breach, presenting themselves as the true defenders of Haiti and its people, the rightful heirs to the ancestors who had won freedom from slavery.

Catlin, the high commissioner of the occupation, was well aware that the resistance movement was steadily growing. The Cacos were not only active in the northeast, where Péralte operated, but also in the Artibonite region, where rebel troops under the command of Benoît Batraville attacked and killed a marine officer in March 1919. Catlin requested—and received—reinforcements from Guantánamo Bay, and he budgeted money for building more roads in the regions where Péralte's Cacos were strongest. But while they publicly exuded confidence that there would be no trouble defeating the Cacos militarily, some U.S. officials were clearly worried. General Alexander S. Williams, the head of the Gendarmerie, moved his residence from the outskirts of Port-au-Prince into the more heavily guarded center of town. Meanwhile, fights between U.S. soldiers and young Haitian men were regularly breaking out in the capital's streets. And in August 1919, the city's residents were infuriated when a deaf-mute teenage boy, leaving his house to tell his relatives about the death of his father, was shot and killed by marines for breaking the curfew.[103]

One night Port-au-Prince was papered with bold posters: "For the last four years, the Occupation has constantly insulted us. Each morning brings some new offense." President Wilson, the posters declared, was a "traitor, brigand, trouble-maker, and thief." Invoking Dessalines and the Haitian Declaration of Independence, the posters announced that a new day, "like that of January 1804," would soon arrive. Haitians needed to "follow the example of Belgium," which had resisted German occupation during World War I by flooding a part of the country and preserving a tiny sovereign territory. In a similar way, Haitians were to take to the mountains to defend their nation from barbarous invaders. The revolt that was already under way in the north would soon spread to the south. "There is no danger. We have weapons. Let us chase away these savage men," the poster exhorted. "Long live independence! . . . Long live just war! Down with the Americans!"[104]

III

With the new Caco movement spreading over much of the country and mobilizing many more insurgents than the resistance of 1915, Péralte allowed different groups of Cacos to operate autonomously to a certain extent. His leadership, though, provided an important measure of coordination and communication. The U.S. authorities grudgingly acknowledged his considerable political skills: one report described him as "a born organizer." A well-educated man, Péralte articulated the political goals of the movement in letters directed to the French and British ambassadors. He also provided a rallying

point for the dispersed Cacos, a visible alternative to being ruled by
U.S. forces and their Haitian collaborators. He sometimes dressed in
a well-tailored black suit and black shoes, with a white panama hat
atop his head. "They were the clothes and the bearing of a head of
state," one of the Cacos later recalled. Péralte was often greeted by
his troops with the presidential hymn of Haiti, and he dubbed himself "General in Chief of the Revolution." Through such symbolism,
Péralte presented himself and his comrades-in-arms as Haiti's rightful, legitimate government.[105]

Those who joined the movement were mostly farmers, some prosperous and some less so, animated by anger over forced labor and
other abuses carried out by the marines. In some ways the revolt
resembled Acaau's 1844 uprising in the south, and like the Piquet
movement, it loaded its demand for institutional change with spiritual overtones. When preparing for a fight, the rebels would often
carry out religious ceremonies. A Haitian gendarme who survived a
Caco raid on his town recalled hearing singing and the sound of a
Vodou drum before the attack. "We realized immediately that it was
a charge, and that there was only one thing to do: retreat." Many of
the Cacos wore red scarves as an homage to Ogou, the god of war in
Haitian Vodou. Péralte, a practicing Catholic, would go into battle
carrying the Haitian flag mounted on a pike that was decorated at
the top with a crucifix.[106]

In open combat with marines, the Cacos were decisively out-
matched, and most encounters ended in defeat and retreat. But the
Cacos nevertheless survived and successfully harassed the U.S.
forces for nearly two years. Marines and gendarmes frequently
found themselves confused by Caco tactics, and on several occasions ended up killing one another during firefights. Terrifying stories circulated among the marines about what happened to those
who were captured by the Cacos, including rumors that they were
flayed alive, had their hearts ripped out, and were cannibalized; the
rebels probably encouraged and sustained such fears. The Cacos set
up camps in high, inaccessible locations and were able to repeatedly

outwit and escape marine missions sent against them. At one point in 1919, marines and gendarmes closed in on one of Péralte's camps, where the Cacos were clearly outnumbered and outgunned. But before they could break into the camp, the attackers saw Péralte and his men appear above them on horseback, having escaped via an unseen path. In another incident, the marines surrounded a camp constructed by Péralte near the border with the Dominican Republic. After four hours of fighting, Péralte and all his men escaped across a river and fled into the Dominican Republic, unmolested by Dominican border guards who had watched the battle unfold. Although the United States was then occupying the Dominican Republic as well and controlled its army, the Americans clearly had little control over the border region. In fact, in a few cases the Cacos formed alliances with groups of Dominican insurgents who were also fighting the U.S. marines, joining in combat against a common enemy.[107]

Haitians fought on both sides of the conflict. "The gendarmes," one Haitian newspaper pointed out, "are the sons, brothers, and cousins of the Cacos." In many engagements, family and friends faced off against one another. Péralte, for his part, actively tried to recruit members of the Gendarmerie. In a 1919 letter to the Gendarmerie office at Maïssade, he addressed himself to "Haitians, sons of the fatherland of Pétion and Dessalines," proclaiming: "you are black, my brothers, and I love you all." He urged them to attack Maïssade and join his revolution. If they did, they would have the "joy" of knowing that they were "defending a just cause." Such efforts had at least some effect: after one attack, in the town of Saut-d'Eau, a gendarme noted that many of the Cacos were wearing Gendarmerie uniforms. In addition, the fear of desertion by gendarmes ultimately sapped their usefulness for the U.S. marines. When a new marine lieutenant arrived to take over the Gendarmerie in July 1919, he discovered that his "predecessors had discouraged target practice on the theory that it was dangerous to teach the native how to shoot."[108]

Péralte's efforts to recruit converts to his cause, however, were

undermined by the Cacos' techniques for obtaining food and supplies. The term "bandits," which the marines and Haitian politicians
preferred to use for the resistance, was not entirely inaccurate: the
Cacos often pillaged houses and farms, sometimes using violence to
get what they needed. One man recounted to Roger Gaillard how
his grandfather, a local farmer, was tied up and struck on the head
by a group of Cacos who came and looted his house and took his
cow. Others claimed that Cacos perpetrated numerous rapes in
some areas and even trafficked in captive women. Some victims of
the pillaging complained to Péralte, assuming that their assailants
were renegades and would be punished by their leader. But Péralte
seems to have tacitly accepted the looting, or was simply unable to
control those operating under his loose command. It is difficult to
say whether such abuses of power were widespread or simply aberrations, though it's clear that over time some farmers and merchants
who had supported the Cacos ultimately turned against them. Still,
one man who recounted stories of pillaging by the rebels also added
that it is crucial to remember that "the abuses of the Cacos were
born of other abuses. They were caused by the abuses of the Occupation." A Haitian bishop interviewed by Gaillard likewise argued
that the Cacos had little choice. "They were both pillagers and
patriots," he declared, and most people were glad that someone was
standing up for Haiti. "They rose up to defend the country: their
intentions were good."[109]

Besides perpetually looking for soldiers, Péralte also understood
that, like the Haitian revolutionaries he hoped to emulate, he needed
allies outside Haiti if he was to succeed. In June 1919, he sent a letter
to the British consul in Port-au-Prince asking for assistance. Calling
on the "humanity" of the consul and on his "great nation that is the
master of the universe," Péralte—drawing on the internationalist language of the time propounded by none other than President Wilson—
argued that it was incumbent upon the powerful to give support to "a
small nation that is trying to save its flag and its territory from the
ambitions of a greedy nation." He declared that he was leading forty

thousand men, "fighting valiantly and with help only from Providence," and pleaded with the British government to at least investigate the abuses perpetrated by the United States. He had been struggling for nine months for a just cause, Péralte lamented, but no other nation was paying attention. In "a time of enlightenment and progress," with people "everywhere preaching justice," Haiti's plight was being forgotten. Soon afterward, Péralte sent a similar message to the French minister in Haiti. This letter, signed by him and a hundred supporters, proclaimed that the Haitian people had suffered four years of "perpetual vexations, unbelievable crimes, assassination, theft, and acts of barbarism" that the United States was carefully covering up. Now their movement was demanding the rights that had been trampled by "Americans without scruples." Neither of these missives got any response: the diplomats simply forwarded them to the U.S. authorities.[110]

Even without outside support, however, the Caco movement was strong enough that the U.S. military decided to deploy a nascent technique against them: aerial bombardment. They brought several planes into the country, set up an aviation station at Gonaïves, and requested a shipment of five hundred bombs. On August 13, 1919, the first mission was carried out, with ground troops attacking a Caco camp supported by airplanes dropping bombs from above. The results were, an officer reported, "very satisfying." They eradicated fifty-two "bandits" and saw a great deal of blood, which suggested that many more had been hurt. "The aviators did splendid work and killed many."[111]

U.S. military officials later downplayed the use of bombing during the occupation, saying that only a few aerial missions had been carried out. Testimonies from Haiti, though, make it clear that the attacks were devastating. Many in rural areas had never seen an airplane before, let alone one dropping bombs; according to one account, the machines became known as "God's bad angels." Unsurprisingly, the aerial bombardments were not always precise in their targets—especially since even the marines on the ground had long

had difficulty distinguishing Cacos from the broader rural population. Furthermore, the Caco camps that were bombed were often
not so much military compounds as temporary villages: the families
of the Cacos settled there, sometimes even growing crops if they
stayed in one place for long enough. The rebels' partners and children were also caught in the aerial attacks.[112]

One Haitian gendarme who participated in a coordinated
ground-air assault later provided a harrowing description of what
he saw. The occupation troops had surrounded a Caco village near
Terre-Rouge by night, and in the morning they were awaiting the
order to charge when they heard people approaching. It was two
women and an eleven-year-old boy, going to get water from a nearby
spring. When they were just steps away from where the gendarmes
were hiding, one of the women stopped. She'd smelled something: a
U.S. cigarette, a foreign smell that she knew could only come from
marines or Haitian gendarmes. The small group turned back toward
the camp to warn the others. The boy ran ahead, until one of the
gendarmes shot and killed him. The two women began to scream,
and the gendarmes were about to charge when an airplane appeared
overhead. "Here come the vultures!" shouted the villagers as the
airplane began its bombing run. The gendarmes heard the screams
of women in the explosions and injured animals braying, as those
who could scattered and ran from the camp. All that was left to do
was finish the work. The marines and gendarmes entered the village,
killed the wounded who had been left behind, counted the dead,
and headed home.[113]

Even with the fearsome new technology on their side, however,
the conflict dragged on. Eventually, the marines decided that there
was a more efficient way of crushing the Caco revolt: assassinating
Péralte. The job fell to two marines, William R. Button—who,
according to a fellow soldier, "could speak all varieties of Creole"
and "pass as a Haitian of any class"—and Herman Hanneken.
Another key figure in the plot was a Haitian man, Jean-Baptiste
Conzé. The three, along with a few other Haitian accomplices,

constructed an elaborate plan for infiltrating the Caco movement and drawing Péralte into a trap.[114]

Conzé came from a prominent family in the town of Grande-Rivière and was a distant relative of Péralte. He had some personal reasons for disliking the Cacos: in 1914, before the occupation, he'd been stopped twice by rebels in the countryside and forced to hand over a ransom to support their cause. By the U.S. military's own accounts, however, Conzé was most of all an opportunist. An American report later described him as having no particular political affiliation and "leaning to whatever side has the most money." Infiltrating the Cacos was not an easy task. Péralte had developed an effective and widespread spy network, depending heavily on market women who circulated throughout the countryside and the towns. Some of these women duly warned the Caco leader about the assassination plot, and specifically about Conzé. Nonetheless, he succeeded in working his way into Péralte's trust, largely through an elaborate ruse. He and Hanneken staged a battle, with Conzé posing as a Caco and the marine pretending to have been defeated and wounded. Impressed with the fake Caco's exploit, Péralte welcomed him into his camp and gave him an officer's commission. Together, they set about engineering a raid on Grande-Rivière.[115]

On the night appointed for the attack, October 31, 1919, Conzé planned to lead Péralte into an ambush. At the last minute, though, Péralte decided to stay back from the battle. Improvising, Hanneken and Button covered their faces in black shoe polish and dressed themselves in tattered clothes. Thus disguised, and accompanied by several Haitian gendarmes, they made it all the way to the small house where Péralte was staying. There, Hanneken shot him twice in the heart at point-blank range.[116]

Péralte had developed a near-legendary status in the country, and the marines could not simply declare that they had killed him: they needed to prove it. So they carried his body down the hill and put it on display in Grande-Rivière. One resident of the town, a friend of

Péralte's, later described watching the procession enter the town, with Jean-Baptiste Conzé proudly in the middle. "I was penetrated with sadness," he recalled. "All at once, my hopes and those of my comrades had collapsed. The Americans would not be chased away."[117]

The next day, Péralte was brought by train to Le Cap and there stripped bare. A piece of cloth was placed over his midsection, and his body was tied to a door and propped up against a wall in the police station. The marines officially identified Péralte by using the file filled out about him when he was in prison in Le Cap, which listed his hair and eye color, his height, and his scars. Then they gathered local residents to come and see the body, including the guard who had helped Péralte escape the previous year—now a prisoner himself—and the French priest serving in Le Cap. Afterward, a marine photographer took a picture of the corpse to show to those who had not seen it for themselves. Several hundred copies of the photo were made, and airplanes dropped them over the countryside in the areas where Cacos were still active.[118]

Even after all of these displays, the marines remained oddly obsessed with Péralte's body, which they didn't quite know where to put. Fearing that the Cacos would attempt to take back the corpse of their leader, they held five different fake funerals in different places to create confusion. Péralte's actual final resting place was carefully chosen: a prison camp at Chabert, not far from Le Cap. An official description of the institution provided to the U.S. Senate in 1921 described it in bucolic terms as a farm worked by convicts to feed the local population and experiment with new agricultural methods. A Haitian newspaper provided a rather different account, referring to the camp as "organized slavery." The crops grown at Chabert were sold for the profit of the occupation, and prisoners there died by the hundreds. The carpenter hired to bury Péralte later recalled that the marines didn't have a coffin to put him in: the prison was out of them. Instead, the soldiers wrapped the body in a Haitian flag and laid it directly in the grave. Then they asked the laborer to pour concrete around it, apparently to make sure that the body couldn't be easily disinterred. A Haitian guard who was among those ordered to stand sentinel over the grave in the following days remembered bitterly: "Charlemagne was buried like a dog."[119]

The Caco war was not yet over, for Benoît Batraville took over the movement's leadership from Péralte and continued to fight for nearly another year. Eventually, however, he, too, was killed, and the remaining insurgents dispersed. Back in the United States, meanwhile, the press published swashbuckling accounts of how Hanneken and Button had tricked and killed Péralte. James Weldon Johnson, an African American writer and critic of the occupation, was among the few to offer a different reading, arguing that the assassination was anything but heroic and represented a "black mark" on the tradition of U.S. military action. The two marines were awarded the Congressional Medal of Honor and were lauded by the Haitian government: in a ceremony on the Champ de Mars in Port-au-Prince, President Dartiguenave pinned Haitian military medals on them to the sounds of the Haitian national anthem and the Marine Corps hymn. The Haitians who had worked with them, including Conzé, got medals, too—but in a separate ceremony.[120]

Lieutenant Button died of malaria in Haiti the following year, while Hanneken went on to a long military career, fighting in Nicaragua and later in the Pacific during World War II. He did not, it seems, take particular pride in his role in Péralte's killing. In 1971, when the Haitian historian Roger Gaillard came to Washington to carry out his research on the occupation in the U.S. National Archives, he managed to find Hanneken's phone number in San Diego. But when he called Hanneken to ask if he could interview him, the ex-marine told him simply: "I'm an old soldier. I don't want to think about that affair anymore."[121]

In Haiti, meanwhile, traveling to the place where Péralte had died, Gaillard found many local residents who kept the memory of the event alive and pointed out to him the precise location where the killing had taken place. In the 1970s it was a lush forest, full of trees offering mangoes, oranges, avocados, guavas, and breadfruit, surrounded by bamboo and fern: perhaps a fitting memorial. For, as Gaillard wrote, while Péralte's assassins were once the ones celebrated and decorated, eventually things changed. "The dialectic of history has reversed the poles, and the one who still lives among us now is Charlemagne Péralte."[122]

It was the marines who, unwittingly, offered Haitians the most lasting and widely known vision of the slain Caco leader. In the photograph taken in 1919, Péralte is nearly naked, with just a cloth covering his groin. Tied to a board propped against a wall, with his head tilted back to one side and his eyes closed, he almost seems to be sleeping. Draped behind him, nestled against his head, is his banner: the Haitian flag, mounted on a flagpole topped with a crucifix. The similarity of this image of the slain Péralte—killed at the age of thirty-three—to the crucified Christ is striking. If the photographer had consciously tried to create a picture of a martyr, he couldn't have done better.[123]

Passed from hand to hand, copies of the photograph of Péralte's corpse circulated throughout Haiti. In 1932, when the journalist and antioccupation activist Félix Viard wrote a poem in honor of Péralte, dubbing him "the last maroon," the publication was illustrated with a sketch of the same photo. Later, Philomé Obin, a painter from Le Cap—once arrested by U.S. marines on suspicion of sympathy with the Cacos—created several works based on the image. In Obin's paintings, the black-and-white of the original is transformed into color, so that the blue and red of the Haitian flag and the yellow of the crucifix stand out against the sky. Obin also added Péralte's mourning mother, clad in black, to the scene. And the title of his work, inscribed directly on the painting, expressed what so many had long seen in the image: "The Crucifixion of Charlemagne Péralte for Liberty."[124]

The name of the marine who snapped the photograph in 1919 is unknown, but he ended up making a lasting contribution to the artistic and political culture of Haiti. The image he produced, meant to make Haitians forget about Péralte, remains the most widely recognized depiction of the U.S. occupation, the ultimate monument to its cruelty and to the resistance it inspired.

7

SECOND INDEPENDENCE

In June 1929, a resplendent new agricultural school was inaugurated in Damien, a suburb north of Port-au-Prince. It was outfitted with laboratories, a geological museum, a collection of Haitian plants, and a dairy farm where imported Jersey and Holstein cows cohabited with a few "indigenous" ones. Haitian and American teachers provided instruction in zoology, botany, agronomy, physics, chemistry, and political economy, and the students got exercise playing soccer, volleyball, and basketball. The school was the crown jewel of a decade-long effort by the United States to transform education and agriculture in Haiti, meant to demonstrate unequivocally that the occupation was a force for progress and civilization. Instead, however, it ended up doing the opposite. Within a few months, the Damien school became the launching pad for a mass student uprising, which eventually helped to do what Péralte's Cacos could not: send the U.S. forces home.[1]

The unrest began on October 31, 1929, when the first class of students at the Damien school learned that the administration was cutting back on promised merit scholarships. They went on strike, marching into Port-au-Prince, where they were soon joined by other high school and university students. The young protesters became heroes for a population fed up with the U.S. presence. Greeted by cheering crowds, they lived an adolescent dream: getting free bus rides, free restaurant meals, even free movie tickets. As a symbol of their protest, they were wore green ribbons, standing for the renewal they hoped to inspire.[2]

When Haitian government employees joined the strike, the U.S. authorities declared martial law and carried out a wave of arrests. Fearing that they were losing control, several officials moved their families out of Port-au-Prince and onto boats in the harbor. Most frightening to them was the fact that the uprising was not limited to the cities: for the first time since the crushing of the Caco revolt, there were mass protests in the countryside as well. In early December, when fifteen hundred rural residents marched on Les Cayes, the tension proved too great: as the protesters entered the town, a marine detachment fired machine guns into the crowd, killing a dozen people and wounding many more.[3]

It was the beginning of the end of the U.S. occupation. The massacre was an international embarrassment, making it clear that the Haitian people were increasingly united across class and regional lines in their opposition to the American presence. Less than five years later, the U.S. Marines formally withdrew. At a simple ceremony in Le Cap, the stars and stripes were taken down and the Haitian flag put back up. Shortly thereafter, the bones of Charlemagne Péralte were disinterred from his cement grave, his skull identified by his mother thanks to a gold tooth. Hastily buried as a bandit in 1919, he was now given a grand state funeral, officially acknowledged as a national hero.[4]

The departure of the marines represented the culmination of two decades of struggle against the occupation. It was supposed to be a new dawn for Haiti; political leaders proclaimed that 1934 was their country's "Second Independence." But that name highlighted the danger as well as the promise of the situation. A hundred and thirty years after Dessalines's 1804 proclamation, Haiti was again starting from scratch in its efforts to secure a place for itself in the world. An entire generation—children when the marines arrived and adults by the time they left—had been deeply marked by the occupation.

Quite a few of them had thrown themselves into the resistance movement, and they could take pride in having finally driven out the invaders. But they and their elders were also forced to think hard about how and why their country had—in clear violation of the key principles set forth by its founders—allowed itself to be taken over by foreigners. Many activists argued that kicking out the United States was only the first step to securing real independence: Haitians also had to transform themselves and their culture. They had to overcome the profound divisions that sapped their strength in the face of outside threats. They had to bridge the gap between the governing elite and the majority who remained on the margins of political life. They had to stop slavishly imitating others and embrace who they were and where they came from.

Like the generation of 1804, though, the activists of the 1930s discovered that the legacy of foreign control was extremely difficult to escape. The U.S. occupation had profoundly changed the country, smashing the political and economic order that had emerged during the nineteenth century and deepening the poverty of the country-side. It had centralized and strengthened the government's authority, giving the country's leaders more power than they had ever had to control the masses and suppress dissent. Many Haitians dreamed in 1934 that their country would finally be able to move forward toward a radically different future. Instead, they found that the years of subjugation were haunting them still.

███

The antipathy that Haitian peasants felt toward the United States was rooted not only in the cruelty of the marines and the ignominy of losing national sovereignty, but also in severe economic suffering. In the early 1910s, when they were urging the State Department to invade Haiti, U.S. bankers and businessmen had argued that an occupation was crucial for making Haiti attractive to foreign investors. Half a decade later, as the country came more and more firmly under U.S. military control, those investors were duly coming in—and life in the Haitian countryside, never easy to begin with, was becoming more and more precarious.

Among the first businesses to profit from the occupation was the Haitian-American Sugar Company, known as HASCO. Founded by Haitian and American entrepreneurs, HASCO aimed to revive large-scale sugar production in the Cul-de-Sac plain outside Port-au-Prince—an area that once had been full of sugar plantations but after independence had been taken over by small farmers who grew cane mostly for rum production in local distilleries. Before the occupation, HASCO had trouble acquiring enough land in the region, but after the American invasion, everything became easier for the company: with the support of the new regime, it simply evicted local peasants to make room. In December 1918, HASCO inaugurated its first Cul-de-Sac sugar mill. The event was touted as a sign of Haiti's progress: President Dartiguenave, the marine brigade commander, and the archbishop of Port-au-Prince all attended, watching intently as the mill's engineers showed off its modern machinery. "In less than half an hour," a Haitian newspaper effused, the cane was transformed into sugar. Although it had taken a long time to get the mill up and running, the newspaper concluded, "all's well that ends well."[5]

But things were not going so well for the farmers who lived near the sugar mill. Even those who had not lost their land directly to HASCO soon found it difficult to make ends meet: the sugar mill replaced the local distilleries and paid the farmers less for their cane. The displaced peasants had the option of working at the mill for wages, but those who accepted jobs there found the conditions and the pay deplorable. Within a few months of the mill's opening, HASCO workers organized the first of many strikes, which brought production to a standstill. Their wages were less than they'd been promised, they complained, and they needed some form of insurance: there were frequent accidents at the mill, sometimes with fatal results. For the company, of course, low wages and low costs were precisely what was attractive about Haiti. They paid their workers no more than thirty cents a day (the equivalent of about $4 in modern currency), a wage one-fifth of that on U.S.-owned plantations in neighboring Cuba.[6]

Other businesses soon followed HASCO's lead. In 1922 the North Haytian Sugar Company acquired a hundred acres of land, and the Haytian Pineapple Company six hundred acres. A few years later, the Haitian American Development Corporation took over 14,000 acres, while the Haytian Agricultural Corporation was granted a 2,200-acre concession. These companies produced a range of products for export to the United States, such as sugar, fruit, and the sisal used to make twine and rope. Their presence was made possible by new laws put in place under the occupation: the 1918 constitution had for the first time allowed foreigners to acquire land in Haiti, while a series of government decrees enacted in the following years provided various legal mechanisms that could be used to take land from rural farmers. Many peasants who cultivated land under the *métayage* system, in which they gave half of what they produced to the landowners but retained significant autonomy regarding how and what they farmed, suddenly found that the fields they'd worked—sometimes for generations—had been sold or leased to American corporations. And even though foreign companies were able to gain control of only a small portion of land in Haiti—no more than 2 percent of the territory was in foreign hands by the 1920s—their impact was outsized. They often monopolized local resources, especially water, and brought about shifts in the local economy that left many peasants increasingly impoverished. To make matters worse, farmers soon discovered that U.S. occupation authorities were substantially more assiduous about collecting taxes than local Haitian authorities had been. During the nineteenth century, rural residents had developed intricate mechanisms for avoiding the state's demands, but now they could no longer do so. Even as their communities were being invaded by U.S. companies, rural Haitians found themselves handing over a sizable portion of their shrinking incomes to subsidize their country's occupation.[7]

The occupation's proponents in the United States and Haiti celebrated the arrival of foreign corporations, insisting that they would help develop the country's economy and thus alleviate poverty. And the new plantations did bring jobs to many regions. But such employment was very poorly paid, ultimately no compensation for the loss of family land and the independence that land ownership had provided. Meanwhile, the promised expansion in the national economy never materialized. The production of coffee, long Haiti's most dependable and profitable export, remained flat throughout the twenty-year occupation. And while HASCO remained in Haiti, most of the other new ventures failed. In many parts of the country, rural communities took on the arriving corporations in a war of attrition and succeeded in driving them away—by refusing dangerous, low-paying work, insistently demanding better conditions, and resisting expropriation of land. It is, in fact, a remarkable testament to the strength of Haiti's counter-plantation system that while American companies successfully built plantations elsewhere in the Caribbean during this period, particularly in Cuba and the Dominican Republic, they were largely unable to do so in Haiti—even though the U.S. directly governed the country for two decades.[8]

The efforts to alleviate rural poverty might have met with more success, perhaps, if the alternatives to large-scale plantation agriculture long embraced by the Haitian population been taken seriously as a foundation for agricultural development rather than simply an obstacle to it. In August 1918, the prominent Haitian intellectual Dantès Bellegarde, then serving as minister of public instruction and agriculture, proposed a sweeping set of reforms aimed at addressing the urgent problems facing rural areas. Among his ideas was creating local councils to share knowledge about more proactive ways of working the fields, and offering microcredit loans to help farmers improve their technology and agricultural techniques. He later testified bitterly, however, that the U.S. authorities were not interested in such "serious projects for agricultural organization and the education of the popular masses" and had ignored his proposals. Most

U.S. officials—and many Haitian leaders, too—believed that the system of small farms had to be swept away and replaced with large plantations in order for the country to prosper.[9]

Although Haiti's farmers largely managed to stop the spread of HASCO-style foreign businesses, the U.S. occupation still contributed to the immiseration of the Haitian countryside. Life had never been easy in rural Haiti, but for generations many communities had done well for themselves by growing their own food and cultivating coffee for export. The political and military transformation brought about by the occupation broke the precarious balance that these communities had relied on. The system of regional ports was dismantled and Port-au-Prince became the dominant hub for trade, concentrating economic power in the hands of a smaller group of merchants. The crushing of the Cacos by the marines in 1918 and 1919 ended the possibility of open resistance to the invaders, while the central government—long kept at bay thanks to the power of local leaders—was greatly strengthened by the U.S. forces. The new state was no more invested in helping rural communities than the old state had been, but now it had a much greater capacity to control the country's population.

The damage done to the rural Haitian communities was magnified by a sustained attack on their ancestral religious practice, as the occupation forces launched a devastating campaign of persecution against Vodou. It was not the first time such attacks had taken place, of course. In the 1860s, the widely publicized trial at Bizoton had demonstrated Fabre Geffrard's desire to rid Haiti of the religion, and in 1896 the Catholic Church—with the support of the government and many intellectuals—had tried to eliminate Vodou so that Haitians could "prove to the world that we are a civilized people." But such campaigns, though traumatic for their victims, had had little broader impact. An 1899 government report concluded that Vodou ceremonies were on the rise, and a French merchant who lived in Haiti between 1904 and 1906 described flourishing temples patronized by local politicians.[10]

Indeed, in the long run, perhaps the most harmful effect of the nineteenth-century anti-Vodou efforts was to develop what Haitian anthropologist Laënnec Hurbon describes as an "ideological wardrobe" awaiting the occupation authorities. When they arrived in the country, U.S. officials noted that Haiti's penal code included two articles outlawing the use of poison and the casting of spells. Like the Boyer-era laws allowing for the use of corvée labor, by 1915 these were legal relics, rarely enforced. What's more, they specifically criminalized only certain practices—the use of spiritual power for negative ends—that most practitioners of Vodou also condemned. But such distinctions were largely ignored by the U.S. authorities, who tended to see the entire complex of popular religious activity in Haiti as a kind of black magic. The old laws about poisons and spell casting were among the only ones—out of the 413 articles that made up Haiti's penal code—to be translated and distributed to U.S. troops governing the rural districts, and the new rulers used them as the legal foundation for a wide-ranging attack on Haitian Vodou in general. Suddenly, for the majority of the population in the country, participation in the many ceremonies that made up their religion's ritual calendar was now a crime.[11]

U.S. authorities began to focus especially intently on Vodou during the Caco wars, seeing it as a key component of the insurrection. Marine reports claimed that leaders like Péralte used religion to frighten otherwise docile and contented Haitian peasants into fighting. "Probably all of the caco chiefs are Vaudoux priests and thus hold together bands which, freed from religious scruples, would abandon their purpose of brigandry," wrote one U.S. visitor. The "elimination" of Vodou was therefore "imperative." In the 1920s, with the Caco war coming to an end and the use of corvée labor falling out of favor, the criminalization of the religion took on a new purpose: it was a convenient way for occupation forces to secure workers. Marine Faustin Wirkus explained that when he needed to build a new police headquarters, he followed the suggestion of a Haitian judge and raided a Vodou ceremony. All those present were arrested and sentenced to up to six months of hard labor on the construction site. Such raids were widespread: Marine General Littleton Waller told the U.S. Senate in 1921 that Vodou "is against the Haitian law . . . but they never enforced the law. We did, and we broke up all their meetings, seized their drums, etc., and wherever a voodoo drum was heard we immediately got on the trail and captured it, and broke it up, as far as we could." A Baptist missionary from the United States similarly testified about the "joy of burning tomtoms and the whole paraphernalia" of the religion, and carrying away "donkey loads of demon-worshipped implements." When a prominent *oungan* was put on trial in Haiti in 1920, the U.S. prosecutor told the marine commission charged with reviewing his case: "Gentlemen, today you have it in your power to aid in ridding humanity of one of its most dangerous and degrading elements. You have it in your power to aid in delivering the Republic of Haiti from a curse which has been on it from the time of its foundation."[12]

For Vodou adherents, service to the *lwa* and to family ancestors involves ongoing ritual responsibilities, and to shirk them is considered both shameful and dangerous. The U.S. occupation thus placed many Haitians before a cruel choice: they could either turn their backs on the *lwa* or risk harassment, prison, and hard labor. Religion had long represented a refuge in Haitian culture, a source of strength for the oppressed; but under the occupation even this realm of life became difficult to defend.

Faced with such assaults, many in the rural communities concluded that there was no choice but to leave their ancestral lands behind. For the first time in its history, Haiti—long a magnet for immigrants from the Caribbean, North America, Europe, and the Middle East—became a country of large-scale emigration. The statistics are startling. In 1912, only about two hundred Haitians had migrated to Cuba; but in 1916—the year after the occupation began—five thousand of them did so, and the numbers increased steadily after that. By 1920, there were already 70,000 Haitians in Cuba, and in that year another 30,000 emigrated there. And throughout the

1920s, about ten thousand Haitians a year left for the Dominican Republic. Yet while they went in search of freedom, the migrants who left the countryside often ended up in precisely the kind of place they and their ancestors had been seeking to escape: the plantation. In Cuba, the Dominican Republic, and other neighboring Caribbean countries, the only places hiring rural refugees were large agricultural enterprises looking for field labor. And there was no escape from U.S. control, either: most of these companies were owned by American corporations.[13]

In 1919, the Haitian consul in Cuba spoke of the conditions experienced by immigrant workers as "very close to slavery": they lived in large, dirty sheds, couldn't leave the plantation without permission, and were under constant guard. An article published in Cuba that same year similarly mentioned the "dark days of slavery" as it described a gruesome scene: the bodies of three Haitian workers hanging from a tree in Oriente province, with no explanation and no investigation of how or why they had been killed. The writer suspected that they had tried to run away and were the victims of plantation guards. In 1922, a Haitian journalist wrote that the migrants were leaving "like our ancestors from the coasts of Ivory and Dahomey," dressed in rags, carrying nothing. Some of them sang as they went, recalling a Vodou song dating back to the days of Saint-Domingue: "I'm leaving this land / This land is not for me."[14]

III

One night in May 1919, in the midst of the Caco war, an elderly *oungan* imprisoned in Croix-des-Bouquets was summoned by the marine commander, Lieutenant Louis A. Brokaw. Along with another prisoner, he was taken to a nearby field by Brokaw, two marine privates, and several Haitian gendarmes. The two men were told to dig their own graves, then shot and killed. The marine authorities who investigated the killing concluded that Brokaw was insane and discharged him from the force. But when the two privates who accompanied him were put on trial, the marine officer defending them insisted they weren't guilty of any crime because such incidents were commonplace—he had "seen many similar cases." Reviewing the case in Washington a few months later, Marine General George Barnett was shocked by the argument that killing prisoners was customary and therefore excusable. Alarmed, he looked into the matter, and he filed a confidential report alerting his superiors that "practically indiscriminate killing of the natives has gone on for some time." The document was leaked to the press, and soon it was all over the front pages. One newspaper decried "slavery in Haiti," while the New York Times wrote of civilians being "slain for sport" by marines, who fired "machine guns from airplanes against defenseless Haitian villages, killing men, women and children in the open market places."[15]

The media attention that followed General Barnett's report was the first time that descriptions of the violence of the occupation circulated widely in the United States, though since 1915 a few determined writers and activists had been trying to get Americans to pay attention to what was being done in their name in Haiti. The Afro-American newspaper had described the occupation as "a stench in the nostrils of all decent people," and in 1917 the Nation had called it "imperialism of the rankest kind." The most prominent critic of the occupation was James Weldon Johnson, a leader of the NAACP, who saw the debate as part of the broader struggle against racism. Asked once about cannibalism in Haiti, Johnson had retorted: "You can take your choice between eating your human flesh without cooking it in that benighted island and cooking your human flesh without eating it in possibly no less benighted Mississippi." Instead of worrying about Vodou practices in Haiti, he suggested, people in the United States should stamp out their own traditions of ritual killing.[16]

In 1920, critics of the occupation found an unlikely supporter in Republican presidential candidate Warren Harding. The occupation in Haiti, Harding realized, provided a perfect opportunity to attack the incumbent Democratic president Woodrow Wilson—a celebrated internationalist and defender of small nations—as a racist hypocrite. Eager to get more details about the brutality of U.S. conduct, Harding met with Johnson, who recalled that the Republican "looked upon the Haitian matter as a gift right off the Christmas tree. He could not conceal his delight." Soon, Harding began regularly referring to the "rape of Haiti" by the Wilson administration. Franklin Delano Roosevelt, the Democratic vice presidential nominee, played right into Harding's hands in a campaign speech when he tried to promote his expertise in foreign affairs by falsely declaring: "You know I have had something to do with the running of a couple of little republics. The facts are that I wrote Haiti's Constitution myself and, if I do say it, I think it is a pretty good Constitution." Harding seized on the comments, explaining that if elected he wouldn't blithely "empower an Assistant Secretary of the Navy to draft a constitution for helpless neighbors in the West Indies and jam it down their throats at the point of bayonets borne by the U.S. Marines."[17]

Harding won the presidency, and in 1921–22 the U.S. Senate carried out an extensive investigation into the occupations of Haiti and the Dominican Republic. The senators heard from U.S. soldiers and marine officers as well as from Haitian witnesses. But while the testimony documented many abuses on the part of the U.S. forces, something strange happened as the investigation went on: it frequently became, instead, a forum for condemnation of Haitian culture. When General Barnett, author of the leaked 1919 report, took the stand, he was peppered with questions about cannibalism and child sacrifice. Was it true that a U.S. marine had been decapitated and that "his skull had been used in some of their incantations there; did you hear of that?" "I did not hear of it, but I can well understand it might be true," Barnett replied. And was it true that some Haitian prisoners were accused of the "butchery of one or more little children, whose blood was necessary in their rituals, in their pagan religious ceremonials"? "Yes," Barnett told the audience. Such questioning was part of a broader pattern. The numerous atrocities carried out by the marines that the investigation exposed were interpreted as aberrations, the fault of a few bad apples. On the other hand, the brutalities of the Cacos—which centered on rumors that the bodies of several marines killed in combat had been ritually mutilated— were regarded as proof of the savagery of Haitians in general. A similar navy investigation of the occupation also included both allegations of Caco brutality and accounts of ritualized violence by U.S. forces: an American ex-soldier described how he and others had crucified Haitian victims, while a priest testified that an officer had the skeleton of an executed prisoner hanging in his house. The headline in the *New York Times*, however, focused exclusively on the anti-Caco stories: "Natives in Haiti Ate Marine Officer," it declared.[18]

The emphasis on the supposed backwardness of Haitian culture had immediate political repercussions: the Senate concluded that the country was not capable of governing itself and that the United States therefore had a responsibility to remain there. As one sociologist put it a few years later, while the occupation might "violate theoretical ideas of national rights," it had not actually "destroyed the right of self-government" in Haiti, because there had never been "real democracy" in the country to begin with. Whatever abuses the United States had brought, "the continuation of former conditions would unquestionably have produced greater ones." John Russell, who served as high commissioner for the occupation from 1922 to 1930, likewise argued that if his forces withdrew, the country would "revert to a condition of chaos when, after a time, the United States would be forced to again occupy Haiti or permit some foreign nation to do so." Russell made a point of socializing with the bourgeoisie in Port-au-Prince, but his opinion of most Haitians was unequivocal: the average "uneducated" citizen was "more or less of an animal" and had "the mentality of a child of not more than seven years of age"—though a seven-year-old, he granted, "reared under advantageous conditions." The general population was "bordering on a state of savagery, if not existing in such a state." Russell considered any suggestions that he should even share power with elected

Haitian leaders to be an "absurdity": "Two men can ride a horse but one must ride behind," he explained. Instead, he said, the United States had to govern Haiti the way the British had ruled when they colonized Egypt from 1882 to 1914, through a "tripartite system." In Egypt "one alien race, the English, have had to control and guide a second alien race, the Turks, by whom they are disliked, in the government of a third race, the Egyptians." In Haiti, as Russell saw it, the United States had to guide and control the Haitian elite, particularly its "mulatto" leaders, in controlling the third group: the mass of the Haitian population. And even the governing elite was never to be fully trusted. In 1919 Russell wrote of Haitian president Sudre Dartiguenave: "At heart he is anti-American, a man of no integrity, a schemer, a Vaudou believer, and he will only work for the good of Haiti when it is to his own personal interests or he is forced to do so by the occupation."[19]

Given such attitudes among the American leadership of the occupation, there was little chance that they would respond to Haitian demands for greater democracy and political participation. But the spate of criticisms that the occupation was attracting in the United States did place the authorities under pressure to make good on the justifications they had given for invading the country—that is, to prove that they were truly engaged in a project of improvement and uplift. Accordingly, during the 1920s, they embarked on a series of ambitious schemes aimed at transforming and modernizing Haiti. At first these efforts garnered support from many prominent Haitians, who hoped that with U.S. assistance they would be able to carry out initiatives they themselves had long envisioned as necessary for their country's advancement. Startlingly quickly, however, the patronizing, top-down approach taken by U.S. officials, and their disregard of the Haitians' own aspirations, would turn that enthusiasm into animosity and rancor.

The Americans' primary partner in their work was Louis Borno, whom they installed as president of Haiti in 1922. Borno—who, back in 1914, had so strenuously protested the USS *Machias* incident—

was not technically eligible to be president: his father was French, and the 1918 constitution required any presidential candidate to have a Haitian father. But he'd been handpicked for the job by the United States, which was, as historian Claude Moïse puts it, the only "real elector" in the country anyway. And Borno agreed with the United States that Haiti wasn't ready for democracy. "Democracy is government by the people through *conscious* popular suffrage," he later explained, and therefore impossible in a country peopled by "totally illiterate" peasants—easy prey for "audacious speculators" who bought their votes.[20]

The only way forward, Borno argued, was to collaborate with the United States in order to carry out an economic and social transformation, which would lay the foundation for the development of a true democracy. "The hour is decisive," he declared in his first presidential message: this was Haiti's chance "to uproot misery and ignorance." The existing situation was a national embarrassment: "a small bourgeoisie, educated, elegant, and refined," coexisting with "an immense popular mass in rags, unable to read or write, plunged into superstition." "This must end," Borno proclaimed; "this social crime must disappear." He promised to create more jobs, construct roads and railroad lines, provide irrigation to help rural farmers, and expand education.[21]

Working with the United States, Borno carried out highly visible public works projects and oversaw the completion of a new National Palace to replace the one destroyed in the 1912 explosion that killed Cincinnatus Leconte. The occupation authorities also won favor by building hospitals in the towns and small clinics in the countryside, which provided significant assistance to many in Haiti. Indeed, the medical personnel who served in Haiti during the occupation left a particularly positive impression on many in the country. "The American doctors," wrote one former Haitian official, "seemed to have given themselves the mission of dressing the wounds inflicted by their peers in the other sectors of the occupation, and of teaching us that their country was not only made up of unscrupulous businessmen and soulless soldiers." The occupation authorities did occasion some protest when they shut down the Haitian-run medical school in Port-au-Prince, which had existed since 1823, and replaced it with one staffed by U.S. doctors; still, the U.S.-run school attracted many students, including a young high school graduate named François Duvalier.[22]

The most ambitious of the U.S. occupation-era projects was the creation of a new bureaucracy, the Service Technique de l'Agriculture et de l'Enseignement Professionnel, to provide technical and agricultural education to Haitians. John Russell, the high commissioner of the occupation, believed that "the one system of education to be pursued in Haiti should be to teach each individual a trade, to make each citizen an asset to his country." As he saw it, the classical education that was traditionally offered in Haiti was useless, even detrimental. "For over one hundred years Haiti has been struggling along, having its schools or semblance of them, giving classical instruction only, and what has been the result?" The answer, Russell thought, was clear: "suffering" and "backwardness," not to mention "political and financial chaos." Technical education, Russell argued, was Haiti's only hope. "It is essential that there be developed in Haiti, as rapidly as possible, a middle class—a class of artisans and skilled laborers, who will become the backbone of the country, and go far to assure the stability of the government."[23]

Over a few years, the Service Technique built sixty-nine farm schools (welcoming 7,500 students in all) and five experimental agricultural stations. It was directed by Dr. George Freeman, who laid out his vision of the schools in a 1925 speech to Haitian students. There was, he explained, no place there for those who were "afraid or ashamed to work with their hands": "Give us men who know labor. Give us men who are not ashamed of honest toil." Having "travelled over your country and studied your natural resources," Freeman intoned, he had "found valleys, rich in fertility, capable of loading thousands of steamers with cargoes of sugar, cotton, bananas, pineapples, and other fruits." But what sprang into his mind, he said, was the "expression of our Holy Master, 'The harvest is ripe but the reapers are few.'" It was a curious analysis, for the country of which Freeman spoke—and which he claimed to have visited and observed carefully—was densely covered with small farms, worked intensely by residents using long-practiced and well-honed agricultural techniques designed for self-sufficiency. If he saw an absence of work there, it was probably in part because he had gone in expecting to see that, thanks to well-established racist ideas about the laziness of Haitians. More importantly, however, for Freeman—as for many others—real agricultural production meant only one thing: large-scale agriculture for export. The counter-plantation system as it was practiced in Haiti registered only as an absence, or an obstacle to progress. In a cynical sleight of hand, he presented the task of producing a new plantation system as mainly a struggle to teach Haitians how to work with their hands.[24]

Freeman's advocacy of technical education was applauded by many prominent Haitian intellectuals. Dantès Bellegarde saw the initiative as a chance to carry out his earlier unrealized proposals for reforming the Haitian countryside, while others took inspiration from Booker T. Washington's ideas of uplift through vocational training. Haitian students enthusiastically enrolled in the new agricultural and technical training schools when they opened, and over time the Service Technique—along with other educational reforms carried out during the occupation—did succeed in expanding the professional classes in the country. But the occupation's educational policies also rapidly generated resentment and resistance. Many of the Haitians who supported the development of agricultural training nevertheless felt it essential to maintain the country's cherished traditions of classical education; they wanted the Service Technique to be an addition, not a replacement. But the U.S. occupation authorities, who controlled the entire state budget of Haiti, wanted instead to carry out a profound reorientation of the country's schools. Over the objections of Haitian leaders, they decided to channel the majority of the education budget to the new agricultural establishments at the expense of all other kinds of classes.[25]

The unbalanced approach taken by the United States convinced many Haitians that a sinister motivation was at work. Like African American critics of vocational education in the United States, such as W.E.B. Du Bois, they worried that the exclusive focus on this training was deliberately designed to maintain Haitians in a subservient role. In view of the strong support given by the occupation to the development of corporate plantation agriculture, they had reason to wonder whether the educational reforms were aimed at transforming all of Haiti into little more than a giant pool of low-wage agricultural and artisanal laborers. When the African American historian Rayford Logan visited Haiti in the late 1920s, he was shocked to discover that U.S. authorities seemed convinced that "vocational training is the *only* kind to which Haitians are suited." Even more galling, the reason the agricultural schools needed so much money was that they were largely staffed by teachers from the United States—"foreign experts" who were paid substantially more than their Haitian counterparts. Given that the teachers' salaries came from Haitian taxpayers, the disparity was particularly infuriating, and the system was not only demeaning but inefficient. The U.S. teachers rarely spoke either French or Kreyòl, so they gave their lectures in English to largely uncomprehending students, or else explained the material to Haitian assistants who then had to teach the classes for them.[26]

The U.S. authorities also alarmed many Haitian intellectuals by proposing that English should become the main language of instruction in all of the country's schools. This was a step too far even for their most steadfast collaborators, including Louis Borno. In one of his few gestures of resistance to the U.S. authorities, Borno insisted that Haitian students be taught in French, and he took the forward-thinking step of allowing Kreyòl to be used in schools as well. The U.S. attempt to impose English on Haiti struck many as a bald attempt at cultural imperialism, stoking the rising resentment about their policies. Such a change, after all, would have represented a kind of cultural amputation: the entire tradition of Haitian political thought and literature, not to mention the country's laws, were in French. Once it had been a colonial language, but now it was a national one, an integral part of Haiti's history and culture. Many saw it as a crucial link with the broader world, allowing Haitians to "to join hands with the world's intellectual elite," as one thinker put it. Indeed, anger at the U.S. occupation pushed many Haitians to affirm their cultural links with France more strongly than ever before. Haitians renarrated their revolution by emphasizing the alliance with French republicans that made it possible. "The first time that a man of the black race was ever a citizen, he was a French citizen," the ex general Alfred Nemours proclaimed in 1919; "the first time that a man of our race was ever an army officer, he was a French officer. And our birth certificate, where is it found? Was it not in France, in the Declaration of the Rights of Man?" The former colonizer was now a useful counterweight to the new empire. Even as the United States gained increasing cultural importance in Haiti, many resisted the trend, a fact symbolized perhaps most clearly in the realm of sports: among the Caribbean countries that were occupied by the United States, Haiti is the only one that never took up baseball, sticking instead with the more European and Latin American game of soccer.[27]

By the time the Service Technique opened its long-awaited flagship school at Damien in 1929, resentments over U.S. educational and cultural policies had been mounting for years, creating a highly combustible situation. When students angry about losing scholarships went to see Dr. Freeman, who was serving as the principal of the school, the encounter summed up everything that frustrated Haitians about the system. The discussion took place through a translator: after seven years of running a major educational initiative in Haiti, the well-paid and powerful Freeman had not learned either French or Kreyòl. Smoking a pipe, he briefly listened to the students but then broke in and told them that he was free to change scholarship policies as he saw fit. When the students pressed him, Freeman got angry and, waving his arms, told them that they could leave the school if they wanted: they would be easy to replace. When he learned that the students were planning to march to Port-au-Prince, Freeman attempted conciliation: there was no need to walk to town, he told them, when they could use the institution's bus. He had not yet realized that something serious was going on. Indeed, he was mystified by the resistance he encountered. These were, after all, supposed to be the most trusted and loyal of the new class of educated Haitians the United States was aiming to produce.[28]

Freeman's surprise is itself surprising: he seemed blind to the fact that for all the buildings, roads, and schools the Americans had constructed, the U.S. presence was still seen by Haitians as an occupation. A commission sent by the U.S. government the following year to evaluate the educational project in Haiti, however, saw clearly where the problem lay. "Had there been less of a disposition to deal with the island as a conquered territory and more to help a sister state in distress," the commission wrote—less "enforced control" and more "helpful cooperation"—perhaps the unrest could have been avoided. Having spoken with many Haitian teachers and students, the group argued that it had been a mistake to overwhelmingly emphasize vocational training, and insisted that U.S. teachers should not be paid out of the Haitian treasury. Their report, however, was ignored, and none of its recommendations were adopted.[29]

Many Haitians were ultimately disappointed, and often infuriated, by an education policy they saw as racist and high-handed. By the mid-1920s, political leaders such as Dantès Bellegarde who had once been willing to work with the United States had turned vociferously against the occupation. And by the early 1930s, it was difficult to find anyone at all who would speak up on behalf of agricultural education. Despite initial goodwill and massive investment—of Haitian money—over the course of several years, the project had failed, largely because it was so disconnected from the population's own vision of the kind of education they needed and wanted. In April

1931, one legislator demanded to know why there were still so many overpaid U.S. teachers working at Damien's and other schools. Perhaps a few of these foreign experts were truly needed, he admitted, but it was time to send most of them home and replace them with the many competent Haitians who could just as easily do the job. "What do these experts do?" he asked bitterly. "Experts in grass, experts in cooking, experts in everything and nothing, experts in strangulation—they're sucking the blood of the people."[30]

III

For Haiti's elites, much of the shock of the U.S. occupation was the long and intimate experience it gave them of American racism. Haitian society had its own intricate forms of social hierarchy, based on skin color, education, and wealth. But for many in the U.S. forces, all Haitians—light-skinned and dark-skinned, uneducated and accomplished alike—were simply "Negroes" or "niggers." Over the course of the occupation, the attitude of the Americans was a constant source of bitterness that profoundly shaped the Haitian social experience. While there was some congenial contact between U.S. troops and Haitians, there were also perpetual tensions, even at the highest levels. Some of these were the result of simple culture shock: U.S. officials, for example, found it odd and amusing that before the start of meetings, Haitian cabinet members might engage in erudite discussions about recent surrealist poetry and similarly unexpected subjects. Others involved more serious snubs, such as an incident when the entire Haitian government was kept waiting for an official mass to begin because of the absence of two marine officers, who in the end never showed up. In their daily lives, meanwhile, Haitians often found the behavior of U.S. troops racist, rude, and uncouth. One evening, a drunk marine threw rocks down on guests listening to a garden piano recital being given by a Haitian who had recently returned from studying at the Paris Music Conservatory. Confronted with such provocations, some young residents answered with violence, ending up in street fights with the occupying forces. Others responded with pugnacious humor, turning the initials of the Marine Corps, USMC, into derisive tags such as "Use Sans Moindre Contrôle" ("has no self-control") or "Un Salaud Mal Costumé" ("a badly dressed jerk").[31]

Much of the tension involved what Haitians saw as a patent hypocrisy on the part of the occupiers regarding race and sex. At a reception for Franklin Roosevelt in 1917, for instance, U.S. officers had danced with Haitian women but commanded their wives to remain in another room to avoid having to dance with Haitian men. American authorities worried constantly about relationships between Haitian men and white women, even as the occupying soldiers created a boom in prostitution and often lived openly with Haitian mistresses. Marine Captain John Houston Craige later recounted the story of one soldier who went on a killing spree in Port-au-Prince, shooting several Haitians after a local woman broke up with him. "Chiquita and her like seldom get into official reports," Craige wrote, "but they have a way of influencing affairs for all of that."[32]

At the same time, for many Haitian elites, the shock of occupation was also a shock of recognition. American attitudes toward Haiti's population and culture, they realized, often uncomfortably paralleled their own. Before the occupation, many had celebrated the United States as a model of economic and political progress; now, the brutal reality of the American regime forced them into a period of soul-searching. Ultimately, the two-decade-long occupation pushed a generation of thinkers to revise their understanding of their own society, spurring new literary and cultural movements that reshaped the intellectual landscape of twentieth-century Haiti.[33]

"A nationality defends itself not only through political action," opposition leader Georges Sylvain wrote in 1918, "but through all the expressions of its thought, which rebels against destruction, against violent absorption." In the face of U.S. occupation, he argued, Haitians needed to study their history to "illuminate the quality and true meaning of our intellectual production." A true political transformation in Haiti, Sylvain insisted, would come only through a cultural transformation. His ideas got a wide hearing: by 1921, his group, L'Union Patriotique, boasted six thousand members.[34]

Musicians were among the first to respond to the call. The singer Candio, who in 1915 had teased the occupation's opponents, soon changed sides and wrote a popular song whose chorus declared: "With faith, hope, work, and unity / Down with the occupation . . . Haiti will remain a nation." The Haitian composer Occide Jeanty, meanwhile, wrote a celebrated orchestral piece called simply "1804." It drew on classical and modern influences, as well as on the music of Haitian Vodou, to celebrate Jean-Jacques Dessalines's revolutionary heritage. Jeanty conducted it weekly in outdoor concerts on the Champ de Mars to rapt audiences, until the U.S. authorities realized that it had become an antioccupation anthem and banned him from performing it.[35]

Over the course of the 1920s, the energy of opposition fueled the development of an increasingly dynamic public sphere. Doctors, lawyers, and teachers created professional organizations, while workers of all stripes—tailors, shoemakers, typographers—founded unions. Several feminist groups came together to lobby for suffrage rights for women and other legal and political reforms. There was no official political outlet for these activities: the U.S. refused to hold legislative elections, and the government insistently harassed the opposition. In 1921, President Dartiguenave had decreed that it was illegal to criticize the Haitian government or the U.S. officials working with them. But the new law could not close the floodgates. There were so many people in the Port-au-Prince jail who had been arrested for writing and publishing articles critical of the government, one U.S. visitor quipped, that you could start an excellent school of journalism there.[36]

President Borno kept a close eye on opponents: his personal archives include a series of letters written by antioccupation activists to their supporters outside the country, intercepted by the police and never delivered. Borno's government also moved to eliminate the traditional lifetime appointments of Haitian judges, many of whom openly opposed the occupation. All these repressive measures, however, only emboldened the opposition. They attacked the occupation regime, and at the same time, they looked past it. Though no elections were scheduled, they campaigned anyway, speaking to the Haitian population and developing political platforms that aimed to tackle the pressing questions of the day: deforestation, environmental protection, immigration, taxation, policing. By creating a political movement independent of the government imposed by the United States, they sought to demonstrate that a democratic order was indeed possible in Haiti.[37]

The Haitian opposition also carried out a vigorous international campaign aimed at embarrassing the United States and connecting with anti-imperial activists elsewhere. Dantès Bellegarde, who was relieved of his government position when he began speaking out against occupation policies, made himself into a sort of roving ambassador for the opposition, convincing a number of international organizations to pass resolutions demanding that the United States withdraw from Haiti. His activism culminated in an eloquent speech to the League of Nations in which he denounced the occupation's hypocrisy and pointed out the damage that it was doing to America's reputation worldwide. A French newspaper applauded Bellegarde's "spirited attack on American imperialism," though it also remarked that most members of the assembly did not want to listen to the message: instead of giving the Haitian speaker "the homage which his courage and talent deserved," they were absorbed in the task of "tracing little figures on sheets of paper." But while diplomats doodled, activists worldwide took note. Bellegarde participated in several Pan-African Congresses alongside luminaries like W.E.B. Du Bois and the Senegalese politician Blaise Diagne, arguing that the United States was promoting the idea of "Haitian inferiority" in part as a way of justifying the disenfranchisement of African Americans. He and other Haitian activists also developed ties with the NAACP and the Women's International League for

Peace and Freedom, which sent a delegation to Haiti and later published a book arguing that an occupation based on the use of force was doomed to fail.[38]

While Bellegarde connected with supporters in Europe and the United States, the energetic activist Joseph Jolibois traveled as a representative for L'Union Patriotique from the Dominican Republic to Argentina, stopping in nearly every Latin American country along the way. In Nicaragua, where U.S. marines had been fighting against resistance forces led by Augusto Sandino—and where they had also begun bombing civilians, as they had done in Haiti—he found a particularly sympathetic audience for his denunciations of American imperialism. Like Pétion a century before, Jolibois sought to connect Haiti's battle for Independence with that of other Latin American nations. The difference, of course, was that in Pétion's time, Haiti had struggled against a European empire and had seen the United States as a potential ally and an inspiration. Now, Haitian activists increasingly regarded the United States as the most dangerous empire of all.[39]

World-traveling intellectuals like Bellegarde and Jolibois were key members of the opposition, but within Haiti itself, the thinker who truly defined the cultural awakening of the 1920s was the teacher and scholar Jean Price-Mars, whose writings became a touchstone for generations of Haitians. Price-Mars claimed a venerable ancestry: he was descended from Jean-Baptiste "Mars" Belley, the African-born man who had represented Saint-Domingue at the French National Convention in 1794 and played a crucial role in the revolution. As a child, Price-Mars had grown up at the crossroads of two religions: his father was a Baptist, converted by African American missionaries, while his grandmother, who largely raised him, was a fervent Catholic. This background made him notably ecumenical: throughout periods of intense religious conflict, Price-Mars often urged Haitians to seek out "compromise and reconciliation" between their different religious traditions.[40]

From 1896 to 1902, when he was in his early twenties, Price-Mars studied on a government scholarship at the Sorbonne and the Collège de France. Wandering into a bookstore one day, he picked up a book by the prominent French social theorist Gustave Le Bon, who had created a typology of human races ranging from "primitive" to "superior," with Africans at the bottom and Europeans at the top. As Price-Mars later recalled, he "revolted against the injustice and insolence of such a judgment," and—like Firmin and Janvier before him—became determined to use "scientific truth" to battle such prejudices. He saw Haitian history itself as a powerful refutation of Le Bon's theories, proof that an oppressed group of Africans could successfully transform their own society. On returning to Haiti, Price-Mars gave a lecture that exemplified the intellectual approach he would develop over the coming decades. Haitians, he argued, suffered from internalizing the racist ideas directed at them by outsiders. In order to productively confront their social and political problems, they first needed to understand and accept that they were the equals of any other people. "Let us persuade ourselves that we are men like other men," he declared.[41]

Price-Mars's belief in the value of Haitian history and culture eventually led him to spend his weekends wandering the countryside, speaking to rural residents about language, music, kinship, and religion. On one of these excursions in 1918, he experienced firsthand the dangers of the U.S. occupation: he was detained by soldiers, and he might have ended up in a corvée labor team somewhere were it not for his status as a well-respected teacher. But he continued his work in the countryside, determined to provide a detailed ethnographic account of Haiti's rural way of life, which he believed should serve as the major reference point for a nation in search of itself.[42]

Price-Mars's ethnographic work, and particularly his readiness to treat Vodou as a subject worthy of serious study, was groundbreaking. Foreign visitors had produced many accounts purporting to describe the "superstitions" of Haiti's population, but Haitian intellectuals had tended to avoid the topic. "We bear very little resemblance to the primitive peoples of Africa, either in physical beauty, spirit, or intelligence," one writer had declared in 1905, explaining that Haitians had more in common with the "Latin part of the white race." Former president François Denys Légitime, speaking in 1911 at a congress in London, had likewise suggested that if Haiti still harbored "a few traces of African fanaticism," it was "only a lingering relic of ancestral traits which a people does not easily suppress." Even Price-Mars's close friend Dantès Bellegarde insisted that Haiti was an "intellectual province of France" and that Vodou was a brake on progress and an all-too-easy justification for racist attitudes. Haiti "would cut a poor figure," Bellegarde declared, if she "divested herself of her French culture and presented herself naked as a little savage" among neighbors clothed in "the magnificent finery of their Western Civilization."[43]

Price-Mars, however, urged Haitians to completely rethink the way they related to their culture. In his classic 1928 book *So Spoke the Uncle*, he drew on his ethnographic work and on a broad range of anthropologist theorists, including Anténor Firmin, to decry the "disconcerting paradox" of Haitian life. Haitians had a past, he said, that was "if not the most beautiful, then certainly the most engaging and moving in the history of the world"—the "transplantation of a human race to a foreign land." And yet they reacted with "an embarrassment barely concealed, indeed shame," when confronted with the fact of their African roots. They were ensnared in the slaveholders' ideology, which presented blacks as "cast-offs of humanity, without history, without morality, without religion." Price-Mars lamented that having overthrown slavery and colonialism, the "black community of Haiti clothed itself in the rags of western civilization." Ever since 1804, the country's leaders had sought to improve Haiti by copying France. "An absurd task, if there ever was one!" Price-Mars exclaimed.[44]

The country's upper classes, Price-Mars argued, had spent two centuries turning away from what really made them who they were: their African heritage, their slave revolution, their rural culture, their religion. All the "authentically indigenous" features of Haitian society were treated with suspicion by the elites, for whom the term "African" had become a "humiliating affront." "The most distinguished man" in Haiti, Price-Mars teased, "much prefers that one find him to bear some resemblance to an Eskimo" rather than "remind him of his Guinean or Sudanese ancestry." Everything, Price-Mars complained, was upside down: instead of glorifying their ancestors, members of the light-skinned elite took pride in the fact that they were descended from "bastard" relationships between French masters and their slaves, from "the anonymous shame of chance encounters." Poignantly summing up, he wrote that "as we gradually forced ourselves to believe that we were 'colored' Frenchmen, we forgot we were simply Haitians."[45]

Price-Mars's eloquent argument and his riveting lectures at the prestigious Lycée Pétion shaped an entire generation of young intellectuals, who agreed that Haiti's lack of cultural independence had paved the way for its loss of political independence. It was dangerous, as Price-Mars put it, for a society to sink into the "ruts of dull and slavish imitation" of other cultures, for that made it seem as if it had made no contribution to human progress—which was a pretext for "nations impatient for territorial expansion, ambitious for hegemony, to erase the society from the map of the world." In failing to acknowledge its own religion and language, traditions and beliefs, Haiti had opened the door to foreign occupation. The lesson was clear: if it wanted to secure independence, Haiti needed to look to its own culture as the necessary foundation of true sovereignty.[46]

⏹ ⏹ ⏹

In February 1930, an official delegation arrived from the United States to investigate conditions in Haiti. Created by President Roosevelt in response to the 1929 student strike and the massacre of protesters at Les Cayes, the commission had a diverse membership: it was led by the banker William Cameron Forbes, a strong advocate of U.S. imperialism, but also included liberal critics of the occupation. Haitian activists knew that this was a crucial opportunity to demonstrate unequivocally that the country wanted to be free from U.S. rule. They filled the streets of Port-au-Prince with protesters holding Haitian flags, mobilized witnesses to testify about the abusive behavior of the marines, and gathered in churches to pray for an end to the occupation. The opposition parties presented the Forbes Commission with a detailed plan for disentangling the two countries, beginning with free elections and the reestablishment of constitutional rights, followed by the withdrawal of U.S. military forces. When they returned to Washington, the Forbes Commission praised many aspects of the occupation, but they also criticized the racism of some U.S. officials and the controversial overemphasis on vocational education. They agreed with the opposition that the only way forward was for the United States to hold a truly open presidential contest and to finally allow legislative elections, which had been deferred for the preceding twelve years. But to the disappointment of many in Haiti, the commission concluded by recommending a slow withdrawal over the course of several years. The country, they believed, was not yet ready for complete control of its own financial and military institutions.[47]

A few months later, Haitians went to the polls for the first free elections since the beginning of the occupation. Though the balloting was organized by the American regime, U.S. officials were under strict orders to make no statements about the candidates, and the marines were kept in their barracks on election day. Energized by the years of opposition activism and by rules allowing for universal manhood suffrage, a record number of Haitians—some three hundred thousand—cast their votes, packing the Senate and the Chamber of Deputies with anti-U.S. activists. Joseph Jolibois, back from his years of traveling across Latin America on behalf of the cause, became the speaker of the Chamber. As the country's president, Haitians elected Sténio Vincent—the former interior minister who had resigned from Dartiguenave's government to protest its submission to U.S. bankers, and who was now a leading member of L'Union Patriotique.[48]

Throughout the 1920s, the Haitian opposition had worked to create an alternative public sphere in the absence of parliamentary democracy. Now they had the parliament back, along with a president who had played a crucial part in the movement against the U.S. presence on the island. Nevertheless, many activists found that progress toward full independence was frustratingly slow. The United States spent four years on a gradual "Haitianization" of the country's institutions, meanwhile maintaining strong control over all financial matters and ruling the countryside through their troops as they had done for the previous decade. The Americans also used these four years to negotiate agreements with the Haitian government that would allow them to maintain a significant level of control even after the formal withdrawal of the marines.

Many antioccupation activists were dismayed to find President Vincent offering enthusiastic support to these agreements. Though he was still committed to ending direct foreign control, Vincent had also become convinced that it was in Haiti's best interest for the United States to maintain a very strong role in the country. He even proposed that a small number of marines should remain in Haiti to provide training and security—a suggestion that infuriated many senators and deputies, who successfully pushed through plans for a full military withdrawal. He also wanted to continue direct U.S. involvement in budgetary and fiscal matters. This, too, angered many representatives, but Vincent outflanked the opposition by waiting until a legislative holiday, then signing a deal with the United States that gave Washington a "fiscal representative" within the Haitian government. The job title sounded innocent enough, but the representative was granted remarkably wide powers: controlling customs collection, inspecting the tax collection system, and approving any changes to tariffs and taxes. The U.S. fiscal representative could also set limits on Haitian government spending, and the officer would remain in place as long as Haiti was still paying off the 1922 loan it had contracted with the United States. Even after the marines departed in 1934, then, the Haitian government still contained a powerful U.S. official. The fiscal representative remained there until 1941, and the Banque Nationale d'Haïti would remain under U.S. supervision until 1947.[49]

In 1932, Vincent and the Haitian Congress rewrote Haiti's constitution to replace the one that had been foisted on the country in 1918. The new constitution, though, maintained the crucial change from that year: granting foreigners the right to own property in Haiti. Eager for investment from the north, Vincent also—despite strenuous opposition from some Haitian congressmen—negotiated an agreement with the powerful U.S.-based Standard Fruit Company that gave them a monopoly on the export of bananas from Haiti. The deal was meant to create an alternative to Haiti's traditional coffee crop, developing a new and profitable export.[50]

In time, the arrangement did succeed in improving the economy in the west of Haiti, with independent small farmers growing the bananas and selling them to Standard Fruit for shipment to the United States. Still, many young activists from the "generation of occupation" were furious at their government's eagerness to concede so much to the Americans. Inspired by Marxist ideas, some of them pressed for a different model of development, one that would avoid foreign investment and control and focus on attacking the massive economic inequalities within Haitian society. Vincent and the United States saw such arguments as dangerous and seditious, however. In 1933, while the marines were still in the country, they worked with Vincent on a campaign targeting leftist leaders, the goal of which was officially described as the "suppression of Bolshevist activities." That same year, in the wake of protests, Vincent declared a "state of siege" in the western part of Haiti, and his interior minister, Élie Lescot, ordered several opposition newspapers shut down. Joseph Jolibois, who had emerged as the most prominent critic of Vincent's cozy relationship with the United States, was arrested and imprisoned. He would remain behind bars for the rest of his life, dying in prison in 1936.[51]

Even before the "Second Independence" was formalized in 1934 with the departure of the U.S. marines, Vincent and his supporters had thus mortgaged away much of what was possible. They argued their position on pragmatic grounds, insisting that there was really no choice but to work with the United States—now Haiti's most important trading partner and clearly the most powerful player in the Caribbean region. In the process, however, they also locked themselves into a relationship with a country whose vision of Haiti would remain profoundly limited and deeply skewed.

Unlike Haitians, citizens of the United States had the privilege of largely overlooking—and in time forgetting—the huge impact their country had had on their neighbor to the south. After the Senate investigations of 1920–21, there was never a broad and public exploration of the occupation. Indeed, there has never been any widespread reckoning of what the United States did in Haiti during those twenty years, and today few people are even aware that the occupation ever occurred. Instead, the most successful writings produced in the United States about the occupation were largely self-congratulatory about its impact, and they portrayed American soldiers and officials as being forced into brutal actions by the backward habits of the Haitian population. These works refined and disseminated a set of tropes about Haiti—stereotypes of naïve and fatalistic peasants, manipulative religious leaders, and a secret world of dark sorcery—that have remained startlingly powerful to this day. The combination of silence about the political and economic impact of the occupation on the one hand, and a great deal of noise about the supposed nature of Haiti and its culture on the other, was in itself a devastating consequence of the U.S. invasion of the country.

The most influential work in the genre was William Seabrook's 1929 book *The Magic Island*. Seabrook had traveled to Haiti eager to see Vodou ceremonies, but at least at first he had no luck: no one was willing to risk imprisonment to satisfy the curiosity of a foreign visitor. In his book, he claims to have eventually gained access to the secrets of the religion by apprenticing with a *manbo*, though it seems that he actually got much of his information from marine reports about their raids on temples. His vivid, exoticized depiction of Vodou helped make the book a commercial success and an influential work among many intellectuals, including participants in the Harlem Renaissance. Seabrook's bestseller was followed in 1931 by *The White King of La Gonave* by the marine Faustin Wirkus, who had served a lengthy tour of duty in Haiti starting in 1916. Wirkus claimed that the local population of the small island of La Gonâve, where he was stationed, had made him their king. Seabrook effused that Wirkus had lived every man's dream: "Every boy ever born, if he is any good, wants, among other things, to be king of a tropical island." The story was, of course, more complicated than that: when Wirkus was the governing marine officer at La Gonâve, local Haitian groups had worked with him—they had no choice—and probably included him in some of their social rituals. This hardly meant that they saw him either as their king or their god. The American readers' expectations, however, were already relatively settled, and the story of Haiti's own long-standing forms of local political and social organization was not part of them. Nor was there much room in these books for soul-searching about the worthiness of occupation itself. When Marine Captain John Houston Craige drafted his memoir, he was at first quite critical of what he had experienced. Before publication, though, he decided that such a work "would knock me out of the Marine Corps because it was brutally frank about political matters," and he rewrote it completely into "a local color book." In his tellingly titled *Black Bagdad* and its sequel *Cannibal Cousins*, Craige's time in Haiti comes across as a humorous romp through a strange and exotic society.[52]

The wave of American occupation-era memoirs was also responsible for sending an unending stream of zombies traipsing through

U.S. popular culture. The 1934 film *White Zombie*, starring Bela Lugosi, even advertised itself as a kind of documentary, "based upon personal observations in Haiti by American writers and research workers." The movie helped spawn an entire genre, which fixed Haiti in many minds as a place of dark ritual and wandering undead, animated by an unending soundtrack of threatening drumming.[53]

By making zombies into generic horror-film monsters, such representations obscured the fact that in Haitian folklore, the *zonbi* is a powerful symbol with a specific, haunting point of reference. It is a person devoid of all agency, under the complete control of a master: that is, a slave. Sometimes the term is used as an insult—to this day, independent farmers in Haiti might call wage workers *zonbi*, insisting that to sell your labor is to sell your freedom. Tales about *zonbi* often reflect fears of an individual or collective loss of control. When the HASCO sugar mill opened in 1918, for instance, a rumor circulated that some of the workers there were *zonbi*. One of the middlemen hired by the company to bring in a gang of field laborers, the story went, had arrived with a group of particularly ragged, dazed, and silent workers whom he had zombified so that he could steal their wages. William Seabrook heard the story and featured it in his book, commenting that it was strange that HASCO—"a modern big business" that looked like "a chunk of Hoboken"— would be connected with "sorcery or superstition." It wasn't really strange at all, though: telling stories about *zonbi* workers at HASCO was probably a way for the local community to articulate the feelings evoked by the reappearance of the plantation in their midst. Indeed, it is the American zombie clichés that have functioned as a kind of intellectual sorcery. They took a religion developed in order to survive and resist slavery—one that had served as central pillar in the counter-plantation system at the core of the Haitian struggle to secure autonomy and dignity—and transformed it into nothing more than a sign of barbarism, further proof that the country would never progress unless it was guided and controlled by foreign whites.[54]

III

A decade before the occupation, Anténor Firmin had predicted that the United States would be the crucial force shaping Haiti's destiny in the twentieth century. The only question, as he saw it, was whether his country would find a way to work productively with their neighbor to the north, or whether it would be swallowed up by the United States altogether. At the dawn of the Second Independence, Vincent and many other Haitian leaders, reviewing the harsh lessons of the previous decades, found themselves agreeing with Firmin's analysis. Accordingly, they sought to maintain a relationship with the United States, though they pushed for one based on cooperation rather than domination. In so doing they seized on the increasingly popular doctrine of Pan-Americanism, which envisioned connections between different countries in the Western Hemisphere based on mutual interest and respect for sovereignty. In Washington, U.S. politicians and statesmen were also seeking to develop a new approach to the Caribbean and Latin America, one with fewer guns and battleships and more free trade and cultural exchange.[55]

For many of Haiti's leftist activists, however, the happy talk about Pan-Americanism was just a smoke screen for continued U.S. dominance. What they wanted instead was a profound reorientation of Haitian politics. A key figure in this movement was Jacques Roumain, who was born into a wealthy Port-au-Prince family, grew up studying in Switzerland, and had come back to Haiti in 1925 to fight the "hated Yankee." During the 1920s Port-au-Prince cultural renaissance, he had published vigorous articles attacking the occupation and promoting the literary style that came to be known as *indigénisme*, which sought to fulfill Jean Price-Mars's call for writing rooted in Haiti's rural culture. Now, with the marines having finally withdrawn in 1934, he founded the Parti Communiste Haïtien, attacking "the excess of the Haitian bourgeoisie and the bourgeois politicians, valets of imperialism and cruel exploiters of the workers and peasants."[56]

The fundamental issue in Haiti, Roumain argued, was one of class: most of the country's population was excluded from political participation and prevented from improving their lot. For generations, Haitian politicians had managed to deflect real challenges to this social structure by focusing instead on issues of color, cultivating conflicts between "blacks" and "mulattoes" and encouraging their followers to believe that getting blacks into power was the answer. But, Roumain insisted, the real problem was that elites of all colors were maintaining the masses in subjection and poverty. The argument was summed up in the motto of the PCH: "Color is nothing, class is everything."[57]

Roumain's movement faced tremendous challenges. Even the remarkably widespread antioccupation protests had largely replicated the country's social divisions, with urban intellectuals and students rarely collaborating directly with rural farmers. But young activists, energized by the artistic and ethnographic celebrations of rural culture, believed that they could overcome the existing divisions, reaching out to the countryside in order to produce real social change in Haiti. They found, however, that they had little room and little time to maneuver. Vincent's government, using the police network set up by the U.S. occupation, quickly and effectively worked to crush the nascent communist party. Roumain was soon arrested and accused of trying to get weapons for an armed uprising from a Haitian communist living in New York. As proof, the police produced letters in which Roumain requested "materials" from his correspondent—though in fact he was requesting pamphlets about the Scottsboro case.[58]

When Roumain was sentenced to three years in prison, there was an international outcry, and the African American writer Langston Hughes—who had met and befriended Roumain during a visit to Haiti in 1931—created an organization to lobby for his release. After a year in jail, during which he contracted malaria, Roumain was allowed to go free but forced to leave the country. Other PCH organizers in Haiti also found that writing articles critical of the government could land them in prison just as easily after the "Second Independence" as back when the marines had been in charge. In 1936, President Vincent decreed that "any profession of communist faith, oral or written, public or private, will be punishable by an imprisonment of six months to one year and by a fine." In the face of such restrictions, Vincent's opponents found other ways to criticize him. Parodying a song that listed his accomplishments, for instance, they sang instead of his failures: "Who made my skin show through my worn out pants? It's President Vincent!" But the political repression was largely effective at silencing the country's leftist movements.[59]

When it came to the question of Haitian democracy, Vincent in fact sounded very much like the U.S. administrators he had once fought against. Arguing for strong limits on political participation, he cited the conclusions of the 1930 Forbes Commission to claim that all "thoughtful and well-intentioned" Haitians knew that most of the population simply wasn't educated enough to choose their leaders responsibly. "Enlightened public opinion," Vincent wrote, represented only a "thin golden fringe" decorating the "primitive clothes of our society." In time, education could expand the basis for popular participation, but until then, too much democracy would lead to instability. "In a country like ours, where the tropical sun exasperates the temperament," he argued, politicians often lost sight of "hard reality" and got lost instead in "vain subtleties" of liberal ideas. In Vincent's opinion, what Haiti needed—what its circumstances and culture required—was a strong president who would override the irrationality and emotionalism all too easily expressed in parliamentary institutions, keeping the nation on track through firm and strict governance.[60]

Vincent made these arguments with a very specific purpose: like any number of presidents who had preceded him in Haiti, he was determined to stay in power as long as possible. In 1935, using a tried-and-true method, he rewrote the constitution to remove the rule that limited presidents to serving one term. Although this change faced stiff congressional opposition, Vincent outmaneuvered it by using the mechanism pioneered by the United States in 1918: a popular referendum, in which Haitians were asked simultaneously to approve the new constitution and to extend Vincent's mandate for another five-year term. The historian Claude Moïse summarizes the electoral farce: "The people said yes. Massively. With more than 99 percent. As usual." The new constitution represented a significant expansion of presidential power. It officially made the president the commander in chief of the armed forces, diminishing the military's independence, and also placed him directly in charge of all internal security. It gave him total control over the naming of all officials in the administration. And it included an alarming symbolic stipulation, declaring that the president "personified the Nation." Indeed, concludes Moïse, the 1935 constitution put into place an "absolute presidential monarchy," providing the president with an assortment of tools to invalidate parliamentary opposition. Vincent was determined to work around congressional resistance to his plans for U.S. investment, such as the Standard Fruit deal, and after his reelection, the new constitution made it much easier for him to push through projects that he saw as essential for Haitian development.[61]

Vincent claimed that his projects would help to alleviate rural and urban poverty, and he even delivered some speeches in Kreyòl to bolster his image as a populist. But he shared with the U.S. occupation authorities a deeply negative view of the typical Haitian peasant. "The man is ignorant, superstitious, has no needs, dissolute morals, no taste for work," Vincent complained. He was a burden on the land, for he "wastes the earth, sterilizes it, exhausting it with his stupid planting," and a burden on Haiti, which staggered under the load of "thousands of examples" of such men. As Vincent saw it, there was no future for the counter-plantation system that the rural population had developed and cultivated for many decades. It needed to disappear, yielding to what he considered to be more advanced forms of agriculture and ways of life.[62]

The most startling illustration of Vincent's distance from his country's population came in 1937, when his first response to a brutal massacre of Haitians living in the Dominican Republic appeared to be one of indifference. The border region between the two countries—Péralte's home territory—had long nourished its own culture, one that was relatively independent from the central authorities and paid little heed to the boundary separating the nations. "Although there were two sides, the people were one, united," a Haitian later recalled. Many Haitians had settled on the Dominican side of the border, acquiring and cultivating land. By the 1930s, some had been there for several generations, and they spoke both Spanish and Kreyòl.[63]

The precise placement of the border between Haiti and the Dominican Republic had long been contested, but in 1936, the Dominican dictator Rafael Trujillo—whose mother was Haitian, though he tended to hide this fact—traveled to Haiti to sign a treaty formally settling the boundary dispute. Newspapers and politicians hailed the moment as a triumph of diplomacy, the beginning of a new era of collaboration between the two neighbors. In a gesture of friendship, Vincent renamed one of the main streets in Port-au-Prince "Avenue Trujillo."[64]

Then, in October 1937, Trujillo took a tour of the border region and made an ominous announcement. "For some months I have travelled and traversed the border in every sense of the word," he declared. "I have seen, investigated, and inquired about the needs of the population." On his journey, Trujillo said, he had heard complaints from Dominicans of "depredations by Haitians living among them, thefts of cattle, provisions, fruits," and he had responded to them, "I will fix this." "We have already begun to remedy the situation," he announced chillingly. "Three hundred Haitians are now dead in Bánica. This remedy will continue."[65]

Over the next days, Dominican troops and civilians rounded up and killed tens of thousands of Haitians along the border. Often the assassins were extremely close to the victims: one officer apparently went into his kitchen and shot the family cook, an elderly Haitian woman. Thousands of Haitians were decapitated with machetes in the town square at Santiago. Others were cut down as they tried to escape across the border, which had been closed by Dominican troops. Decades later, a survivor, still carrying visible scars on her shoulders and neck, recalled how her entire extended family—twenty-eight people—had set out as a group early one morning to march toward Haiti and escape. At the border, however, Dominican soldiers were not letting any Haitians pass. When some tried to make a run for it, a guard began murdering the prisoners. "He killed everyone. I was the only one who was saved. They thought I was dead because they had given me a lot of machete blows. I was soaked in blood—all the blood in my heart. They killed my entire family . . . I was the only one to survive."[66]

There was almost no media coverage of the massacre, and Trujillo denied any personal responsibility, presenting the events as a spontaneous reaction against Haitians by local Dominicans. The official response of the Haitian government, meanwhile, was startling in its timidity. President Vincent said nothing until cabinet members pressured him to criticize Trujillo and demand an explanation for the killings. Meanwhile, the United States, concerned about the implications for regional stability, stepped in and quietly helped broker a deal between Vincent and Trujillo. The Dominican dictator agreed to pay Haiti an indemnity of $750,000—a tepid apology for a genocide. (He eventually paid only two-thirds of that, the equivalent of less than $8 million in today's currency.) Even after the indemnity agreement was signed, sporadic massacres of Haitians continued for years in the southern border region between the two countries, now directed at Haitian cane workers. The Haitian government, again, did nothing.[67]

Jacques Roumain, now living in France, described the events as a "massive lynching" of Haitians, their bodies "thrown to the sharks." He accused Trujillo of ordering the attacks and Vincent of being complicit in the massacre. Though seemingly safe in exile, Roumain was once again pursued for speaking out: he was arrested and put on trial in a French court by representatives of Trujillo's government, who accused him of "outrage against a foreign head of state." (He was not convicted.) In Haiti itself, almost no one wrote about the massacre at the time; Trujillo and Vincent had effectively established a code of silence around the entire incident. Though the massacre was one of largest genocides to take place in the Americas during the twentieth century, there has never been any official trial or investigation of what happened. To this day, it remains a disturbing specter in both countries, largely unacknowledged and unmemorialized.[68]

III

Vincent's lack of respect for Haiti's rural population and his penchant for repressive government combined to spell trouble for the religious culture of the countryside. After the U.S. forces withdrew in 1934, the laws used by the marines to justify the persecution of Vodou were revoked. The following year, however, President Vincent passed a new decree outlawing "superstitious practices," defined as "the ceremonies, rites, dances, and meetings in the course of which are practiced, in offering to so-called divinities, sacrifices of cattle or fowl." The 1935 law also targeted all practices that "exploited the public by making them think that it is possible, by occult means, either to change the luck or situation of a person, or prevent something bad from happening through procedures unknown to medical science." Those who organized or attended such ceremonies could be imprisoned for up to six months. The legislation was a stark signal that the ethnographic movement of the 1920s, despite its profound impact on Haitian literature, music, and theater, had failed to transform the way the Haitian government itself related to the country's population.[69]

Vincent's effort to eliminate this fundamental component of Haitian culture led to a particularly absurd situation a few years later, when Élie Lescot—now serving as the Haitian ambassador to Washington—was invited to bring a troupe of dancers and drummers to the city's Constitution Hall. (In 1939, that institution had famously refused to let the African American opera star Marian Anderson sing there because of the color of her skin, and Eleanor Roosevelt had riposted by organizing a concert for her on the steps of the Lincoln Memorial instead; the 1941 performance by the Haitian group would, in fact, be the first breach of the color line at the hallowed hall.) U.S. organizers planning the visit had initially pushed for an "authentic" musical group from the countryside, headed by an *oungan* and ready to perform traditional Vodou songs. But Lescot warned the organizers that one could not be sure of "what would happen" with such a group. If the dancers "got under the power," he said—that is, went into possession—"we might not be able to stop them." Instead, he proposed bringing a nascent troupe made up of young dancers drawn from prominent Port-au-Prince families, who were studying traditional dances as part of a broader folkloric education.*[71]

Lescot's approach put the dancers into a peculiar position. As they prepared for their journey to Washington, their teacher took them to a Vodou ceremony so that they could observe firsthand the performance styles that they were learning. The experience, one of the dancers later recalled, was both thrilling and frightening for someone who had long been taught to stay away from Vodou. "What adventure! What anxiety!" It was also illegal, and when the police decided to enforce the law that night, the ceremony was broken up and the young dancers were carted off to jail. Their teacher managed to get them released, but the irony of the situation was undeniable. In the process of preparing for what the Haitian state had asked them to do—perform traditional dances in the United States—the dancers had ended up breaking the state's own laws.[72]

Shortly after the performance at Constitution Hall, Lescot succeeded Vincent as the president of Haiti. Despite his promotion of

---

* The distinction was lost on a reporter from the *Washington Post*, who described "wild-eyed" dancers "falling to the floor palpably voodooed," and explained that they "weren't professionals but girls and boys from the bush" who had "worked themselves into an incipient jungle fever" backstage.[70]

the folkloric dance troupe, though, he was no more inclined than his predecessor to support the actual practice of Vodou. Indeed, in 1941, when the Catholic Church began organizing a nationwide "anti-superstition" campaign aimed at pressuring Haitians to renounce Vodou, Lescot signed an order asking "civil and military authorities to give their most complete assistance" to the church in its struggle against "fetishism and superstition." For several months, members of the Garde d'Haïti and local officials accompanied Catholic priests on their raids, collecting ritual implements to be burned in pyres. The campaign also left permanent scars on the Haitian landscape. In many communities, ancient trees were considered holy by those who practiced Vodou, understood to be a kind of home for some of the *lwa*, to eliminate such sites of worship, Catholic priests ordered these trees to be chopped down.[73]

The 1941 anti-Vodou campaign was part of a trilateral religious conflict that had been simmering in Haiti for several decades. The occupation years had brought to Haiti an increasing number of Protestant missionaries, who were attracting many converts. As the Swiss anthropologist Alfred Métraux noted, some Protestant denominations, such as Pentecostals, were particularly appealing to Haitians because they found there "an atmosphere that reminded them of that of Vaudou sanctuaries." The Protestants often saw Catholicism and Vodou as twin enemies; one Baptist missionary declared that "the Roman Catholic Church in Haiti is a bastard production of Voodooism, witchcraft, and other African heathenish cults with a gloss of Roman Catholicism." Catholics, for their part, returned the favor, portraying the Protestants as a spiritual menace and accusing them of doing "Satan's work" in Haiti.[74]

By the 1940s, many Haitian rural communities had become battlegrounds for tremendously complex spiritual warfare involving Catholic priests, Protestant missionaries, and *oungans* and *manbos* of the Vodou religion. Still, Vodou bore the brunt of the attacks. When Métraux arrived in Haiti for a vacation in 1941, he was shocked to see "an enormous pyramid of drums and 'superstitious objects'" taken from Vodou temples, piled in the presbytery of a church and awaiting a "solemn auto-da-fé." The scene reminded him of stories about Spanish priests engaging in the "suppression of idolatry" during the conquest of the Americas. The French priests in twentieth-century Haiti, Métraux later wrote, would have impressed their long-dead forebears with their zeal and intensity. When he pleaded that at least some of the items should be saved for scientific or aesthetic reasons, he was told that "the honour of Haiti was at stake and all must be destroyed."[75]

Even Jacques Roumain—who, as a committed Marxist, held that religion in general was an obstacle to human progress—insisted that the anti-Vodou methods used by the Catholic Church were inhumane and ultimately counterproductive. In the long run, he argued, the attacks only ended up confirming the spiritual power of the sites and objects that the church tried to destroy. "We must, naturally, rid the Haitian masses of the mystical shackles," Roumain wrote; but he believed that Vodou would disappear quite naturally once the ignorance and poverty that sustained it were gone. In his opinion, Haitian peasants went to the Vodou priest for healing because there were no health clinics. "What we need in Haiti," he said, "is not an anti-superstition campaign, but an anti-misery campaign."[76]

Roumain had returned to Haiti from his European exile after Lescot assumed the presidency. He had made little headway on the political front, and the "anti-superstition" campaign made it clear that, seven years after the departure of the United States, the social and religious divisions in Haiti were as deep as ever. Still, like other activists, Roumain had faith that cultural work could open the way for societal change. He began working on a novel called *Masters of the Dew*, which was meant to depict and confront Haiti's problems. The title of the book came from an ironic and wistful moniker he had heard rural residents use for themselves: we are masters of the dew, they said, implying that they were masters of nothing else. Roumain's novel, published in 1944, brought together much of the experience of Haiti's rural population from the previous years, telling the story of a man named Manuel who, returning from years as a cane worker in Cuba, tries to save a village from drought. At once tragic and hopeful, the novel (which was translated into English by Langston Hughes a few years later) is considered perhaps the greatest work of twentieth-century Haitian literature.[77]

Masters of the Dew was—and remains—so powerful because it dreamed of a different future for Haiti: one in which the migrants scattered to Cuba and the Dominican Republic could come home, the water that was so badly needed could flow once again, and Haiti's rural population would occupy the center of the story rather than being perpetually condemned to its margins. In both his political and his aesthetic work, Roumain tried to make a connection between the elite world into which he had been born and what he knew was the core and foundation of his country: the farmers and families of the countryside. But it was an uphill struggle. A decade after the departure of the United States, the political order was as closed to the majority of the population as ever. The rural population had seen its situation largely grow worse and had suffered two major assaults—the massacres along the Dominican border in 1937, and the religious persecution of 1941. The possibility of change that many had seen at the dawn of the "Second Independence" now seemed increasingly distant, even impossible.

Roumain himself died a month before his masterpiece was published. He was a young man—barely thirty-seven—but the years of imprisonment and exile had taken their toll. When he had been behind bars in the 1930s, he had taken solace in writing short poems for his young son. One of them described water coming down from the mountain and flowing to the prison, where it gives news of the outside world to a prisoner named "Little Jacques." Another described a ship heading out onto the open sea—"that great indigo tub"—toward an island in the distance. But alongside these hopeful poems was one that transformed a comforting children's song—"I'm going to the river"—into a haunting lament. In Roumain's version, when the speaker gets to the river, he finds it dry.

Nearby he sees a threatening presence, a white person, cutting wood. The elliptical poem—the only one Roumain ever wrote in Kreyòl—captured the sense of unshakable menace he felt shadowing Haiti: the threat of outsiders taking away the country's resources, and its own sources of power and renewal drying up.[78]

8

AN IMMATERIAL BEING

For six months in 1967, Marie Vieux-Chauvet shut herself in her house in Port-au-Prince to write. In the trilogy of novels she produced—*Love, Anger, Madness*—men with guns are taking over Haiti: its land, its people, even its spirit. Dressed in red and black, the gunmen shoot songbirds out of trees and, just as casually, mow down fleeing victims in the streets. "Where do these men come from?" wonders one character. "Who is their leader? They suddenly showed up in the country and have taken over without any of us being able to put up a fight. Have we become that weak and spineless?" "They're here to bring us news of the death of our freedom," an elderly man explains. Even the soldiers, however, don't really understand who is controlling them. "I am only a cog in an immense machine," one says. "The one who gives us our orders is like God, invisible and all-powerful." Vieux-Chauvet's characters try to fight back, seeking to fulfill their responsibilities to each other, to their ideals, and to their ancestors. But neither open revolt nor escape proves possible. By the end of the trilogy, they are trapped in a nightmarish dead end, with nowhere to go but the grave.[1]

Vieux-Chauvet's women find themselves in particularly horrifying situations, as sexual violence and control become a currency of power. In the first novel, *Love*, a police commander brutalizes a local woman simply because he finds her haughty and insufficiently submissive. In the second, a young woman tries to save her family and their land by submitting to the repeated sexual assaults of a powerful officer, her body spread out for him as if in a crucifixion. Throughout the novels, hope is never far from hopelessness. "Wasn't it her role," one mother wonders, "to shower her children with love, to quietly help them conquer their terror, to shut her eyes and let them take action, all with the conviction that they too would meet with failure?"[2]

In the years before she wrote the trilogy, Vieux-Chauvet had sought to create a refuge for art by organizing weekly meetings for Haitian writers in her home. They called themselves Les Araignées du Soir—"the Spiders of the Night." "Like actual spiders," explains novelist Edwidge Danticat, "they hoped to weave a protective web around themselves and keep out predatory pests." But Vieux-Chauvet was also driven to describe—to bear witness to—what was going on outside her doors. She knew that she had to be careful: during the 1960s, many intellectuals and artists had found themselves in prison, forced into exile, or worse. Three members of Vieux-Chauvet's extended family had been killed by government forces in previous years. So she set her trilogy in a vague, unspecified period of Haitian history. It started at some point after the U.S. occupation, but nothing specifically dated it to the reign of François Duvalier. Though Vieux-Chauvet was obviously writing about the omnipresent roving militia forces that Duvalier had created, she never used the nickname given to them by Haitians: Tontons Makouts. (That moniker came from a frightening character in Haitian folktales who carries away naughty children in his *makout*, or bag, and it captured the way in which the militia lurked somewhere between reality and nightmarish imagination.) The fact that Vieux-Chauvet didn't feel she could even say their name was a testament to their power.[3]

When she was finished writing *Love, Anger, Madness*, Vieux-Chauvet sent the manuscript off to the leading French press Gallimard. A few months later, she heard that they were going to publish it. Ecstatic, she threw a party at her house and, for the first time,

read excerpts from the book to her friends. As they listened, however, some of them became increasingly worried. They saw clearly
what she hadn't seen, or perhaps hadn't wanted to see: despite the
care she had taken not to name Duvalier, it was obvious that the
work was a critique of his regime. In 1962, the president had
declared, "I am even now an immaterial being," and it was all too
easy to conclude that Vieux-Chauvet's portrait of a ghostly, all-
powerful leader was meant to describe him. If she published the
work, friends warned Vieux-Chauvet, she would endanger not only
herself but potentially her acquaintances and family as well.[4]

At first Vieux-Chauvet ignored these warnings and told Gallimard
to go ahead with the publication. But when the Haitian ambassador
in Paris received an advance copy, he, too, said that she would probably be targeted if the book was released. Vieux-Chauvet, now more
frightened—this new warning had come from an official government
figure—asked the press to stop distributing the book. Her husband
apparently tracked down the small number of copies that had arrived
in Haitian bookstores, purchased them, and destroyed them, and they
soon fled into exile. It would take several decades before the trilogy
finally gained a wide readership and the critical recognition it deserves
as one of the great works of twentieth-century Haitian literature.[5]

Today, Vieux-Chauvet's novels vividly transport readers back to
the claustrophobia and terror of the years when Duvalier steadily
eliminated, neutralized, and co-opted all of the independent institutions in Haitian society. A careful student of his country's history
and politics, Duvalier offered a brutally successful response to the
decades of political crisis that had followed the U.S. occupation,
tapping into a long tradition of authoritarian rule in Haiti and
carrying it to new heights of cynicism and effectiveness. *Love, Anger,
Madness* captures the stunningly effective construction of this
regime, portraying a time when many found that there was nowhere
to turn but inside—only to discover that even their interior life was
inescapably haunted by the specter of oppression.

I I I

By the mid-1940s, many Haitians found themselves increasingly frustrated with the rule of President Élie Lescot. A decade after the end of the U.S. occupation, a new generation of student activists felt that Haiti's political class was once again selling out the mass of the population to foreign interests. Lescot found himself particularly vulnerable to such charges not only because of his involvement in the antisuperstition campaign of 1941, but also because of the negative impact of one of his major economic initiatives: the attempt to bring rubber cultivation to Haiti. A development project designed in close collaboration with the United States, the rubber cultivation scheme highlighted the profound divisions that still remained between Haiti's governing elite and the rural majority.

When Lescot first launched the project, it had seemed like a perfect plan: World War II had greatly increased demand for rubber in the United States, and Haiti offered the ideal climate for growing it. A $5 million loan from an American bank (equivalent to about $68 million today) powered the creation of the Société Haitiano-Américaine de Développement Agricole, or SHADA. The agricultural development society was hailed as a model of Haitian-American collaboration: SHADA was headed by a U.S. agronomist, but its vice president was Haitian minister of agriculture Maurice Dartigue. A botany professor from the University of Michigan traveled to the Philippines to identify and collect the best *hevea* trees (from which rubber is harvested) for transplantation to Haiti. With the plants and capital in hand, the Haitian state provided the final piece of the puzzle: land.[6]

That land, of course, had to be taken from someone. For rural Haitians, SHADA thus represented another assault of the kind now wearily familiar. The government expropriated family fields, forced residents to leave, and razed their houses. The scale of the dispossession was staggering: nearly fifty thousand acres of land throughout Haiti were cleared to make way for imported *hevea* seedlings. In the process, decades of agricultural work by rural farmers was destroyed.

In Jérémie, as many as a million fruit trees were chopped down, while the destruction of rice fields led to a significant rise in food prices across the country. Maurice Dartigue, alarmed by SHADA's tactics, pleaded with the U.S. head of the company to take into consideration "the mentality and the legitimate interests" of Haitians and to use less brutal measures for acquiring land from the peasants. But he quickly found that although he held the title of vice president of the company, he had little power to change its policies. What's more, hopes that rubber production would bring prosperity were quickly dashed. The 1943–44 harvest was a poor one, and by the following year—with World War II ending—demand for the particular kind of rubber produced by SHADA had declined. In the end, the project left little in its wake but dislocated families, their fields emptied of trees that had once provided breadfruit, mangoes, and other crops to the local population. An embittered Lescot asked for a new loan from the United States in 1945, but was turned down.[7]

The SHADA fiasco emboldened leftist activists who had long argued that U.S. involvement in Haiti was a menace rather than an opportunity. They lambasted Lescot for having been too eager to collaborate with the United States and too weak to resist the American designs on rural Haiti. More broadly, they accused him of having failed to address the overall issue of Haitian poverty. In January 1946, students poured out of schools in downtown Port-au-Prince, shouting anti-Lescot chants, singing the national anthem, and heading for the National Palace. Workers and state employees joined in. A panicked Lescot escaped by hiding in the back of a U.S. embassy car, and he warned that the Garde d'Haïti would take "the most drastic measures to re-establish public order." The next day, when the widow of Jacques Roumain led a march to the National Cathedral, soldiers fired into the crowd, killing two and wounding several others. As word spread about the deaths, crowds stormed police stations and ransacked the houses and stores of government ministers. Outside the city, drums and bamboo pipes rallied the population, and several government-owned factories were burned to the ground.[8]

With Haiti apparently on the verge of a revolution, several leaders of the Garde d'Haïti, including a high-ranking officer named Paul Magloire, stepped in and sent Lescot on the well-trodden path to political exile. In his place, the military established a three-man executive council and announced that they would be overseeing new presidential and parliamentary elections. The population of Port-au-Prince took to the streets in jubilation, shaking palm fronds—as one would on Palm Sunday—to announce a rebirth. It was a watershed moment, the first time a U.S.-supported regime in the Americas was overthrown by a popular uprising. At the same time, however, it set a dangerous precedent: the young student activists had initiated the uprising, but it was the Garde d'Haïti that harvested political power as a result, placing itself in charge of the balloting. In the elections that followed, none of the leftist groups won political office, and when they accused the Garde d'Haïti of electoral fraud, the response from the military council was all too familiar: the imposition of martial law and a ban on protests.[9]

Still, while leftist parties didn't gain political power directly, they did shape the policies of the candidate who was ultimately elected by the parliament to succeed Lescot: Dumarsais Estimé, a teacher at the Lycée Pétion. A dark-skinned man from a modest background, Estimé was a brilliant orator: the American writer Edmund Wilson, who heard him speak, proclaimed that Estimé possessed a "style and a sweep of historical imagination well beyond the reach of any living white statesman known to me, not excluding Winston Churchill." Once in power, Estimé launched a range of progressive programs, expanding educational opportunities for poorer Haitians, organizing the beginnings of a social security system, increasing the minimum wage, and instituting new labor laws. His new constitution included protections for unions and far-sighted environmental stipulations, and he initiated irrigation and reforestation projects to improve agricultural productivity and fight the degradation of farmland.[10]

Estimé knew that his progressive social policies would go nowhere if he didn't address the country's economic difficulties, and he energetically sought to secure what he called Haiti's "financial emancipation." But like all Haitian leaders going back to Boyer, he found himself hamstrung by the problem of debt: the government was still paying off the occupation-era loan contracted with the United States in 1922. Estimé pleaded with the U.S. government to forgive the debt, but to no avail, and with Haiti's state budget sapped by debt payments, many of Estimé's ambitious ideas remained nothing more than that. In a bid to increase government revenues, he nationalized the banana industry that had been run by the Standard Fruit Company; but Haitian ships lacked the necessary refrigeration capabilities and this, coupled with mismanagement, led to what one historian calls an "unmitigated disaster." Soon, the once-thriving business was in shambles.[11]

After the nationalization of the banana industry failed, Estimé looked to another possible solution to his country's economic problems: tourism. In 1949, hoping to draw visitors to Haiti, he organized a bicentennial exposition commemorating the two hundredth anniversary of the founding of Port-au-Prince. The event was widely covered in the U.S. media, helping to spread positive images of the country and showcasing the art of various Haitian painters. The American dancer Katherine Dunham, meanwhile, helped bring Haitian culture to eager audiences abroad. Estimé's plan worked to some extent, and for a time Haiti became a fashionable destination for wealthy whites and African Americans who wanted to purchase Haitian paintings and watch performances of Vodou music and dances. But the promotion came with a sizable price tag. The bicentennial exhibition cost $4 million (the equivalent of over $37 million in today's currency)—nearly a quarter of the Haitian government's total annual budget. And ultimately, Estimé's investment in publicity did not pay off. The number of tourists who came to Haiti steadily grew during the next decade, reaching over sixty thousand in 1956; but Haiti never became an attraction on the level of Jamaica or Cuba, and tourism's impact on the broader economy always remained relatively small.[12]

By the late 1940s, Estimé found himself increasingly frustrated in his attempts to transform the economic order in Haiti, and his opponents grew more vocal and hostile. Critics on the left accused him of spending too much money on trying to impress foreigners and not enough on helping his own people, while those on the right declared that his social welfare policies were radically leftist. A Haitian army officer in the Dominican Republic complained that Estimé's administration was "composed exclusively of blacks of the lowest social level" and accused him of trying to replace Catholicism with the "barbarous and primitive voodoo cult, the ritual of which is bloody sacrifice." Another opponent dubbed him "cannibal, thief, and bandit" and his regime "the most dangerous Bolshevik cell in the Antilles." In 1950, Estimé tried to revise the constitution so that he could extend his time in power, but the parliament refused to cooperate. After a group of angry Estimé supporters responded by ransacking the Senate, the military officer Paul Magloire took control and forced the president into exile.[13]

Once again, as in 1946, Magloire declared that he would supervise a transition to a new government. This time, however, the transition he oversaw was to himself. Styling himself as a "citizen-soldier" who would ensure stability, Magloire was elected by the parliament to be Haiti's next president. In sharp contrast to Estimé, he made the suppression of leftist activity a hallmark of his regime: he signed an anticommunist pact with the Dominican dictator Rafael Trujillo and actively attacked union organizers. "The people of Haiti are immune to Communism," he announced, "because the goods are well distributed among everybody."[14]

Magloire was well aware that such declarations were music to the ears of American policymakers during the Cold War, and he made the most of the situation. Where Estimé had insisted that Haiti should pursue economic independence and self-sufficiency, Magloire eagerly sought out U.S. investment and financial assistance. On a visit to the United States, Magloire was honored with a ticker-tape parade in New York, and in Washington he declared to a joint session of

Congress that Haiti's "destiny" was "closely linked to that of the great American democracy, for better or worse." Soon, aid money from the United States, the United Nations, and the World Health Organization began pouring into the country, along with new groups of volunteers and missionaries, who established schools and hospitals. The foreign assistance enabled Magloire to rebuild roads that had fallen into disrepair and to construct a dam in the Artibonite Valley for hydroelectric power and irrigation. In 1954, he also organized massive celebrations of the sesquicentennial of Haitian independence, with the African American singer Marian Anderson performing a concert at the ruins of Christophe's Sans-Souci palace. These projects made the early years of Magloire's presidency popular with many Haitians: one observer has dubbed his time in office a "golden age" for Haiti, a period of stability and relative prosperity that made the regime's reactionary rigidity less conspicuous.[15]

Ultimately, though, Magloire's conservative approach and his courting of foreign aid were no more successful than Estimé's progressive policies at arresting Haiti's economic decline. Agricultural production, which accounted for more than 80 percent of the gross national product, was stagnating, having sunk by some accounts to levels as low as those of the worst stretches of the nineteenth century. Deforestation and soil erosion were an increasingly dire threat, and rural residents continued to leave for Port-au-Prince in droves. In 1954, the situation was worsened dramatically by a massive hurricane that killed five thousand people, left a quarter of a million homeless, and destroyed much of the year's coffee and cocoa crops. Almost a decade after a popular uprising had removed Lescot from power, the country's situation seemed as desperate as ever. As Haitians began talking about who would succeed Magloire at the end of his term, one commentator declared that "the choice of the future president is for the laboring classes a matter of life and death."[16]

Back in 1950, Magloire had intervened to depose Estimé when he tried to extend his time in office. As the end of Magloire's own term approached in 1956, however, he proved no more willing to relinquish power and refused to call an election. When that decision was met with protests, he declared a state of siege. The result was a violent, year-long struggle over control of the presidency, and when the fighting ended, it was a relative unknown—a doctor, writer, and occasional activist—who had taken power. Having carefully watched what had happened to the previous leaders, François Duvalier would offer his own response to Haiti's situation: a twisted synthesis of Estimé's populism and Magloire's conservatism, with a ferocious cult of personality at the center.[17]

| | |

The 1956 tug-of-war over the presidency was not Duvalier's first venture into Haitian politics. As a student at the prestigious Lycée Pétion, he had counted Estimé and Jean Price-Mars among his teachers, and after graduating from medical school, he combined his work as a doctor with writing for newspapers. By 1934 he was publishing regular columns about literature and politics under the memorable pen name Abderrahman, in reference to Abd-al-Rahman, a tenth-century Muslim caliph in Spain who founded the medical school in Córdoba.[18]

In one of his newspaper columns, Duvalier railed against the "useless elite, bloated with pride, stupid, and imbecile" that governed Haiti. His own career, though, was rapidly propelling him from a middle-class childhood—his father was an elementary school teacher, and his mother worked in a bakery—toward the elite ranks. In the early 1940s he was hired to be part of a U.S.-sponsored program aimed at the eradication of yaws, an infectious tropical disease that left many crippled in Haiti. Because he spoke some English, Duvalier became the interpreter for the American leader of the project, and soon he was named to head one of the anti-yaws clinics. The prestige of his work as a doctor also contributed to his social advancement: in 1939 he had married Simone Ovide Faine, the daughter of a wealthy light-skinned merchant from the prosperous neighborhood of Pétionville. The match highlighted the complicated ways in which class and color interacted in shaping the hierarchies of Haitian society. Though light-skinned Haitian families often considered dark-skinned suitors like Duvalier to be unsuitable, education and professional success could overcome such barriers. Simone would eventually accompany Duvalier to the heights of power, playing a vital role behind the scenes.[19]

Despite his firsthand experience with the fluidity of Haiti's social system, in his political thought Duvalier held fast to the idea that there was a fundamental opposition between "black" and "mulatto" groups in Haiti. Leftist thinkers such as Jacques Roumain had sought to direct political debate toward issues of class, pointing out that in Haiti discussions of color merely served to hide the more difficult truth: governing elites of all colors had consistently marginalized the population. Duvalier, though, saw the two as inseparable. For him, color was class, and class was color. In a 1946 essay, Duvalier and his friend Lorimer Denis noted that the vast majority of Haiti's people were black descendants of Africans. But this group, they argued, had always been dominated and oppressed by the country's light-skinned elites. Dessalines—whom they described as "the first Haitian socialist"—was assassinated by the light-skinned Pétion, they said, because he had planned to distribute land to the ex-slaves. Peasant leaders like Acaau had been likewise crushed by the elites. This nineteenth-century pattern, Duvalier and Denis maintained, had continued through the twentieth century, and it was time to break it. The country needed new black leaders, true heirs to Dessalines, who would finally complete the decolonization begun by the Haitian Revolution.[20]

The historical narrative presented by Duvalier and Denis was decidedly selective. Christophe was largely absent: his story didn't fit well into their narrative about the perpetual exclusion of the black majority. Duvalier and Denis also elided the fact that it was Pétion who had distributed land to his army, thereby helping to lay the foundation for *lakou* culture. Such details would have muddied the point. In any case, the essay was really less about the past than about the future. As Duvalier launched himself into politics, he realized that the social resentments felt by many darker-skinned Haitians could be effectively channeled into an invitingly simple political argument: remove the light-skinned elite, replace them with black leaders, and Haiti would be saved.[21]

After Lescot was forced into exile in 1946, the question of color became a central issue in the election. It did not escape activists' notice that all four presidents installed through U.S. support—Dartiguenave, Borno, Vincent, and Lescot—had been light-skinned. "The mulatto is a mulatto before being a Haitian," one newspaper article proclaimed. Another writer declared that blacks were tired of the "contempt and arrogance of the Nazis of Haiti"—that is, the light-skinned elites. Duvalier himself briefly considered running for president, but then decided that it was too early for such a move. Instead, he wound up serving in the administration of his former teacher Estimé, where he witnessed both the president's attempts at reform and the strenuous resistance they encountered. The provocatively racist tone used by some of Estimé's opponents confirmed Duvalier's sense that color conflict was indeed the key to Haitian politics. When Magloire came to power, he dismissed a number of the middle-class blacks hired by Estimé, including Duvalier, who returned to his work in the anti-yaws campaign.[22]

Throughout the Magloire years, Duvalier continued to write, further developing his theories about what ailed Haiti and what could heal it. In addition to insisting on the need for black leadership, he also delved into the question of what particular style of government was best suited for Haitians. Like many intellectuals of his generation, Duvalier considered himself an heir to Jean Price-Mars, convinced by the ethnographer's argument that Haitian cultural and political development had been stunted by subservience to French values. Duvalier's version of this viewpoint, however, represented an important shift from the approach taken by his mentor. Whereas Price-Mars had emphasized the way that Haitian culture had been forged by the country's history, Duvalier stressed what he saw as the essential, transhistorical qualities of the African race. In making this argument he drew from a surprising source: the nineteenth-century French racial theorist Arthur de Gobineau, who had postulated that there were fundamental biological differences between the personalities of different racial groups. Gobineau had specifically cited Haiti as proof of the inferiority of blacks, describing the manners of its people as being "depraved, brutal, and savage." Back in 1885, Anténor Firmin had energetically attacked these theories in his *On the Equality of the Human Races*. Duvalier, however, was taken by the idea that there were distinct African and European personalities, and particularly by Gobineau's suggestion that Africans were naturally inclined to "paternalistic" and "despotic" forms of government. Elaborating on Gobineau, Duvalier proposed that Africans were "communal" in nature, rather than "individualistic" as Westerners were. As a result, he concluded, Africans—and, by extension, Haitians—needed strong leaders, rulers who would be less interested in safeguarding individual rights than in pursuing the good of the national community as a whole.[23]

When the political chaos began in 1956, Duvalier decided that the time had come to transform his ideas into action. The situation was muddled and treacherous. After refusing to call elections, Magloire had been forced out of power, and over the next seven months, Haiti had passed through the hands of five temporary governments. Eventually, three major players emerged: the wealthy Louis Déjoie, a descendant of the nineteenth-century president Fabre Geffrard; the working-class leader Daniel Fignolé; and Duvalier. All of them were experienced political operators, who knew both how to deploy public demonstrations and how to work behind the scenes. Déjoie was an agronomist who had studied in Belgium, directed an agricultural school during the U.S. occupation, and worked as a chemist for HASCO before being elected senator; he had the support of many powerful Haitians. Fignolé, a charismatic former mathematics professor, was the most popular of the leftist candidates who had been kept from office by Magloire's military council in 1946, and he continued to command an impressive following among the masses in Port-au-Prince. Fignolé's supporters, ready to pour out into the streets at his call, were known as his "steamroller." The fifty-year-old Duvalier seemed, in comparison, to have a much smaller chance of capturing the presidency. But he had many contacts in the countryside, was admired for his medical work, and presented himself as the heir to Estimé, accumulating a significant following among those committed to increasing black political power.[24]

Supporters of the three candidates often clashed violently, and Duvalier proved particularly masterful in the tactics of ground-level political conflict. He made especially effective use of a network of hired thugs, known as *cagoulards* for the *cagoules*, or masks, they wore over their faces. Duvalier's *cagoulards* disrupted the process of voter registration with demonstrations and attacks on electoral offices, and even invaded an official mass in the National Cathedral, starting a melee that left several dead. At night they visited the houses of Duvalier's opponents, and they seem to have carried out a string of bombings aimed at sowing a climate of fear. Duvalier also cultivated support within the military. The army was initially divided between different candidates—at one point a showdown between two rival groups of soldiers in the streets of Port-au-Prince came complete with artillery fire and a bombing raid—but as the election approached, most of it united behind Duvalier. In May 1957 Fignolé was appointed provisional president, but within weeks he was overthrown by high-ranking military officers and forced out of the country, leaving his supporters without a candidate. When they surged into the streets to protest, the army responded with gunfire, pursuing them into their neighborhoods and killing as many as five hundred.[25]

On September 22, 1957, Haitians finally went to the polls. Duvalier was declared the victor, with nearly 680,000 votes, compared to just under 267,000 for Déjoie—though many were convinced at the time, and remain convinced, that his victory was in fact the result of fraud. His sympathizers also secured fifty-six out of the fifty-eight seats in the Congress of Deputies. Déjoie pointed out that Duvalier's father was not Haitian-born but had immigrated from Martinique, and that therefore (according to the same constitutional provision that should have disqualified Louis Borno) Duvalier was not eligible to be president. Though Déjoie was technically correct, he no longer had any real power, and Duvalier simply ignored the issue. Widespread accusations that he had manipulated the electoral process and stolen the presidency also left Duvalier unfazed. When asked how he had won, Duvalier responded smilingly, "The peasants love their doc." But he also made it clear that his power was not subject to question. "As President I have no enemies and can have none," he declared. "There are only the enemies of the nation. And these the nation must judge."[26]

III

"No one is untouchable, and nothing is sacred." This, writes the Haitian historian Claude Moïse, was the message Duvalier rapidly broadcast from the first days of his presidency. Duvalier's remorseless suppression of dissent "stupefied" all the other traditional power holders in the country—the church, the political elites, the army, foreign government representatives—and reshaped the entire political landscape. "Duvalierist violence appeared limitless," writes the Haitian anthropologist Michel-Rolph Trouillot, and its "logic lay precisely in the fact that it seemed limitless" and almost random. "A tally of its casualties would count more scapegoats, more victims of sheer arbitrariness, of accidents of birth, or of presence at inopportune times and places than opponents who represented any real menace to the regime." The randomness was part of the point: "The victims were so many sacrificial offerings, confirming the permanence of power, a reminder to the people of their smallness in regard to the state, a reminder to the executioners of the omnipotence of

their chief." Though no one will likely ever know how many perished at the hands of Duvalier's regime, estimates range from twenty
thousand to as high as sixty thousand killed over the course of three
decades. As Moïse puts it, Duvalier became an innovator: his "origi-
nality was to elevate repression to a level of brutality and perfection
that had never before been achieved."[27]

Duvalier did initially send out some reassuring signals about the
kind of regime he had in mind. His cabinet brought together men
from a wide range of political and social backgrounds, including a
few Marxists, and he garnered strong support from many prominent political and intellectual figures. The new constitution adopted
in 1957 preserved the basic civil rights laid out in the previous version of the document, and even expanded some of them in significant ways. Though it did not explicitly name Kreyòl as an official
language—that would have to wait another thirty years—Duvalier's
constitution broke new ground by decreeing that Kreyòl could be
used in official contexts when necessary to protect "the material and
moral interests of citizens who do not speak the French language
sufficiently." The new constitution was also the first to give women
the right to vote, while a section on family law established equal economic rights within marriage.[28]

At the same time, however, the constitution paved the way for an
attack on democratic institutions. Duvalier knew that previous
presidents had often encountered powerful opposition in the Haitian Senate, so he abolished the bicameral legislature, which dated
back to 1816, replacing it with a single and more tractable house
that combined the Senate and the Chamber of Deputies. The members of this new parliament also had shorter terms than representatives had enjoyed before. In addition, the new constitution put into
place a ban on strikes by government employees and gave the executive the right to "militarize" the public sector when necessary.
Most significantly, it expanded the government's right to declare a
state of siege: Duvalier could now do so not only in case of foreign
invasion but also in response to "civil disturbances" within the

country. The term was intentionally vague, so that it could be applied to almost anything—strikes, demonstrations, conspiracies, even mere rumors of any of these. Since a state of siege brought with it a suspension of civil and political rights, the executive was now armed with an extremely powerful mechanism for establishing near-total control. As Claude Moïse notes, this simple-seeming clause within the constitution allowed the president to dispense at will with the entire legal edifice that surrounded it. And Duvalier did not hesitate to take advantage of this ability: indeed, "the entire Duvalier regime can be summarized as an almost uninterrupted chain of states of siege and special powers."[29]

Over the next years, Duvalier created an ever-widening web of repression and terror. Occasionally, his efforts at establishing total control were frustrated: a Cuban opened a clandestine radio station in Haiti that broadcast anti-Duvalier messages, for example, and the police were never able to locate it, even though it was based in a butcher shop across the street from the National Palace. But what the regime lacked at first in surveillance skills, it made up for with ruthlessness that shocked and ultimately silenced most opponents. No one was exempt from the brutality; prominent women, in particular, suffered some remarkably vicious attacks. In early 1958, a group of *cagoulards* sent by Duvalier entered the home of Yvonne Hakim-Rimpel, an admired feminist activist who had criticized the new regime, beat up her two daughters, and carried her away. The next day, she was discovered dumped along a roadside, unconscious and almost naked.[30]

The repression was motivated in part by a series of attempted coups against Duvalier in the early years of his regime. In July 1958, three exiled Haitian officers backed up by a handful of U.S. mercenaries (including two deputy sheriffs from Florida) sailed into Haiti, hijacked a bus, and briefly took over the garrison in downtown Port-au-Prince before being killed by Duvalier's forces. A year later a small group of rebels landed at Les Cayes, but the Haitian military—working with the U.S. marines—rapidly crushed the uprising and carried out brutal reprisals against those suspected of having aided the insurgents. In April 1961, the leftist activist Jacques-Stephen Alexis arrived with four other Haitians from Cuba, intending to start a popular uprising, but they were quickly captured. After several days of torture, Alexis and his companions were executed in a particularly gruesome way: local residents were ordered to publicly stone the men to death. "Revolutions must be total, radical, inflexible," Duvalier declared afterward. "I have conquered the country. I have conquered power. I am the new Haiti. To wish to destroy me is to wish to destroy Haiti itself. It is thanks to me that it breathes, thanks to me that it even exists."[31]

Duvalier seized upon these attacks to justify the creation of his own security forces, transforming the informal bands of *cagoulards* that had helped him to win the election into a more formal organization under his direct command. Although the Haitian army had played a crucial role in getting him into power, Duvalier was extremely wary of it, realizing that it was one of the few institutions that could effectively stand up to him. Accordingly, he routinely purged the armed forces of anyone he suspected might oppose him, kept the military off balance with frequent firings and demotions, and closed down the military academy to eliminate a source of potentially independent-minded officers. Meanwhile, his longtime collaborator Clément Barbot was placed in charge of creating a new civil militia, which began taking in recruits in 1959. These recruits were paid relatively little, but through their connection with the regime they gained social prestige and nearly limitless power, especially in rural areas. Within a few years, the force was given the official name of National Security Volunteers, while many Haitians had started referring to them as Tontons Makouts. Ultimately, the security forces became twice as large as the Haitian army itself, and by the mid-1960s they were consuming more than two-thirds of the entire government budget.[32]

These new troops—the men with guns who pop up everywhere in Vieux-Chauvet's novels—were quickly deployed by Duvalier to assert complete control over all political activity. Early in 1960, a group of them entered the house of Dantès Bellegarde in downtown Port-au-Prince. The former minister of agriculture had retired from public life several years before and now spent much of his time cultivating his garden, a small oasis in the increasingly run-down center of the capital. But this disengagement didn't offer him protection: his status as a renowned intellectual was enough to make him a potential threat who needed to be intimidated into silence. The men held a gun to him and ransacked his residence, ripping up his papers and throwing his books on the ground. Bellegarde was comparatively lucky: the intruders, having roughed him up, left him in his home. Many others simply disappeared. When six senators from Duvalier's slate spoke up against some of his actions in late 1959, the president declared them "enemies of the Republic" and accused them of terrorism. Five of them fled into exile, but one, an Episcopalian minister named Yvon Emmanuel Moreau, stayed behind. He declared that he was "a believer in democracy" and just doing his job as a senator. Within days, Moreau was arrested, and he was never heard from again.[33]

Well-known activists and politicians were not the only ones Duvalier saw as a danger to his regime. In September 1960 he arrested several young university students, accusing them of "subversive activities." When other students went on strike in protest, Duvalier closed the university, declaring an early vacation, and reorganized the university system in a way that gave him firmer control over the institution. During the same period, four of Haiti's major newspapers were shut down, their premises destroyed, and their journalists imprisoned and tortured. Duvalier also attacked unions, arresting the president of the country's largest labor organization. "All popular movements will be repressed with utmost rigor," he announced. "The repression will be total, inflexible and inexorable." Among the groups he banned under this edict was the Haitian Boy Scouts.[34]

The violence infused everyday interactions with terror and uncertainty. To protect themselves from being harmed by the state, people sought to tie themselves to it in whatever way they could. At the same time, government connections became a sort of trump card that could put an end to any argument. "In the course of daily life anyone could claim a relationship, even fictitious, to the sole center and source of power in order to ensure a place on the side of the survivors," notes Trouillot. "Thousands of everyday disputes, from a parent's arguments about a child's school grades to a brawl at a nightclub over a dancing partner," led "one or another of the contending parties" to invoke the regime as a way of gaining the upper hand. This habit constantly reinforced and solidified the state's claims to power, sundering links of friendship and conviviality. Over time, people coped with the situation in different ways. Some chose to work with the regime, seeing this as the only way to guarantee a certain level of security for themselves. Others sought simply to minimize their interactions with the state and go about their daily lives as quietly as possible. Many went into exile, waiting and hoping that they could one day return to a land free of Duvalier. Year after year, however, the regime seemed only to get stronger.[35]

"Do you know why I have succeeded where other intellectuals, like Firmin and Bobo, failed?" Duvalier once asked a group of army officers. "I was the first to have a pen in one hand and a gun in the other." Drawing skillfully on his own involvement in the decades of intellectual and cultural effervescence that began in the 1920s, Duvalier presented himself as the embodiment of the aspirations of an awakened Haitian nation. His regime, he insisted, was the fulfillment of the powerful demands made during and after the occupation for a more authentic, indigenous form of governance. "The Haitian democracy is not the German or the French democracy," Duvalier declared a few years after his election. "It is neither the Latin American or U.S.-type democracy. It is defined in full, according to the ethnic background of the people, its history, its traditions, its sociology, all overflowing with humanism." Those who opposed him abroad, he proclaimed, were participating in a form of "masqueraded colonialism." "No power in the world can come and give us a lesson in democracy," he belligerently announced in 1963.[36]

Duvalier's self-presentation as a champion of authentic Haitian culture made expert use of the language of Haiti's cultural renaissance. The irony—and indeed tragedy—of the situation was that he twisted the argument for culturally rooted forms of governance into nothing more than a justification of authoritarian rule, stifling any hope for actually achieving social change. Like many leaders before him, Duvalier trumpeted the virtues of Haitian independence and sovereignty while doing little to address the profound social and economic difficulties facing the population. And though he played up his devotion to the rural Haitian masses, most of them remained profoundly disempowered. His regime offered them little more than symbolic inclusion, frequently busing in large numbers of supporters from the countryside to listen to his speeches in Port-au-Prince. Duvalier became a patron for popular singers, and he sponsored celebrations in his honor that showcased the traditional *rara* music played by musicians during the carnival season. But Haitians who tried to exercise the traditional right to parody long granted to carnival acts found that this, too, had been taken away from them. One performer in 1962 built a castle out of papier-mâché and carried it through the streets, demanding pennies for "maintenance"—a humorous reference to the government's habit of demanding coerced "contributions" for new construction projects. Many laughed at the joke, until the Tontons Makouts came to arrest the man. Another group pantomimed a forceful critique of life under Duvalier: they worked on repairing the road, but whenever they asked their boss for their wages, he pulled out a mimed gun and pointed it at them. These performers, too, soon found themselves facing the quite real guns of the militia, and were taken off to prison.[37]

Observers of Duvalier's implacable hold on power have often dwelled, sometimes obsessively, on one aspect of his rule: his use of the symbols of Haitian Vodou. Some have claimed that in order to spread fear among the population, Duvalier consciously dressed so as to make himself look like the Vodou *lwa* Bawon Samèdi, who wears a dark suit and top hat and is associated with the realm of the dead. Duvalier was widely reputed to be a practitioner of Vodou, even an *oungan* himself, leading many to conclude that Vodou was one of the central pillars of the regime and its practitioners near-automatic Duvalier supporters. In fact, however, Duvalier approached Vodou in the same way that he handled all other institutions in Haitian society, through a combination of co-optation and repression. He eliminated those *oungans* and *manbos* who resisted his regime and rewarded those who supported him. In the countryside, where religious leaders wielded significant influence, Duvalier did recruit many of them as militia members or local enforcers; but this was a strategic decision, meant both to draw on the existing rural power structures and to make them subordinate to the state. Overall, Duvalier's use of Vodou was opportunistic, and he did little to change the status of the religion in the country. Indeed, laws outlawing "superstitious practices" remained in effect throughout his time in power. As for the loyalty of Vodou practitioners, the extremely diverse and decentralized nature of the religion meant that it was never a monolithic political force. Vodou rituals were deployed both to support the regime and to resist it, depending on the region, the circumstance, and the individuals involved.[38]

Duvalier's attitude toward the Catholic Church was similarly driven by political calculations rather than any overarching principle. As a young intellectual, Duvalier had made a name for himself in part by criticizing the Church for its 1941 antisuperstition campaign, and many Catholic priests in the country remembered this with bitterness: during the 1956 election, a prominent bishop had opposed Duvalier's candidacy by calling on Haitians to "vote Catholic." Once in power, however, Duvalier frequently used Catholic imagery to present himself as Haiti's moral leader. A newspaper published an image of Christ tapping Duvalier's shoulders and declaring "I have chosen him," and a popular portrait of the president showed him at his desk with Jesus standing behind him, like a patron and protector.[39]

While he embraced Catholic imagery, however, Duvalier saw the established Catholic Church in Haiti as a potential threat to his power, an institution that might provide opponents with a sanctuary and a platform for airing their grievances. Soon he found the perfect pretext to attack the Church, one that fit well with his image as an ardent nationalist: he denounced it as a foreign establishment. It was an easy charge to make: in the early 1960s, the Catholic Church in Haiti was still staffed almost completely with priests from France, Canada, and Belgium. Duvalier also took advantage of the simmering anger in the countryside about the anti-Vodou campaign, accusing a foreign priest of having destroyed "archaeological and folkloric riches" in his diocese.[40]

Such claims, along with more direct accusations of sedition, formed the basis for a systematic purge of priests and bishops who were critical of the Duvalier regime. The attacks were carried out with startling brazenness: at one point, Duvalier sent troops to break up a prayer meeting in the Port-au-Prince cathedral and briefly arrested the bishop. Eventually, he negotiated with the papacy to secure the nomination of five Haitian bishops, who distinguished themselves by their steadfast support of the regime. Still, as with Vodou, Duvalier's co-opting of the Catholic Church was never complete, and it continued to harbor pockets of resistance to his rule throughout the years—resistance all the more meaningful because now the Church was largely Haitian.[41]

III

While Duvalier was extremely adept at gaining control over the institutions of Haitian civil society, that would not have been enough to sustain his regime if he had not also been able to outmaneuver the most powerful outside force he faced: the United States. At the time, Washington's approach to Haiti was (as it so often has been) uneven and fragmented, with different actors—the president and Congress, the State Department and the diplomatic corps in Haiti, the CIA and the U.S. military—each pursuing their own agenda. Duvalier understood that, and he also understood that the broader Cold War context provided him with ample opportunities to manipulate the U.S. government to his own ends.

When the 1956 election began, the U.S. State Department had initially come out in support of Déjoie, not Duvalier. But some U.S. officials in the country noted that Déjoie was distinctly oriented toward France, while Duvalier had long-standing professional connections with the United States. Duvalier also offered what some Americans saw as an appealingly limited project of reform, an anticommunist agenda that did not call for overthrowing existing economic hierarchies. Many Haitians became convinced that Duvalier was the U.S. government's preferred candidate, and though there was in fact division among the ranks of American officials, just before the election, the U.S. embassy openly endorsed him. Duvalier responded in kind: in his first press conference as president, he announced his hope that Haiti would become the "spoiled child of the United States, with the help of American capital." The example of Puerto Rico's prosperity, he said, was an inspiration.[42]

As soon as he was installed in office, Duvalier hired a New York public relations firm headed by John Roosevelt, the son of Franklin, to promote Haiti and the Duvalier regime. (This was the first of many U.S. firms hired by Duvalier, who at one point turned to Lehman Brothers for advice on economic reforms.) The publicity efforts soon paid off. A *New York Times* editorial concluded that, despite the problems with the election, Duvalier should be "accepted as the legitimate president of Haiti": what was done was done, and it was in the best interests of the United States to work with the country's new ruler. And in May 1958, a Marine Corps training team, led by a veteran of the U.S. occupation, arrived to work with the Haitian army. Though quite small, the marine presence was symbolically significant, buttressing Duvalier's power during his crucial first years. Direct financial aid also began to pour in from the United States: $7 million in 1959, and over $9 million in 1960—30 percent of the state budget in that year. By 1961, the $13.5 million received from the United States (the equivalent of over $100 million in today's currency) made up 50 percent of the Haitian budget. In addition, both the Haitian military and the Tontons Makouts were largely armed with U.S. weapons: the Americans sent about two million dollars' worth of equipment in 1959, including rifles, mortars, and machine guns. Though the weapons were technically U.S. property under control of the marine mission, they were in fact widely distributed and stockpiled by Duvalier's militia units. U.S. officials working in Haiti were well aware of the violence of Duvalier's regime. But Duvalier's repressive approach also gave his government unusual stability—something that the United States had long wanted to see in Haiti, and that they found particularly appealing in the wake of the 1959 Cuban Revolution.[43]

For a brief moment in the 1960s, the U.S. government did seem poised to turn decisively against Duvalier. The John F. Kennedy administration, pursuing a new approach for economic and political collaboration with Latin America known as the Alliance for Progress, saw Haiti, in the words of Secretary of State Dean Rusk, as a "disgrace to this hemisphere." "We were very concerned about Haiti," Rusk later recalled. The country was "a political and social cesspool," plagued by problems of "poverty, illiteracy, superstition, inadequate public services of the most minimum sort, human rights—make your own list." One U.S. official who served in Haiti during this time summed up Duvalier's regime as "unconstitutional, uncooperative, unreliable, unresponsive, unfriendly, inhumane, insincere and ineffective." Americans also felt that Duvalier represented a strategic liability. The Alliance for Progress, as one official put it, was supposed to "encourage the growth of reasonably stable governments capable of absorbing reform and change, secure from both the extreme Left and the extreme Right," and Duvalier did not fit the bill. They feared that he could end up being for Haiti what Batista had been for Cuba: a brutal dictator who opened the way for a communist revolution. In addition, U.S. officials were worried about Duvalier's new militia, which they rightly perceived as usurping the role of the traditional military. Since creating the Garde d'Haïti, the U.S. military had maintained close contacts with the Haitian army and indeed trained a number of Haitian officers, and Washington considered that institution an important conduit for the transmission of U.S. ideals.[44]

The showdown between Duvalier and the Kennedy administration began in earnest in May 1961. Haiti's constitution established a six-year presidential mandate, which meant that Duvalier was supposed to leave office in 1963. In the previous decades, every Haitian president approaching the end of his term had tried to extend his time in power; Duvalier decided to get an early start on the process. In 1961 he called a referendum on a yes-or-no question: Should he continue to serve as president until 1967? The U.S. considered the election a farce: under the watchful eyes of the president's militia, voters filed in and had to publicly ask for either a yes or a no ballot. Unsurprisingly, a massive majority voted in favor of the extension. In protest, Kennedy withdrew his ambassador and cut off direct military aid, though the United States continued to supply some assistance to the country. The goal was to establish distance from Duvalier himself and search for a political alternative within Haitian society, while trying to avoid a social upheaval by continuing to provide humanitarian assistance.[45]

With Kennedy's approval, the CIA gave some financial support and military training to groups of exiles who volunteered to invade the country. One plan, optimistically, hoped to kill two birds with one stone: a joint force of Haitian and Cuban exiles would topple Duvalier, then Castro. But support for such schemes was halfhearted at best, and the exile groups who eventually did attack Haiti from the United States in the 1960s would do so largely on their own initiative. In the meantime, the CIA explored other possible ways to influence Haiti: for a short time they apparently bought editorial control of the astrological forecast of the French magazine *Horoscope*, which they believed Duvalier read avidly, hoping to manipulate him through the stars.[46]

As Rusk himself later admitted, the United States found the Haitian dictator to be "extraordinarily resistant." In the wake of the Cuban Revolution, Duvalier astutely played on U.S. fears about the spread of communism in the Caribbean. "Haiti has to choose between the two great poles of attraction in the world today to realize her needs," he threatened in a 1960 speech. At a key meeting of the Organization of American States in January 1962, when the United States was pushing for the expulsion of Cuba from the OAS, the Haitian foreign minister met with Dean Rusk and offered his support in return for a promise of aid. The U.S. secretary of state agreed, and Haiti cast the swing vote. A burst of aid to Haiti soon followed. The pointed joke among staffers in Washington was that on his return from the meeting, Rusk submitted a receipt for expenses that read, "Breakfast: $2.25. Lunch with Haitian Foreign Minister: $2,800,000.00."[47]

Even as he held the United States at bay, however, Duvalier faced continuing threats of coups and insurrections in his own country. Many of these plots originated right next door, in the Dominican Republic. After his election Duvalier had signed a pact with the Dominican dictator Rafael Trujillo: the two agreed to protect each other by suppressing any such conspiracies within their borders. Trujillo was nearing his third decade in power, and he planned to stay seemingly indefinitely; at one point he declared that he would still be running the Dominican Republic in the year 2000. In May 1961, however, he was assassinated. The longtime Trujillo opponent Juan Bosch returned from exile, won the ensuing election, and embarked on a far-reaching project of reform. Bosch made no secret of his distaste for Duvalier, and he allowed groups of Haitian exiles planning to overthrow the president to gather and train in the Dominican Republic. One of these groups flew planes over Port-au-Prince dropping leaflets announcing that they would destroy "all noxious insects who accompany the gorilla Duvalier" and calling on army officers to join in the uprising.[48]

As tensions mounted, Duvalier rarely appeared in public, and when he did, he was always surrounded by groups of Tontons Makouts. "It was a marvel," wrote a pair of U.S. journalists, "that Duvalier was not killed accidentally amid the ocean of cocked pistols waving around him." At the same time, he baited his opponents, declaring a celebratory "month of gratitude" in his own honor. Dr. Jacques Fourcand, the head of the Haitian Red Cross and a loyal Duvalierist, set the standard for defiant pugnacity in his speech at the celebrations. If anyone tried to attack Duvalier, he declared, Haiti would become a "Himalaya of corpses . . . Blood will flow in Haiti as never before. The land will burn from north to south, from east to west. There will be no sunrise or sunset—just one big flame licking the sky. The dead will be buried under a mountain of ashes." Fourcand also lashed out against the American criticisms of the Duvalier term-extension referendum. Given the segregation and racial violence in the U.S. South, and Americans' own history of invading Haiti, he said, "what right have they to advise us and give us a lesson in constitutional law?" In a final insult, he dubbed the United States a "democracy of sluts."[49]

A few days after Fourcand's speech, the car bringing Duvalier's children to school was ambushed by gunmen. The precise goal of the attack was unclear, and the children were able to flee unharmed into their school, though their bodyguards were killed. Duvalier's reprisals were immediate, furious, and indiscriminate. When suspicion fell on François Benoît, an army officer who had been trained as a sharpshooter by the United States, Duvalier's militia stormed his house. Benoît himself wasn't there—he had fled to the Dominican embassy—but his parents were on the porch when the Tontons Makouts arrived, along with a family servant and a neighbor. The militia opened fire, killing them all. Afterward, they burned the house down; inside was Benoît's baby, who died in the flames.[50]

Angry that Dominicans were shielding suspected conspirators, Duvalier sent his militia into the Dominican embassy, where they roughed up the lone secretary who was there at the time. The Dominican ambassador had already moved to his own, better-guarded residence, along with the group of Haitians who had requested refuge;

but Duvalier's forces surrounded the house, making it impossible for anyone to go in or out. "Only a government of savages, of criminals, is capable of violating the sanctity of a foreign embassy," a furious Bosch declared. In the capital of the Dominican Republic, crowds threw stones at the Haitian embassy, and the Haitian ambassador himself decided to resign and go into exile, announcing that he felt compelled to join "the forces fighting to regain the prestige my country deserves." Summing up the situation, Bosch said that "Haiti is a powder keg and we are a lake of gasoline," adding that if outside governments wanted to prevent a crisis, they should "send a psychiatrist down to examine Duvalier."[51]

Alarmed by the developments, the OAS dispatched a mission to Haiti. Duvalier brought in huge crowds of supporters to the National Palace and delivered a blistering speech to the visitors. "I am the personification of Haiti," he declared. "Those who seek to destroy Duvalier seek to destroy our fatherland . . . God and the people are the source of all power. I have twice been given the power. I have taken it and, damn it, I will keep it forever." "I am here to continue the tradition of Toussaint Louverture and Dessalines," he went on. "No foreigner is going to tell me what to do." Duvalier's representative to the United Nations, meanwhile, complained that criticisms of Haiti were part of a racist conspiracy aimed at "bringing about the death of the only Negro republic on the American continent."[52]

For all their strong language, neither Kennedy nor Bosch was willing to carry out a direct assault against Duvalier. A bigger threat, as it turned out, was someone much closer to home: Clément Barbot, the man who had been one of Duvalier's most important partners during his rise to power. Barbot had overseen the creation of the Tontons Makouts, and in 1959 he had briefly taken over the reins of government while Duvalier was recovering from a heart attack. When the president got better, Barbot stepped down. He ended up paying for his loyalty: Duvalier concluded that his longtime ally, having tasted power, was now a threat, and threw him into prison. Eighteen months later, without explanation, Barbot was set free. He kept out of sight for a while, but eventually decided to use the very networks he had created to support Duvalier to overthrow him. The attempt to kidnap the president's children was in fact his doing, though Duvalier didn't suspect so at the time, and he followed it up with a series of guerrilla attacks. "Duvalier is a madman," Barbot told a U.S. reporter who managed to interview him during this period. "Duvalier is not a communist, a democrat, or anything else. He is an opportunist." A few months later, Duvalier's forces tracked down Barbot and his small group of supporters. The rebels fled into a nearby sugarcane field, but Duvalier's militia set it on fire and shot the men as they tried to escape the flames.[53]

A similarly bleak fate awaited a rebel group led by a young man named Hector Riobé, whose father had been executed by the Tontons Makouts. Tracked down by government forces, Riobé's band fled into the mountains above Pétionville, where they holed up in a cave stocked with guns and ammunition, holding the militiamen at bay for days. Duvalier dispatched his best troops, a unit of marine-trained soldiers armed with mortars, but they, too, were beaten back. Eventually, he sent Riobé's mother, on muleback, to the entrance of the cave to plead with him to surrender. Inside, the lone survivor of the earlier battles, Riobé shot himself.[54]

With these battles raging in and around Port-au-Prince, many were convinced that Duvalier's days were numbered. The United States positioned warships around Haiti and developed a plan for a provisional government; Duvalier himself booked seats on a flight to Paris. But he never had to use them. The military structure he had built, it turned out, was strong enough to withstand both foreign pressure and internal insurrection. In September 1963, after just seven months in power, Juan Bosch was overthrown by a military coup in the Dominican Republic. Two months later, Kennedy was assassinated. Duvalier had outlasted them both. Just to make sure that no more rebel groups could attack him from the Dominican Republic, Duvalier ordered his troops to create a no-man's-land several miles wide along the Dominican border. All the houses in the region were burned, and the residents who lived there were forced out; anyone found moving through the area could be shot on sight.[55]

Even with the odds overwhelmingly against them, though, some Haitian exiles still hoped to overthrow Duvalier and reclaim their country. One of the best-organized attempts came from a U.S.-based group of thirteen men who could boast degrees from Harvard and NYU and training from the U.S. military and the CIA. The rebels, who called themselves Jeune Haïti, disembarked in August 1964 on Haiti's southern peninsula and carried out what Marine Colonel Robert Heinl described as "the most hard-fought guerrilla campaign Haiti had seen since the days of Péralte." As always, the government's reprisals were brutal and terrifyingly arbitrary. Because most of the members of Jeune Haïti had roots in Jérémie, Duvalier's forces killed several hundred people in the town, often on the flimsiest of pretexts. A family called the Sansaricqs fell under suspicion, for example, because one member of the family was studying abroad in the United States. As a result, they were almost entirely wiped out; the victims included a handicapped grandmother and a two-year-old child.[56]

The Jeune Haïti fighters managed to keep Duvalier's militia at bay for a month, but one by one they were eventually tracked down and killed. By the end of October, Duvalier declared "total victory" over the rebels, publishing pictures of the severed heads of three of them. Two captured members of Jeune Haïti were shot by a firing squad in a public ceremony attended by a large crowd and televised live on government TV. Duvalier distributed a leaflet at the execution explaining that he had "crushed and will always crush the attempts of the antipatriots," whose goal was to put Haiti back under the "whip" of foreign masters. "No force will stop the invincible march of the Duvalierist revolution," he proclaimed. "It carries the strength of a torrent."[57]

There has never been full documentation or public recognition of all the victims of the Duvalier regime. The stories of many of those who lost their lives during this period remain untold. But what happened to one of them can perhaps stand in for the unpredictable and devastating cost exacted by the Haitian state during this period. The soccer player Joe Gaetjens, part of a prominent Port-au-Prince family, was a legend in Haiti both because of his professional playing in the country and for a goal he had scored during the 1950 World Cup—not for Haiti, but for the United States. Gaetjens was living in New York at the time, and thanks to lax regulations about player citizenship, he was recruited to play for the Americans. It was a brilliant choice: against the heavily favored English team, Gaetjens scored on a diving header, and the U.S. won 1–0 in one of the most famous upsets in the history of soccer. When Gaetjens returned to Haiti in 1953, he was greeted by a cheering throng and a banner declaring him "the best player in Haiti, the U.S.A. and the Whole World." Settling down in his native country, he ran a laundromat and coached youth soccer. A few of his brothers were active in politics, supporting Louis Déjoie in 1957 and later joining an anti-Duvalier group, and in 1964 most of the Gaetjens family decided to flee abroad. Joe, however, was convinced that—given his fame and the fact that he had stayed out of politics—he was not in danger. He was wrong. On June 8, 1964, two Tontons Makouts stopped him and carried him off to the infamous Fort Dimanche prison. The family never heard from him again. Eventually, the Haitian government confirmed that he had died behind bars. After the fall of the Duvaliers, one of Gaetjens's relatives visited Fort Dimanche and saw the only trace left of Joe: his name scrawled on the wall of one of the cells.[58]

I I I

By 1964, after several years of crisis and violent conflict, there was no room left in Haiti's public sphere for anything but strident assertions of loyalty. When Duvalier presented a new constitution to the Haitian Congress that would make him president for life, representatives competed with each other to express the loudest approbation. One exclaimed that followers of the "Duvalierist Revolution" should be ready to sacrifice themselves for the cause; another riposted they should also be ready to sacrifice "their father, their mother, their brother." After being approved by Congress, the constitution was presented to the Haitian people for a national referendum. There was only one kind of ballot: it said "yes." By now Haitian voters knew what they needed to do to avoid trouble, and over 2,800,000 of them cast the preprinted ballots. The three thousand or so who wrote "no" on the cards were in danger of arrest—for defacing their ballots. A few days before the voting, Duvalier had predicted the result. "There will never again be an election to elect a chief of state on the soil of Haiti," he told a group of judges. "I shall be lord and master." Along with a lifetime presidency, the new constitution gave Duvalier a series of titles that recalled the elaborate court of Henry Christophe: Supreme Chief of the Haitian Nation, Uncontestable Leader of the Revolution, Apostle of National Unity, Renovator of the Fatherland, and Worthy Heir of the Founders of the Haitian Nation.[59]

"Duvalier is the professor of energy," declared a Haitian newspaper in March 1964. "Like Napoleon Bonaparte, Duvalier is an electrifier of souls." The government issued a new catechism to be recited by schoolchildren. "Who are Dessalines, Toussaint, Christophe, Pétion and Estimé?" it asked, in what could seem at first an innocent enough introduction to some of Haiti's historical leaders. The answer, however, was not about history but the inescapable present: "Dessalines, Toussaint, Christophe, Pétion and Estimé are five distinct Chiefs of State who are substantiated in and form only one and the same President in the person of François Duvalier." A new version of the Lord's Prayer enabled Haitians to pray for the success of their ruler: "Our Doc, who art in the Palais National for life, hallowed be Thy name by present and future generations. Thy will be done in Port-au-Prince as it is in the provinces. Give us this day our new Haiti and forgive not the trespasses of those antipatriots who daily spit upon our country; lead them into temptation and, poised by their own venom, deliver them from no evil." The country, writes the historian Claude Moïse, was "saturated with portraits, slogans, posters and speeches constantly reminding people that Duvalier was president-for-life, the supreme chief, and the personification of the nation."[60]

Duvalier also remade the Haitian flag, getting rid of the traditional blue and red horizontal stripes and replacing them with vertical stripes in black and red. The change was a return to the flag used by Dessalines when he was emperor and by Christophe when he was king. It carried a potent meaning: the blue and the red had long been considered symbols of Haiti's two social groups—red for the lighter-skinned people of mixed ancestry, blue for the darker-skinned blacks. Changing the blue to black made the blacks' presence more prominent. Switching the orientation of the stripes from horizontal to vertical, meanwhile, meant that instead of having both colors share an equal attachment to the flagpole, the black now became the only color that connected to the mast—just as black leaders, Duvalier argued, should have pride of place. Having remade the design, the president placed a neon sign in front of the National Palace flashing a message with his signature at the bottom: "I am the Haitian flag, One and Indivisible—François Duvalier."[61]

While Duvalier presented himself as the heir to Louverture and Dessalines, he had come most of all to resemble the authoritarian Jean-Pierre Boyer. The political order he created was the most powerful and long-lasting government in Haiti since Boyer's time. Indeed, Boyer's ability to control the population was significantly limited in comparison to Duvalier's. Building on the legacy of centralization from the U.S. occupation, and using his powerful, well-armed militia, Duvalier had established an iron grip on the country beyond anything that Boyer could have imagined. And unlike Boyer, who struggled for years to gain international recognition and only bought it at the steep price of the 1825 indemnity, by the mid-1960s, Duvalier had managed to stare down the United States and win. After Kennedy's assassination, President Johnson had resumed diplomatic relations with Haiti. A new ambassador was sent from Washington, and he declared that his government looked forward to "close cooperation and solidarity" with Duvalier.[62]

American journalists, for their part, found Duvalier a fascinating subject. The president for life had a friendly chat with a visiting reporter from *Newsweek* magazine, and when asked about malnutrition among Haitian peasants, had "goggled with disbelief." "Do you know how many mangoes they eat a year?" he asked, and then "answered himself with a spur-of-the-moment statistic: '400 million.'" Duvalier, the journalist wrote, "impressed me as Big Brother masquerading as the Mad Hatter." Much of the coverage tended toward the sensationalistic, and recalled the outlandish visions of Haiti cultivated during the U.S. occupation. "Foreign journalists and scholars in search of exotic buffoons," notes Michel-Rolph Trouillot, "enjoyed painting François Duvalier as an incoherent madman, a black Ubu, a tropical Caligula who would spout any amount of nonsense at any time."[63]

While Duvalier denounced negative depictions of Haiti, he also played a complicated double game, cultivating the idea that his form of despotism was the country's only viable form of governance. He hired a publicity director named Herbert Morrison, a one-time Hollywood press agent, who in an NBC interview gave credence to the idea that Duvalier used Vodou to keep his hold on power. Morrison claimed that Duvalier's office had a "voodoo altar" with two dolls of U.S. officials—former president Eisenhower and former secretary of state John Foster Dulles, the latter with pins stuck around his pancreas. Such descriptions were calculated to appeal to U.S. stereotypes of voodoo dolls, which are not a part of most Haitian Vodou practice. But they also served Duvalier's political interests, urging viewers to conclude that Haiti had the leader it needed and deserved. Many in the United States decided that the Haitian population as a whole was primitive and irrational. In 1957 a *New York Times* editorial described Haitians as a "highly emotional people, who have little but tribal rule and superstition to guide their thinking" and who were therefore "notoriously susceptible to demagogic political appeal." A decade later, a study carried out by the State Department said that Duvalier had a "paranoid personality" that "approached psychotic proportions at times." However, the document went on, that made him a fitting president for Haitians, who were a "paranoid" group in general. Even Haitians who had a "veneer of education," the study argued, were burdened by a belief in "animism."[64]

The logic of such reports was that while Duvalier might be brutal, he was the inevitable product of Haitian culture. As during the U.S. occupation, depictions of the supposed religious and cultural backwardness of Haiti conveniently neglected to consider the effects of America's massive economic and military involvement in the country. The exoticizing representations of Haiti and Duvalier both justified U.S. support of his regime and buttressed his hold on power, legitimizing it by delegitimizing the idea of Haitian democracy.

A few American reporters did manage to talk to ordinary Haitians, who described a life plagued not only by state violence but by ever-increasing poverty. "Duvalier has performed an economic miracle," one Haitian told a U.S. journalist in 1964. "He has taught us to live without money and eat without food." Indeed, while after his election Duvalier had promised to give the population "the opportunity to liberate itself from the throes of misery," the Haitian economy worsened significantly during his time in power. He created a strong state, but it was essentially the shell of a state: it served almost entirely to assure control over the people rather than to serve their needs for health care, education, or land reform. Duvalier's regime perfected the forms of extraction long practiced by Haitian leaders, using monopoly control over a number of industries— tobacco, flour, sugar, automobiles, alcohol, and other goods—as a way of indirectly taxing the rural population. Much of the budget went into officials' individual accounts, enabling widespread corruption that enriched those tied to the regime even as it sucked resources from the rest of the country. And while Haiti's population grew and the cost of living increased dramatically, sources of income—particularly agriculture—stagnated. The GNP went from $338 million in 1962 to $329 million in 1967, and coffee exports dropped by 31 percent between 1960 and 1967.[65]

In perhaps the most cynical profiteering of all, the Haitian government worked out a deal with the Dominican Republic to earn money from the emigration of laborers who wanted to work on Dominican sugar plantations. Driven to leave their country by the increasingly difficult economic conditions, Haitian workers found themselves indentured to their own government. In the late 1950s and early 1960s, migrant workers had to pay the Haitian government the significant sum of $10 (approximately equivalent to $75 today) to gain the right to go to the Dominican Republic. The plantation owners there paid an additional $15 to the Haitian government for each worker, and subsequently deposited half of each worker's wages into special accounts held by the Haitian state. Like much of the other money that went into government coffers, these fees mostly flowed to Duvalier and his close associates. By 1981, the Haitian government was charging Dominican planters a fee of $182 per Haitian worker, collecting nearly three million dollars that went into hidden accounts. The garnishment of wages made it extremely difficult for Haitian laborers to do what many had intended to do—work in the Dominican Republic for a while and then return home with savings to buy land. Instead, they were left destitute and stranded.[66]

While Haitian migrants were being squeezed by their own government, the rural residents who remained behind were suffering as well. The massive network of rural Tontons Makouts in the countryside used their extensive control to levy arbitrary "taxes" on farmers and market women, and to deprive people of their land under one pretext or another. The prominent anti-Duvalier activist Jean Dominique described the regime as a "dictatorship that systematically organized the pillage, exploitation, spoliation and dispossession" of the poor, leaving them with only two options: "to flee or to fight." Documenting the sporadic uprisings that took place through the Duvalier years, Dominique compared them to the ancient forms of resistance practiced by the enslaved against their colonial masters. Residents arrested after one such revolt, he noted, sang songs dating back to the Haitian Revolution to taunt and shame their guards.[67]

For a short time in the late 1960s, groups of young urban activists sought to tap rural resentments against Duvalier to create a national movement against the dictatorship. Some advocated armed struggle, explicitly presenting themselves as new maroons resisting a new kind of slavery. They were, however, no match for Duvalier's police apparatus. Students, labor leaders, and others suspected of leftist sympathies were imprisoned, executed, or forced into exile; at one point, Duvalier's forces attacked the headquarters of an activist group, killing twenty of its members. Duvalier also appropriated the imagery of the resistance, constructing a statue dedicated to the "Unknown Maroon"—a kind of "tomb of the unknown soldier" for those who had resisted slavery and laid the foundation for Haiti's independence. The message was clear: Duvalier was the one true representative of the Haitian nation, the authentic descendant of the country's revolutionary founders. The era of resistance was past; the present was for obedience, and the only revolution was the one led by Duvalier himself.[68]

Duvalier's suppression of leftist groups impressed the Nixon administration, which began to strengthen its ties with the regime. In July 1969, Nelson Rockefeller, then the governor of New York, came to Haiti in a high-profile visit and was photographed smiling and shaking hands with Duvalier. The visit marked an era of intense and open cooperation. A new U.S. ambassador to Haiti, Clinton Knox, lobbied so intensely for aid to the Duvalier regime that some Haitian officials apparently dubbed him an honorary Tonton Makout. Soon the Nixon government officially ended the embargo on the sale of arms to Haiti that had been put in place after Duvalier's 1963 attack on the Dominican embassy, and in 1971, one million dollars' worth of weaponry was bought by Haiti from the United

States. In the early 1960s, the Kennedy administration had considered Duvalier a threat to democracy and Caribbean stability; a decade later, he had firmly established himself as one of America's most favored client governments in the region.[69]

* * *

Standing on the balcony of the National Palace with Duvalier in 1969, Nelson Rockefeller realized that he had to hold up the president as he waved to the crowd below. The sixty-two-year-old Duvalier was in poor health and becoming increasingly frail. But in an odd if telling oversight, he hadn't indicated in the 1964 constitution that made him president for life what would happen when that life ended. In 1970, Duvalier explained to his close associates that there was only one solution: his presidency would become a dynasty, passed on to his only son, Jean-Claude. (Though he had older daughters, Duvalier did not consider handing power to them.) Jean-Claude, however, posed a problem: he was only nineteen. He couldn't even vote, and he certainly couldn't be president—the constitution required a person to be at least forty years old to take that position. So Duvalier, talking of the need to include Haitian youth more fully in political life, changed the age of majority from twenty-one to eighteen and revised the 1964 constitution to make Jean-Claude Duvalier's accession to power possible. "That a Duvalier should one day succeed a Duvalier," the ailing president declared in January 1971, "should alarm nobody." The next month, Haitians were once again called to the polls. They were asked the following question: "Citizen Dr. François Duvalier has chosen Citizen Jean-Claude Duvalier to succeed him as President-for-Life of the Republic. Does this choice respond to your aspirations and your desires? Do you ratify it?" According to the official results, there were 2,391,916 yes votes. Scholars differ on the question of how many voted against the measure: some say 1, others 0.[70]

The United States, eager to see an untroubled transfer of power in the country, sent warships to patrol the waters between Miami and Haiti to make sure no exiles decided to use the moment to launch an attack. The Duvalier regime knew precisely what kind of language to use to appeal to the Americans. The Duvalierist official Luckner Cambronne proclaimed that "in the Caribbean basin, this crossroads of civilization," Haiti represented "an enviable example of political and economic stability." The country, he said, was a "barrier" to leftist ideologies that were seeking "the destruction of the spiritual and moral values of a Western civilization based on humanistic and Christian values." François Duvalier died on April 21, 1971; the next day, Jean-Claude was sworn in as the new president for life. In his first speech, he declared: "The United States will always find Haiti on its side against communism."[71]

The younger Duvalier was widely considered a protected playboy lacking the political skills of his father, and many thought that his reign would not last long. But despite a series of family dramas that intrigued and entertained many observers, he would stay in power for fourteen years. It helped, of course, that he inherited his father's well-established system of control and extraction, as well as his close ties with the U.S. administration. During his time in office, Haiti's relationships with the United States and other countries continued to improve, and an increasing amount of foreign investment began coming into the country. Corporations eager to take advantage of the low cost of labor in Haiti built factories to produce wigs, clothes, and baseballs. There was some incongruity to the last item, since Haitians themselves never took up the American sport. Soon, however, every baseball used in the U.S. professional leagues was made in Haiti.[72]

Many commentators and economists were optimistic that foreign investment would help transform Haiti into a prosperous nation; one went so far as to imagine it becoming a new Taiwan. By 1984, there were as many as thirty thousand people working in factories around Port-au-Prince, and Haiti was competing with countries like Mexico, Malaysia, Singapore, and Hong Kong in the production of assembled export goods. Still, even Jean-Claude Duvalier himself admitted that export industries did little to address the overall problem of poverty in Haiti, declaring in a 1981 speech that they "remained enclaves with a weak level of integration into the economy." A bigger transformation came from two other trends, whose impact continues to be felt to this day: the rapidly growing presence of private foreign aid groups, which came flooding into Haiti in the 1980s, and the creation of a massive diaspora as Haitians increasingly left the country to settle abroad.[73]

The amount of aid that came into Haiti during the Jean-Claude Duvalier years was staggering: between 1972 to 1981 alone it amounted to $584 million (roughly equivalent to $2 billion today), with 80 percent of that coming from the United States. But foreign governments were well aware that Duvalier and his associates were simply taking much of the official aid money sent to the country for their own private gain. Loath to stop sending assistance altogether for fear of the social and political consequences, the donor countries found an elegant solution: channeling more and more of their aid into what were then called private voluntary organizations, or PVOs, which now largely go under the name of nongovernmental organizations (NGOs). Giving money to independent groups bypassed the Duvalier government while still promoting stability by addressing poverty, lack of health care, and agricultural problems. Soon Haiti became a magnet for evangelical religious groups and secular relief agencies alike, in part because of what one scholar describes as the "marketing of its paganism and poverty." By 1984 there were at least four hundred PVOs, and probably more, operating in the country. Two years later, a Haitian association set up to assist the work of voluntary agencies reported that a new aid group was arriving in Haiti every week. In time this process created what some critics today refer to as the "Republic of NGOs," with a bewildering patchwork of foreign aid organizations playing a central role in Haiti's economic and political life.[74]

In at least one case, U.S. involvement ended up being devastating for rural Haitians. In 1983, the U.S. Agency for International Development and the Haitian government carried out a campaign to prevent the spread of swine flu among pigs in the country. The only way to stop the disease from spreading, they insisted, was to slaughter the entire existing pig population in Haiti. Unlike many other government efforts in the countryside, this one was carried out with remarkable efficiency. "We didn't imagine the Haitian state was capable of such determination and effectiveness," an economist who studied the situation later remarked. "And it's too bad that they don't apply them to more constructive projects." Over the course of a few months, nearly two million pigs throughout Haiti were collected and killed. The Haitian government and the aid groups saw this as a logical public health measure, but from the perspective of rural Haitians it was a brutal assault. Haiti's indigenous black breed of pigs, known as creole pigs, were crucial to rural survival. Descended from animals first introduced to the island by the Spanish in the early sixteenth century, the black pigs were well adapted to the environment, nourishing themselves with local plants, familiar with what they could eat and what was poisonous.[75]

USAID and the Haitian government promised to provide compensation for the slaughtered pigs: assistance with purchasing white pigs, to be brought in from the United States. But the reimbursement plan turned out to be much less effectively run than the eradication program, and many Haitians got nothing in return for what they had lost. Moreover, those peasants who did get access to the new pigs rapidly learned that they were effectively useless. Unsuited to the climate, they frequently got sick and died; few of them bore young, and any piglets also usually died quickly. The imported white pigs had to be kept in pens to protect them, and they had to be fed special feed—imported from the United States—that the farmers could not afford. Indeed, as some noted bitingly, the new pigs required food and health care of a kind far superior to what the peasants themselves had access to. As one farmer told journalist Amy Wilentz a few years later, "the big white American pigs . . . cost too much, they eat too much, they eat fancy feed, not garbage and mango skins like the little Haitian pigs, they need lots of water, and who has lots of water? And then you'd have to find a sty to house them in, because the American pigs aren't used to Haitian soil . . . They get sick. They die, and you've wasted all your money." In a way, the moment symbolized all of the contradictions of Duvalier rule: a regime that insistently presented itself as the defender and embodiment of the Haitian nation had allowed outsiders to target a cornerstone of rural life, slaughtering the black pigs and offering foreign white ones in return.[76]

As foreign aid groups struggled to find their way, for many Haitians the most important source of external assistance came not from any well-meaning outsiders but from their own connections and relatives abroad. By the early 1980s, Haitians themselves had become the country's most significant export. The three decades of Duvalier rule were a time of massive exodus, of a scale and breadth never before seen in Haitian history. In one of the many ironic twists in the Duvalier saga, it was money coming from Haitians driven into exile that in many ways propped up the economy during Jean-Claude Duvalier's rule. In 1960, remittances from immigrants overseas had made up 5 percent of all the money coming into the country; by the early 1980s, that had increased to one-third of the total amount.[77]

In the late 1950s and early 1960s, those who left Haiti had been mostly wealthier officials and professionals who feared political repression and who were often able to secure visas to travel by airplane to the United States, Canada, or Europe. By the middle of the 1960s, observers estimated that as many as 80 percent of Haiti's professionals were outside the country; physicians, psychiatrists, and other medical personnel fled in droves. But in time the exodus claimed people from every social group and region in the country. Poorer residents, seeking to avoid the exploitation of working on the sugarcane plantations in the Dominican Republic, began escaping by boat to other parts of the Caribbean and to Florida. Many left hoping for temporary exile, but for most it became permanent. By 1970 there were already 35,000 Haitians in the Bahamas, and the number would continue to increase in the coming decade. A tally of Haitians in New York City found approximately 150,000 of them there in 1976, and that figure would climb to at least 400,000, and probably significantly more, by the end of the 1990s. Although a precise count is difficult to come by, it is estimated that up to a million Haitians—about 15 percent of the country's population—fled during the thirty years of Duvalier rule.[78]

By the early 1980s, Haiti had become what it remains today: a vast and seemingly boundless territory made up of communities not only within the borders of the country but in Boston, New York, Miami, Montréal, Paris, Guadeloupe, French Guiana, the Bahamas, and many other places as well. This diaspora was later dubbed the "Tenth Department"—an international supplement to the nine official districts within Haiti itself—as a way of acknowledging both how essential it is to Haiti's present and future and how firmly established these emigrants have become in their adopted lands. The novelist Edwidge Danticat, who came to New York as a child in 1981, recalls noting a particularly poignant turning point in the history of that diaspora. For a long time, when a Haitian died in New York, the body would be sent back to Haiti to be buried near family. One day, Danticat heard the news that a Haitian resident of New York had been traveling in Haiti and had died there, and the body was being sent back to New York, to be buried in the new place—the surest sign that it had now become home.[79]

III

Those in the "liberated territory" of the diaspora had the freedom to speak out against Duvalier, and many took the opportunity to do so. The New York radio station WRUL, for instance, broadcast a daily program in Kreyòl with news about Haiti and sharp attacks against the Duvalier regime; Duvalier tried hard to jam the signal, but many Haitians were able to tune in nonetheless. Within Haiti itself, criticizing the president was still difficult and fraught with danger. In the mid-1970s, though, courageous activists in Haiti began increasingly to test Duvalier's regime. Newspapers and magazines spoke out against the government, and with the spread of transistor radios, a series of new radio stations popped up, enabling journalists to reach a far greater audience. Some of them began reporting from the countryside, providing accounts of the suffering of rural residents, which in turn emboldened the rural population to organize protests against local officials.[80]

Activists in Haiti got a significant boost when Jimmy Carter was elected president of the United States in 1976. He instituted a new approach to foreign policy in Latin America, putting pressure on U.S. allies to demonstrate a commitment to human rights in return for continued aid. In response, Duvalier eased restrictions on the press and allowed for local elections. Two non-Duvalierist political parties were formed, and the population in Le Cap shocked the regime by taking the liberalization seriously enough to elect an independent political leader to Congress. Activists created the Haitian League of Human Rights, which collected testimony by victims of the government, while delegations from the OAS published reports detailing the disappearances and government-sponsored torture. During the 1979 carnival, one group of revelers took the bold step of parading through the streets in Fidel Castro masks.[81]

Carter did not win a second term, though, and Ronald Reagan's election in 1980 dealt a profound blow to the Haitian prodemocracy movement. Within weeks of the U.S. elections, realizing that American foreign policy was about to change, Duvalier carried out a sudden wave of arrests, attacking those who had spoken out against his regime over the previous years. Opposition radio stations were ransacked and shut down, journalists imprisoned and tortured. Reagan, for his part, sent Coast Guard ships patrolling the waters between Haiti and the United States in order to stop Haitians fleeing their country from making it to Florida. The goal was to prevent Haitians from setting foot on U.S. soil, where they had the right to apply for political asylum. Only a tiny number of Haitians were ever granted such asylum—despite the widely reported political repression in Haiti, the "boat people" were systematically categorized as "economic refugees"—but the U.S. government wanted to avoid having to carry out such hearings altogether. The Haitians who were intercepted on the seas were often shipped back to Haiti, where they risked severe punishment from the Duvalier government. Others were held at Guantánamo Bay or in the Krome detention camp in Florida, sometimes for years. Activists in the United States lambasted the policy, insisting that it was both unethical and racist, especially given the continuing welcome of refugees fleeing Cuba during the same years. But Haiti remained a U.S. ally, and immigration policies flowed from that.[82]

Facing hostility abroad and continued repression at home, Haitians found their horizons closed off in every direction. But the flowering of opposition in the late 1970s was impossible to suppress completely. Journalists continued to brave the threat of arrest and torture, and young people carried out ever-bolder street protests against the regime. The disastrous pig eradication campaign pushed rural Haitians to criticize local power structures with increasing fervor. And Haitian Catholic leaders, influenced by the broader currents of 1970s liberation theology, added their voices to the demands for reform. A young priest named Jean-Bertrand Aristide attracted large and impassioned crowds with his riveting preaching, packed with wordplay and complex symbolism and fearless in its attacks on Duvalier. "We must end this regime where the donkeys do all the work and horses prance in the sunshine," he declared in 1982 in his first sermon as an ordained priest. The following year, Haitian Catholics got high-profile encouragement for their efforts when Pope John Paul II visited the country and declared to a crowd that included Jean-Claude Duvalier: "Something must change here."[83]

The Duvalier family, meanwhile, seemed increasingly unhinged from the population. In 1984, the first lady, Michèle Bennett, held a lavish benefit dinner to raise money for her pet project, a hospital in Port-au-Prince. "If Nero were to come back to earth and throw a party, this was the party he would throw," one of the guests said of the proceedings. Bennett made sure that the entire evening was televised: the Haitian population was meant to see the luxurious event as a symbol of how much their rulers cared about them. The next year, Bennett took two dozen of her friends to Paris for a $1.7 million shopping spree. U.S. officials and Haitian industrialists, longtime supporters of the regime, worried that such provocations would make a revolution inevitable. Even Duvalier's loyalists began to perceive him as a liability.[84]

In November 1985, an incident in the town of Gonaïves opened the way for the final push against the dictator. As a student demonstration raged in the street outside, a student named Jean-Robert Cius was leaning against the wall in the courtyard of his school with a notebook in his hands. Cius himself wasn't demonstrating, but when government militiamen trying to suppress the protests fired into the courtyard, a bullet hit him squarely in the chest. He fell dead to the ground, the bullet-pierced notebook still clasped against his body. Two other students were also killed that day. One of them, who had shouted out in protest after watching Cius die, was chased into a dead-end alley and shot by a militiaman at point-blank range. The other, wounded by militia gunfire, was beaten to death as he lay on the ground.[85]

Somehow, after all the tens of thousands of killings, after the decades of political repression and poverty that had sent more than a million fleeing Haiti, these three murders tipped the scale. Students poured into the streets in Gonaïves and other towns; fifty thousand protesters marched in Le Cap. Invoking the spirit of Dessalines, they proclaimed that a new revolution was imminent, and that Duvalier had to go. "Get out, Satan!" Aristide cried in a sermon. In January 1986, Duvalier apparently called a delegation of leading Vodou *oungans* to the National Palace to get advice about how he should respond to the situation. He got an earful, as the leader of the delegation, Max Beauvoir, laid out the grievances of the Haitian people against the regime. A few days later, Beauvoir delivered the verdict: "The spirits are annoyed and angry." For many months, he said, "the spirits have wanted you to leave." The U.S. embassy in Port-au-Prince gave Duvalier the same message, arranging for him to be carried out of the country to a comfortable life in France—sustained there by a Swiss bank account filled over the previous decades with millions of dollars from the Haitian treasury.[86]

The thirty years of Duvalier rule left behind a devastated country. As many as a million Haitians had fled into exile. The treasury was empty. The civil institutions that had previously provided an alternative means of organizing Haitian society had been largely demolished or absorbed by the state. Haiti was still burdened by crushing foreign debt and battered by foreign involvement in its affairs. And while international investment and aid had helped to build up some aspects of the country's infrastructure, what remained of the state had little capacity to maintain it. The only truly functioning institution that Duvalier left behind was a massive military apparatus. By the early 1980s, perhaps as many as three hundred thousand individuals were incorporated into the Tontons Makouts hierarchy. The army, meanwhile, had long ago been purged of its opposition elements and now was composed of men who had also loyally served the dictator. The militia chiefs and the army officers had little desire to let go of the social and political power that the regime had given them, and they retained tremendous influence even after Jean-Claude Duvalier himself was gone.[87]

The protesters who had at last succeeded in overthrowing Duvalier, however, were buoyed by a sense that radical change was truly possible. The uprising of 1985–86, and the years of activism that preceded it, had created a network of grassroots organizations that seemed poised to reconstitute a democratic order in the country. The moment had come, they hoped, to finally put an end to Haiti's perpetual cycle of violence and poverty. Stripping politics to its core, the student demonstrators had demanded: "Long live life! Down with death!"[88]

EPILOGUE

"We have become the subjects of our own history," announced
Jean-Bertrand Aristide in 1987, "and we refuse from now on to be
the objects of that history." Aristide's exultation captured the hope
and determination of the moment. The 1986 overthrow of Duvalier
was spoken of as the "uprooting": the tree planted by decades of
dictatorship had to be completely destroyed before something else
could grow in its place. Under the aegis of a transitional military
government known as the Conseil National de Gouvernement (CNG),
an assembly set about writing a new constitution aimed at undoing
the three decades of Duvalierism. The resulting document was a
watershed in the country's constitutional history, the first attempt at
creating a truly participatory democracy in Haiti.[1]

The 1987 constitution explicitly identified the central problem in
Haitian political culture: the gap between the mass of the population and the political class. The aim of the new political order, it
declared, should be to "eliminate all discrimination between urban
and rural populations, through the acceptance of a community of
language and culture and the recognition of the right to progress,
information, education, health, work and leisure for all citizens." To
that end, the constitution for the first time made Kreyòl an official
language of the country on a par with French, requiring the government to disseminate all laws, decrees, and international agreements

in both French and Kreyòl in the press and on the radio. Taking aim at the political culture of the Duvalier regime, the constitution also announced that "the cult of personality is formally outlawed," and it ordered that no streets, public buildings, or works of art could be named after living individuals. It prohibited those who had carried out torture or committed other crimes under Duvalier from serving in office for ten years. And it created a new electoral commission, charged with overseeing the political process and assuring the legitimacy and fairness of elections.[2]

Almost immediately after its ratification, though, the ambitious new constitution ran into a wearily familiar challenge: the military seemed determined to stay in power. They refused to apply the new laws and seemed intent on putting off the transition to democracy for as long as possible. Haiti was stuck in what Michel-Rolph Trouillot dubbed "Duvalierism after Duvalier": the dictator was gone, but his generals and his tactics were still in place. It seemed possible that, as had happened so many times before, the popular uprising would find itself stifled, blocked off, and ultimately evanescent. A song by the musical group Les Frères Parent pointed out that Haitians had spent almost all of the twentieth century struggling against leaders they couldn't trust: "Vincent let Lescot rise up / Lescot was succeeded by Estimé / Estimé left Paul Magloire / Our misery did not abate . . . / Magloire gave us Duvalier the father / Duvalier the father gave us Duvalier the son / Duvalier the son gave us the CNG / And that's why we have to watch them!" Still, activists kept speaking out, through songs and sermons, newspaper columns and street demonstrations, and after years of repression by the military, they finally prevailed. In 1990, the CNG, yielding to the pressure, named the supreme court justice Ertha Pascal-Trouillot to the post of provisional president—making her Haiti's first female head of state—and put her in charge of organizing an election.[3]

The field of candidates was large and diverse; among others, it included Louis Déjoie Jr., the son of Duvalier's 1956 opponent. But the competition shifted dramatically when, a few weeks before the election, Jean-Bertrand Aristide announced that he was running. Since his participation in the anti-Duvalier movement of the early 1980s, Aristide had become one of the most prominent voices of protest in Haiti, speaking out boldly against the CNG and criticizing many aspects of U.S. policy in Haiti. Infuriated by his blistering speeches from the pulpit, the military regime had carried out several assassination attempts against him; but although they killed dozens of his parishioners and burned his church to the ground, they never got Aristide himself. These repeated escapes from death were seen by many of Aristide's supporters as evidence of divine protection, and they helped to establish him as the embodiment of the popular push for democracy in Haiti.[4]

Aristide called his party Lavalas, "the flood," after a popular anti-Duvalier song that likened the demonstrators to a deluge that would carry away the oppressive regime. As his symbol he chose a white rooster, a symbol of strength and combativeness. It decorated his campaign posters, the pro-Aristide murals that sprang up throughout the country—and the ballots that about two-thirds of the voters put into the urns. Not since the 1930 elections, when the end of the U.S. occupation was in the offing, had an electoral process generated such enthusiasm, and the levels of participation were significantly higher than ever before. At last, many Haitians hoped, there would be a real connection between the country's population and its government institutions. A song produced for the electoral commission summed up the ebullient mood: "We are the state . . . / The state is us."[5]

The day after his inauguration as president, Aristide led a march to the notorious Fort Dimanche prison and declared that it should be made into a museum documenting the crimes of the Duvalier years. Families of the prison's victims carried photographs of the dead and disappeared and placed them around the site. Many hoped for a reckoning with the crimes of the recent past and a fundamental transformation of the political order. But while the movement to overthrow the Duvalier regime had created a flowering of new organizations and institutions, they emerged in a landscape scarred by the repression of civil society. The state was essentially a shell, offering few services to the Haitian population. And despite the efforts of the previous years, the army was in fact far from uprooted and still had support from influential sectors of Haitian society. With Aristide promising sweeping changes that threatened their power, the military leadership struck back. On September 30, 1991—less than eight months after Aristide's inauguration—a group of army officers organized a coup. Aristide was able to escape to the United States, but the army carried out brutal reprisals against his supporters, killing at least twelve hundred over the next few days and many thousands more in the following years.[6]

Aristide returned to the presidency in 1994, escorted by U.S. troops ordered to Haiti by President Bill Clinton with the sanction of the United Nations. Once back in office, Aristide disbanded the Haitian army entirely, convinced that if left in place it would represent a recurrent threat to the fragile democratic regime. Foreign troops—first from the United States, and then from a U.N. mission—took over some of the army's duties. Aristide had long spoken about the need for Haitians to emancipate themselves from foreign influence, but the conditions of his return in fact helped establish a long-term foreign military presence in the country.[7]

In the three years of Aristide's absence, the economic situation in Haiti had gotten even worse: an embargo put in place after the military coup had taken a deep economic toll. As a condition of their support, international financial institutions insisted that Aristide follow the neoliberal economic doctrine and remove all protectionist tariffs—a policy which, as Clinton himself would later admit, devastated Haiti's rice growers and deepened the country's dependency on imported food. When Aristide attempted to resist, he found himself facing the threat of withheld aid and loans. With the government in tremendous debt, he also had difficulty financing state projects that might have improved the lives of the population. And he was given little time: the United States counted Aristide's years in exile as part of the five-year presidential term and insisted that he step down and allow a new presidential election in 1995. René Préval, a member of the Lavalas party, was voted in as his successor. Aristide remained a powerful political figure, however, and at the end of Préval's term, he was elected president once again. This succession of presidential elections was a landmark in some respects: they represented largely peaceful and democratic transfers of power of a kind rarely seen before in Haitian history. Nevertheless, especially after Aristide's second election, there were complaints of electoral fraud, and the next years saw increasing political conflict as his opponents tapped into popular frustration at the lack of improvement in the country. Protests against him increased, and Port-au-Prince and other cities were racked by violent street confrontations.[8]

The year 2004 was supposed to be a moment of triumph for Haiti: the bicentennial of the country's independence. Aristide had prepared elaborate celebrations and invited international guests to attend. He also issued a challenge to France, accusing the country of having condemned Haiti to poverty through the 1825 indemnity and demanding that France pay it back. But the bicentennial instead became the occasion for an uprising: in February 2004, a small group of former military officers took up arms against Aristide, approaching Port-au-Prince from the north. The U.S. government made it clear that it would not intervene to support him, and at the end of the month, Aristide left the country in circumstances that remain the subject of tremendous controversy. He was escorted by U.S. troops and officials, who claimed that they were simply helping him to flee to safety; Aristide himself, however, described the event as a kidnapping. Exiled for a second time, Aristide would remain abroad until 2011, when, despite strenuous objections from the United States, he returned to Haiti as a private citizen. Aristide's return came just a few months after Jean-Claude Duvalier astonished virtually everyone by similarly reappearing in Haiti, and the political life of both men is probably far from over.

What happened to Aristide between 1990 and 2004? Why did the promise of the uprooting remain unfulfilled? The question still haunts political debate. There were powerful people both inside and outside Haiti who always distrusted Aristide, and they played a crucial role in undermining his regime. But in time he and his party also lost the support of many close allies, some of whom accused Aristide of sinking into the very patterns of authoritarianism and corruption he had once so eloquently denounced. His defenders, meanwhile, continue to insist that such accusations are largely ideological fabrications and that his attempts to bring democracy and reform to Haiti were crushed by the policies of foreign governments and international financial organizations. Given the recentness of these events, and the fact that many of those involved are still playing central roles in Haitian political life today, the dispute is an intense and often hyperbolic one, a tangle of accusations and counteraccusations of bewildering complexity. But the larger lessons to be learned must be less about individuals than about structure, about the long-term historical processes that came bearing down on Haiti in the wake of Duvalier. Regardless of their opinion of Aristide, all those who look back at the 1990s can share a sense of mourning that yet another moment that seemed to offer hope for real and profound change in Haiti fell prey to the seemingly inescapable cycle of crisis and decline.[9]

I I I

Twenty-five years after the overthrow of Duvalier, Haitians are still largely the objects rather than the subjects of the political and economic order under which they live. Their capacity to shape the direction taken by their country remains extremely limited. Elections, understood as the necessary precondition for political stability, are instead occasions for shadowy and often violent political conflict. State institutions are weak and largely unresponsive. And the population has no control at all over foreign governments and organizations, which in many ways call the shots in contemporary Haiti.

Those institutions—including the U.N. military mission (known as MINUSTAH), official U.S. aid agencies, and NGOs and missionary organizations—make up a startlingly fragmented and complex network. Their actual functioning and impact are difficult to analyze or evaluate with much precision; indeed, trying to count how many nongovernmental groups are operating in Haiti is itself a remarkable challenge. NGO employees, young volunteers, missionaries, and U.N. soldiers from a bewildering array of countries with their national flags on their uniforms are a constant presence throughout most of the country.

Some political activists compare the current foreign presence in Haiti with the era of the U.S. occupation. René Préval, who was elected president again in 2005, has been accused of selling out to the United States: at one point, graffiti comparing him to Jean-Baptiste Conzé, the Haitian who led marines into the camp of Charlemagne Péralte, popped up on walls in Port-au-Prince. The comparison is politically potent, but it is also somewhat misleading: the foreign presence today operates in rather different ways and on different terms than it did in the early twentieth century. The various organizations are dispersed, decentralized, and largely uncoordinated. Members of the Haitian diaspora are also heavily involved in seeking to address pressing issues in the country, adding another dimension to the international presence. As the novelist Edwidge Danticat puts it, "Every Haitian is an NGO." Haiti's new president, Michel Martelly, spent a number of years living in the United States, and the Haitian diaspora was actively involved in his campaign.[10]

The current situation does have one major characteristic in common with the occupation years, however: now, as then, the setup leaves most individuals within Haiti almost completely disempowered. To survive, they continue to depend, as they long have, on their informal rural and urban networks and on deeply rooted practices of self-reliance. They draw what they can from the shifting and unpredictable terrain of aid. At times, they gain assistance from foreign organizations for projects that are truly valuable for their communities. When taken as a whole, however, it is clear that the current aid schemes are simply not working to address the larger issues: poverty, ecological devastation, insufficient educational opportunities for the youth who make up the majority of the population, a dire lack of water, food, and health care. Hope for real change is difficult to summon. Demonstrators often chant simply "Nou bouke!"—"We're tired!"

The devastating 2010 earthquake profoundly deepened the country's problems, destroying much of the infrastructure in Port-au-Prince and leaving millions homeless. It also starkly exposed the Haitian state's inability to help its people in times of crisis. A global response provided emergency assistance to the country in the days and weeks after the disaster, and an array of governments and organizations mobilized to try to contribute to rebuilding the country. But it is now also abundantly clear that the tremendous difficulties of reconstruction are part of much deeper and older problems: the aftershocks of a long history of internal conflict and external pressures that has left Haiti's population vulnerable and exposed.

In December 2010, nearly a year after the earthquake, Ricardo Seitenfus, the Brazilian head of the OAS mission in the country, offered a frank and devastating analysis of Haiti's condition to the Swiss newspaper *Le Temps*. He described the U.N. presence in Haiti as wasteful and even harmful: "Haiti is not an international menace. There is no civil war." Rather, he said, the country was in the midst of low-intensity conflict between "various political actors who do not respect the democratic process." In such a context, the U.N. approach—which results in "freezing" the existing power structures—would "resolve nothing, and only make things worse." The U.N. troops, Seitenfus said, were there only to prop up a bankrupt vision for the country. "We want to make Haiti a capitalist country, a platform for export to the U.S. market. It's absurd." Echoing the historian Steven Stoll, who has called for a "Second Haitian Revolution" that would allow Haiti's "subsistence cultures" of agrarian self-sufficiency to exist on their own terms instead of being forced to reform or disappear, Seitenfus proclaimed that "Haiti must return to what it is, a primarily agricultural country."[11]

Seitenfus was as withering in his analysis of NGOs as he was about the United Nations. "There is a malicious and perverse relationship between the force of NGOs and the weakness of the Haitian state," he declared. He described the NGO relationship to Haiti as a relatively cynical one: the country, he lamented, has been reduced to a handy place for "professional training" for an increasingly youthful group of workers. "And Haiti, I can tell you, is not the place for amateurs." The complex interrelationships between state officials, community leaders, businesses, and other foreign aid groups in the country often mystify and deeply frustrate new volunteers, while the proliferation of different aid organizations—which often do not coordinate their work, and sometimes directly compete with each other—leads to tremendous amounts of duplicated effort.[12]

What was blocking a "normalization" of the situation in Haiti, the interviewer asked Seitenfus? In order to answer, the Brazilian official looked back to the country's founding. "Haiti's original sin, in the international theatre, was its liberation," he said. "Haitians committed the unacceptable in 1804." The world "didn't know how to deal with Haiti," and time and time again simply turned to force and coercion. Two centuries on, Seitenfus concluded, it was clear that outsiders' efforts to shape Haiti to their own liking were ineffective. If there was hope for improvement, it would come from the realization of the original dreams of self-determination that had launched Haiti into the world. "Two hundred years ago, Haiti illuminated the history of humanity and of human rights. Now we must give Haitians the chance to confirm their vision."[13]

Seitenfus's remarks hit a nerve. The OAS pulled him from his position several months early, displeased with his unflinching critique of essentially every aspect of international work in Haiti. Many Haitians, however, applauded and celebrated the controversial interview, pleased that complaints they had often made themselves were now being voiced by a prominent figure in the international community.

They noted that surprisingly few aid workers speak either French or Kreyòl, and that NGOs are subject to very little oversight from the Haitian government, essentially reporting only to their donors. As in the later years of the U.S. occupation, Haitian critics also pointed out that the money spent on salaries and living expenses for foreign workers could go much further if it were used to employ people from within the country. In March 2011, President Préval honored Seitenfus by naming him a Knight of the Republic of Haiti. The entire incident, in a way, only confirmed the continuing distance between the different groups who all have the same general aim—improving Haiti—but harbor completely different visions of what that actually means.

Looking back on the history of Haiti and its recent struggles, it is sometimes difficult not to succumb to hopelessness, to the feeling that nothing can be done. But in truth, none of what has happened in Haiti during the past two hundred years has been inevitable. Haiti's current situation is the culmination of a long set of historical choices that date back to its beginnings as a French plantation colony. And it is the consequence of the ways that powerful political leaders and institutions, inside and outside the country, have ignored and suppressed the aspirations of Haiti's majority.

It's easy, in the abstract, to identify what makes for a successful democracy: a strong state, civil society, popular participation, an effective legal system. Many of these have in fact existed at one time or another in Haitian history. But the devastating combination of internal conflict and external intervention has stymied their consolidation into a network of sustainable and responsive political institutions. Remarkably, however, the history of repression has not snuffed out the Haitian struggle for dignity, equality, and autonomy. Haiti's people have steadfastly sustained the counter-plantation system that they created through their founding revolution and painstakingly anchored in the countryside over the course of the nineteenth century. Generation after generation, they have demonstrated their ability to resist, escape, and at times transform the oppressive regimes they have faced.

"A different Port-au-Prince is possible," graffiti declared on the walls of the city a few years ago. A different Haiti is—always, and still—possible too. That is because Haitians have never accepted what so many have announced, over and over again, during the past two hundred years: that democracy is not for them, that it cannot flourish in their land. They have kept their political imagination alive, and the story of how they have done that for so long should spur us on toward a still unwritten future. When the situation is at its worst, we should remember how this story began, and what the ancestors of today's Haitians accomplished two hundred years ago. In the midst of a brutal plantation system, they imagined a different order, one based on freedom, equality, and autonomy. But they did more than imagine it. They built it out of nothing—with fury, solidarity, and determination. Out of a situation that seemed utterly hopeless, they created a new and better world for themselves. Two hundred years later, that remains a reminder of what is possible: if it happened once, perhaps it can happen again.

NOTES

INTRODUCTION

1. Louis-Joseph Janvier, *La république d'Haïti et ses visiteurs (1840–1882)* (Paris: Mappon et Flammarion, 1883), i.

2. Ibid., 11–12, 22, 56, 67, 74.

3. David Brooks, "The Underlying Tragedy," *New York Times*, January 14, 2010.

4. I tell the story of Haiti's colonial history and its revolution in Laurent Dubois, *Avengers of the New World: The Story of the Haitian Revolution* (Cambridge, Mass.: Belknap Press of Harvard University Press, 2004). The slave trade to Haiti reflects the broader pattern of the Middle Passage, which brought 90 percent of enslaved Africans to either the Caribbean or Brazil. For the precise numbers of known arrivals from Africa to Saint-Domingue, see the Trans-Atlantic Slave Trade Database at http://www.slavevoyages.org. Additional slaves were brought, often illegally, through transshipment from nearby colonies.

5. My interpretation of this process is based on the pioneering work of Jean Casimir, *La culture opprimée* (Delmas, Haïti: Lakay, 2001)—Casimir uses the term "counter-plantation" system to describe what emerged in Haiti after the revolution; I also draw on Gérard Barthélemy, *L'univers rural haïtien: Le pays en dehors* (Paris: L'Harmattan, 1990), which draws on and extends Casimir's approach.

6. My analysis of the state in Haiti draws on the expert analyses presented in Michel-Rolph Trouillot, *Haiti, State Against Nation: The Origins and Legacy of Duvalierism* (New York: Monthly Review Press, 1990);

Robert Fatton Jr., *The Roots of Haitian Despotism* (Boulder Colo.: Lynne Rienner, 2007); and Alex Dupuy, *Haiti in the World Economy: Class, Race, and Underdevelopment Since 1700* (Boulder, Colo.: Westview Press, 1989). The materials collected in Charles Arthur and Michael Dash, eds., *Libète: A Haiti Anthology* (Princeton: Markus Weiner, 1999), form an excellent introduction and overview of key issues in Haitian history.

7. My interpretation of Haitian political history is guided by the magisterial two-volume work of Claude Moïse, *Constitutions et luttes de pouvoir en Haïti, 1804–1987: La faillite des classes dirigeantes (1804–1915)* (vol. 1) and *Constitutions et luttes de pouvoir en Haïti, 1804–1987: De l'occupation étrangère à la dictature macoute (1915–1987)* (vol. 2) (Montréal: Éditions du CIDIHCA, 1988). My analysis differs in its angle of interpretation and emphasis from two other important works of general history: the detailed and influential R. D. Heinl, N. G. Heinl, and M. Heinl, *Written in Blood: The Story of the Haitian People, 1492–1995*, 2nd ed. (Lanham, Md.: University Press of America, 1996), and the most recent survey, first published in 2005 and reissued in 2010: Philippe R. Girard, *Haiti: The Tumultuous History—from Pearl of the Caribbean to Broken Nation* (New York: Palgrave Macmillan, 2010).

8. François Blancpain, *Un siècle de relations financières entre Haïti et la France (1825–1922)* (Paris: L'Harmattan, 2001), 24 and chap. 3. Calculating equivalences between nineteenth-century French and Haitian currency and contemporary dollars is extremely difficult, as is figuring out precisely how much long-term Haitian debt can be directly attributed to the indemnity. In 2004, when Haitian president Jean-Bertrand Aristide demanded that France repay Haiti for the indemnity, he calculated that between the original levy, the debt burden it produced, and the interest on the money that was lost because of it, the former colonial power owed its former colony about $21 billion in today's currency. More recently, a fake news story announcing that France was repaying the debt—circulated by an activist organization—put the amount owed at 17 billion euros.

9. Janvier, *La république d'Haïti*, 17.

10. Georges Anglade, *Atlas critique d'Haïti* (Montréal: Groupe d'études et de recherches critiques d'espace, UQAM, 1982), vividly illustrates the shifts caused by the U.S. occupation.

11. L. Trouillot, *Street of Lost Footsteps*, trans. Linda Coverdale (Lincoln: University of Nebraska Press, 2003), 1.

12. Janvier, *La république d'Haïti*, 15–16.

1: INDEPENDENCE

1. A translation of the declaration is available in Laurent Dubois and John D. Garrigus, *Slave Revolution in the Caribbean, 1789–1804: A Brief History with Documents* (New York: Bedford/St. Martin's, 2006), 188–91. Throughout this chapter I draw on Laurent Dubois, *Avengers of the New World: The Story of the Haitian Revolution* (Cambridge, Mass.: Belknap Press of Harvard University Press, 2004). For a brief overview, see also the introduction to Dubois and Garrigus, *Slave Revolution*.

2. Dubois and Garrigus, *Slave Revolution*, 188–91.

3. David Patrick Geggus, *Haitian Revolutionary Studies* (Bloomington: Indiana University Press, 2002), chap. 13.

4. On the colony's population and the plantation system, see Dubois, *Avengers*, chap. 1.

5. On the history of free people of color in the colony, see John D. Garrigus, *Before Haiti: Race and Citizenship in French Saint-Domingue* (New York: Palgrave Macmillan, 2006), and Stewart R. King, *Blue Coat or Powdered Wig: Free People of Color in Pre-revolutionary Saint Domingue* (Athens: University of Georgia Press, 2007).

6. Sidney Wilfred Mintz, *Sweetness and Power: The Place of Sugar in Modern History* (New York: Viking, 1985).

7. Statistics on slave imports are drawn from the Trans-Atlantic Slave Trade Database at http://www.slavevoyages.org. The most detailed exploration of the role of the African-born in shaping Haitian culture is Gérard Barthélemy, *Créoles, bossales: Conflit en Haïti* (Petit-Bourg, Guadeloupe: Ibis Rouge, 2000). The pioneering studies on the African dimensions of the Haitian Revolution, and particularly on the place of enslaved people from the Kongo in Saint-Domingue, are from John K. Thornton, "I Am the Subject of the King of Congo: African Political Ideology and the Haitian Revolution," *Journal of World History* 4 (Fall 1993): 181–214, and John K. Thornton, "African Soldiers in the Haitian Revolution," *Journal of Caribbean History* 25, nos. 1 and 2 (n.d.): 58–80. A remarkable reconstruction of the life of one African-born woman in Saint-Domingue is offered in Rebecca Scott and Jean Michel Hébrard, "Les papiers de la liberté: Une mère africaine et ses enfants à l'époque de la révolution haïtienne," *Genèses* 66 (March 2007): 4–29.

8. The song was heard by the French anthropologist Odette Mennesson-Rigaud, who wrote out the words in papers now preserved in the Bibliothèque Haïtienne des Pères du Saint-Esprit in Port-au-Prince.

9. The song is recorded on Wawa and Racine Kanga, *The Haitian Roots*, vol. 1 (Geronimo Records). For analyses of the history of Vodou, see Karen McCarthy Brown, *Mama Lola: A Vodou Priestess in Brooklyn* (Berkeley: University of California Press, 1991); Joan Dayan, *Haiti, History, and the Gods* (Berkeley: University of California Press, 1995); and Leslie G. Desmangles, *The Faces of the Gods: Vodou and Roman Catholicism in Haiti* (Chapel Hill: University of North Carolina Press, 1992). An excellent introduction is provided in Laënnec Hurbon, *Voodoo: Search for the Spirit* (New York: H. N. Abrams, 1995).

10. For a detailed and convincing analysis of the history of Haitian Kreyòl, see Michel Degraff, "Relexification: A Reevaluation," *Linguistic Anthropology* 44, no. 4 (2002): 321–414, and Michel Degraff, "Against Creole Exceptionalism," *Language* 79, no. 2 (2003): 391–410. On Kreyòl theater, see Bernard Camier and Laurent Dubois, "Voltaire et Zaïre, ou le théâtre des lumières dans l'aire atlantique française," *Revue d'histoire moderne et contemporaine* 54, no. 4 (2007): 39–69; on poetry see Deborah Jenson, *Beyond the Slave Narrative: Politics, Sex, and Manuscripts in the Haitian Revolution* (Liverpool, U.K.: Liverpool University Press, 2011), chaps. 6 and 7.

11. Thornton, "African Soldiers in the Haitian Revolution."

12. King, *Blue Coat or Powdered Wig*; Garrigus, *Before Haiti*; Doris Lorraine Garraway, *The Libertine Colony: Creolization in the Early French Caribbean* (Durham, N.C.: Duke University Press, 2005).

13. Louverture has had many biographers over the years. For some of the most important works, see Victor Schoelcher, *Vie de Toussaint Louverture*, 2nd ed. (Paris: P. Ollendorff, 1889); Aimé Césaire, *Toussaint Louverture: La révolution française et le problème colonial* (Paris: Club Français du Livre, 1960); and Madison Smartt Bell, *Toussaint Louverture: A Biography*, 1st ed. (New York: Pantheon Books, 2007).

14. For a vivid narrative of this process, see Jeremy D. Popkin, *You Are All Free: The Haitian Revolution and the Abolition of Slavery* (New York: Cambridge University Press, 2010). On Sonthonax's pivotal role, see Robert Louis Stein, *Léger Félicité Sonthonax: The Lost Sentinel of the Republic* (Rutherford, N.J.: Fairleigh Dickinson University Press, 1985).

15. Mats Lundahl, *Politics or Markets? Essays on Haitian Underdevelopment* (London: Routledge, 1992), chap. 8; Michel Hector, "Problèmes du passage à la société postesclavagiste et postcoloniale (1791–1793/1820–1826)," in *Genèse de l'état haïtien (1804–1859)*, ed. Michel Hector and

Laënnec Hurbon (Paris: Éditions de la Maison des Sciences de l'Homme, 2009), 93–117.

16. On the role of women in these assemblies, see Gérard Barthélemy, *L'univers rural haïtien: Le pays en dehors* (Paris: L'Harmattan, 1990), 93–94, and Carolyn E. Fick, *The Making of Haiti: The Saint Domingue Revolution from Below*, 1st ed. (University of Tennessee Press, 1990), 168–80; for first-hand accounts of the assemblies, see the documents in Dubois and Garrigus, *Slave Revolution*, 138–44.

17. The classic study of slave gardens is Sidney Wilfred Mintz, "The Origins of the Jamaican Market System," in *Caribbean Transformations* (New York: Columbia University Press, 1989), 180–215.

18. Jean Casimir, *La culture opprimée* (Delmas, Haïti: Lakay, 2001). See also the discussion of this broad process in Robert Fatton Jr., *The Roots of Haitian Despotism* (Boulder Colo.: Lynne Rienner, 2007), 62–68.

19. Dubois, *Avengers*, 226–30.

20. On refugees from Saint-Domingue in the United States, see Ashli White, *Encountering Revolution: Haiti and the Making of the Early Republic* (Baltimore: Johns Hopkins University Press, 2010).

21. The best study of the 1801 constitution is Claude Moïse, *Le projet national de Toussaint Louverture: La constitution de 1801* (Port-au-Prince: Mémoire, 2001).

22. Lundahl, *Politics or Markets?*, chap. 8.

23. Paul Roussier, ed., *Lettres du général Leclerc, commandant en chef de l'armée de Saint-Domingue en 1802* (Paris: Société de l'Histoire des Colonies Françaises et E. Leroux, 1937), 263–74, 306–7.

24. I recount the war of independence in Dubois, *Avengers*, chaps. 12 and 13; the most detailed history of the war is C. B. Auguste and M. B. Auguste, *L'expédition Leclerc, 1801–1803* (Port-au-Prince: Henri Deschamps, 1985).

25. Deborah Jenson, "From the Kidnapping(s) of the Louvertures to the Alleged Kidnapping of Aristide: Legacies of Slavery in the Post/Colonial World," *Yale French Studies* 107 (July 2005).

26. Antoine Métral, *Histoire de l'expédition des français à Saint-Domingue: Sous le consulat de Napoléon Bonaparte, 1802–1803* (Paris: Éditions Karthala, 1985), 83; Dubois, *Avengers*, chap. 13.

27. Dubois, *Avengers*, 285–86; Roussier, *Lettres*, 199–206, 219.

28. Dubois, *Avengers*, 288–89.

29. Ibid., 291–92; Auguste and Auguste, *L'expédition Leclerc, 1801–1803*.

30. Dubois, *Avengers*, 289–92; Marcus Rainsford, *An Historical Account of the Black Empire of Hayti* (London: J. Cundee, 1805).

31. Dayan, *Haiti*, 40.

32. Thomas Madiou, *Histoire d'Haïti*, vol. 3 (Port-au-Prince: Henri Deschamps, 1985), 324.

33. Ibid., 3:139–91; Philippe R. Girard, "Caribbean Genocide: Racial War in Haiti, 1802–4," *Patterns of Prejudice* 39, no. 2 (2005): 138–61. Firsthand accounts of the killings are presented in Jeremy D. Popkin, *Facing Racial Revolution: Eyewitness Accounts of the Haitian Insurrection* (Chicago: University of Chicago Press, 2007).

34. Dubois, *Avengers*, 1, 300; Rayford Whittingham Logan, *The Diplomatic Relations of the United States with Haiti, 1776–1891* (Chapel Hill: University of North Carolina Press, 1941), 173.

35. Dubois and Garrigus, *Slave Revolution*, 191–96. For examples of a white French officer serving in Dessalines's regime, see Madiou, *Histoire d'Haïti*, 3:367–68.

36. Jenson, *Beyond the Slave Narrative*, chaps. 2 and 3.

37. Logan, *Diplomatic Relations*, chaps. 4 and 5; Tim Matthewson, *A Proslavery Foreign Policy: Haitian-American Relations During the Early Republic* (Westport, Conn.: Praeger, 2003). A detailed analysis of Dessalines's foreign policy and diplomatic negotiations is presented in the recent work of Julia Gaffield: "'The good understanding which ought always to subsist between the two islands': Haiti and Jamaica in the Atlantic World, 1803–1804," presented at "Haiti's History: Foundations for the Future" at Duke University, April 22–24, 2010; and "'Liberté, Indépendance': Haitian Anti-slavery and National Independence," presented at "Anti-slavery in the 19th Century," a symposium at the University College of Dublin, April 30–May 1, 2010.

38. On the French occupation of Santo Domingo, see Jenson, *Beyond the Slave Narrative*, chap. 3.

39. Dubois and Garrigus, *Slave Revolution*, 191; Claude Moïse, *Constitutions et luttes de pouvoir en Haïti, 1804–1987: La faillite des classes dirigeantes (1804–1915)*, vol. 1 (Montréal: Éditions du CIDIHCA, 1988), 29–33.

40. Madiou, *Histoire d'Haïti*, 3:351; Gaétan Mentor, *Histoire d'un crime politique: Le Général Etienne Victor Mentor* (Port-au-Prince: Fondation Sogebank, 1999).

41. Michel-Rolph Trouillot, *Silencing the Past: Power and the Production of History* (Boston: Beacon Press, 1995), chap. 3; Vergniaud Leconte, *Henri Christophe dans l'histoire d'Haïti* (Paris: Berger-Levrault, 1931), 144.

42. I am indebted to Jean Casimir, who pointed out this feature of the declaration to me and who sees it as an intentional marker of exclusion. For the text of the declaration, see Dubois and Garrigus, *Slave Revolution*, 188–91.

43. Moïse, *Constitutions*, 1:34; Lundahl, *Politics or Markets?*, chap. 9; Madiou, *Histoire d'Haïti*, 3:330.

44. Madiou, *Histoire d'Haïti*, 3:344–45, 349, 368–72, 404–5. On the economic history of the south, see Garrigus, *Before Haiti*.

45. Madiou, *Histoire d'Haïti*, 3:405; Dayan, *Haiti*, 39–45.

46. On Ogou and Dessalines, see Dayan, *Haiti*, esp. 30–31, and Brown, *Mama Lola*, chap. 4.

2: THE CITADEL

1. Earl Leslie Griggs and Clifford H. Prator, eds., *Henry Christophe and Thomas Clarkson: A Correspondence* (Berkeley: University of California Press, 1952), 88.

2. Ibid., 134–35.

3. H. Trouillot, *Le gouvernement du Roi Henri Christophe* (Port-au-Prince: Imprimerie Centrale, 1972), 11.

4. For detailed analyses, see Vergniaud Leconte, *Henri Christophe dans l'histoire d'Haïti* (Paris: Berger-Levrault, 1931), 367–70, and H. Trouillot, *Gouvernement*, 1–27. One of the best-known literary accounts of the construction of the Citadel is Alejo Carpentier, *The Kingdom of This World*, trans. Harriet De Onís (New York: Farrar, Straus and Giroux, 2006).

5. The Voltaire quote appeared on the masthead of the *Gazette Royal d'Hayti* for several months in 1807; copies are in the British National Archives, Colonial Office, 137/120.

6. Claude Moïse, *Constitutions et luttes de pouvoir en Haïti, 1804–1987: La faillite des classes dirigeantes (1804–1915)*, vol. 1 (Montréal: Éditions du CIDIHCA, 1988), 35.

7. Dantès Bellegarde, "President Alexandre Pétion," *Phylon* 2, no. 3 (3rd qtr. 1941): 205–6; Laurent Dubois, *Avengers of the New World: The Story of the Haitian Revolution* (Cambridge, Mass.: Belknap Press of

Harvard University Press, 2004), 65–67, 234, 254; Leconte, *Christophe*, 2; Hubert Cole, *Christophe, King of Haiti* (New York: Viking, 1967), 31; Thomas Madiou, *Histoire d'Haïti*, vol. 3 (Port-au-Prince: Henri Deschamps, 1985), 328–29; Claude Moïse, *Constitutions et luttes de pouvoir en Haïti, 1804–1987: De l'occupation étrangère à la dictature macoute (1915–1987)*, vol. 2 (Montréal: Éditions du CIDIHCA, 1988), 29–33.

8. Cole, *Christophe*, 31–32; Leconte, *Christophe*, 1–3.

9. Moïse, *Constitutions*, 1:39–44.

10. Cole, *Christophe*, 162–90; Leconte, *Christophe*, 205–45.

11. Beaubrun Ardouin, *Études sur l'histoire d'Haïti*, vol. 7 (Paris: Chez l'Auteur, 1856), 14–15, 21, 24.

12. Ibid., 7:21; Georges Corvington, *Port-au-Prince au cours des ans* (Montréal: Éditions du CIDIHCA, 2007), 2:50–52.

13. Ardouin, *Études*, 7:12, 31–43.

14. Robert K. Lacerte, "The First Land Reform in Latin America: The Reforms of Alexandre Pétion, 1809–1814," *Inter-American Economic Affairs* 28, no. 4 (Spring 1975): 77–85.

15. William F. Lewis, "Simón Bolívar and Xavier Mina: A Rendezvous in Haiti," *Journal of Inter-American Studies* 11, no. 3 (July 1969): 458–60. The most detailed study of the relationship with Bolívar is Paul Verna, *Pétion y Bolívar: Cuarenta años (1790–1830) de relaciones haitianovenezolanas y su aporte a la emancipación de Hispanoamérica* (Caracas, 1969), quote p. 524.

16. Moïse, *Constitutions*, 1:45, 53.

17. Ibid., 1:53–58. For a comparative analysis of Haiti's early constitutions, see Julia Gaffield, "Complexities of Imagining Haiti: A Study of National Constitutions, 1801–1807," *Journal of Social History* 41, no. 1 (Fall 2007): 81–103.

18. Michel-Rolph Trouillot, *Silencing the Past: Power and the Production of History* (Boston: Beacon Press, 1995), chap. 3; Leconte, *Christophe*, 144.

19. Cole, *Christophe*, 190–93; Clive Cheesman and Marie-Lucie Vendrynes, eds., *The Armorial of Haiti: Symbols of Nobility in the Reign of Henry Christophe* (London: College of Arms, 2007), 18.

20. H. Trouillot, *Gouvernement*, 61–63; Leconte, *Christophe*, 397.

21. Cheesman and Vendrynes, *The Armorial of Haiti*, 72, 90, 168.

22. H. Trouillot, *Gouvernement*, 72–77. On the theater in Le Cap, see Moreau de Saint-Méry's note from October 19, 1816, in Centre des Archives d'Outre-Mer, F3 141 bis fol. 316.

23. Chris Bongie, *Friends and Enemies: The Scribal Politics of Post/Colonial Literature* (Liverpool, U.K.: Liverpool University Press, 2008), 115–16.

24. Cheesman and Vendrynes, *Armorial of Haiti*, 6.

25. Aimé Césaire, *The Tragedy of King Christophe: A Play* (New York: Grove, 1970). The 1997 performance, which I attended, was at the Théâtre de la Colline in the 20th arrondissement of Paris.

26. Michel Hector, "Une autre voie de construction de l'état-nation: L'expérience christophienne (1806–1820)," in *Genèse de l'état haïtien (1804–1859)*, ed. Michel Hector and Laënnec Hurbon (Paris: Éditions de la Maison des Sciences de l'Homme, 2009), 248.

27. Henry Christophe, "Loi concernant la Culture," in *Code Henry*, vol. 7 (Au Cap-Henry: Chez P. Roux, Imprimeur du Roi, 1812), 10, 14, http://www.archive.org/details/codehenry00hait.

28. Ibid., 5.

29. Ibid., 5–6.

30. Ibid., 2.

31. Ibid., 11; Leconte, *Christophe*, 322.

32. Prince Sanders, *Haytian Papers: A Collection of the Very Interesting Proclamations and Other Official Documents, Together with Some Account of the Rise, Progress, and Present State of the Kingdom of Hayti* (Boston: Caleb Bingham, 1818); Griggs and Prator, *Christophe and Clarkson*, 45.

33. Alyssa Goldstein Sepinwall, *The Abbé Grégoire and the French Revolution: The Making of Modern Universalism* (Berkeley: University of California Press, 2005), 182.

34. Ibid.

35. Deborah Jenson, *Beyond the Slave Narrative: Politics, Sex, and Manuscripts in the Haitian Revolution* (Liverpool, U.K.: Liverpool University Press, 2011), 195–98.

36. Ibid., 199–206.

37. Griggs and Prator, *Christophe and Clarkson*, 70–71. H. Trouillot, *Gouvernement*, 49, 108.

38. Job B. Clement, "History of Education in Haiti: 1804–1915," *Revista de Historia de América*, no. 88 (December 1979): 35; Madiou, *Histoire d'Haïti*, 3:328–29; Hector, "Une autre voie," 255.

39. Rayford W. Logan, "Education in Haiti," *Journal of Negro History* 15, no. 4 (October 1930): 412–16; Hector, "Une autre voie," 255; Leslie François Manigat, "Le Roi Henry Christophe et l'éducation nationale 1807–1820," in *Éventail d'histoire vivante d'Haïti*, vol. 1, Collection du CHUDAC

(Port-au-Prince: CHUDAC, 2001), 293–309; Cole, *Christophe*, 256–57; H. Trouillot, *Gouvernement*, 87–91.

40. Hector, "Une autre voie," 255; Logan, "Education in Haiti," 416; Manigat, "Roi Henry Christophe," 293–309; Cole, *Christophe*, 256–57; H. Trouillot, *Gouvernement*, 87–91.

41. Griggs and Prator, *Christophe and Clarkson*, 187.

42. William Woodis Harvey, *Sketches of Hayti: From the Expulsion of the French, to the Death of Christophe* (London: L. B. Seeley and Son, 1827), 249–51.

43. Griggs and Prator, *Christophe and Clarkson*, 162; Sanders, *Haytian Papers*; Arthur O. White, "Prince Saunders: An Instance of Social Mobility Among Antebellum New England Blacks," *Journal of Negro History* 60, no. 4 (October 1975): 526–35. On the history of African American emigration to Haiti, see Chris Dixon, *African America and Haiti: Emigration and Black Nationalism in the Nineteenth Century* (Westport, Conn.: Greenwood Press, 2000).

44. Griggs and Prator, *Christophe and Clarkson*, 162.

45. Michel-Rolph Trouillot, *Haiti, State Against Nation: The Origins and Legacy of Duvalierism* (New York: Monthly Review Press, 1990), 57–58; François Blancpain, *Un siècle de relations financières entre Haïti et la France (1825–1922)* (Paris: L'Harmattan, 2001), 43–44.

46. Jean-François Brière, *Haïti et la France, 1804–1848: Le rêve brisé* (Paris: Kharthala, 2008), 19, 23.

47. Ibid., 22.

48. Ibid., 27.

49. Griggs and Prator, *Christophe and Clarkson*, 200.

50. Blancpain, *Un siècle*, 43–44.

51. Ibid., 45.

52. Ibid., 45–46.

53. Ibid., 46.

54. Ibid., 47.

55. Ibid., 49; Brière, *Haïti et la France*, illustration facing 156.

56. Griggs and Prator, *Christophe and Clarkson*, 155, 173.

57. Ibid., 174–75.

58. Ibid., 175–76.

59. Ibid., 196, 202.

60. Ibid., 202.

61. Leconte, *Christophe*, 370; George E. Simpson and J. B. Cinéas,

"Folk Tales of Haitian Heroes," *Journal of American Folklore* 54, no. 213/214 (December 1941): 176–85.

62. Cole, *Christophe*, 260–74; Griggs and Prator, *Christophe and Clarkson*, 213–19; H. Trouillot, *Gouvernement*, 168–70.

63. Griggs and Prator, *Christophe and Clarkson*, 238; Cole, *Christophe*, 274.

64. Cole, *Christophe*, 274–75; Clement, "History of Education in Haiti," 38–39.

65. For a detailed examination of the question of color in Haitian politics, see the classic work by David Nicholls, *From Dessalines to Duvalier: Race, Colour, and National Independence in Haiti*, rev. ed. (New Brunswick, N.J.: Rutgers University Press, 1996), xliii, 1. Nicholls admits that some Haitian friends consider him a bit too obsessed with color; one teased him that he always wore "bi-color" glasses when looking at Haitian history. But he insists, as others have, that the question of color has been a major cause of political conflict in Haiti.

66. Madiou, *Histoire d'Haïti*, 3:330.

67. Lacerte, "First Land Reform," 82–83; Ardouin, *Études*, 7:32, 43; Corvington, *Port-au-Prince*, 49, 59; Mimi Sheller, *Democracy After Slavery: Black Publics and Peasant Radicalism in Haiti and Jamaica* (Gainesville: University Press of Florida, 2000), 93.

3: STALEMATE

1. Hérard Dumesle, *Voyage dans le nord d'Hayti; ou, révélation des lieux et des monuments historiques* (Aux Cayes: Imprimerie du Gouvernement, 1824), 2. For biographical details, see Daniel Supplice, *Dictionnaire biographique des personnalités politiques de la république d'Haïti, 1804–2001*, 1st ed. (Haïti: D. Supplice, 2001), 235.

2. Dumesle, *Voyage*, 7–8, 333. On Buffon, see Joan Dayan, *Haiti, History, and the Gods* (Berkeley: University of California Press, 1995), 228, 237–40.

3. For the Dalmas account, which was written in 1793 but not published until 1814, see Laurent Dubois and John D. Garrigus, *Slave Revolution in the Caribbean, 1789–1804: A Brief History with Documents* (New York: Bedford/St. Martin's, 2006), 89–90. On the different accounts of this ceremony, see Léon-François Hoffman, "Un mythe national: La cérémonie du Bois-Caïman," in *La république haïtienne: État des lieux et perspectives*, ed. Gérard Barthélemy and Christian Girault (Paris: Kharthala,

1993), 434–48; the essays in Laënnec Hurbon, ed., *L'insurrection des esclaves de Saint-Domingue (22–23 août 1791)* (Paris: Kharthala, 2000); and the detailed analysis of the sources provided by David Patrick Geggus, *Haitian Revolutionary Studies* (Bloomington: Indiana University Press, 2002), chap. 6. For narratives that place the ceremony within the broader context of the 1791 insurrection, see Laurent Dubois, *Avengers of the New World: The Story of the Haitian Revolution* (Cambridge, Mass.: Belknap Press of Harvard University Press, 2004), 94–102, and Carolyn E. Fick, *The Making of Haiti: The Saint Domingue Revolution from Below*, 1st ed. (Knoxville: University of Tennessee Press, 1990), chap. 4.

4. Dumesle, *Voyage*, 88; Dubois and Garrigus, *Slave Revolution*, 87–88. Dumesle published two versions of the speech, one in French and one in Kreyòl, which raises complex issues regarding the precise translation of one line. The phrase "Bondié blancs mandé crime, et part nous vlé bienfets" is usually translated as "The God of the whites pushes them to crime, but ours wants good deeds," suggesting that there are two gods, one white and one black, asking for different things. In the French, however, Boukman is quoted as saying "Leur culte leur engage au crime, et le nôtre aux bienfaits," which can be translated as "Their religion pushes them to crime, and ours to good deeds." Rather than suggesting that there are two gods, the French version emphasizes a difference of interpretation of God's will between two religions—the one practiced by the whites versus that practiced by the blacks. The question of translation is thus also one of theology: in one case there are two gods with different messages, in the other, one god whose message is understood differently by different groups of humans. Since Catholicism and Vodou share a belief in the existence of one God—known as *bondyé* in Kreyòl—it seems likely to me that Boukman's speech was meant in the latter sense, contrasting whites using religion to justify slavery and the insurgents drawing on religion to overthrow it. But the exact meaning of this line remains open to debate and interpretation.

5. For a description of one contemporary Vodou priest's vision of the Bois Caïman ceremony, see Laurent Dubois, *A Colony of Citizens: Revolution and Slave Emancipation in the French Caribbean, 1787–1804* (Chapel Hill: Published for the Omohundro Institute of Early American History and Culture, Williamsburg, Virginia, by the University of North Carolina Press, 2004), 432–34.

6. Rayford W. Logan, *Haiti and the Dominican Republic* (London: Oxford University Press, 1968), 32–33; Job B. Clement, "History of Education

in Haiti: 1804–1915," *Revista de Historia de América*, no. 88 (December 1979): 39.

7. Chris Dixon, *African America and Haiti: Emigration and Black Nationalism in the Nineteenth Century* (Westport, Conn.: Greenwood Press, 2000), 39–46.

8. Ibid., 47; Claude Moïse, *Constitutions et luttes de pouvoir en Haïti, 1804–1987: La faillite des classes dirigeantes (1804–1915)*, vol. 1 (Montréal: Éditions du CIDIHCA, 1988), 59.

9. Victor Schoelcher, *Colonies étrangères et Haïti: Résultats de l'émancipation anglaise*, vol. 2 (Paris: Pagnerre, 1843), 180–81.

10. Ibid., 2:197–207; Benoît Joachim, *Les racines du sous développement en Haïti* (Port-au-Prince: Henri Deschamps, 1979), 104; Clement, "History of Education in Haiti," 38–39.

11. Joseph-Anténor Firmin, *M. Roosevelt, président des États-Unis et la république d'Haïti* (Paris: F. Pichon et Durand-Auzias, 1905), 339–40.

12. Jean-François Brière, *Haïti et la France, 1804–1848: Le rêve brisé* (Paris: Kharthala, 2008).

13. Ibid., 111–12, 121–22.

14. Ibid., 108–9.

15. Ibid., 109, 328–29.

16. Ibid., 111–12.

17. Ibid., 113–14.

18. Ibid., 118.

19. François Blancpain, *Un siècle de relations financières entre Haïti et la France (1825–1922)* (Paris: L'Harmattan, 2001), 66; Brière, *Haïti et la France*, 156.

20. Brière, *Haïti et la France*, 117.

21. Blancpain, *Un siècle*, 66–67.

22. Brière, *Haïti et la France*, 133.

23. Schoelcher, *Colonies*, 2:279–80; Gusti-Klara Gaillard, *L'expérience haïtienne de la dette extérieure; ou, une production caféière pillée: 1875–1915* (Port-au-Prince: Henri Deschamps, 1990).

24. On the idea of the "counter-plantation" system, see Jean Casimir, *La culture opprimée* (Delmas, Haïti: Lakay, 2001); on *métayage* see Alex Dupuy, *Haiti in the World Economy: Class, Race, and Underdevelopment Since 1700* (Boulder, Colo.: Westview Press, 1989), esp. 91.

25. Mimi Sheller, *Democracy After Slavery: Black Publics and Peasant Radicalism in Haiti and Jamaica* (Gainesville: University of Florida Press,

2000), 96–97; Blancpain, *Un siècle*, 63–64; Dupuy, *Haiti in the World Economy*, 95–96.

26. Dupuy, *Haiti in the World Economy*, 96.

27. Michel-Rolph Trouillot, *Haiti, State Against Nation: The Origins and Legacy of Duvalierism* (New York: Monthly Review Press, 1990), 74–75.

28. Rémy Bastien, *Le paysan haïtien et sa famille: Vallée de Marbial* (Paris: Kharthala, 1985), 150–54.

29. Ibid., 21–22.

30. Gérard Barthélemy, *L'univers rural haïtien: Le pays en dehors* (Paris: L'Harmattan, 1990), 28.

31. Bastien, *Paysan haïtien*, 56.

32. Barthélemy, *L'univers*, 38; Leslie François Manigat, *La révolution de 1843: Essai d'analyse historique d'une conjoncture de crise*, Les cahiers du CHUDAC vol. 1, no. 5 and 6 (Port-au-Prince, 1997), 22; Trouillot, *Haiti*, 75.

33. The most detailed study of the complex patterns of land ownership in Haiti is Drexel G. Woodson, "Tout Mounn Se Mounn, Men Tout Mounn Pa Menm: Microlevel Sociocultural Aspects of Land Tenure in a Northern Haitian Locality" (Ph.D. dissertation: Johns Hopkins University, 1990).

34. Barthélemy, *L'univers*, 31; Bastien, *Paysan haïtien*, 59.

35. Bastien, *Paysan haïtien*, 62–66; Barthélemy, *L'univers*, 33.

36. Barthélemy, *L'univers*, 31. An excellent exploration of the relationships to ancestors in Haitian Vodou is provided in Karen McCarthy Brown, *Mama Lola: A Vodou Priestess in Brooklyn* (Berkeley: University of California Press, 1991).

37. Anglade's atlas remains the classic work of historical geography on Haiti: Georges Anglade, *Atlas critique d'Haïti* (Montréal: Groupe d'Études et de Recherches Critiques d'Espace, UQAM, 1982), notes p. 37. For an excellent study of merchant women in Jamaica see Gina A. Ulysse, *Downtown Ladies: Informal Commercial Importers, a Haitian Anthropologist, and Self-Making in Jamaica* (Chicago: University of Chicago Press, 2007).

38. On different groups of immigrants, see Eugène Aubin, *En Haïti: Planteurs d'autrefois, nègres d'aujourd'hui* (Paris: A. Colin, 1910), xxii.

39. Schoelcher, *Colonies*, 2:171.

40. Ibid., 2:261, 266.

41. Ibid., 2:243–244.

42. Louis-Joseph Janvier, *La république d'Haïti et ses visiteurs (1840–1882)* (Paris: Mappon et Flammarion, 1883), 23; Schoelcher, *Colonies*, 2:215.

43. Trouillot, *Haiti*, 59; Alex Dupuy describes this process in detail and

dubs it a "stalemate" in *Haiti in the World Economy: Class, Race, and Underdevelopment Since 1700* (Boulder, Colo.: Westview Press, 1989), chap. 4.

44. Trouillot, *Haiti*, 60.

45. Ibid., 36–38. For an overview of the agricultural and environmental history of coffee in Haiti, see Roger Michel, *L'espace caféier en Haïti* (Genève: IUED, 2005), chap. 1. On the history of coffee during colonial times, see Stewart R. King, *Blue Coat or Powdered Wig: Free People of Color in Prerevolutionary Saint Domingue* (Athens: University of Georgia Press, 2007).

46. Trouillot, *Haiti*, 71.

47. Ibid., 61; Blancpain, *Un siècle*, 17.

48. For an excellent analysis of this process that argues that it created a durable "political habitus" in Haiti, see Robert Fatton Jr., *The Roots of Haitian Despotism* (Boulder, Colo.: Lynne Rienner, 2007), 7.

49. Sheller, *Democracy*, 113–14; David Nicholls, *From Dessalines to Duvalier: Race, Colour, and National Independence in Haiti*, rev. ed. (New Brunswick, N.J.: Rutgers University Press, 1996), 42–43; Schoelcher, *Colonies*, 2:182–83.

50. Moïse, *Constitutions*, 1:71.

51. Ibid; Sheller, *Democracy*, 115–17; Manigat, *La révolution de 1843*, 12; Schoelcher, *Colonies*, 2:184–89. The 1838 address is printed in full in F. E. Dubois, *Précis historique de la révolution haïtienne de 1843* (Paris: Bourdier, 1866), 11–17. Dubois, one of the members of the opposition, provides a rich firsthand account of the political activism of the period.

52. Schoelcher, *Colonies*, 2:180.

53. Sheller, *Democracy*, 118–19; Manigat, *La révolution de 1843*, 12–14.

54. Schoelcher, *Colonies*, 2:268–70; Sheller, *Democracy*, 119–20.

55. Manigat, *La révolution de 1843*, 25; Logan, *Haiti and the Dominican Republic*, 33.

56. Moïse, *Constitutions*, 1:79–81.

57. Sheller, *Democracy*, 122–25; Moïse, *Constitutions*, 1:83–85.

58. Sheller, *Democracy*, 126–27; Manigat, *La révolution de 1843*, 28.

59. Moïse, *Constitutions*, 1:91.

60. Ibid., 1:93–94.

61. Ibid., 1:88–90; Sheller, *Democracy*, 133.

62. Moïse, *Constitutions*, 1:102–3.

63. Manigat, *La révolution de 1843*, 29.

64. Maxime Reybaud, *L'empereur Soulouque et son empire* (Paris: Michel Lévy Frères, 1860), 111–13; Sheller, *Democracy*, 135–36.

65. Sheller, *Democracy*, 137; Moïse, *Constitutions*, 1:169–70; Nicholls, *Haiti in Caribbean Context*, 167, 174–76.

66. Sheller, *Democracy*, 132–39; Nicholls, *Haiti in Caribbean Context*, 171–72; Moïse, *Constitutions*, 1:170; Manigat, *La révolution de 1843*, 39.

67. Reybaud, *Soulouque*; Sheller, *Democracy*, 136–39; Nicholls, *Haiti in Caribbean Context*, 176.

68. Sheller, *Democracy*, 136–37; Moïse, *Constitutions*, 1:105–6.

69. Moïse, *Constitutions*, 1:109–10; Sheller, *Democracy*, 138; Clive Cheesman and Marie-Lucie Vendrynes, eds., *The Armorial of Haiti: Symbols of Nobility in the Reign of Henry Christophe* (London: College of Arms, 2007), 50.

70. Moïse, *Constitutions*, 1:119–20.

71. Sheller, *Democracy*, 138; Moïse, *Constitutions*, 1:111–12.

72. Leslie François Manigat, "La dichotomie Villes-Campagnes en Haïti à l'époque de la société traditionelle épanouie (1838–1896)," in *Éventail d'histoire vivante d'Haïti*, vol. 2, Collection du CHUDAC (Port-au-Prince: CHUDAC, 2002), 78.

73. Sheller, *Democracy*, 135–36; Manigat, *La révolution de 1843*, 44; Blancpain, *Un siècle*, 189.

4: THE SACRIFICE

1. John E. Baur, "The Presidency of Nicolas Geffrard of Haiti," *The Americas* 10, no. 4 (April 1954): 438–39; Matthew J. Clavin, *Toussaint Louverture and the American Civil War: The Promise and Peril of a Second Haitian Revolution* (Philadelphia: University of Pennsylvania Press, 2010), 53–54.

2. Clavin, *Toussaint Louverture*, 51–53, 204n85.

3. Ibid., 48, 54.

4. Alain Turnier, *Les États-Unis et le marché haïtien* (Montréal: Saint-Joseph, 1955), 23–26.

5. Laurent Dubois, *Avengers of the New World: The Story of the Haitian Revolution* (Cambridge, Mass.: Belknap Press of Harvard University Press, 2004), 268; Rayford Whittingham Logan, *The Diplomatic Relations of the United States with Haiti, 1776–1891* (Chapel Hill: University of North Carolina Press, 1941), 173–74; David Nicholls, *From Dessalines to Duvalier: Race, Colour, and National Independence in Haiti*, rev. ed. (New Brunswick, N.J.: Rutgers University Press, 1996), 37.

6. Logan, *Diplomatic Relations*, 173.

7. Turnier, *Marché*, 121–136.

8. Logan, *Diplomatic Relations*, 187, 197–98, 214–15.

9. Ibid., 195–96, 200.

10. Ibid., 207–9.

11. Ibid., 214.

12. Ibid., 223–27.

13. Clavin, *Toussaint Louverture*, 73. Louverture was celebrated by contemporaries such as William Wordsworth in a poem originally published in the *Morning Post*, reprinted in the online version of William Wordsworth, *The Complete Poetical Works* (London: Macmillan, 1888), http://www.bartleby.com/br/145.html, as well as in the widely read account of Marcus Rainsford, *An Historical Account of the Black Empire of Hayti* (London: J. Cundee, 1805). In the 1850s his memoirs were published in France by Joseph Saint-Remy, ed., *Mémoires du général Toussaint-Louverture, écrits par lui-même, pouvant servir à l'histoire de sa vie* (Paris: Pagnerre, 1853), and translated into English in John Relly Beard, *Toussaint L'Ouverture: A Biography and Autobiography* (Boston: J. Redpath, 1863).

14. Logan, *Diplomatic Relations*, 233–34.

15. Laënnec Hurbon, *Religions et lien social: L'église et l'état moderne en Haïti* (Paris: Cerf, 2004), 136–41; Philippe Delisle, *Le catholicisme en Haïti au XIXe siècle* (Paris: Kharthala, 2003), 15, 20. The most detailed study of the negotiations with the papacy is Adolphe Cabon, *Notes sur l'histoire religieuse d'Haïti de la révolution au concordat (1789–1860)* (Port-au-Prince: Petit Séminaire Collège Saint-Martial, 1933).

16. Hurbon, *Religions*, 145–50; Delisle, *Catholicisme*, 15–16, 33; Micial M. Nérestant, *Religions et politique en Haïti (1804–1990)* (Paris: Karthala, 1994), 69–75.

17. Delisle, *Catholicisme*, 15–16; Thomas F. O'Connor and Joseph Bp, "Joseph Rosati, C. M., Apostolic Delegate to Haiti, 1842, Two Letters to Bishop John Hughes," *The Americas* 1, no. 4 (April 1945): 492–93.

18. Delisle, *Catholicisme*, 20; Hurbon, *Religions*, 139–41.

19. Hurbon, *Religions*, 159; Murdo J. Macleod, "The Soulouque Regime in Haiti, 1847–1859: A Reevaluation," *Caribbean Studies* 10, no. 3 (October 1970): 35–48, quotes p. 47. For negative depictions of Soulouque, see Maxime Reybaud, *L'empereur Soulouque et son empire* (Paris: Michel Lévy frères, 1860), and Cham [pseud.], *Soulouque et sa cour: Caricatures* (Paris: Au Bureau du Journal Le Charivari, 1850).

20. Macleod, "Soulouque," 35–36; Hurbon, *Religions*, 141.

21. Macleod, "Soulouque," 36, 44; Joan Dayan, *Haiti, History, and the Gods* (Berkeley: University of California Press, 1995), 10.

22. Dayan, *Haiti*, 12; Spenser St. John, *Hayti; or, The Black Republic* (New York: Scribner & Welford, 1889), 187.

23. Millery Polyné, *From Douglass to Duvalier: U.S. African Americans, Haiti and Pan Americanism, 1870–1964* (Gainesville: University Press of Florida, 2010), 29. On Panama, see Aims McGuinness, *Path of Empire: Panama and the California Gold Rush* (Ithaca: Cornell University Press, 2008), and David G. McCullough, *The Path Between the Seas: The Creation of the Panama Canal, 1870–1914* (New York: Simon and Schuster, 1977).

24. Robert E. May, *The Southern Dream of a Caribbean Empire, 1854–1861*, 2nd ed. (Gainesville: University Press of Florida, 2002), 5–6.

25. Logan, *Diplomatic Relations*, 249–50.

26. Ibid., 249–55.

27. Macleod, "Soulouque," 46; Rayford W. Logan, *Haiti and the Dominican Republic* (London: Oxford University Press, 1968), 33–42.

28. Leslie François Manigat, "L'Essentiel sur la question de la navase," in *Éventail d'histoire vivante d'Haïti*, vol. 2, Collection du CHUDAC (Port-au-Prince: CHUDAC, 2002), 224–41. See also Ted Widmer, "Little America," *New York Times*, June 30, 2007.

29. Ibid. See also Widmer, "Little America."

30. Manigat, "Navase."

31. Ibid., 236–41.

32. Clavin, *Toussaint Louverture*, 2.

33. Ibid., 3, 58–59.

34. Ibid., chap. 3.

35. Logan, *Diplomatic Relations*, 293–302.

36. Ibid., 297–98.

37. Ibid., 303–5.

38. J. C. Dorsainvil, *Manuel d'histoire d'Haïti* (Port-au-Prince: Henri Deschamps, 1924), 228–38; David M. Dean, *Defender of the Race: James Theodore Holly, Black Nationalist and Bishop* (Newton Center, Mass.: Lambeth Press, 1979), 33–38; Chris Dixon, *African America and Haiti: Emigration and Black Nationalism in the Nineteenth Century* (Westport, Conn.: Greenwood Press, 2000), chap. 4 and p. 186.

39. Dean, *Defender*, 18, 36–38, 41; Dixon, *African America and Haiti*, 187–90; Howard Holman Bell, ed., *Black Separatism and the Caribbean, 1860* (Ann Arbor: University of Michigan Press, 1970).

40. Dean, *Defender*, 44, 67, 96; Dixon, *African America and Haiti*, 190.

41. Dean, *Defender*, chaps. 5 and 6, esp. pp. 66–71.

42. Delisle, *Catholicisme*, 20–22; Nérestant, *Religions et politique en Haïti (1804–1990)*, 105–21.

43. Delisle, *Catholicisme*, 39–43.

44. Ibid., 33, 44–48. For a detailed study of the *plaçage* system, see Serge-Henri Vieux, *Le plaçage, droit coutumier et famille en Haïti* (Paris: Publisud, 1989).

45. Delisle, *Catholicisme*, 49–70; Rayford W. Logan, "Education in Haiti," *Journal of Negro History* 15, no. 4 (October 1930): 436–37; Job B. Clement, "History of Education in Haiti: 1804–1915," *Revista de Historia de América*, no. 88 (December 1979): 51–52.

46. Delisle, *Catholicisme*, 61–67.

47. Philippe Delisle, *Catholicisme*, 22.

48. Laënnec Hurbon, *Le barbare imaginaire* (Paris: Cerf, 1988), 112–14; Kate Ramsey, "Prohibition, Persecution, Performance: Anthropology and the Penalization of Vodou in Mid-20th-Century," *Gradhiva* 1 (2005): 165n2.

49. Delisle, *Catholicisme*, 83–84; Hurbon, *Religions*, 145, 153.

50. On the issue of witchcraft within Vodou, see Hurbon, *Barbare*. The best study of secret societies in contemporary Haiti is Rachel Beauvoir-Dominique, *Savalou E* (Havana: Casa de las Americas, 2003); see also Pierre Pluchon, *Vaudou, sorciers, empoisonneurs: De Saint-Domingue à Haïti* (Paris: Karthala, 1987).

51. St. John, *Hayti*, 216.

52. Ibid., 215–18.

53. Hurbon, *Barbare*, 116–17; St. John, *Hayti*, 218.

54. St. John, *Hayti*, 208.

55. Ibid., 192–208.

56. Ibid., 222; Delisle, *Catholicisme*, 88–90.

57. Samuel Hazard, *Santo Domingo, Past and Present: With a Glance at Hayti* (New York: Harper & Bros., 1873), 419.

5: LOOKING NORTH

1. Joseph-Anténor Firmin, *M. Roosevelt, président des États-Unis et la république d'Haïti* (Paris: F. Pichon et Durand-Auzias, 1905), 463.

2. Joseph-Anténor Firmin, *Lettres de Saint-Thomas: Études sociologiques,*

historiques et littéraires (Port-au-Prince: Imprimerie Centrale, 1976), 91–92; Firmin, *Roosevelt*, 468–69.

3. Firmin, *Roosevelt*, 478, 480.

4. Ibid., 131; Watson Denis, "Les 100 ans de Monsieur Roosevelt et Haïti," *Revue de la société haïtienne d'histoire et de géographie* 81è année, no. 226 (September 2006): 17–18.

5. Firmin, *Roosevelt*, 477, 480.

6. Jean Price-Mars, *Anténor Firmin* (Port-au-Prince: Séminaire Adventiste, 1964), 14–17; J. C. Dorsainvil, *Manuel d'histoire d'Haïti* (Port-au-Prince: Henri Deschamps, 1924), 239–42; Rayford Whittingham Logan, *The Diplomatic Relations of the United States with Haiti, 1776–1891* (Chapel Hill: University of North Carolina Press, 1941), 319.

7. Logan, *Diplomatic Relations*, 320–21; Alain Turnier, *Les États-Unis et le marché haïtien* (Montréal: Saint-Joseph, 1955), 198–201.

8. Logan, *Diplomatic Relations*, 320–21; Ludwell Lee Montague, *Haiti and the United States, 1714–1938* (Durham, N.C.: Duke University Press, 1940), 100–101.

9. Claude Moïse, *Constitutions et luttes de pouvoir en Haïti, 1804–1987: La faillite des classes dirigeantes (1804–1915)*, vol. 1 (Montréal: Éditions du CIDIHCA, 1988), chap. 7; Dorsainvil, *Histoire d'Haïti*, 243–51; Price-Mars, *Anténor Firmin*, 14–23; Turnier, *Marché*, 202.

10. Moïse, *Constitutions*, 1:272.

11. Eugène Aubin, *En Haïti: Planteurs d'autrefois, nègres d'aujourd'hui* (Paris: A. Colin, 1910), 14–15.

12. Alain Turnier, *Avec Mérisier Jeannis: Une tranche de vie jacmélienne et nationale* (Port-au-Prince: Le Natal, 1982), 23–24. Turnier's book provides a detailed biography of one general who rose from relative poverty as a peasant to become a significant regional power holder.

13. For the clearest analysis of the regional system of Haiti in the nineteenth century, see Georges Anglade, *Atlas Critique d'Haïti* (Montréal: Groupe d'Études et de Recherches Critiques d'Espace, UQAM, 1982).

14. Moïse, *Constitutions*, 1:176, 261, 264–65.

15. Kethly Millet, *Les paysans haïtiens et l'occupation américaine d'Haïti, 1915–1930* (La Salle, Québec: Collectif Paroles, 1978), 10.

16. Moïse, *Constitutions*, 1:258–60, 268; for a detailed analysis of the long-term construction of an "authoritarian political habitus" in Haiti, see Robert Fatton Jr., *The Roots of Haitian Despotism* (Boulder, Colo.: Lynne Rienner, 2007).

17. Moïse, *Constitutions*, 1:258.

18. Turnier, *Avec Mérisier Jeannis*, provides the most detailed local account of the military and political conflicts of this era.

19. Rémy Bastien, *Le paysan haïtien et sa famille: Vallée de Marbial* (Paris: Kharthala, 1985), 166.

20. Brenda Gayle Plummer, *Haiti and the United States: The Psychological Moment* (Athens: University of Georgia Press, 1992), 78–79; see also Fatton, *Roots*, 138–39.

21. Logan, *Diplomatic Relations*, 356–57; David Nicholls, *Haiti in Caribbean Context: Ethnicity, Economy, and Revolt* (New York: St. Martin's Press, 1985), 109; François Blancpain, *Un siècle de relations financières entre Haïti et la France (1825–1922)* (Paris: L'Harmattan, 2001), 81; Fatton, *Roots*, 138–39.

22. Moïse, *Constitutions*, 1:214.

23. Blancpain, *Un siècle*, 81–88.

24. Ibid., 23; François Blancpain, *Haïti et les Etats-Unis, 1915–1934: Histoire d'une occupation* (Paris: L'Harmattan, 1999), 35. For a detailed examination of state corruption during this period, see Leslie J. R. Péan, *Haïti: Économie politique de la corruption*, vol. 2: *L'état marron (1870–1915)* (Paris: Maisonneuve et Larose, 2005).

25. Blancpain, *Un siècle*, 89–103.

26. Millery Polyné, *From Douglass to Duvalier: U.S. African Americans, Haiti and Pan Americanism, 1870–1964* (Gainesville: University Press of Florida, 2010), 35; Montague, *Haiti*, 94.

27. Polyné, *Douglass to Duvalier*, 25–26, 38.

28. Rayford W. Logan, *Haiti and the Dominican Republic* (London: Oxford University Press, 1968), 39–46; Polyné, *Douglass to Duvalier*, 34.

29. Logan, *Diplomatic Relations*, 345–46.

30. Logan, *Haiti and the Dominican Republic*, 45; Logan, *Diplomatic Relations*, 352; Polyné, *Douglass to Duvalier*, 35. For the newspaper report, see *New York Herald*, February 2, 1869.

31. Montague, *Haiti*, 107–10; Polyné, *Douglass to Duvalier*, 36–40.

32. Logan, *Diplomatic Relations*, 349–50.

33. Ibid., 351.

34. Denis, "100 Ans," 22–24.

35. Leslie F. Manigat, "La substitution de la prépondérance américaine à la prépondérance française en Haïti au début du XXe siècle: La

conjoncture de 1910–1911," *Revue d'histoire moderne et contemporaine* 14, no. 4 (December 1967): 323.

36. Denis, "100 Ans," 10–11; David Nicholls, *From Dessalines to Duvalier: Race, Colour, and National Independence in Haiti*, rev. ed. (New Brunswick, N.J.: Rutgers University Press, 1996), 102–7.

37. Nicholls, *From Dessalines to Duvalier*, 113–17.

38. Denis, "100 Ans," 10–11.

39. Firmin, *Lettres de Saint-Thomas*, 111–15; Joseph-Anténor Firmin, *The Equality of the Human Races* (New York: Garland, 2000), xvi. The arguments in Louis-Joseph Janvier, *La république d'Haïti et ses visiteurs (1840–1882)* (Paris: Mappon et Flammarion, 1883), were also shaped by his encounter with contemporary French anthropology.

40. Firmin, *Equality*, 325–28.

41. Ibid., 198.

42. On the broader history of Firmin's work and impact, see Carolyn Fluehr-Lobban's introduction to Firmin, *Equality*.

43. Dorsainvil, *Histoire d'Haïti*, 267–70; Moïse, *Constitutions*, 1:226.

44. Georges J. Benjamin, *La Diplomatie d'Anténor Firmin: Ses péripéties, ses aspects* (Nancy, France: Grandville, 1957), 43–45; Denis, "100 Ans," 31–32.

45. Polyné, *Douglass to Duvalier*, 30, 46–47; Logan, *Diplomatic Relations*, 398–400.

46. Logan, *Diplomatic Relations*, 416–17, 425–26.

47. Ibid., 420; Dorsainvil, *Histoire d'Haïti*, 269–71.

48. Denis, "100 Ans," 32; Montague, *Haiti*, 146–47; Logan, *Diplomatic Relations*, 408.

49. Logan, *Diplomatic Relations*, 411–14; Montague, *Haiti*, 147.

50. Logan, *Diplomatic Relations*, 426; Polyné, *Douglass to Duvalier*, 6.

51. On the role of descendants of migrants from Saint-Domingue in politics in Louisiana, see Rebecca J. Scott, *Degrees of Freedom: Louisiana and Cuba After Slavery* (Cambridge, Mass.: Harvard University Press, 2005).

52. Mimi Sheller, *Democracy After Slavery: Black Publics and Peasant Radicalism in Haiti and Jamaica* (Gainesville: University Press of Florida, 2000), 69.

53. Moïse, *Constitutions*, 1:246.

54. Ibid., 1:247.

55. Logan, *Diplomatic Relations*, 429–30.

56. Ibid., 432–33; Montague, *Haiti*, 147.

57. Logan, *Diplomatic Relations*, 438.

58. Frederick Douglass, "Haïti and the United States. Inside History of the Negotiations for the Môle St. Nicolas. II," *North American Review* 153, no. 419 (October 1891): 456–57; Logan, *Diplomatic Relations*, 406–7, 433–34.

59. Frederick Douglass, "Haïti and the United States. Inside History of the Negotiations for the Môle St. Nicolas. I," *North American Review* 153, no. 418 (September 1891): 339–40; Logan, *Diplomatic Relations*, 447–48.

60. Montague, *Haiti*, 148–49; Logan, *Diplomatic Relations*, 436, 442, 447–48; Douglass, "Haïti and the United States. Inside History of the Negotiations for the Môle St. Nicolas. I," 343–44.

61. Logan, *Diplomatic Relations*, 441–44.

62. Ibid., 448–49.

63. The full correspondence is published in Firmin, *Roosevelt*, 497–501. See also Logan, *Diplomatic Relations*, 448–50, and Benjamin, *Diplomatie*, 91–96.

64. Firmin, *Roosevelt*, 498–500.

65. Denis, "100 Ans," 14; Marc Péan, *L'échec du Firminisme* (Port-au-Prince: Henri Deschamps, 1987), 52–53.

66. Firmin, *Roosevelt*, 497–501; Logan, *Diplomatic Relations*, 437–38, 451.

67. Denis, "100 Ans," 14; Firmin, *Lettres de Saint-Thomas*, 117–18.

68. Denis, "100 Ans," 14.

69. Dorsainvil, *Histoire d'Haïti*, 274–75; Montague, *Haiti*, 178–79.

70. Dorsainvil, *Histoire d'Haïti*, 275–78; Péan, *Firminisme*, 66.

71. Péan, *Firminisme*, 69–71, 81.

72. Ibid., 100–105.

73. Price-Mars, *Anténor Firmin*, 20–23.

74. Péan, *Firminisme*, 110–19.

75. Ibid., 122–30.

76. Ibid., 133–34.

77. Ibid., 157–59.

78. Denis, "100 Ans," 38, 39; Marc Péan, *La ville éclatée (Décembre 1902–Juillet 1915)*, vol. 3 (Port-au-Prince: Imprimeur II, 1993), 93–95.

79. Denis, "100 Ans."; Firmin, *Roosevelt*, 477; Patrick Bellegarde-Smith, *In the Shadow of Powers: Dantès Bellegarde in Haitian Social Thought* (Atlantic Highlands, N.J.: Humanities Press International, 1985), xiv.

80. Firmin, *Roosevelt*, 472–73.

81. Claude Moïse, *Constitutions et luttes de pouvoir en Haïti, 1804–1987: De l'occupation étrangère à la dictature macoute (1915–1987)*, vol. 2 (Montréal: Éditions du CIDIHCA, 1988), 12.

6: OCCUPATION

1. François Blancpain, *Haïti et les États-Unis: 1915–1934: Histoire d'une occupation* (Paris: L'Harmattan, 1999), 33–34.

2. Ibid., 33–35; François Blancpain, *Un siècle de relations financières entre Haïti et la France (1825–1922)* (Paris: L'Harmattan, 2001), 75–76.

3. Hans Schmidt, *The United States Occupation of Haiti, 1915–1934* (New Brunswick, N.J.: Rutgers University Press, 1995), 33, 61. The most detailed study of the shift in financial power is Leslie François Manigat, "La substitution de la prépondérance américaine à la prépondérance française en Haïti au début du XXe siècle: La conjoncture de 1910–1911," *Revue d'histoire moderne et contemporaine* 14, no. 4 (December 1967): 321–55.

4. Blancpain, *Un siècle*, 32; Alain Turnier, *Les États-Unis et le marché haïtien* (Washington, 1955), 209; Manigat, "La substitution," 322–23.

5. Blancpain, *Haïti et les États-Unis*, 32.

6. Ibid., 36–37.

7. Ibid., 37–38.

8. Kethly Millet, *Les paysans haïtiens et l'occupation américaine d'Haïti, 1915–1930* (La Salle, Québec: Collectif Paroles, 1978).

9. For an excellent textual and visual overview of this economy, see Georges Anglade, *Atlas critique d'Haïti* (Montréal: Groupe d'Études et de Recherches Critiques d'Espace, UQAM, 1982).

10. Millet, *Les paysans*, 44, 52.

11. Roger Gaillard, *Charlemagne Péralte le caco* (Port-au-Prince: R. Gaillard, 1982), 119–23.

12. J. C. Dorsainvil, *Manuel d'histoire d'Haïti* (Port-au-Prince: Henri Deschamps, 1924), 287–89; Mary A. Renda, *Taking Haiti: Military Occupation and the Culture of U.S. Imperialism, 1915–1940* (Chapel Hill: University of North Carolina Press, 2001), 91.

13. Gaillard, *Charlemagne*, 124–25; Schmidt, *Occupation*, 64–65, 71; Renda, *Taking Haiti*, 80–81; Claude Moïse, *Constitutions et luttes de pouvoir en Haïti, 1804–1987: De l'occupation étrangère à la dictature macoute (1915–1987)*, vol. 2 (Montréal: Éditions du CIDIHCA, 1988), 26–27. For a detailed study of Bobo's biography and movement, see Roger Gaillard, *Les cent-jours de Rosalvo Bobo; ou, une mise à mort politique*, 2nd ed. (Port-au-Prince: R. Gaillard, 1987).

14. Roger Gaillard, *Premier écrasement du cacoïsme* (Port-au-Prince: R. Gaillard, 1981), 12.

15. Ibid., 11.

16. Renda, *Taking Haiti*, 96; Schmidt, *Occupation*, 57.

17. Schmidt, *Occupation*, 48.

18. Ibid., 55.

19. Renda, *Taking Haiti*, 99–100.

20. Schmidt, *Occupation*, 66; Dantès Bellegarde, *L'occupation américaine d'Haïti, ses conséquences morales et économiques* (Port-au-Prince: Chéraquit, 1929), 5.

21. Rayford Logan, *Haiti and the Dominican Republic* (London: Oxford University Press, 1968), 125–27.

22. Gage Averill, *A Day for the Hunter, a Day for the Prey: Popular Music and Power in Haiti* (Chicago: University of Chicago Press, 1997), 36.

23. Renda, *Taking Haiti*, 84–85.

24. Gaillard, *Écrasement*, 13, 21; Schmidt, *Occupation*, 67.

25. Gaillard, *Écrasement*, 14–15; Schmidt, *Occupation*, 67.

26. Moïse, *Constitutions*, 2:28; Gaillard, *Écrasement*, 53.

27. Roger Gaillard, *La destinée de Carl Brouard: Essai accompagné de documents photographiques* (Port-au-Prince: Henri Deschamps, 1966), 6; Renda, *Taking Haiti*, 85.

28. Gaillard, *Écrasement*, 20.

29. Moïse, *Constitutions*, 2:28–30; Schmidt, *Occupation*, 71–72.

30. Moïse, *Constitutions*, 2:28–30; Schmidt, *Occupation*, 71–72.

31. Moïse, *Constitutions*, 2:30–31; Gaillard, *Écrasement*, 111–12. On Dartiguenave's background and presidency, see Barthelemieux Danache, *Le président Dartiguenave et les américains* (Port-au-Prince: Imprimerie de l'État, 1950).

32. Moïse, *Constitutions*, 2:32.

33. Gaillard, *Écrasement*, 53–55; Moïse, *Constitutions*, 2:28.

34. Gaillard, *Écrasement*, 57–58.

35. Ibid., 59–60.

36. Ibid., 100–103.

37. Ibid., 113.

38. Ibid., 98–99.

39. Danache, *Le président Dartiguenave*, 47; Moïse, *Constitutions*, 2:36–39; Blancpain, *Haïti et les États-Unis*, 64–65; Gaillard, *Écrasement*, 141–42.

40. Moïse, *Constitutions*, 2:39–40; Claude Moïse, *Constitutions et luttes de pouvoir en Haïti, 1804–1987: La faillite des classes dirigeantes (1804–1915)*, vol. 1 (Montréal: Éditions du CIDIHCA, 1988), 301.

41. The song is reprinted in full, and translated into French, in Gaillard, *Écrasement*, 148–51, 227–29. See also Averill, *Hunter*, 48–49, and Moïse, *Constitutions*, 2:40–41.

42. Moïse, *Constitutions*, 2:40–41; Select Committee on Haiti and Santo Domingo Congress, *Inquiry into Occupation and Administration of Haiti and Santo Domingo* (Washington, D.C.: United States Congress, 1921), 395.

43. Moïse, *Constitutions*, 2:42–43.

44. Gaillard, *Écrasement*, 144.

45. Ibid., 38–39.

46. Ibid., 38–40.

47. Ibid., 105, 109.

48. Ibid., 117, 152.

49. Renda, *Taking Haiti*, 78–80.

50. Hans Schmidt, *Maverick Marine: General Smedley D. Butler and the Contradictions of American Military History* (Lexington: University Press of Kentucky, 1987), 84, 87; Renda, *Taking Haiti*, 155–56; Schmidt, *Occupation*, 144–45.

51. Renda, *Taking Haiti*, 141, 155, 156; H. P. Davis, *Black Democracy: The Story of Haiti* (New York: L. MacVeagh, Dial Press, 1929), 224.

52. Renda, *Taking Haiti*, 140–43; Gaillard, *Écrasement*, 162.

53. Gaillard, *Écrasement*, 167; Renda, *Taking Haiti*, 117, 142.

54. Schmidt, *Maverick Marine*, 75, 78; Schmidt, *Occupation*, 146; Renda, *Taking Haiti*, 13.

55. Gaillard, *Charlemagne*, 108.

56. Gaillard, *Écrasement*, 184–89; Schmidt, *Maverick Marine*, 81.

57. Gaillard, *Écrasement*, 184–88; Renda, *Taking Haiti*, 146; Lowell Jackson Thomas, *Old Gimlet Eye: The Adventures of Smedley D. Butler as*

Told to Lowell Thomas (New York: Farrar and Rinehart, 1933); Schmidt, *Maverick Marine*, 90.

58. Gaillard, *Écrasement*, 188.

59. Congress, *Inquiry*, 398; Renda, *Taking Haiti*, 135; Gaillard, *Charlemagne*, 200.

60. Moïse, *Constitutions*, 2:46. The most detailed institutional history of the Gendarmerie (later renamed the Garde d'Haïti) is James H. McCrocklin, *Garde d'Haiti, 1915–1934: Twenty Years of Organization and Training by the United States Marine Corps* (Annapolis: United States Naval Institute, 1956). On Butler, see Schmidt, *Maverick Marine*, 83–84.

61. B. Davis, *Marine! The Life of Lt. Gen. Lewis B. (Chesty) Puller, USMA (ret.)* (Boston: Little, Brown, 1962), 27.

62. François Blancpain, *Louis Borno, président d'Haïti* (Port-au-Prince: Éditions Regain, 1998), 172.

63. Renda, *Taking Haiti*, 147–48; Schmidt, *Occupation*, 148.

64. Gaillard, *Charlemagne*, 44; Renda, *Taking Haiti*, 150.

65. Renda, *Taking Haiti*, 166–67.

66. Ibid., 80, 171.

67. Gaillard, *Charlemagne*, 34–36.

68. Ibid., 33–38.

69. Congress, *Inquiry*, 553; Roger Gaillard, *Hinche mise en croix* (Port-au-Prince: Le Natal, 1982), 29.

70. Renda, *Taking Haiti*, 154; Schmidt, *Occupation*, 146.

71. This transformation is emphasized in Anglade, *Atlas critique d'Haïti*.

72. Michel-Rolph Trouillot, *Haiti, State Against Nation: The Origins and Legacy of Duvalierism* (New York: Monthly Review Press, 1990), 106.

73. Gaillard, *Hinche*, 26–27; Schmidt, *Occupation*, 110–11.

74. Congress, *Inquiry*, 606; Gaillard, *Hinche*, 31.

75. Moïse, *Constitutions*, 2:63; Renda, *Taking Haiti*, 148–50; Gaillard, *Hinche*, 176, chap. 4; Congress, *Inquiry*, 658.

76. Gaillard, *Hinche*, 213–14; Renda, *Taking Haiti*, 148–50.

77. Gaillard, *Hinche*, 215–16.

78. Ibid., 32, 220, 223–24.

79. Ibid., 217–18; Congress, *Inquiry*, 658.

80. Gaillard, *Hinche*, 224.

81. Ibid., 33–39.

82. Roger Gaillard, *La république autoritaire* (Port-au-Prince: R. Gaillard, 1981), 28.

83. Moïse, *Constitutions*, 2:59.

84. Ibid., 2:49–57.

85. Ibid., 2:56–59.

86. Ibid., 2:60–61; Schmidt, *Occupation*, 97–98; Howard Zinn and Anthony Arnove, *Voices of a People's History of the United States*, 2nd ed. (New York: Seven Stories Press, 2009), 251–52.

87. Moïse, *Constitutions*, 2:64; Schmidt, *Occupation*, 98–99.

88. Moïse, *Constitutions*, 2:62–65; Schmidt, *Occupation*, 98–99; Rayford W. Logan, "Education in Haiti," *Journal of Negro History* 15, no. 4 (October 1930): 450.

89. Moïse, *Constitutions*, 2:65–67. On the impact of U.S. investment and commerce in Haiti in the early twentieth century, see Turnier, *Marché*, esp. chap. 10; on Roosevelt and the constitution, see Schmidt, *Maverick Marine*.

90. Moïse, *Constitutions*, 2:67; Mirlande Manigat, *Traité de droit constitutionnel haïtien* (Port-au-Prince: Université Quisqueya, 2000), 532–43.

91. Gaillard, *Hinche*, 177–79.

92. Ibid., 180–81.

93. Ibid., 180–81, 187–88, 225.

94. Ibid., 199–209; Millet, *Les paysans*, 90.

95. Gaillard, *Hinche*, 175–76; Renda, *Taking Haiti*, 149–50.

96. Gaillard, *Charlemagne*, 68–71, 87.

97. Ibid., 68–71.

98. B. Davis, *Marine!* 43; Renda, *Taking Haiti*, 151, 156–57; the photograph from the *Crisis* is reprinted in Gaillard, *Charlemagne*, 337.

99. Gaillard, *Charlemagne*, 237.

100. Ibid., 147–48.

101. Ibid., 101, 140.

102. Ibid., 139–48; David Nicholls, *From Dessalines to Duvalier: Race, Colour, and National Independence in Haiti*, rev. ed. (New Brunswick, N.J.: Rutgers University Press, 1996), 146.

103. Gaillard, *Charlemagne*, 98–100; Schmidt, *Occupation*, 105.

104. Gaillard, *Charlemagne*, 96.

105. Ibid., 247.

106. Ibid., 188, 292.

107. Ibid., 160–61; Renda, *Taking Haiti*, 173–74.

108. Gaillard, *Charlemagne*, 113, 164–65, 187, 214–16; Schmidt, *Occupation*, 103; Millet, *Les paysans*, 101.

109. Gaillard, *Charlemagne*, 126–36.

110. Ibid., 184–86, 201.

111. Ibid., 206.

112. Ibid., 208–12.

113. Ibid., 212–14.

114. Renda, *Taking Haiti*, 171–72.

115. Gaillard, *Charlemagne*, 222–23, 333.

116. Ibid., 298–306.

117. Ibid., 308–9.

118. Ibid., 317–18.

119. Renda, *Taking Haiti*, 150; Congress, *Inquiry*, 606; Gaillard, *Hinche*, 26–27; Moïse, *Constitutions*, 2:63; Millet, *Les paysans*, 109; Gaillard, *Charlemagne*, 322–23.

120. Gaillard, *Charlemagne*, 325–26.

121. Ibid., 334.

122. Ibid., 308, 335.

123. The photograph is reproduced among the illustrations following p. 134 in Schmidt, *Occupation*.

124. Gaillard, *Charlemagne*, illustrations following p. 335. My thanks to LeGrace Benson for providing me with these details about Obin's paintings of Péralte.

7: SECOND INDEPENDENCE

1. François Blancpain, *Louis Borno, président d'Haïti* (Port-au-Prince: Éditions Regain, 1998), 175–76; Rulhière Savaille, *La grève de 29: La première grève des étudiants haïtiens, 31 Octobre 1929* (Port-au-Prince: Ateliers Fardin, 1979), 18–19.

2. Savaille, *Grève*, 24–34.

3. Claude Moïse, *Constitutions et luttes de pouvoir en Haïti, 1804–1987: De l'occupation étrangère à la dictature macoute (1915–1987)*, vol. 2 (Montréal: Éditions du CIDIHCA, 1988), 158–59; Savaille, *Grève*, 47–54; Kethly Millet, *Les paysans haïtiens et l'occupation américaine d'Haïti, 1915–1930* (La Salle, Québec: Collectif Paroles, 1978), 131. For a summary of the situation in rural Haiti under the occupation see Suzy Castor, *L'occupation américaine d'Haïti* (Port-au-Prince: Société Haïtienne d'Histoire, 1988), chap. 5.

4. Matthew J. Smith, *Red and Black in Haiti: Radicalism, Conflict, and Political Change, 1934–1957* (Chapel Hill: University of North Carolina

Press, 2009), 10; Georges Michel, *Charlemagne Péralte and the First American Occupation of Haiti*, trans. Douglas Henry Daniels (Dubuque, Iowa: Kendall/Hunt, 1996), 45–47; Andrew Walker, "Contested Sovereignty: Haitian Politics and Protest in the Era of U.S. Occupation, 1915–1934" (B.A. thesis, Duke University, 2011), 4–5.

5. Roger Gaillard, *Charlemagne Péralte le caco* (Port-au-Prince: R. Gaillard, 1982), 27–28.

6. Alex Dupuy, *Haiti in the World Economy: Class, Race, and Underdevelopment Since 1700* (Boulder, Colo.: Westview Press, 1989), 136; Millet, *Les paysans*, 123; Gaillard, *Charlemagne*, 90–92; Castor, *L'occupation américaine d'Haïti*, 95–96; Kate Ramsey, *The Spirits and the Law: Vodou and Power in Haiti* (Chicago: University of Chicago Press, 2011), n. 254.

7. Millet, *Les paysans*, 107–9; Karen E. Richman, *Migration and Vodou* (Gainesville: University Press of Florida, 2005), 102–11; Castor, *L'occupation américaine d'Haïti*, 91–97; Ramsey, *Spirits*, 124. For a contemporary critical account of the dispossession of rural land, see Perceval Thoby, *Dépossessions: Le latifundia américain contre la petite propriété d'Haiti*, vol. 1 (Port-au-Prince: Impr. de "La Presse," 1930).

8. Blancpain, *Borno*, 176, 198.

9. Patrick Bellegarde-Smith, *In the Shadow of Powers: Dantès Bellegarde in Haitian Social Thought* (Atlantic Highlands, N.J.: Humanities Press International, 1985), 63–66; Millery Polyné, *From Douglass to Duvalier: U.S. African Americans, Haiti and Pan Americanism, 1870–1964* (Gainesville: University Press of Florida, 2010), 69; Blancpain, *Borno*, 175–76.

10. Laënnec Hurbon, *Le Barbare Imaginaire* (Paris: Cerf, 1988), 119–20; David Nicholls, *From Dessalines to Duvalier: Race, Colour, and National Independence in Haiti*, rev. ed. (New Brunswick, N.J.: Rutgers University Press, 1996), 155; Eugène Aubin, *En Haïti: Planteurs d'autrefois, nègres d'aujourd'hui* (Paris: A. Colin, 1910), 54–60.

11. Ramsey, *Spirits*, 128–30.

12. Hurbon, *Barbare*, 121–23; John Dryden Kuser, *Haiti: Its Dawn of Progress After Years in a Night of Revolution* (Boston: R. G. Badger, 1921), 57–58; Ramsey, *Spirits*, 131, 146, 149, 200.

13. Millet, *Les paysans*, 108–9; Castor, *L'occupation américaine d'Haïti*, 97–101.

14. Gaillard, *Charlemagne*, 31, 93–95, 171–74; Marc C. McLeod, "Undesirable Aliens: Race, Ethnicity, and Nationalism in the Comparison of Haitian and British West Indian Immigrant Workers in Cuba, 1912–1939,"

Journal of Social History 31, no. 3 (Spring 1998): 599–623; Catherine C. Legrand, "Informal Resistance on a Dominican Sugar Plantation During the Trujillo Dictatorship," *Hispanic American Historical Review* 75, no. 4 (November 1995): 555–96.

15. Ramsey, *Spirits*, 133–34, 137–38; Mary A. Renda, *Taking Haiti: Military Occupation and the Culture of U.S. Imperialism, 1915–1940* (Chapel Hill: University of North Carolina Press, 2001), 159–60; Hans Schmidt, *The United States Occupation of Haiti, 1915–1934* (New Brunswick, N.J.: Rutgers University Press, 1995), 119; Gaillard, *Charlemagne*, 237–39.

16. Polyné, *Douglass to Duvalier*, 61–62; Renda, *Taking Haiti*, 186. For Johnson's statements, see the *Crisis* (February 1922), p. 182.

17. Polyné, *Douglass to Duvalier*, 62; Renda, *Taking Haiti*, 188–96; Schmidt, *Occupation*, 114–20.

18. Ramsey, *Spirits*, 134–37, 182, 315n80.

19. Ulysses G. Weatherly, "Haiti: An Experiment in Pragmatism," *American Journal of Sociology* 32, no. 3 (November 1926): 366; Robert Fatton Jr., *The Roots of Haitian Despotism* (Boulder, Colo.: Lynne Rienner, 2007), 164–65, 189; Schmidt, *Occupation*, 124–29; Gaillard, *Charlemagne*, 239.

20. Moïse, *Constitutions*, 2:105, 137.

21. Ibid., 2:110–111. The most detailed study of Borno's political life is Blancpain, *Borno*.

22. Georges Corvington, *Le palais national de la république d'Haïti* (Port-au-Prince: Henri Deschamps, 2004); Barthelemieux Danache, *Le président Dartiguenave et les américains* (Port-au-Prince: Imprimerie de l'État, 1950); cited in Blancpain, *Borno*, 172–73; Bellegarde-Smith, *Shadow*, 64–65; Rayford W. Logan, "Education in Haiti," *Journal of Negro History* 15, no. 4 (October 1930): 450.

23. Blancpain, *Borno*, 184–86.

24. Ibid., 175–76; Savaille, *Grève*, 18–19; Schmidt, *Occupation*, 184.

25. Bellegarde-Smith, *Shadow*, 61–62; Magdaline W. Shannon, *Jean Price-Mars, the Haitian Elite and the American Occupation, 1915–1935* (New York: St. Martin's Press, 1996), 23; Polyné, *Douglass to Duvalier*, 77–79; Philippe Delisle, *Le catholicisme en Haïti au XIXe siècle* (Paris: Kharthala, 2003), 66.

26. Polyné, *Douglass to Duvalier*, 76; Logan, "Education in Haiti," 440–48; Blancpain, *Borno*, 188.

27. Blancpain, *Borno*, 179–81; Bellegarde-Smith, *Shadow*, 122–23, 155–57, 164.

28. Savaille, *Grève*, 9–14, 47–54, 107; Moïse, *Constitutions*, 2:158–59; Schmidt, *Occupation*, 197.

29. Polyné, *Douglass to Duvalier*, 83–86.

30. Blancpain, *Borno*, 188–89; Savaille, *Grève*, 101.

31. Schmidt, *Occupation*, 149; Gaillard, *Charlemagne*, 171; Bellegarde-Smith, *Shadow*, 63–64; Nadève Ménard, "The Occupied Novel: The Representation of Foreigners in Haitian Novels Written During the United States Occupation, 1915–1934" (Ph.D. dissertation: University of Pennsylvania, 2002).

32. Schmidt, *Occupation*, 138–39; Renda, *Taking Haiti*, 132–33.

33. Michel-Rolph Trouillot, *Haiti, State Against Nation: The Origins and Legacy of Duvalierism* (New York: Monthly Review Press, 1990), 130–31. For detailed studies of how the occupation shaped the thought of particular Haitian intellectuals, see Bellegarde-Smith, *Shadow*; Shannon, *Price-Mars*; and J. Michael Dash, *Literature and Ideology in Haiti, 1915–1961* (Totowa, N.J.: Barnes & Noble Books, 1981).

34. Gaillard, *Charlemagne*, 62–63; Shannon, *Price-Mars*, 55.

35. On Jeanty, see Michael D. Largey, *Vodou Nation: Haitian Art Music and Cultural Nationalism* (Chicago: University of Chicago Press, 2006), chap. 2. On Candio, see Gage Averill, *A Day for the Hunter, a Day for the Prey: Popular Music and Power in Haiti* (Chicago: University of Chicago Press, 1997), 49–50.

36. Shannon, *Price-Mars*, 57–61; Moïse, *Constitutions*, 2:93–94; Nicholls, *From Dessalines to Duvalier*, 150; Walker, "Contested Sovereignty," chap. 3. On the history of struggles for women's rights in Haiti see Madelaine Sylvain Bouchereau, *Haïti et ses femmes* (Port-au-Prince: Les Presses Libres, 1957).

37. Blancpain, *Borno*, 171; Moïse, *Constitutions*, 2:128–35; Schmidt, *Occupation*, 128, 195.

38. Bellegarde-Smith, *Shadow*, 66–77.

39. Schmidt, *Occupation*, 208; Moïse, *Constitutions*, 2:149; Shannon, *Price-Mars*, 64; Emily Greene Balch, *Occupied Haiti* (New York: Writers Publishing, 1927).

40. Shannon, *Price-Mars*, 14–15.

41. Ibid., 16–23.

42. Ibid., 59; Ramsey, *Spirits*, 126.

43. Hurbon, *Barbare*, 119–20; Nicholls, *From Dessalines to Duvalier*, 132, 155; Shannon, *Price-Mars*, 59; Bellegarde-Smith, *Shadow*, 104, 127.

44. Jean Price-Mars, *Ainsi parla l'oncle: Essai d'ethnographie* (Port-au-Prince: Compiègne, 1928), i–ii. While I have largely followed the translation provided in Jean Price-Mars, *So Spoke the Uncle*, trans. Magdaline Shannon (Washington, D.C.: Three Continents Press, 1983), I have also retranslated some passages. For an analysis of Price-Mars and his relation to Firmin, see Gérarde Magloire-Danton, "Anténor Firmin and Jean Price-Mars: Revolution, Memory, Humanism," *Small Axe* 9, no. 2 (September 2005): 150–70.

45. Price-Mars, *Ainsi parla l'oncle*, 2–3; Price-Mars, *Uncle*, 8–9.

46. Price-Mars, *Ainsi parla l'oncle*, 2; Price-Mars, *Uncle*, 8; Ramsey, *Spirits*, 178–81.

47. Smith, *Red and Black*, 9; Schmidt, *Occupation*, 210–12; Moïse, *Constitutions*, 2:160–61.

48. Moïse, *Constitutions*, 2:168.

49. Ibid., 2:191–95; Schmidt, *Occupation*, 224–26.

50. Moïse, *Constitutions*, 2:191–95, 212; Schmidt, *Occupation*, 224–26; Polyné, *Douglass to Duvalier*, 79–80.

51. Moïse, *Constitutions*, 2:194–95; Smith, *Red and Black*, 18.

52. Ramsey, *Spirits*, 149–50, 162–66; John Houston Craige, *Black Bagdad* (New York: Minton, Balch, 1933); John Houston Craige, *Cannibal Cousins*, 1st ed. (New York: Minton, Balch, 1934); Renda, *Taking Haiti*, chap. 2.

53. Ramsey, *Spirits*, 171.

54. Ramsey, *Spirits*, 170–173; Richman, *Migration and Vodou*, 111; Laënnec Hurbon, "American Fantasy and Haitian Vodou," in *Sacred Arts of Haitian Vodou*, ed. Donald Cosentino (Los Angeles: UCLA Fowler Museum of Cultural History, 1995). The best discussion of the symbolism and meaning of the *zonbi* in Haiti is Hurbon, *Barbare*. Wade Davis argues that the practice of zombification does exist among secret societies in Haiti who use neurotoxins against certain enemies; see Wade Davis, *Passage of Darkness: The Ethnobiology of the Haitian Zombie* (Chapel Hill: University of North Carolina Press, 1988), which was popularized in his *The Serpent and the Rainbow* (London: Collins, 1986) and later in a rather unfortunate movie version by horror film director Wes Craven.

55. Chantalle Verna, "Haiti's 'Second Independence' and the Promise of Pan-American Cooperation, 1934–1956" (Ph.D. dissertation: Michigan State University, 2005).

56. Jacques Roumain, *Oeuvres complètes*, ed. Léon-François Hoffmann (Paris: Allca XX, Collection Archivos, 2003), introduction and p. 429; Smith,

Red and Black, 18–20. For insights into the broader cultural movements of this time, see Ramsey, *Spirits*, 178; Roger Gaillard, *La destinée de Carl Brouard: Essai accompagné de documents photographiques* (Port-au-Prince: Henri Deschamps, 1966); and Dash, *Literature and Ideology in Haiti, 1915–1961*, chaps. 2–4.

57. Smith, *Red and Black*, 19–22.

58. Ibid., 20–21.

59. Moïse, *Constitutions*, 2:194–95; Smith, *Red and Black*, 22; Averill, *Hunter*, 50.

60. Sténio Vincent, *En posant les jalons* (Port-au-Prince: Imprimerie de l'État, 1939), 334–35; Moïse, *Constitutions*, 2:194–95, 214–15.

61. Smith, *Red and Black*, 41–43; Moïse, *Constitutions*, 2:217–23, 235–36.

62. Ramsey, *Spirits*, 182; Gérard Barthélemy, *L'univers rural haïtien: Le pays en dehors* (Paris: L'Harmattan, 1990), 47.

63. Richard Lee Turits, "A World Destroyed, a Nation Imposed: The 1937 Haitian Massacre in the Dominican Republic," *Hispanic American Historical Review* 82, no. 3 (August 2002): 595.

64. Ibid., 610; Richard Lee Turits, *Foundations of Despotism: Peasants, the Trujillo Regime, and Modernity in Dominican History* (Stanford: Stanford University Press, 2003). See also Eric Roorda, *The Dictator Next Door: The Good Neighbor Policy and the Trujillo Regime in the Dominican Republic, 1930–1945* (Durham, N.C.: Duke University Press, 1998), and Lauren Hutchinson Derby, *The Dictator's Seduction: Politics and the Popular Imagination in the Era of Trujillo* (Durham, N.C.: Duke University Press, 2009).

65. Turits, "World Destroyed," 613.

66. Ibid., 614; Brenda Gayle Plummer, *Haiti and the United States: The Psychological Moment* (Athens: University of Georgia Press, 1992), 154.

67. Plummer, *Haiti and the United States*, 156–57; Smith, *Red and Black*, 34; Turits, "World Destroyed."

68. Roumain, *Oeuvres*, 682–88.

69. Ramsey, *Spirits*, 181–91; Hurbon, *Barbare*, 124.

70. Kate Ramsey, "Without One Ritual Note: Folklore Performance and the Haitian State, 1935–1946," *Radical History Review* 84 (Fall 2002): 22.

71. Ramsey, *Spirits*, 231–32; Ramsey, "Ritual Note," 20–21.

72. Ramsey, *Spirits*, 177, 181–91, 231–36; Ramsey, "Ritual Note," 20–22; Hurbon, *Barbare*, 124.

73. Ramsey, *Spirits*, 194, 196, 200–202; and Smith, *Red and Black*, 49–50.

74. Smith, *Red and Black*, 48–49; Ramsey, *Spirits*, 185–86, 198–200.

75. Alfred Métraux, *Voodoo in Haiti*, trans. Hugo Charteris (New York: Schocken Books, 1972), 17.

76. Roumain, *Oeuvres*, 745-52.

77. Ibid., 247–54; Jacques Roumain, *Masters of the Dew*, trans. Langston Hughes and Mercer Cook (New York: Reynal & Hitchcock, 1947).

78. Roumain, *Oeuvres*, 88–94.

8: AN IMMATERIAL BEING

1. Marie Vieux-Chauvet, *Love, Anger, Madness: A Haitian Trilogy* (New York: Modern Library, 2009), xxi–xxii, 160, 230, 265. On Vieux-Chauvet within the broader context of twentieth-century women's writing in Haiti see Myriam Chancy, *Framing Silence: Revolutionary Novels by Haitian Women* (New Brunswick, N.J.: Rutgers University Press, 1997), chap. 5.

2. Ibid., 228.

3. Ibid., xiii, 24–25; Patti M. Marxsen, "In Perpetual Revolt," *Women's Review of Books*, April 2010.

4. Vieux-Chauvet, *Love, Anger, Madness*, xxii; Marxsen, "In Perpetual Revolt"; Bernard Diederich and Al Burt, *Papa Doc: The Truth About Haiti Today*, 1st ed. (New York: McGraw-Hill, 1969), 216–17.

5. Vieux-Chauvet, *Love, Anger, Madness*, xiv–xv, xxii; Marxsen, "In Perpetual Revolt."

6. Matthew J. Smith, *Red and Black in Haiti: Radicalism, Conflict, and Political Change, 1934–1957* (Chapel Hill: University of North Carolina Press, 2009), 43–44.

7. Ibid., 45–46; Diederich and Burt, *Papa Doc*, 50–51; Claude Moïse, *Constitutions et luttes de pouvoir en Haïti, 1804–1987: De l'occupation étrangère à la dictature macoute (1915–1987)*, vol. 2 (Montréal: Éditions du CIDIHCA, 1988), 236–37.

8. Smith, *Red and Black*, 77–79; Patrick Bellegarde-Smith, *In the Shadow of Powers: Dantès Bellegarde in Haitian Social Thought* (Atlantic Highlands, N.J.: Humanities Press International, 1985), 147–48; Moïse, *Constitutions*, 2:235.

9. Moïse, *Constitutions*, 2:252–54; Smith, *Red and Black*, 73, 80–82.

10. Smith, *Red and Black*, 90–99, 110–13; Patrick Bellegarde-Smith,

Haiti: The Breached Citadel, 2nd ed. (Toronto: Canadian Scholars Press, 2004), 121; Edmund Wilson, *Red, Black, Blond, and Olive; Studies in Four Civilizations: Zuñi, Haiti, Soviet Russia, Israel* (New York: Oxford University Press, 1956), 91; Moïse, *Constitutions*, 2:282–88; Bellegarde-Smith, *Shadow*, 148.

11. Millery Polyné, *From Douglass to Duvalier: U.S. African Americans, Haiti and Pan Americanism, 1870–1964* (Gainesville: University Press of Florida, 2010), 138–39; Smith, *Red and Black*, 114–16.

12. Smith, *Red and Black*, 107, 143–44; Gage Averill, *A Day for the Hunter, a Day for the Prey: Popular Music and Power in Haiti* (Chicago: University of Chicago Press, 1997), 63–65; Polyné, *Douglass to Duvalier*, chaps. 4 and 5, esp. 146–47; Katherine Dunham, *Island Possessed*, 1st ed. (Garden City, N.Y.: Doubleday, 1969); Polly Pattullo, *Last Resorts: The Cost of Tourism in the Caribbean* (New York: Monthly Review Press, 2005).

13. Smith, *Red and Black*, 139, 142, 145–47.

14. Moïse, *Constitutions*, 2:315; Smith, *Red and Black*, 149–62; Diederich and Burt, *Papa Doc*, 68.

15. Diederich and Burt, *Papa Doc*, 64–65, 68; Smith, *Red and Black*, 164–65; James Ferguson, *Papa Doc, Baby Doc: Haiti and the Duvaliers* (Oxford: B. Blackwell, 1988), 35. On the Schweitzer hospital, see Barry Paris, *Song of Haiti: The Lives of Dr. Larimer and Gwen Mellon at Albert Schweitzer Hospital of Deschapelles*, 1st ed. (New York: Public Affairs, 2000). For a detailed firsthand account of Magloire's regime, see Bernard Diederich, *Bon Papa: Haiti's Golden Years* (Princeton: Markus Wiener, 2008).

16. Smith, *Red and Black*, 164–66, 169; Diederich and Burt, *Papa Doc*, 68.

17. Smith, *Red and Black*, 161; Ferguson, *Duvaliers*, 32–33; Moïse, *Constitutions*, 2:327.

18. Diederich and Burt, *Papa Doc*, 30–38.

19. Ibid., 38, 45; Ferguson, *Duvaliers*, 33. For extended reflections on color in Haitian politics, see David Nicholls, *From Dessalines to Duvalier: Race, Colour, and National Independence in Haiti*, rev. ed. (New Brunswick, N.J.: Rutgers University Press, 1996).

20. François Duvalier, *Oeuvres essentielles* (Port-au-Prince: Presses Nationales d'Haïti, 1966), 1: 311–12; Nicholls, *From Dessalines to Duvalier*, 194–95.

21. Duvalier, *Oeuvres essentielles*, 1: 311–12; Nicholls, *From Dessalines to Duvalier*, 194–95; Smith, *Red and Black*, 23–24; Robert Fatton Jr., *The Roots of Haitian Despotism* (Boulder, Colo.: Lynne Rienner, 2007), 179.

22. Nicholls, *From Dessalines to Duvalier*, 185–88; Smith, *Red and Black*, 97–99, 110–13, 161; Ferguson, *Duvaliers*, 32–33; Moïse, *Constitutions*, 2:327.

23. Nicholls, *From Dessalines to Duvalier*, 113–17, 154–55; Smith, *Red and Black*, 23–26.

24. Moïse, *Constitutions*, 2:330, 334–35; Diederich and Burt, *Papa Doc*, 78–79, 86.

25. Smith, *Red and Black*, 168–85; Moïse, *Constitutions*, 2:344–45, 352–58; Diederich and Burt, *Papa Doc*, chap. 8; Bellegarde-Smith, *Breached Citadel*, 125–26.

26. Moïse, *Constitutions*, 2:344–45, 366–67; Smith, *Red and Black*, 168–85; Nicholls, *From Dessalines to Duvalier*, 208–9; Diederich and Burt, *Papa Doc*, 99–100; Bellegarde-Smith, *Breached Citadel*, 128.

27. Moïse, *Constitutions*, 2:366, 381, 396; Michel-Rolph Trouillot, *Haiti, State Against Nation: The Origins and Legacy of Duvalierism* (New York: Monthly Review Press, 1990), 169; Fatton, *Roots*, 182; Ferguson, *Duvaliers*, 37, 57.

28. Moïse, *Constitutions*, 2:372–73; Ferguson, *Duvaliers*, 39.

29. Moïse, *Constitutions*, 2:374–77.

30. Diederich and Burt, *Papa Doc*, 102, 105; Moïse, *Constitutions*, 2:380–81.

31. Diederich and Burt, *Papa Doc*, 113–20, 145; Ferguson, *Duvaliers*, 41; Robert Debs Heinl, Nancy Gordon Heinl, and Michael Heinl, *Written in Blood: The Story of the Haitian People, 1492–1995*, 2nd ed. (Lanham, Md.: University Press of America, 1996), 593; Moïse, *Constitutions*, 2:385–88.

32. Diederich and Burt, *Papa Doc*, 156, 190; Moïse, *Constitutions*, 2:376; Trouillot, *Haiti*, 144–45; Fatton, *Roots*, 107; Bellegarde-Smith, *Breached Citadel*, 132; Heinl, Heinl, and Heinl, *Written in Blood*, 557–58.

33. Bellegarde-Smith, *Shadow*, 86; Heinl, Heinl, and Heinl, *Written in Blood*, 553; Moïse, *Constitutions*, 2:396; Diederich and Burt, *Papa Doc*, 147.

34. Moïse, *Constitutions*, 2:396; Bellegarde-Smith, *Breached Citadel*, 133; Heinl, Heinl, and Heinl, *Written in Blood*, 554, 560; Diederich and Burt, *Papa Doc*, 159.

35. Trouillot, *Haiti*, 179; Vieux-Chauvet, *Love, Anger, Madness*.

36. Heinl, Heinl, and Heinl, *Written in Blood*, 607; Diederich and Burt, *Papa Doc*, 187, 198. Most of Duvalier's speeches and writings are collected in Duvalier, *Oeuvres essentielles*.

37. Diederich and Burt, *Papa Doc*, 183–84; Averill, *Hunter*, 74–75; Trouillot, *Haiti*, 194.

38. Fatton, *Roots*, 102–103; Heinl, Heinl, and Heinl, *Written in Blood*, 561, 574–75; Moïse, *Constitutions*, 2:413; Paul Christopher Johnson, "Secretism and the Apotheosis of Duvalier," *Journal of the American Academy of Religion* 74, no. 2 (2006): 420.

39. Laënnec Hurbon, *Religions et lien social: L'église et l'état moderne en Haïti* (Paris: Cerf, 2004), 222–23; Fatton, *Roots*, 102; Averill, *Hunter*, 74.

40. Hurbon, *Religions*, 220–26; Diederich and Burt, *Papa Doc*, 191.

41. Hurbon, *Religions*, 222–26; Moïse, *Constitutions*, 2:391–94; Nicholls, *From Dessalines to Duvalier*, 234; Trouillot, *Haiti*, 194; Bellegarde-Smith, *Breached Citadel*, 135.

42. Smith, *Red and Black*, 172–85; Diederich and Burt, *Papa Doc*, 99–100; Bellegarde-Smith, *Breached Citadel*, 125–26.

43. Moïse, *Constitutions*, 2:366–368; Bellegarde-Smith, *Breached Citadel*, 123, 132; Diederich and Burt, *Papa Doc*, 99–100, 126–27, 136–37, 226–27; Heinl, Heinl, and Heinl, *Written in Blood*, 567.

44. Brenda Gayle Plummer, *Haiti and the United States: The Psychological Moment* (Athens: University of Georgia Press, 1992), 184; Moïse, *Constitutions*, 2:400–401; Heinl, Heinl, and Heinl, *Written in Blood*, 566–67, 580; Robert David Johnson, "Constitutionalism Abroad and at Home: The United States Senate and the Alliance for Progress, 1961–1967," *International History Review* 21, no. 2 (June 1, 1999): 418; Diederich and Burt, *Papa Doc*, 133.

45. Johnson, "Constitutionalism Abroad and at Home," 421–22.

46. Diederich and Burt, *Papa Doc*, 133, 242; Plummer, *Haiti and the United States*, 186–87; Heinl, Heinl, and Heinl, *Written in Blood*, 606.

47. Heinl, Heinl, and Heinl, *Written in Blood*, 564–67.

48. Plummer, *Haiti and the United States*, 180; Diederich and Burt, *Papa Doc*, 202, 224, 240. For Bosch's own account of his time as president, see Juan Bosch, *The Unfinished Experiment: Democracy in the Dominican Republic* (New York: Praeger, 1965). On relations with the United States, see Bernardo Vega, *Kennedy y Bosch: Aporte al Estudio de las Relaciones*

Internacionales del Gobierno Constitucional de 1963 (Santo Domingo: Fundación Cultural Dominicana, 1993).

49. Moïse, *Constitutions*, 2:402–3; Diederich and Burt, *Papa Doc*, 194–95, 202–3.

50. Diederich and Burt, *Papa Doc*, 204–9; Moïse, *Constitutions*, 2:403.

51. Diederich and Burt, *Papa Doc*, 210–14, 223–24, 233.

52. Ibid., 216–17, 223.

53. Diederich and Burt, *Papa Doc*, 221–22, 237; Heinl, Heinl, and Heinl, *Written in Blood*, 578–79.

54. Diederich and Burt, *Papa Doc*, 244–45.

55. Heinl, Heinl, and Heinl, *Written in Blood*, 579–80; Diederich and Burt, *Papa Doc*, 240, 289–99; Ferguson, *Duvaliers*, 45–46. On the coup in the Dominican Republic and its effects, see Piero Gleijeses, *The Dominican Crisis: The 1965 Constitutionalist Revolt and American Intervention* (Baltimore: Johns Hopkins University Press, 1978).

56. Robert Heinl was the head of the marine mission in Haiti starting in 1958 but came into conflict with Duvalier and was withdrawn by the United States several years later. Upon his return to the United States, he cowrote a long history of Haiti that presented a damning portrait of the dictator. Heinl, Heinl, and Heinl, *Written in Blood*, 579–81; Ferguson, *Duvaliers*, 45–48; Diederich and Burt, *Papa Doc*, 289–99, 300–312; Plummer, *Haiti and the United States*, 180, 190. The most detailed account of the repression in Jérémie is Albert D. Chassagne, *Bain de sang en Haïti: Les macoutes opèrent à Jérémie*, 2nd ed. (n.p.: 1977).

57. Heinl, Heinl, and Heinl, *Written in Blood*, 582; Diederich and Burt, *Papa Doc*, 311–12.

58. Alexander Wolff, "The Hero Who Vanished," *Sports Illustrated*, March 8, 2010. For documentation on abuses in the prison, see Patrick Lemoine, *Fort-Dimanche, Fort–La Mort*, 2nd ed. (Port-au-Prince: Éditions Regain, 1996).

59. Moïse, *Constitutions*, 2:405–11; Diederich and Burt, *Papa Doc*, 280–82; Heinl, Heinl, and Heinl, *Written in Blood*, 555, 583.

60. Heinl, Heinl, and Heinl, *Written in Blood*, 583; Diederich and Burt, *Papa Doc*, 271, 283; Moïse, *Constitutions*, 2:412–13; Ferguson, *Duvaliers*, 53; Averill, *Hunter*, 8–9.

61. Heinl, Heinl, and Heinl, *Written in Blood*, 582–83; Nicholls, *From Dessalines to Duvalier*, 155, 234–35; Moïse, *Constitutions*, 2:409; Ferguson, *Duvaliers*, 52–53.

62. Heinl, Heinl, and Heinl, *Written in Blood*, 583.

63. Heinl, Heinl, and Heinl, *Written in Blood*, 588; Diederich and Burt, *Papa Doc*, 320, 328–31; Trouillot, *Haiti*, 192.

64. Heinl, Heinl, and Heinl, *Written in Blood*, 583; Polyné, *Douglass to Duvalier*, 185; Bellegarde-Smith, *Breached Citadel*, 139. Duvalier harshly attacked Graham Greene, for instance, whose popular novel *The Comedians* presented a dark portrait of life in Haiti. Ferguson, *Duvaliers*, 51.

65. Moïse, *Constitutions*, 2:398; Ferguson, *Duvaliers*, 53–54; Alex Dupuy, *Haiti in the World Economy: Class, Race, and Underdevelopment Since 1700* (Boulder, Colo.: Westview Press, 1989), 164–65; Diederich and Burt, *Papa Doc*, 320–21; Heinl, Heinl, and Heinl, *Written in Blood*, 570.

66. Ferguson, *Duvaliers*, 54; Simon M. Fass, *Political Economy in Haiti: The Drama of Survival* (New Brunswick, N.J.: Transaction Books, 1988), 50.

67. Jean Dominique, "La fin du marronage haïtien: Éléments pour une étude des mouvements de contestation populaire en Haïti," *Collectif Paroles* 32 (December 1985): 39–46.

68. Ferguson, *Duvaliers*, 53, 55; Averill, *Hunter*, 8–9, 94–97; Plummer, *Haiti and the United States*, 194–95.

69. Ferguson, *Duvaliers*, 54–55; Heinl, Heinl, and Heinl, *Written in Blood*, 594, 596, 616.

70. Moïse, *Constitutions*, 2:415–19; Ferguson, *Duvaliers*, 56–57; Heinl, Heinl, and Heinl, *Written in Blood*, 598.

71. Moïse, *Constitutions*, 2:416; Ferguson, *Duvaliers*, 53, 55; Heinl, Heinl, and Heinl, *Written in Blood*, 612.

72. The most detailed account of Jean-Claude Duvalier's presidency to date is Bernard Diederich, *L'Héritier* (Port-au-Prince: Henri Deschamps, 2011).

73. Ferguson, *Duvaliers*, 54–55; Heinl, Heinl, and Heinl, *Written in Blood*, 594, 596, 616; Fass, *Political Economy in Haiti*, 39, 43, 67; Cary Hector, "Des 'prises de démocratie' de la société civile au renouvellement des pratiques de pouvoir (1975–1983)," *Collectif Paroles* 32 (December 1985): 12.

74. Fass, *Political Economy in Haiti*, 22–23; Plummer, *Haiti and the United States*, 195.

75. Fritz Deshommes, *Haïti: La nation écartelée* (Port-au-Prince: Éditions Cahiers Universitaires, 2006), 65–69; Bernard Diederich, "Swine Fever Ironies," *Caribbean Review* 14:1 (1985): 16–17, 41.

76. Deshommes, *Haïti*, 65–70; Amy Wilentz, *The Rainy Season: Haiti Since Duvalier* (New York: Simon and Schuster, 1989), 157.

77. Fass, *Political Economy in Haiti*, 48–49.

78. Heinl, Heinl, and Heinl, *Written in Blood*, 586–87; Averill, *Hunter*, 110–11. For rich portraits of aspects of life in the Haitian diaspora, see Karen McCarthy Brown, *Mama Lola: A Vodou Priestess in Brooklyn* (Berkeley: University of California Press, 1991), and Nina Glick Schiller and Georges Eugene Fouron, *Georges Woke Up Laughing: Long-Distance Nationalism and the Search for Home* (Durham, N.C.: Duke University Press, 2001). On Catholic institutions and the diaspora, see Regine O. Jackson, "After the Exodus: The New Catholics in Boston's Old Ethnic Neighborhoods," *Religion and American Culture: A Journal of Interpretation* 17, no. 2 (July 1, 2007): 191–212, and Margarita A. Mooney, *Faith Makes Us Live: Surviving and Thriving in the Haitian Diaspora* (Berkeley: University of California Press, 2009).

79. Jean-Pierre Jean, "The Tenth Department," *NACLA Report on the Americas*, 1994. On family and migration, see Karen E. Richman, *Migration and Vodou* (Gainesville: University Press of Florida, 2005). Edwidge Danticat told the story about the burials during a presentation at Duke University on February 15, 2011; she tells her family's story in the searing memoir *Brother, I'm Dying*, 1st ed. (New York: Alfred A. Knopf, 2007).

80. Heinl, Heinl, and Heinl, *Written in Blood*, 592.

81. For excellent overviews of these changes, see Hector, "Prises de démocratie"; Moïse, *Constitutions*, 2:420–25; and Dominique, "Fin du marronage." For the Castro masks, see Bruce Chatwin, *Under the Sun: The Letters of Bruce Chatwin*, 1st ed. (New York: Viking, 2011), 312.

82. Moïse, *Constitutions*, 2:425–30; Hector, "Prises de démocratie"; Dominique, "Fin du marronage"; Paul Farmer, *The Uses of Haiti*, 2nd ed. (Monroe, Maine: Common Courage Press, 2003); Robert Lawless, *Haiti's Bad Press* (Rochester, Vt.: Schenkman Books, 1992); Laurent Dubois, "L'accueil des réfugiés haïtiens aux États-Unis," *Hommes et Migrations* 1213 (June 1998): 47–59; Richman, *Migration and Vodou*.

83. Dominique, "Fin du marronage"; Conférence épiscopale d'Haïti, *Présence de l'église en Haïti: Messages et documents de l'épiscopat, 1980–1988* (Paris: Éditions S.O.S., 1988); Jean-Bertrand Aristide, *Aristide: An Autobiography* (Maryknoll, N.Y.: Orbis Books, 1993); Peter Hallward,

Damming the Flood: Haiti, Aristide, and the Politics of Containment (London: Verso, 2007), 23.

84. Elizabeth Abbott, *Haiti: The Duvaliers and Their Legacy* (New York: McGraw-Hill, 1988), 293–94.

85. Martin-Luc Bonnardot and Gilles Danroc, eds., *La chute de la maison Duvalier: Textes pour l'histoire* (Paris: Karthala, 1989), 39, 55, 63; Abbott, *Haiti*, 295–96.

86. David Nicholls, "Haiti: The Rise and Fall of Duvalierism," *Third World Quarterly* 8, no. 4 (October 1, 1986): 1239–52; Bonnardot and Danroc, *La chute de la maison Duvalier*, 55; Hallward, *Damming the Flood*, 22; Abbott, *Haiti*, 299; Averill, *Hunter*, 159.

87. Abbott, *Haiti*, 302 and chap. 13; Trouillot, *Haiti*, chap. 7.

88. Bonnardot and Danroc, *La chute de la maison Duvalier*, 55, 63; Abbott, *Haiti*, 299.

EPILOGUE

1. Peter Hallward, *Damming the Flood: Haiti, Aristide, and the Politics of Containment* (London: Verso, 2007), xxxv. For descriptions of events in 1986, see Amy Wilentz, *The Rainy Season: Haiti Since Duvalier* (New York: Simon and Schuster, 1989), and Gage Averill, *A Day for the Hunter, a Day for the Prey: Popular Music and Power in Haiti* (Chicago: University of Chicago Press, 1997), chap. 8. On the constitution, see Claude Moïse, *Constitutions et luttes de pouvoir en Haïti, 1804–1987: De l'occupation étrangère à la dictature macoute (1915–1987)*, vol. 2 (Montréal: Éditions du CIDIHCA, 1988), 463–66. A complete list of members of the Constituent Assembly is available at http://www.haiti-reference.com/histoire/notables/assemb_const87.php (consulted April 14, 2011).

2. See the detailed analysis of the constitution in Moïse, *Constitutions*, 2:463–80, which reprints the document on pp. 495–548.

3. Michel-Rolph Trouillot, *Haiti, State Against Nation: The Origins and Legacy of Duvalierism* (New York: Monthly Review Press, 1990), 221; Wilentz, *Rainy Season*, 113; Averill, *Hunter*, 171; Hallward, *Damming the Flood*, xxxv.

4. Moïse, *Constitutions*, 2:463; Trouillot, *Haiti*, chaps. 7 and 8; Averill, *Hunter*, 173–75. The most detailed account of Aristide during this period is Wilentz, *Rainy Season*.

5. Averill, *Hunter*, 185–90; Robert Fatton Jr., *Haiti's Predatory*

Republic: The Unending Transition to Democracy (Boulder, Colo.: Lynne Rienner, 2002), 77–80.

6. Averill, *Hunter*, 185–93, 196. For a detailed analysis of the political suppression of this period, and the use of rape as a tool by the military, see Erica Caple James, *Democratic Insecurities: Violence, Trauma, and Intervention in Haiti* (Berkeley: University of California Press, 2010).

7. Philippe R. Girard, *Clinton in Haiti: The 1994 U.S. Invasion of Haiti* (New York: Palgrave Macmillan, 2004); Bob Shacochis, *The Immaculate Invasion* (New York: Viking, 1999); Stan Goff, *Hideous Dream: A Soldier's Memoir of the U.S. Invasion of Haiti*, 1st ed. (New York: Soft Skull Press, 2000).

8. The most detailed studies of this period are Wiener Kerns Fleurimond, *Haïti de la crise à l'occupation: Histoire d'un chaos, 2000–2004* (Paris: L'Harmattan, 2009); Alex Dupuy, *The Prophet and Power: Jean-Bertrand Aristide, the International Community, and Haiti* (Lanham, Md.: Rowman & Littlefield, 2007); and Fatton, *Haiti's Predatory Republic*, chap. 6.

9. The most detailed political analyses of Aristide's regime are Dupuy, *Prophet and Power*, and Fatton, *Haiti's Predatory Republic*. A powerful critique of U.S. policy in recent years is Paul Farmer, *The Uses of Haiti*, 2nd ed. (Monroe, Maine: Common Courage Press, 2003). Two works that defend Aristide and insist that foreign governments purposely undermined his regime are Randall Robinson, *An Unbroken Agony: Haiti, from Revolution to the Kidnapping of a President* (New York: Basic Civitas Books, 2007), and Hallward, *Damming the Flood*.

10. Edwidge Danticat made this comment during a lecture at Duke University on February 15, 2011.

11. Arnaud Robert, "Haïti est la preuve de l'échec de l'aide internationale," interview with Ricardo Seitenfus, *Le Temps*, December 21, 2010; Steven Stoll, "Toward a Second Haitian Revolution," *Harper's Magazine*, April 2010.

12. Robert, "Haïti est la preuve." For a lucid and illuminating analysis of these issues, see Paul Farmer's recent *Haiti After the Earthquake* (New York: Public Affairs, 2011).

13. Robert, "Haïti est la preuve."

ACKNOWLEDGMENTS

This book was conceived in the immediate aftermath of the January 2010 earthquake in Haiti, a time of shock, mourning, and mutual support. I offer it up in the hope both that it will help illuminate the country's present and spur further debate and research about Haiti's history. In these pages I draw on the work of a remarkable group of scholars, many of whom I am deeply fortunate to have as both colleagues and friends.

Chief among them is Jean Casimir, whom I first met in 2004, and who had just arrived to spend a semester as a Mellon Visiting Professor at Duke at the beginning of January 2010. The first meeting of a class we taught together on twentieth-century Haiti took place just a few days after the disaster. Our conversations in class and outside of it, our work together on a short essay called "Reckoning in Haiti" for an SSRC forum, and his ability to channel the long history of Haiti into a meaningful interpretation of the present all deeply shaped the structure and analysis of this book.

I have also been delighted to work with my Duke colleague Deborah Jenson, with whom in September 2010 I began codirecting a Humanities Laboratory focused on Haiti, thanks to the imagination and generosity of Ian Baucom, director of the Franklin Humanities Center. I have learned much from her work, and collaborating with her on a range of Haiti-related projects has been an amazing experience. Working with the other faculty members of the Haiti Lab—Haitian linguist Jacques Pierre, Global Health faculty member Kathy Walmer, and Law School professor Guy Uriel-Charles—has been an inspiration as well. We were able to host a series of remarkable visitors in 2010 and 2011—including Edwidge Danticat, Edouard Duval-Carrié, and Erica James—whose work is a constant inspiration. I also thank Vincent Brown, my new colleague at Duke and a companion in thinking through Caribbean and Atlantic history, for all that he continues to teach me.

Duke has been a remarkable institution to be at during the past years because of its innovative support of Haitian and Caribbean studies. During that time, I have been blessed to work with an extraordinary group of graduate and undergraduate students. Julia Gaffield has already helped to transform the public's understanding of Haiti's history through her research on the early independence period. UNC graduate student Laura Wagner, who has written powerfully about the 2010 earthquake, has shared with me her deep understanding of the presence of the past in contemporary Haiti. Christy Mobley's commitment to understanding Africa and Haiti has been an inspiration. And Andrew Walker, who as an undergraduate studied with me in the spring of 2010 and is now going on to graduate school, gave me invaluable help as a research assistant. He will soon be helping to change the way we think about twentieth-century Haitian and U.S. history.

These links are just one part of a larger web of connections that have sustained me for the past decades of work on Haiti. Mentors on Haiti and the Caribbean at Princeton (especially Barbara Browning, Colin Dayan, and Peter Johnson) and the University of Michigan (particularly Fernando Coronil, Simon Gikandi, and Rebecca Scott) illuminated the way forward, while Robert Fatton Jr. and Michel-Rolph Trouillot served as intellectual touchstones and encouraging colleagues.

Chantalle Verna, whom I began working with when I started my first teaching job at Michigan State University, has been as much a teacher as a student over the years. She is part of a generation of exceptional young scholars who are rewriting twentieth-century Haitian history, and their friendship and writing has been crucial in shaping the approach taken in this book. Millery Polyné and Thor Burnham have shared their insights with me, while Matthew Smith's work and his participation in an April 2010 conference at Duke have been critical for me. As a leader of the Haitian Studies Association, which plays such a vital role in sustaining research and conversation in the field, he honored me with an invitation to give a keynote address to the group in November 2010. The event allowed me to test out key aspects of this work with a dauntingly expert audience. Kate Ramsey also joined us at Duke in April 2010 and returned for a lecture in the spring of 2011. She was kind enough to share with me chapters of her forthcoming book, which transformed my interpretation of religion and the U.S. occupation.

Part of the inspiration for this work came from the many conversations I have had about Haiti with journalists covering the 2010 earthquake. Among them, Damien Cave of the *New York Times* and Jeb Sharp of BBC's *The World* have been particularly impassioned and committed to tying past to present. I thank both of them for their work and for the ways that their questions prodded me to articulate and interpret Haitian history.

The Triangle French Studies Workshop and the Haiti Lab Working Group both read drafts of early chapters of the book, and the comments of participants were a tremendous help. During our collective experience of the 2010 World Cup in South Africa, conversations with Paul Gilroy, Achille Mbembe, Sarah Nutall, and Vron Ware provided direction and inspiration.

In Haiti, dialogues with Pierre Buteau, Fritz Deshommes, Michel Hector, Patrick Tardieu, Lyonel Trouillot, and students at the Université d'État helped shape my thinking on key issues. And though I know him only through his work, Claude Moïse has been a constant companion. His research and analysis have been fundamental for me in writing this book. So, too, has the work of Georges Anglade, who was among the hundreds of thousands who died on January 12, 2010, and who left behind an illuminating body of work that makes Haiti's past live on. My ongoing friendship and dialogue with Erol Josué has also been crucial in framing my approach.

Honor and respect are due to my amazing editors at Metropolitan Books, Sara Bershtel and Grigory Tovbis, for tremendous patience and fortitude, keen and lucid critique, and endless intellectual generosity. It would simply have been impossible for me to write this book without them, and I feel undeservedly lucky to have had the chance to work with them. I am also grateful to my agent, Wendy Strothman, for helping me develop the project and shepherding it to the perfect place.

Finally, to my son, Anton Dubois—who has gotten used to having to interrupt me by asking, "Are you talking about Haiti again?"— and my coconspirator in all things, Katharine Brophy Dubois, I owe gratitude for all the sustenance that makes it possible to think and write.

INDEX

ABOUT THE AUTHOR

LAURENT DUBOIS is the author of *Avengers of the New World: The Story of the Haitian Revolution*, a *Los Angeles Times* Best Book of 2004. The Marcello Lotti Professor of Romance Studies and History at Duke University, Dubois has written on Haiti for the *Los Angeles Times*, *The Nation*, and *The New Yorker* Web site, among other publications, and is the codirector of the Haiti Lab at the Franklin Humanities Institute. He lives in Durham, North Carolina.